Strategic Interpersonal Communication

LEA's COMMUNICATION SERIES
Jennings Bryant/Dolf Zillmann, General Editors

Selected titles in Interpersonal/Intercultural Communication (W. Barnett Pearce, Advisory Editor) include:

Cupach/Spitzberg • The Dark Side of Interpersonal Communication

Daly/Wiemann • Strategic Interpersonal Communication

Hewes • The Cognitive Bases of Interpersonal Communication

Kalbfleisch • Interpersonal Communication: Evolving Interpersonal Relationships

Leeds-Hurwitz • Semiotics and Communication: Signs, Codes, Cultures

For a complete list of other titles in LEA's Communication Series, please contact Lawrence Erlbaum Associates, Publishers.

Strategic Interpersonal Communication

Edited by

John A. Daly
University of Texas, Austin

John M. Wiemann
University of California, Santa Barbara

LEA LAWRENCE ERLBAUM ASSOCIATES, PUBLISHERS
1994   Hillsdale, New Jersey   Hove, UK

Lawrence Erlbaum Associates, Inc., Publishers
365 Broadway
Hillsdale, New Jersey 07642

Cover Design by Cheryl Minden

Library of Congress Cataloging-in-Publication Data

Strategic Interpersonal Communication / edited by John A. Daly, John M. Wiemann.
    p.   cm.
    Includes bibliographical references and index.
    ISBN 0-8058-957-1
    1. Interpersonal communication.   2. Social interaction.   I. Daly,
John A. (John Augustine), 1952–   .   II. Wiemann, John M.
BF637.C45C638   1993
153.6–dc20   92-45190
                                                        CIP

Books published by Lawrence Erlbaum Associates are printed on acid-free
paper, and their bindings are chosen for strength and durability.

Printed in the United States of America
10 9 8 7 6 5 4 3 2 1

Contents

Introduction:
Getting Your Own Way

John M. Wiemann
University of California, Santa Barbara

John A. Daly
University of Texas, Austin

This book is about how people go about achieving their social goals through human symbolic interaction. Our collective presumption is that there are more or less typical ways that people attempt to obtain desired outcomes, be they persuasive, informative, conflictive, or the like, through communication.

In many ways, this book represents a first summary of research done by scholars, primarily in the communication discipline, over the past 15 years seeking to identify and understand how it is that people achieve what they want through social interaction. Under the very broad label of strategies, this research has sought to (a) identify critical social goals such as gaining compliance, generating affinity, resolving social conflict, and offering information; (b) specify, for each goal, the ways, or strategies, by which people can go about achieving these goals; and (c) determine predictors of strategy selection—that is, why does a person opt for one strategy over others to obtain the desired end. It reflects the attention the field of communication has given to strategy issues in the past 15 years. Today it is difficult to open a journal or attend a conference where one does not regularly hear people talking of research on some strategy.

The chapters that follow, in a somewhat catalog fashion, describe research on the ways in which people achieve different goals. Each chapter summarizes existing research and theory on the attainment of some social goal.

Reading the chapters that follow should be done with two thoughts in mind: First, that the reader will gain insight into the varied ways in which people go about achieving their social goals. Each chapter summarizes research on a particular goal or related set of goals and then lays out research on the different ways people may accomplish that goal. Second, though, the reader would be wise to treat these chapters as exemplars—there are clearly many social goals that are not covered in this book. Looking at each chapter should offer the reader some insight into many of the issues that exist regardless of the strategy being discussed. Thus, whereas we don't have chapters on topics such as ways people elicit or offer disclosure, ways people demonstrate anger, or ways people create guilt, the issues that appear consistently throughout the various chapters should apply equally to these.

In this introduction, we highlight some important aspects of strategy research that are relevant to all of the chapters, including some assumed characteristics of strategic communication, the state of research in this area, and some of its limitations.

CHARACTERISTICS OF STRATEGIC COMMUNICATION

A careful reading of the literature leads us to conclude that researchers concerned with strategic interpersonal communication assume certain characteristics are common to such behavior.

The first assumption is that the strategy/tactic/goal relationship is hierarchical and fluid. That is to say, on the one hand, goals are pursued by implementing strategies composed of tactics. On the other hand, today's strategy may turn out to be tomorrow's tactic. Goal attainment may be seen as a strategic move in itself, useful in attaining a more distant or higher order goal.

This is not exactly a confusion of terms, although the fluid nature of the definitions of strategy and tactic can certainly lead to conceptual confusion. Exactly what sort of behavior might constitute a strategy is not clear. In the literature the concepts of strategy and tactic are often used interchangeably, and the relationship of strategy to tactic and their joint relevance to goal attainment often goes unspecified. The ambiguities make comparison among studies and conceptual rigor difficult at times. Yet, these ambiguities accurately portray the fluid relationship among and between these concepts, both in the laboratory and in real life.

A consensus definition of *strategy* is that it is a plan of action to achieve a goal or goals. *Tactics*, on the other hand, are specific moves made to implement a strategy. One way to think about tactics is to treat them as constituted by microbehaviors (discrete behaviors), which is especially the case in conversation. Communication is strategic when behavior (utterances, nonverbal displays) are "formulated in a particular way because it is projected that they will have social utility" (Sanders, 1987, p. 3).

The proactivity of communicators in goal attainment is a second assumption frequently made by strategy researchers. This assumption equates strategic communication with intentional communication. The implicit or explicit assumption of most researchers is that strategy selection is a cognitive process that is preformed with some intention and more or less consciously. The frequent use of concepts such as *schema* and *planning* in the strategy literature underscores the presumed intentionality of the behavior. The implication: Performances that are not "rational" are not—cannot be, by definition—strategic. But the work of some scholars (Buck, 1984, 1988; Cronkhite, 1986; Motely, 1986) raises the possibility that we might have a repertoire of emotionally based strategies. It is certainly worth considering the possibility that arousal of various kinds leads to performances that can easily be seen as goal directed and, thus, strategic. Giving emotion primacy over planning could be considered an *a*rational approach to strategic communication. A more rational alternative to interpersonal strategies, but one that is inconsistent with the prevailing view that strategic behavior requires planning, and so on, is one that views ongoing (online) construction of strategies as part of the conversational process. This view of communication as strategic is consistent with the theoretical orientations of symbolic interactionism (Blumler, 1969) and coordinated management of meaning (Pearce & Cronen, 1980), although scholars from these traditions do not typically talk about communication in terms of strategic choice.

Untried, novel, or little-used strategies are probably implemented consciously and, thus, clearly fit with the prevailing view of strategic communication. Similarly, specific contexts may increase the consciousness of strategy selection as well as the salience of making the "correct" selection (e.g., deciding what to say as you watch the policeman who just pulled you over approach in your rearview mirror). Some strategies, however, are overlearned and seem to drop from consciousness (e.g., *greeting* strategies). A specific situation or person can automatically evoke a particular strategy (and, possibly, a specific tactic associated with that strategy). Such strategies can usefully be seen as default options, which at some level are intentional, are clearly not invoked at full levels of consciousness. The emotional triggering of strategies likely works the same way. Arousal of a specific type, or arousal associated with a specific stimulus set might predictably evoke some communication strategy and relevant tactics associated with it. This proposition, of course, needs further exploration.

Habituation is a related issue in strategy selection. Are people creatures of habit when it comes to interpersonal strategies? Do they find one strategy that works for them and then stick with it, ignoring the possibility of other strategies? Moreover, are there strategy "habits" within relationships? Perhaps people walk into Relationship X and drop into a schema for strategies that is different than one they have for Relationship Y—to either functional or dysfunctional ends.

Does the same model of strategy selection work for every goal? Can we generalize from research on strategy selection in, say, compliance, to strategy selection in affinity work? Or do we have to develop separate models for each area? This ideograph is an important one. Another variant is this: It may well be that different strategies work for different people, and we may lose valuable information by cutting across people. In different relationships, people may find that different strategies work better or worse.

This last point is relevant to the third assumed characteristic of strategic communication, although it is infrequently acknowledged by those committed to the prevailing rational model of strategy selection. Known successful strategies are not necessarily employed. People, for sometimes good and rational reasons, do not always do what they know will work (Vause & Wiemann, 1981). Conversely, unsuccessful or dysfunctional strategies are not always abandoned. Reasons vary, of course; for example, I know spending time with a person induces liking; I want you to like me, but I won't spend time with you because I have other obligations.

One explanation of this arational behavior might be that the naive theories (see Bradac, Wiemann, & Schaefer, this volume) upon which people base their understandings of social situations and social behavior are either wrong or at odds with "sophisticated" strategies of communication researchers. It is clear that, at times, naive strategists are often out of touch with the link between their actual strategy use and what they report are useful or "good" strategies.

This assumed characteristic of strategic interpersonal communication raises several questions. What sort of theories do just plain folks use to guide strategic/tactical choices? How do these "naive theories" compare with the "informed" theories of communication scholars? For example, our students disparage the "What's your name?" "What's your major?" get-acquainted strategies, but rely on these types of strategies when they are faced with getting acquainted. Further, they readily admit that they are put off by people who use nonstandard strategies (e.g., skipping small talk) in get-acquainted episodes. But these discrepancies should not be lightly dismissed as ignorance or the like. Their study holds promise for helping us understand how strategies are selected or constructed and how these are later evaluated.

The State of Strategic Communication Research

In general, the state of research in strategic interpersonal communication is healthy, as the following chapters testify. Various literatures related to strategic communication are reviewed in these chapters. Here we merely offer some general observations about the area and how it has progressed. This research has generally sought to: (a) identify critical social goals (e.g., compliance-gaining; see Cody, Canary, & Smith, this volume); (b) specify for each goal the ways (strategies) by which people can go about achieving these goals; and (c) determine predictors of strategy selection (Why does a person opt for one strategy over another?). The first two of these goals have been more fully addressed than the third.

Strategy research typically acknowledges that communicators are proactive, especially when conscious planning is involved as was just mentioned. This may sound like a surprising observation, but consider that much work in our discipline implies a different view; for example, interpersonal attraction work typically focuses on person characteristics such as physical attractiveness or attitudinal similarity, ignoring that such characteristics can be manipulated by interactants. The emphasis on proactivity leads us to conclude that strategy-oriented research can be integrative of the literature in an area.

Strategy research accomplished to date does have some general limitations; we suggest four. We note that progress is already being made in each of these areas and we believe that the articulation of these general limitations should hasten our collective progress in understanding strategic communication.

First, it is important that the nature of goals be clarified. Strategies are goal-driven, but there are a wide variety of types of goals. Three important types that have been only loosely considered in the literature are *personal*, *relational* (mutual), and *institutional* goals. Personal goals are relevant primarily to one individual. These goals are carried around with that individual, if you will. We might assume that he or she will seek out persons or situations that will allow him or her to accomplish these goals, but from this perspective the goals of other people are only marginally relevant. In multiple-goal situations, the question still remains as to the procedures used by people in choosing one goal over another.

Contrast individual to relational goals, which are mutually constructed and agreed on. Here the focus is to move the relationship (rather than any one individual) from here to there, so to speak. When relational goals are considered, a new set of questions comes to the fore. For example, it becomes important to understand both the goal construction process and how these goals are related to the individual goals of the people in the relationship. Under what circumstances do individual goals take precedence? How are potentially conflicting goals accommodated? Can we predict the circumstances under which optimization of relational outcomes give way to maximization of individual outcomes?

Institutional goals are those that involve groups organized to achieve some task. Group size can vary from dyads to massive industrial organizations. The important characteristic here is that people are interacting not for personal reasons or to foster a close relationship, but to perform a non-relational task (e.g., write a group term paper, build a car, make a profit). A set of questions similar to those just listed needs answering. Our point is that goals at this level probably differ from and interact with those at the other two levels. Strategy researchers have to become more sensitive to the various types of goals and how they differ—and how these differences influence communication.

Another aspect of the nature of goals is whether they are *process* or *outcome* goals. The contrast can be seen as "How do I accomplish this (or any or every) goal?" versus "Did I accomplish this particular goal?" The concept of process strategies is a prospect that heretofore has not been systematically considered. One example that comes to mind is *tenacity*. People may strategically use such an implementation strategy in addition to outcome-directed strategies. For instance, an outcome-directed strategy in affinity (see Daly & Kreiser, this volume) might be "to show positive self"; the process strategy represents an implementation model: to do it with tenacity—to stick to that move over any other. It may well be that the big constant variables in strategy work aren't the typologies we have now for different goals, but rather the implementation strategies that are applicable across substantive strategies. Process strategies are the "how" for the substantive strategies.

Another little-explored aspect of the nature of goals is the difference between predefined and emergent goals. Are they approached in the same way? Probably not, but what are the consequences for communication behavior? Relatedly, how are multiple and/or shifting goals evaluated in strategy selection?

Importantly, are there generic goals that subsume situation specific goals? A conceptualization of generic goals might lead to an escape from the limitations of situation or goal-specific typologies. We say more on this later.

A second limitation of strategy research is the preoccupation with typologies. Typological research has led to important gains in our understanding interpersonal strategies, but this line of work can only go so far. A major conceptual issue is: How do we know we have incorporated the universe of strategies? At what point is our catalog complete? Does every communication episode have associated with it a typology of strategies that might accomplish that episode? Coming up with a core group of strategies would be important. Clearly, the chapters in this book reflect the helter-skelter approach research has taken. What may be necessary is a broad theory of communication purposes that then allows a derivation of the particular strategies. As it stands now, typological work tends to be context-specific and *a*theoretical. Results are method-bound, a fact vividly illustrated by the dispute over the validity of check-off versus free response measures.

A third limitation of current strategy research is that there is little (if any) integrating theory. It can be argued that we didn't know enough to construct good theory until recently. It seems to us that we are now in a position to begin serious theory construction and to expect research to be theory-driven.

A final limitation we want to point out is that little attention is paid to strategy selection processes. Is it always a cognitive process? As we have argued, there is good evidence to suggest emotion has a role to play. Habituation clearly plays a role. Another nagging question is: How are equally "good" competing strategies evaluated so that one can be selected? How do we decide to shift from one strategy to another when confronted with multiple strategies—each appearing equally desirable? Social creativity comes from the unusual mixing of different strategies.

Tied to this notion is the issue of weighting strategies—in most cases people don't simply engage in only one. Rather, what they do is put together a composite. The composite may shift over time. Assume the following hypothetical model: A person has five alternative strategies available: a1, a2, a3, a4, a5. Think of them forming a vector. That vector has weights associated with each of the strategies. At Time 1 of the interaction, the weights (w1, w2, w3, w4, w5) are different from the weights at Time 2. The shift in weights becomes interesting.

One solution to at least some of these problems may lie in the identification of functions of communication, which can be seen as metagoals (Kellermann, 1988). Wiemann and his colleagues (Wiemann, 1977; Wiemann & Bradac, 1989; Wiemann & Giles, 1988; Wiemann & Kelly, 1981; also see Patterson, this volume) have argued that from a relationally oriented/systemic view, communication (at all levels of analysis) can be seen as functioning to achieve a small set of general or ubiquitous goals (Dance & Larson, 1976). These functions, which are accomplished at what Watzlawick, Beavin, and Jackson (1967) called the metalevel of communication, include the negotiation of control distribution in the relationship and the acceptable level of expressed affiliation. The enactment of control distribution and expressed affiliation can be said to define the relationship along these dimensions. A third important function is the "task orientation" displayed by the partners in the relationship. That is to say, the degree to which important or defining tasks are attended to by the partners.

Strategies can be seen as directed at both specific goals and these general functions simultaneously. This sort of analysis, which is still in much need of specification, offers the promise of cross-context comparisons. To the extent that a small set of functions are, indeed, ubiquitous, strategies enacted in the general service of these functions can be compared for efficacy, appropriateness, efficiency (Kellermann, 1988; Kellermann & Kim, 1991), and satisfaction. The functions translate into goals at the relational level in that people have specific relationship definitions as goals.

This approach to the analysis of goals also recognizes goal hierarchies. Further, it suggests answers to questions about reconciliation of competing goals and strategies.

Conclusion

One question that remains is where strategy work will go. It hasn't been that generative of subsequent research. Yes, we have integrative topologies and we can tell that different strategies are used in different situations, but what after that? Perhaps the reason for this is the lack of any strong theoretical models.

Why hasn't theory in this area developed more? Perhaps because it was driven not by a theory but, rather, by observation and inductive categories. Our challenge now is to create that theory.

The essays collected in this volume provide not only a summary of what has been accomplished to date, but also an initial theoretic map for future research concerning strategic interpersonal communication.

REFERENCES

Blumler, H. (1969). *Symbolic interactionism: Perspective and method*. Englewood Cliffs, NJ: Prentice-Hall.

Buck, R. (1984). *The communication of emotion*. New York: Guilford.

Buck, R. (1988). Emotional education and mass media: A new view of the global village. In R. Hawkins, J. M. Wiemann, & S. Pingree (Eds.), *Advancing communication science: Merging mass and interpersonal processes* (pp. 44–76). Newbury Park, CA: Sage.

Cronkhite, G. (1986). On the focus, scope, and coherence of the study of human symbolic activity. *Quarterly Journal of Speech, 72*, 231–246.

Dance, F. E. X., & Larson, C. E. (1976). *The functions of human communication*. New York: Holt, Rinehart, & Winston.

Kellermann, K. (1988). *Understanding tactical choice: Metagoals in conversation*. Paper presented at the Temple University Discourse Conference, Philadelphia.

Kellermann, K., & Kim, M-S. (1991, May). *Working within constraints: Tactical choices in the pursuit of social goals*. Paper presented at the annual meeting of the International Communication Association, Chicago, IL.

Motely, M. T. (1986). Consciousness and intentionality in communication: A preliminary model and methodological approaches. *Western Journal of Speech Communication, 50*, 3–23.

Pearce, W. B., & Cronen, V. E. (1980). *Communication, action, and meaning: The creation of social realities*. New York: Praeger.

Sanders, R. E. (1987). *Cognitive foundations of calculated speech: Controlling understandings in conversation and persuasion*. Albany, NY: SUNY Press.

Vause, C., & Wiemann, J. M. (1981). Communication strategies for role invention. *Western Journal of Speech Communication, 45*, 239–249.

Watzlawick, P., Beavin, J., & Jackson, J. J. (1967). *Pragmatics of human communication*. New York: Norton.

Wiemann, J. M. (1977). Explication and test of a model of communicative competence. *Human Communication Research, 3*, 195–213.

Wiemann, J. M., & Bradac, J. J. (1989). Metatheoretical issues in the study of communicative competence: Structural and functional approaches. *Progress in Communication Sciences, 9*, 261–284.

Wiemann, J. M., & Giles, H. (1988). Interpersonal communication. In M. Hewstone, W. Stroebe, J-P. Codol, & G. M. Stephenson (Eds.), *Introduction to social psychology* (pp. 199–221). Oxford: Blackwell.

Wiemann, J. M., & Kelly, C. W. (1981). Pragmatics of interpersonal competence. In C. Wilder-Mott & J. H. Weakland (Eds.), *Rigor and imagination: Essays from the legacy of Gregory Bateson* (pp. 183–197). New York: Praeger.

Chapter 1

Acquiring Social Information

Charles R. Berger
University of California, Davis

Kathy Kellermann
University of California, Santa Barbara

The considerable diversity of social goals for which strategic communicators strive is reflected in the variety of titles of this volume's chapters. In their interactions with others, social actors and actresses seek to achieve such goals as controlling their conversations, comforting others, gaining compliance from others, and inducing others to like them (Graham, Argyle, & Furnham, 1980; Kellermann & Kim, 1991). In these and other endeavors, persons employ their knowledge of themselves and others, their knowledge about social interaction processes and their communication skills to achieve their goals. These three components of goal-oriented communicative action do not always work together; that is, persons may know the optimal strategies for achieving a particular interaction goal but be unable to muster the requisite communication skills to do so. Conversely, some persons may have high communication skill levels but be prevented from successful goal attainment by faulty knowledge.

Although faulty knowledge or lack of skill may prevent interactants from achieving their social goals, these deficits are not immutable. Persons are capable of acquiring information necessary for generating new knowledge, correcting faulty knowledge, and remediating skill deficits. This chapter focuses on the first of these three problems; nevertheless, the importance of the latter two should not be minimized. Knowledge may be power, but in the domain of strategic communication, *praxis* assumes an equally important role in the production of optimal performance. We assume that although individuals bring general knowledge about persons and interaction procedures with them to particular interaction episodes, they must acquire specific information about their interaction partners and the current interaction context to achieve their interaction goals. Even individuals who possess large amounts of general knowledge about persons and interaction procedures must acquire specific information in order to be successful; thus, the acquisition of social and personal information is an important goal in almost every strategic communication episode.

We take it as a given that most interaction situations involve the simultaneous pursuit of a number of interaction goals (Berger, 1988a). For instance, when an individual tries to persuade a friend to go to a movie, he or she may actually be trying to accomplish two or more goals at once, for example, persuasion and maintaining the friendship. The pursuit of multiple goals can constrain the choice and implementation of interaction strategies. The existence of a friendship-maintenance goal might prevent an individual from employing certain aversive compliance-gaining strategies and tactics. The goal of acquiring information about others is frequently pursued along with other social goals and in many cases may be a precondition for the attainment of other goals as the procurement of information about others is crucial in retrieving or developing plans to reach social goals. Although our discussion focuses on the goal of information acquisition, one should not lose sight of the fact that such a focus ignores the complex goal and planning interactions that accrue from the simultaneous striving for multiple interaction goals.

It is also important to recognize that as persons engage in strategic interactions their goals may change (Berger, 1988a). Thus, the goal of becoming a friend to another may transmute to the goal of becoming a lover as a relationship progresses. Goal metamorphosis is especially important in the social information-gathering context. We suspect that social information acquisition is undertaken generally to achieve such social goals as ingratiation, compliance-gaining, and the like. Once sufficient information is gathered, the social information acquisition goal transmutes to one of these more primary goals. Of course, the goal of acquiring social information might reemerge later in an ongoing interaction if a primary goal is not being reached. Understanding goal hierarchies and their dynamics is crucial to the study of strategic communication (Berger, 1988a; Lichtenstein & Brewer, 1980; McCann & Higgins, 1988).

Within the context of the assumptions and caveats just outlined, in the remainder of this chapter we explore the following issues related to social information acquisition. First, the functions served by social information acquisition are considered. Second, various strategies used to acquire social information are examined. Third, research findings concerning the use of information acquisition strategies are presented. Finally, some directions for future research are suggested.

WHY SEEK SOCIAL INFORMATION?

The understandings that persons have of their social interactions are deter-mined by their interpretations of: (a) the context within which the interaction occurs, (b) the actions of their interaction partners, and (c) their own actions. These interpretations are, in part, the product of the processing of inputs by various schemata. We now turn our attention to the functions served by social information acquisition in schematic processing.

Instantiating Appropriate Schemata

Taylor and Crocker (1981) argued that well-articulated schemata speed infor-mation processing. In order to gain the advantages of more rapid information processing, however, it is necessary to find schemata from a long-term store that are appropriate for processing inputs from the present situation. Although a voluminous literature exists concerning the effects of schemata on memory for persons and events (Hastie et al., 1980; Wyer & Srull, 1984), relatively little is known about the schemata selection process. Presumably, certain criti-cal cues "point to" potentially appropriate schemata. For example, if a per-son says little in interactions with others, avoids eye contact while speaking, and prefers reading books to going to parties, a fellow interactant might be led to instantiate an introvert schema with which to understand and respond to the person during their interactions. There is, of course, the nagging ques-tion of how perceivers know that these cues point to an introvert prototype in the first place. Do persons need schemata to understand the cues that point to still other schemata?

Indications are that in initial interactions between strangers, persons ask questions that may aid them in selecting schemata for processing subsequent inputs from their interactions. Several studies show that the first few minutes of interactions between strangers are dominated by the asking and answering of questions (Berger, 1973; Berger & Kellermann, 1983; Calabrese, 1975; Kellermann, 1984a). These questions are predominantly concerned with such background and demographic characteristics of the interactants as occupation, place of birth, current residence, and so on. Answers to these questions may determine directly what schemata are called up, and the paralinguistic and other nonverbal cues that accompany questions and answers may also provide input for the selection of appropriate schemata (Scherer, 1979). Berger (1975) reported that the background information exchanged during the first few minutes of initial interactions is used to predict attitudes and opinions not yet disclosed by the interaction participants. This finding suggests that persons may use background information to select schemata and develop predictions from the selected schemata.

Filling in Incomplete Schemata

Persons may access relevant schemata for processing; however, for a variety of reasons these schemata may be incomplete. Young children frequently experience this problem, but adults may also find themselves processing persons and situations with gap-ridden schemata. For example, a child who has been to several restaurants and developed a rudimentary script for processing restaurant action sequences may be befuddled when the waiter delivers cold forks (for eating salad) or when the waiter vacuums up crumbs from the tablecloth with a small vacuum cleaner. Even adult diners might be taken aback when hot towels for washing their face and hands are delivered after being seated. Similar kinds of gaps can occur in both person and role schemata with equally confounding effects.

Persons can respond in at least three ways to gaps in their knowledge structures. First, persons can ask questions of others who are perceived to have the requisite knowledge to fill in their gaps. The child who does not know what to do with a cold fork might ask a parent "Why is this fork cold?" or "What do I do with this fork?" Second, persons can watch what others do and imitate them. We suspect that for reasons related to self-esteem maintenance and projecting a sophisticated and knowledgeable persona, many adults are more likely to follow the latter course of action, whereas children are more likely to ask questions. A third potential response to an incomplete schemata might be to act without acquiring any information and to see whether one's actions produce desired outcomes. This trial-and-error process would seem to be the least efficacious of the three; however, we suspect that it is employed when self-presentational concerns are salient to some individuals.

Fabricating Schemata

There are times when persons lack schemata for processing information about persons or event sequences. Again, this situation is more likely to arise with children, but adults may experience this condition with its attendant uncertainties. The problem here is not one of missing pieces but the complete lack of knowledge concerning the focal situation or person. Although this type of situation might seem intractable in terms of both understanding and the generation of meaningful action, the fact is that both adults and children manage to act in non-random ways in such circumstances. How is this possible?

There are at least two answers to this question. First, although the focal person or situation may be completely unique, information processors may see some similarities between the focal person or situation and persons or situations that are already known. This reminding process is at the heart of Schank's (1982) model of memory processes. Given these remindings, persons can feel that they understand the person or the situation and can respond in potentially meaningful ways. It is difficult to imagine many persons or situations in which individuals would be at a complete loss to respond in more or less understandable ways, although children might be more prone to experience such complete losses of ability to respond. Second, through both observation and interaction persons can acquire the information necessary to build schemata. This bottom-up processing is both time consuming and effortful, but once schemata are constructed, they can be utilized in a top-down fashion at a later time. Much of the research done under the rubric of social cognition carries with it the assumption that persons already have numerous schemata for processing both person and event information. As a consequence, the process of schemata fabrication has been little researched and, as a result, is little understood.

Nonepistemic Functions

Gathering social information to instantiate appropriate schemata, to fill gaps in them, and to fabricate new ones points to the epistemic function served by social information seeking. It would be a critical error to assume, however, that all social information-gathering activity subserves this function. Persons may deploy actions ostensibly aimed at acquiring information but they may actually have quite different intentions. There are several possible nonepistemic functions that social information-gathering activities can serve; moreover, particular actions may fulfill both epistemic and nonepistemic functions simultaneously.

Mishler (1975) argued that question asking can be used by parents to exert *control* in conversations with their children. Parents ask questions that obligate their children to answer. Many adults recall that, as children, when they arrived home from elementary school their parents would frequently begin conversations with them by asking what they did in school that day. Their answers to this question prompted more follow-up questioning from their parents, thus allowing parents to continue their role as question askers. We do not mean to imply that parents question their children about their day at school solely to control their children's behavior. No doubt, many parents pay considerable attention to the answers their children provide and wish to know how their children are doing at school. Nevertheless, the parallel control function played by question asking cannot be overlooked.

Questions can also be used as directives (Ervin-Tripp, 1976). A parent trying to induce a child to choose a particular article of clothing at a store might say, "That's a nice one, isn't it?" Or, instead of saying "Let's go to the movies tonight," one friend might say to another, "Wouldn't it be nice to go to a movie tonight?" In both examples, the "right" answer or the answer desired by the asker is embedded within the question itself. In research related to the directive function of questions, Merritt (1976) discovered the conditions under which questions are interpreted as requests for information versus requests for service in customer–salesperson transactions, again demonstrating the multifunctionality of question asking.

Although the foregoing discussion has focused on various nonepistemic functions served by question asking, information-gathering activities other than question asking also can be multifunctional. For example, in order to ingratiate one's self to another, a person might be highly attentive to the other during a conversation. Showing interest may involve not only such verbal behaviors as asking questions, but such nonverbal behaviors as eye contact, touch, gesticulation, and the like. In addition, persons might reduce the amount of talking they do to effect perceptions of attentiveness. Some of these actions, for example, talking less and increasing eye contact, might increase both perceived attentiveness and information intake about the other. The lesson to be gleaned here is that singular actions may serve multiple functions. Information-seeking activities like question asking and increased attentiveness may subserve the epistemic goals of schemata instantiation, gap filling, and schemata fabrication; moreover, such actions may be the means for reaching ingratiation, conversational control, persuasion, and other nonepistemic goals. The remainder of this chapter focuses on strategies and tactics for acquiring social information, however, the issue of the multifunctionality of strategic actions should be kept in mind.

STRATEGIES FOR ACQUIRING
SOCIAL INFORMATION

We now consider general strategies for gathering social information. First, however, it is important to differentiate between *strategies* and *tactics*, a distinction that has frequently been ignored in discussions of strategic communication (Berger, 1985). We view strategies as cognitive phenomena like plans or scripts that provide general guidelines for action. Berger (1988a) has compiled a number of definitions of the plan construct (Miller, Galanter, & Pribram, 1960; Schank & Abelson, 1977; Wilensky, 1983) and suggested the following synthetic definition of a plan: "A plan specifies the actions that are necessary for the attainment of a goal or several goals. Plans vary in their levels of abstraction. Highly abstract plans can spawn more detailed plans. Plans contain alternative paths for goal attainment from which the social actor can choose" (Berger, 1988a, p. 96). Plans are not the actions themselves but abstract cognitive representations of action sequences; they represent kinds of strategies.

In contrast to plans or strategies, tactics are specific actional realizations of abstract cognitive representations. Thus, for example, if one chooses to try to induce another to comply with a request by using a threat strategy, one can choose from a very large repertoire of verbal and nonverbal actions those that will be used to represent the strategy; that is, the threat strategy can be realized tactically in a very large number of ways. Much of the research to be discussed later in the chapter concerns tactical representations of plans or strategies. At this juncture we consider the strategies that generate these tactics.

Information Acquisition Strategies

We have found it useful to distinguish among three general information-acquisition strategy classes. Within each of these three general classes of strategies are several substrategies. These general classes and substrategies have been described elsewhere (Berger, 1979, 1988b; Berger & Bradac, 1982); we only briefly consider them here.

Passive Strategies. Individuals can acquire considerable information about persons and situations simply by observing them. If the observer is unobtrusive, passive strategies have the same advantages as nonreactive measurement procedures (Webb, Campbell, Schwartz, & Sechrest, 1966). Persons who do not have to interact with the target of their observations need not be preoccupied with self-presentational concerns, so they can free more cognitive resources for processing information because they do not have to monitor their own actional outputs. Communication researchers and others who study social information gathering have tended to ignore the fact that considerable social information can be gleaned through unobtrusive observation.

Berger (1979) suggested several potential passive substrategies. First, social information seekers try to observe targets in situations where the target is most likely to be *reactive* rather than passive or solitary. In addition, based on social comparison theory (Festinger, 1954; Suls & Miller, 1977), observers seek to observe targets interacting with persons whom the observers judge to be similar to themselves. Finally, observers prefer to gather information about targets in situations where the targets' behaviors are less constrained by formal norms.

Active Strategies. This class of strategies includes those in which the information seeker actively alters the physical or the social environment and then observes how the target individual responds to these alterations. No direct interaction between the observer and target occurs. Thus, an observer might seat an unknown other next to a friend at a dinner party to see how the unknown other responds to the known friend. The observer alters the environment to assess the target's responses to these alterations. These kinds of environmental alterations may be thought of as informal social experiments performed by observers to gather information about targets. A second substrategy included in this general class is asking third parties for information about targets. Considerable social information is gleaned from one's social networks, and under certain conditions, persons evaluate this information carefully (Doelger, Hewes,

& Graham, 1986; Hewes & Graham, 1989; Hewes, Graham, Doelger, & Pavitt, 1985; Hewes, Graham, Monsour, & Doelger, 1989; Hewes & Planalp, 1982).

Interactive Strategies.   These strategies involve direct interaction between the observer and the target; that is, the information seeker becomes a participant–observer. One might conjecture that interactive strategies are superior to both passive and active strategies because the observer can exert considerably more direct control over the target. For example, the observer can interrogate the target and if the target does not provide satisfactory answers to questions, the observer can ask still more questions. Although this line of reasoning has some merit, it is also possible that interaction between the observer and the target might increase the likelihood of impression management or outright deception by the target. Furthermore, in the interactive context observers must be more concerned with their own self-presentations and, in so doing, are less able to muster cognitive resources for monitoring the actions of their targets (Gilbert, 1989). Thus, the increased control afforded the observer in interactive information-gathering contexts comes at a cost and that cost may be considerable.

Several interactive substrategies have been proposed (Berger, 1979; Berger & Bradac, 1982; Berger & Kellermann, 1983; Kellermann & Berger, 1984). Beyond the obvious strategy of interrogation, two additional strategies have been suggested. The disclosure strategy, predicated on the reciprocity norm (Gouldner, 1960), involves persons disclosing particular pieces of information about themselves under the assumption that their targets will reveal similar information about themselves. In other words, instead of requesting information (interrogation strategy), persons disclose information with the hope their disclosures will be reciprocated. A third interactive strategy is relaxing the target. Using this strategy, persons relax targets so that the targets will be more inclined to talk about themselves. This strategy is similar to the one used in client-centered therapy (Rogers, 1951). In the client-centered approach, therapists avoid being directive and prescriptive. Instead, therapists seek to encourage clients to talk about their problems in a nonevaluative environment.

Berger (1979) also suggested that social information gatherers must somehow assess the veracity of the information provided them by targets. Although this problem may be less acute when the information seeker makes unobtrusive observations, it can become more significant when active and interactive strategies are employed. In addition to the problems associated with detecting outright deception by targets are those related to the evaluation of incoming information using a number of other criteria. When persons seek information about targets from persons who know them, are they concerned with the possibility that reports obtained from such persons might be biased in some way? The question here is not necessarily one of intentional deception by third-party information sources, but the possibility that such sources might be overly positive or negative when evaluating target persons for observers. An extensive research program investigating the phenomenon of second-guessing has revealed how social information processors deal with these problems (Doelger et al., 1986; Hewes & Graham, 1989; Hewes et al., 1985; Hewes et al., 1989; Hewes & Planalp, 1982).

In addition to the problem of evaluating data provided by third-party sources are issues concerned with the assessment of directly obtained data (Berger, 1988b). Are social information seekers sensitive to the representativeness of their behavior observations of others? That is, are persons adequate intuitive samplers? If persons perform the kinds of social experiments suggested in the discussion of active strategies, do they have a grasp of the problems associated with experimental control and the necessity for establishing meaningful baselines against which to assess experimental effects? Finally, are social information seekers sensitive to the reliability and validity of the empirical indicators they use to index dispositional qualities of others; that is, are social information seekers adequate intuitive psychometricians (Kunda & Nisbett, 1986)?

Although evidence indicates that persons' judgments of themselves and others may be biased in a variety of ways (Hogarth, 1980; Kahneman, Slovic, & Tversky, 1982; Nisbett & Ross, 1980), thus suggesting that persons may not be very adept samplers, experimenters, or psychometricians, there is reason to believe that some of the biases reported in the judgment literature may not be as pervasive or as severe as has been thought in the past (Berger & Kellermann, 1983; Dailey, 1985; Doelger et al., 1986; Hewes & Graham, 1989; Hewes et al., 1985; Hewes & Planalp, 1982; Kellermann & Berger, 1984; Trope & Bassok, 1982). Furthermore, language comprehension processes (i.e., the use of conversational implicatures) may underlie some of the "supposed" judgment fallacies in comprehending social information (Kellermann, Burrell, Mulcrone, Lim, & Kang, 1987; Kellermann, Lim, Kang, Burrell, & Mulcrone, 1987). Given the possibility that individuals may exhibit considerable sensitivity to the potential for biases in their judgments, it would be prudent to explore in greater depth individuals' adequacy as intuitive social scientists.

Generating Social Information-Gathering Strategies

Having discussed the functions served by social information seeking and the passive, active, and interactive strategies for gathering social information, we now briefly consider the processes by which these strategies are formulated. As we noted at the beginning of this section, strategies can be viewed as plans for reaching social goals. These plans can be accessed from a long-term store (Hammond, 1989; Riesbeck & Schank, 1989) or they can be fabricated on-line while a person interacts. Human planning exhibits both top-down and bottom-up processes and is opportunistic in nature; that is, persons take into account changing environmental circumstances to modify their plans rather than remaining inexorably committed to a preconceived course of action (Bratman, 1987). However, overcommitment to action plans that are less than optimal for goal achievement can occur (Hayes-Roth & Hayes-Roth, 1979).

Plans serve two crucial functions (Wilensky, 1983). First, persons seeking to comprehend others' actions frequently base their understandings of observed actions on inferences they make about the goals and plans being pursued by others (Abbott & Black, 1986; Bruce, 1980; Bruce & Newman, 1978; Hobbs & Evans, 1980; Lichtenstein & Brewer, 1980; Schank & Abelson, 1977; Schmidt, 1976; Wilensky, 1983). Second, plans are critical to the production of social action (Berger, 1988a; Brand, 1984; Bratman, 1987; Miller et al., 1960; Sacerdoti, 1977). Furthermore, as Bruce and Newman (1978) persuasively demonstrated, individuals may take into account the goals and plans of others as they generate plans to reach their own goals. Failure to consider others' goals and plans may result in the development of less than optimal plans or complete failure to reach goals.

We assume that both plan selection from a long-term store and plan fabrication are governed by meta-goals and meta-plans. Wilensky (1983) argued that the processes of plan selection and plan building are controlled by the meta-goal of *efficiency*. Wilensky assumed that planners seek to develop the most efficient plans possible. We suggest that the meta-goal of *social appropriateness* is also critical to the conduct of strategic communication (Berger, 1988a; Berger & Kellermann, 1983; Kellermann & Berger, 1984). Research on politeness (Brown & Levinson, 1978) and self-disclosure (Derlega & Grzelak, 1979) reinforces the importance of social appropriateness as a meta-goal guiding the planning of social behavior.

These two meta-goals of efficiency and social appropriateness may be either compatible or incompatible depending on the primary goals of interactants (Kellermann, 1988; Kellermann & Kim, 1991). For example, when one's goal is to ingratiate one's self to another, the most efficient ways to accomplish this goal are also most likely to be socially appropriate. Persons might use opinion agreement and the rendering of compliments to reach an ingratiation goal (Jones, 1964; Jones & Wortman, 1973). Such ingratiation tactics generally involve the enactment of positive actions that are very likely to be judged socially appropriate. By contrast, asking questions may be a highly efficient way to acquire social information; however, by its very nature question asking is an intrusive activity, especially when the questions are directed toward ascertaining attributes of the other person. We also pointed out earlier that question asking may serve a social control function (Mishler, 1975). As a result, question asking may be highly efficient for gathering social information, but may also be quite intrusive (i.e., socially inappropriate).

Individuals who have better-articulated plans for achieving goals are more likely to be successful than those who have sketchy or poorly integrated plans. The degree of plan articulation depends on the general complexity of the plan.

For example, persons may or may not build into plans contingencies that can be invoked when progress toward a goal is blocked. In addition to having more contingencies, better articulated plans are ones in which more abstract planning levels are translated into more concrete actions; that is, having only a general idea of what one will do is less preferable to having a more specific idea of a line of action. There is one caveat that must be introduced here, however. One can envision circumstances in which a relatively simple plan might be more effective than a highly convoluted plan. Plans might be complex to the point that social actors are unable to discern the most productive paths to social goals from the vast array of options available in the plan. Moreover, a given complex plan might not contain the most efficient and socially appropriate option or options among the many present; by contrast, a simple plan might contain the optimal path to the desired goal. Nevertheless, when a particular course of action fails to produce the intended goal state, complex planners are in a better position to respond with further goal-seeking actions than are their less complex counterparts.

We believe that considerably more can be learned about the planning capabilities of individuals when they fail to reach goals than when they are successful at reaching goals, provided, of course, that they continue to pursue their goals in the face of failure. As we just noted, complex planners have available to them an extensive repertoire of alternative action sequences for attaining their goals. Immediate success in reaching a goal may reveal only a few of these options. It is when persons fail to reach goals and are forced to pursue other courses of action that a broader range of their planning options is exposed.

SOCIAL INFORMATION ACQUISITION RESEARCH

We now consider research that has been conducted to explore various strategies for acquiring social information. Most of this research has been descriptive and has been conducted at the tactical level of analysis. In general, the research to be discussed in this section has neither indexed information acquisition plans or strategies directly nor studied their relationships to information acquisition tactics; instead, it has focused on the alternative actions that persons take when they gather social information. Frequently, inferences have been made about cognitive structures believed to guide these actions; however, the structures themselves have not been indexed. Also, this research has generally ignored the multiple goals problem outlined previously. Typically, research participants are given a singular goal to accomplish. Virtually no attention has been paid to how persons might vary information-gathering tactics as a function of other primary or secondary goals. Keeping these limitations in mind, we now turn to a review of these studies.

Passive Strategies

Anticipated Interaction Effects.   When persons anticipate that they will interact with a stranger in the future and they are given the opportunity to acquire information about that person before meeting him or her, they are likely
to acquire more information about the stranger than about strangers whom
they believe they will not encounter in the future. Considerable evidence supports this generalization. Berscheid, Graziano, Monson, and Dermer (1976)
reported that persons who were led to believe they would be dating a particular individual spent more time observing that individual during a videotaped
discussion and remembered more about that individual than they did about
other persons involved in the discussion. In a similar investigation, Harvey,
Yarkin, Lightner, and Towne (1980) found that persons who anticipated they
would interact with a person who was part of a videotaped discussion group
remembered more about that person than they did about other discussion group
members with whom they did not anticipate interaction. Finally, Douglas (1985)
demonstrated that persons anticipating interaction with a stranger remembered
more biographic and demographic information disclosed by that person than
biographic and demographic information disclosed by a person with whom they
did not anticipate interaction.
   The studies cited involved anticipated first interactions with strangers.
Research examining relationships between anticipated future interaction and
information gathering in the situation where persons have already met for the
first time and are or are not anticipating future interaction reveal that anticipated interaction does not necessarily promote increased information gathering (Calabrese, 1975; Douglas, 1987a; Kellermann, 1986). Calabrese (1975),
however, found that persons anticipating a second interaction tended to gather
more biographic/demographic information from their conversational partners
than those not anticipating a second interaction. One potential explanation
for the sharp differences in information-acquisition activity observed between
these two anticipated interaction paradigms is simply that persons who will
never meet each other have little reason to acquire information about that person; thus, in the anticipated first interaction with a stranger paradigm there
are large differences between anticipators and non-anticipators. By contrast,
in the anticipated second interaction paradigm, regardless of their anticipated
interaction assignment, persons can easily gather information because they are
already involved in a face-to-face interaction. Those anticipating future interactions have no need to increase their informational intake in this situation
relative to those not anticipating information; that is, the information needs
of those anticipating a second interaction may be met by information gleaned
during the first interaction. Because of the wealth of information available in
face-to-face interactions, it may also be possible that in this situation antici-

pators cannot increase their information intake because they are in danger of experiencing cognitive overload.

Although both information intake and memory for persons are enhanced under conditions of anticipated interaction before initial encounters, anticipated interaction produces other cognitive effects. For example, persons who were given the opportunity to judge the information value of various situations in which to view a target stranger and who were led to believe that they would interact with the stranger after making their judgments, generally found informal situations in which the target was present to be more informative than formal situations. Moreover, persons who anticipated interacting with the target person judged themselves to be more similar to the target than did persons not anticipating interaction with the target (Berger & Douglas, 1981). It was also demonstrated that persons who anticipate interaction with others judge their own speech to be more similar to the others' speech than when they do not anticipate future interaction with them (Larsen, Martin, & Giles, 1977).

Increasing one's intake of information and preferring to observe target persons in informal rather than in formal situations are two useful strategies for acquiring social information. The first one needs no further comment. The advantage of observing persons in informal social contexts is that in such circumstances persons are more likely to display a wide variety of responses. This line of reasoning is similar to that presented by Jones and Davis (1965) in their discussion of correspondent inference theory. They argued that out-of-role behavior provides more information about underlying dispositions than does in-role behavior. In-role behavior does indicate to observers that actors are aware of socially prescribed norms and rules; however, when persons conform to role demands, they behave like many other persons. It is when persons fail to adhere to role demands that they are perceived to have unique qualities that set them apart from others. This highly diagnostic, out-of-role behavior is more likely to be exhibited in informal social situations.

Increased perceptions of similarity when observers anticipate interacting with targets may be the product of the desire to have at least some similarity with the stranger when he or she is finally encountered. Because initial interactions are expected to be at least slightly positive (Kellermann, 1984b), assuming similarities may be a way of generating attraction (Byrne, 1971). Rosenbaum (1986), however, suggested that perceived similarities may not be responsible for attraction, and perceived dissimilarities may be the cause of decreased attraction. One potential problem with assuming similarities between one's self and a person with whom interaction is anticipated is that the assumed similarities may countervail against the development of veridical judgments during the interaction itself. Assumed similarities developed before the interaction takes place might undermine the quality of the information obtained once the interaction commences.

Situational Informativeness.   The previous discussion has focused on the effects that anticipated interaction has on the acquisition and processing of social information using passive strategies. There are, in addition to this research, studies that have explored the kinds of strategies that persons use to maximize their information about another when they do not necessarily anticipate meeting the person. In a series of studies (Berger & Douglas, 1981; Berger & Perkins, 1978, 1979) persons were asked to judge the informativeness of slide pictures of target persons shown in a variety of solitary and social situations. Multidimensional scaling analyses (MDPREF) of pair comparison judgments of the slides revealed that observers judged: (a) social situations to be more informative than solitary situations; (b) situations in which the target person was interacting with others to be more informative than those where the target was simply present with others; and (c) informal situations to be more informative than formal ones when observers anticipated interacting with the target. In general, these findings support the view that social information seekers using unobtrusive observation methods prefer to gather information about targets in social situations where the target is an active participant, probably because such situations afford observers the opportunity to sample greater variability in the targets' behaviors.

Active Strategies

Naive Social Experiments.   At present, we have little research evidence to support the view that persons alter various aspects of their physical and social environments to gain information about others. As a result, we have little idea about the formal properties of the naive social experimentation substrategy. However, after informally describing this substrategy to persons, they have been able to think of occasions when they have performed these informal experiments. For example, some informants claimed to have introduced a target person to a person whom they knew well to see how the target would respond to the well-known other. In their study of "secret tests" used to assess the degree of relational partners' commitment to relationships, Baxter and Wilmot (1984) reported that persons sometimes use well-known others to help them assess persons with whom they are interested in developing close relationships. It is clear that persons engage in some form of naive social experimentation to acquire information about others; however, more work is needed to determine how these experiments are conducted and how adequately they are set up by social information gatherers.

Asking Third Parties.   An active substrategy that has received considerable research attention is one that involves an observer asking a third-party source who knows the target to provide information about and evaluations of the target. The recent emphasis on understanding social networks provides some insight into social information acquisition through interrogation of third parties. For example, persons understand their relational partner better the more they communicate with members of their social network (Parks & Adelman, 1983). Typically, persons learn about others through their social networks by asking third parties for information on a target's occupation, location, age, gender, hobbies, organizational membership, and marital status (Bernard, Killworth, & McCarty, 1982; Killworth, Bernard, & McCarty, 1984). The information sought through social networks is similar to information sought directly by persons in initial encounters (Kellermann, Broetzmann, Lim, & Kitao, 1989). Such information can provide the biographic and demographic base needed to predict the opinions and attitudes of target others prior to interacting with them (Berger, 1975).

In general, the research conducted with respect to this strategy has focused on the question of whether observers who receive information from third-party sources are sensitive to the possibility that such information may be tainted in some way by the third-party source. Another question pursued in this research concerns the extent to which observers will second-guess these third-party sources and compensate for the biases in those sources' information (Hewes & Planalp, 1982). Apparently, both college students and non-college students obtain a considerable amount of information about persons in their social networks from third-party sources. Hewes et al. (1985) found that persons estimated that they obtain about 30% of their information about others from third parties in their social networks. This indirectly obtained information was rated as only somewhat less useful than directly acquired information. In fact, respondents felt that third-party sources might be able to provide them with information about events involving the target that they could not directly witness. Furthermore, respondents indicated that third-party sources might provide them with valuable insights about targets. Respondents recognized that information provided by third parties might be tainted in some way and 71% of them reported that they could rectify these distortions using various debiasing techniques.

In a subsequent investigation, Doelger et al. (1986) identified various cues that prompt observers to second-guess the veracity of information provided by third parties. Among the 16 cues identified were: (a) third party distorts information for his or her own benefit, (b) third party distorts for altruistic reasons (e.g., to avoid embarrassing the target or the observer), (c) third party has rigid knowledge structures (always sees things from the same perspective even when it is inappropriate), (d) third party is a habitual liar, (e) third party's information distorted by availability heuristic, (f) third party's information distorted by representativeness heuristic, (g) third party's information distorted by fundamental attribution error, and (h) message provided by third party is internally inconsistent. The results of this investigation revealed that persons were consistently able to recognize that messages containing the cues might be biased along the lines implied by the particular cue.

These two studies suggest that persons acquire considerable information about others through third-party sources and whereas they find this information to be useful, they are aware of the possibility that it might be biased in some way. Furthermore, when bias cues are present in messages from third parties, observers recognize these cues. A more recent version of second-guessing theory has been presented by Hewes and Graham (1989), and Miller (1989) and Roloff (1989) provided commentary on this revised model.

Interactive Strategies

Interrogation. Perhaps the most obvious way to gather social information in ongoing interactions is to ask questions directly to one's interaction partner. Question asking and question answering have both been studied from a wide variety of perspectives including communication, computer science, education, linguistics, philosophy, and psychology (see Dillon, 1982, 1986; Van der Meij, 1986, for reviews). Here we are only concerned with the roles that questioning plays in the informal social interaction context.

Not surprisingly, the initial few minutes of interactions between strangers are saturated with question-asking and question-answering events (Berger, 1973; Berger & Kellermann, 1983; Calabrese, 1975; Kellermann, 1984a). After approximately one minute of interaction, question-asking rate drops sharply and then slowly declines from that point. This exponential decrease in overall question-asking rate has been observed in at least three studies (Berger & Kellermann, 1983; Calabrese, 1975; Kellermann, 1984a). The questions typically asked during the first few minutes of initial interactions are focused on biographic and demographic characteristics of interactants. Berger and Kellermann (1983) found that 62% of some 1,096 questions asked during 5-minute interactions between 48 unacquainted dyads were questions about aspects of the partner's self. Another 24% were concerned with general information, and 11% were verbal prompts like, "Oh, really?" that were in the form of questions. The remaining 3% of the questions focused on third parties outside of the dyad.

Although the overall rate of question asking in initial encounters shows an exponential decrease over time, the proportion of questions about the partners' selves shows a cyclical pattern of change over the same time period (Berger & Kellermann, 1983). One interpretation offered for this cyclical pattern is that persons may use questions about their co-interactant's self to help rejuvenate their conversations if they begin to wane. This particular interpretation of the cyclical pattern of questions about partners' selves illustrates the potential multifunctionality of question asking. Again, questions most probably subserve epistemic, conversational control, and other functions simultaneously in initial interactions between strangers.

Berger and Kellermann (1983) varied the information-acquisition goals of research participants by giving them instructions before their initial interactions. Some persons were told to find out as much as possible about their partner (High Seekers). Others were instructed to find out as little as possible about their partners during their interactions (Low Seekers). Other persons were simply told to have a normal, get-acquainted conversation (Normals). Individuals with these instructions were placed into High Seeker–High Seeker, High Seeker–Low Seeker, Low Seeker–Low Seeker, or Normal–Normal dyads. Low Seekers asked significantly fewer questions than either the Highs or the Normals. Furthermore, when compared with the other three dyad types, the Low Seeker–Low Seeker dyads displayed a much higher probability of statements by one interactant being followed by statements by the partner. Thus, Low Seekers not only avoided asking questions to achieve their goal, they also proffered statements. High Seekers asked no more questions than did Normals, but they did ask more questions concerned with their partners' goals and future plans. High Seekers also asked their partners to explain their actions more frequently than did the Normals or the Lows. High Seekers generally achieved their information acquisition goals by converting their floor possessions into question-asking opportunities.

Judges' ratings of the efficiency and the social appropriateness of the interactants' behavior revealed a strong positive relationship ($r = .74$) between the number of questions asked by High Seekers and their efficiency in goal achievement. A negative relationship between the same two variables was found for the Low Seekers ($r = -.39$). In other words, question asking increased the efficiency of High Seekers while decreasing the efficiency of Low Seekers. This finding implies that question asking is perceived to be an efficient means of acquiring social information. Social appropriateness was also affected by tactical choices of Low and High Seekers. Low Seekers were significantly less socially appropriate than either the Highs or the Normals. This finding suggests that the Low Seekers deployed socially inappropriate behaviors to put off their interaction partners and thus reach their conversational goal. However, the more questions High Seekers asked, the more inappropriate they were perceived to be, indicating that question asking can be sufficiently intrusive so as to make it socially inappropriate.

Although the questioning behaviors of the High Seekers seem to be ones that would maximize their information gain, some research suggests that when persons attempt to test hypotheses about others, they are likely to ask questions that confirm rather than disconfirm the existence of a trait (see Snyder, 1981). In this research, participants were asked to select from lists of questions those they would ask a target person to see whether the target possessed a particular personality trait, for example, introversion. The question lists were structured so that some questions were biased toward detecting the trait whereas others were biased toward disconfirming the trait; still other questions were neutral with respect to the trait. Several investigations demonstrated that when given a trait to test, persons tend to choose questions that will confirm the existence of the trait rather than following the optimal strategy of asking both confirming and disconfirming questions. The word "asking" is used advisedly here as almost all of the research done in this area was conducted using paper-and-pencil measures, thus depriving the information seeker of the opportunity to ask questions based on responses given by the target.

Beyond the obvious ecological flaws in Snyder's studies is evidence that under certain conditions, persons are more likely to seek diagnostic information to test hypotheses about others regardless of whether the information confirms or disconfirms their hypothesis (Trope & Bassok, 1982). Given this study as well as our own findings, we are considerably more optimistic about the ability of persons to ask questions that provide them with useful information about their co-interactants. Furthermore, the previously discussed research of Hewes and his colleagues supports the view that persons may be both more critical consumers of social information and more sensitive to information-seeking biases than Snyder's research suggests.

Disclosure.   Although interrogation is an interactive substrategy with the potential for high efficiency, it can become intrusive quickly. Persons may ask either too many questions or ask questions that are too probing for their interaction partners to answer. In either case, interrogation might suffer on the social appropriateness dimension. A somewhat less efficient but potentially more socially appropriate substrategy is to volunteer information about one's self with the hope that one's co-interactant will reciprocate the information disclosed. As we noted earlier, Gouldner (1960) argued that persons tend to reciprocate behaviors and considerable evidence exists that this norm of reciprocity operates in social interaction situations (Jourard, 1971; Sermat & Smyth, 1973; Worthy, Gary, & Kahn, 1969). Furthermore, postinteraction protocols completed by participants in the previously discussed Berger and Kellermann (1983) study showed that disclosure was the second most frequently mentioned interactive strategy for gaining information from others.

One problem with the reciprocity construct concerns its precise meaning. There are any number of dimensions along which disclosures can be "reciprocated." For example, persons can reciprocate the sheer amount of information exchanged without regard to any other characteristics. Or, persons can focus on the intimacy of the information exchanged. More important from the perspective of information seeking is the utility of the information for achieving goals. It is possible that neither quantity of information exchanged nor its intimacy level are necessarily tied to goal achievement. A small number of specific pieces of information that are not particularly intimate may be the most useful ones to social information seekers. For example, Kellermann (1984a) reported that relatively trivial information from the standpoint of intimacy was often judged to be informative by social actors. Similarly, Berger and Kellermann (1985) found evidence suggesting that informativeness is unrelated to the intimacy of social information. This notion of information utility has been ignored by most self-disclosure researchers but it is a crucial concept for those interested in strategic communication.

Another difficulty with the reciprocity concept concerns the timing of reciprocal exchanges. A liberal view of reciprocity holds that persons may reciprocate a particular piece of information at any point in an interaction. A more conservative view contends that reciprocity must occur on the next conversational turn in order for a particular interaction event to be "reciprocal" (Dindia, 1982). Although it is certainly true that when a social information seeker obtains a critical piece of information that may be vital to goal achievement, many times the important issue is whether the information is procured at all. As a result, from our perspective the more liberal view of disclosure reciprocity is probably more useful.

Although considerable research has been reported concerning the disclosure reciprocity issue, there is relatively little information about disclosure as an information-gaining strategy. Research stemming from the self-disclosure tradition has found that disclosure by one person tends to elevate the disclosure level of a conversational partner (Jourard & Resnick, 1970). In a sense, the receipt of a disclosure places an obligation on the recipient, requiring a disclosure in return (Archer, 1980). However, proportionately less is revealed by the low discloser as the high discloser reveals more and more (Levin & Gergen, 1969). Thus, the efficiency of self-disclosure as an information-seeking strategy might be somewhat less than that of question asking. However, the loss of efficiency might be offset by potentially more socially appropriate behavior. Typically, the use of the interrogation strategy inhibits disclosure (Berger & Kellermann, 1983) and too little disclosure is perceived to be inappropriate (Chaikin & Derlega, 1974). These findings highlight the importance of efficiency and social appropriateness as meta-goals in the planning and tactical deployment of social information seeking.

Our own research indicates that persons use disclosure as a strategy, but the ways this strategy is realized at the tactical level are still not well understood, though presently being explored. One preliminary result from our work is that the disclosure strategy is composed of structural tactics rather than content-based tactics. The strategy alters the frequency of statements and questions but does not alter the intimacy of the information exchanged. For example, instead of asking where a person is from, social actors will state where they are from, hoping the other will reciprocate. The disclosure strategy is an important means of acquiring information about others. This strategy is consistently used to gain information; more research effort needs to be focused on it.

Relaxing the Target. Of the three interactive substrategies we have isolated, this one is the least intrusive. As we noted before, the aim of the information seeker is to put the target at ease so that he or she will be more prone to disclose information. The lack of intrusiveness of this strategy is, however, counterbalanced by its potential low efficiency. When information seekers use interrogation or disclosure, they can exert considerable control over their partners. The degree of direct control when using relaxation is minimal by comparison. Thus, one might relax a target and encourage the target to disclose personal information, but the target might not disclose the desired information. In psychotherapeutic contexts, such relaxation tactics as "approval-supportive" and "reflection-statement" techniques garnered less information from clients than "open disclosure" (Powell, 1968) or "probing" (Vondracek, 1969).

Kellermann and Berger (1984) studied the behaviors that persons employ to instantiate the relaxation strategy. They found a number of behaviors to be associated with perceived attempts to relax partners. This study revealed that greater fluency, increased pause frequency, and longer switching pause durations were associated with greater relaxation of the partner. Also, increases in head nods, durations of forward body lean, and verbal backchannels were associated with increased attempts to relax co-interactants. High Seekers displayed many more of these relaxing behaviors than did Low Seekers, prompting the speculation that High Seekers may use these positive nonverbal behaviors to compensate for the intrusiveness of their questioning. This possibility raises the issue of whether the relaxation substrategy is actually a separate interactive strategy or whether it is used to blunt the negative impact of other interactive strategies. Evidence adduced by Kellermann and Berger (1984) favors the former interpretation because, in their postinteraction protocols, persons mentioned using relaxation as a strategy, although it was mentioned less frequently
than either interrogation or disclosure. Nevertheless, the deployment of positive nonverbal behaviors by High Seekers may demonstrate that they were attempting to achieve at least two interaction goals simultaneously, that is, acquire social information and leave a positive impression.

Remaining Opaque to Others

Up to this point, our presentation has emphasized the strategies that persons use to ferret out social information. It would be an egregious oversight, however, to ignore the other side of the information seeking coin, that is, the strategies persons use to avoid revealing personal information to others. In a society where persons value their right to privacy, it is important to understand how persons defend this right in the face of excessively inquisitive others. Granted, competent speakers of English are perfectly capable of informing social information seekers that certain things are none of their business; however, the social appropriateness meta-goal is likely to prevent persons from invoking this defensive alternative very often. There must be more subtle ways persons can evade their co-interactants' information-seeking attempts.

These evasiveness strategies were examined by Berger and Kellermann (1989). This study was similar in design to the previously discussed Berger and Kellermann (1983) research; however, in this study High Seekers were paired with persons given different conversational goals. Some High Seekers conversed with persons who were told to reveal as much about themselves as possible during their interactions (High Revealers). Other High Seekers interacted with persons who were instructed to reveal as little about themselves as possible during the interaction (Low Revealers). A third group of High Seekers spoke with persons who were asked to have a normal get-acquainted conversation (Normals).

Compared with High Revealers and Normals, Low Revealers provided information judged to be low in specificity, importance, intimacy, and clarity. Low Revealers were also judged to provide less information and to be less responsive, cooperative, and relaxed than High Revealers and Normals. Interactions involving Low Revealers were judged to be less coordinated. Analyses of various speech parameters showed that Low Revealers produced a larger number of switching pauses, more frequent vocal hesitations, and longer pause durations. In general, these findings suggest that Low Revealers tried to achieve their conversational goal by slowing down the conversation and providing information that was relatively uninformative and ambiguous. These verbal and nonverbal tactics are generally defensive in nature. The postinteraction protocols suggested an offensive tactic that did not manifest itself in the interaction data. Some of the Low Revealers reported that they tried to achieve their goal by becoming High Seekers. Obviously, if one is a successful High Seeker, one can avoid disclosing information about one's self. Apparently, however, not enough Low Revealers employed this offensive tactic to reverse the defensive trends found in the analyses of the interaction data.

The meta-goals of social appropriateness and efficiency were again demonstrated to be of considerable importance in the generation of tactical behavior. Low Revealers evading their inquisitive partners (High Seekers) were found to become less efficient though more socially appropriate over the course of their conversations. By contrast, High Revealers accommodating their inquisitive partners initially gained in both efficiency and social appropriateness, though continuing increases in efficiency were accompanied by corresponding decreases in appropriateness. In other words, evasion of social information-seeking attempts is difficult to maintain over time and is socially inappropriate. However, individuals can also reveal too much about themselves as well as too little.

Although self-disclosure researchers have concerned themselves with the determinants of disclosure, they have not done the kind of fine-grained analyses of evasive tactics reported here. This is a major oversight for at least two reasons. First, simply measuring amount or intimacy of self-disclosure does not reveal the complexities of how disclosure is accomplished or avoided in ongoing interactions. Traditional self-disclosure measures only tap the residues of interactions. Second, failure to achieve an understanding of how persons seek information and avoid disclosing it prevents the development of ways to improve the skills of such communication practitioners as interviewers and therapists. The approach taken in this research also avoids the trap of encouraging value judgments about self-disclosure; it takes as a given the presumption that persons may wish to be opaque or transparent to others for good reasons. Although detailed analyses of interaction data are both difficult and time consuming, the information they reveal about tactical variations are more than worth the effort.

Responses to Failed Information Acquisition Goals

In the previous section we reviewed evidence bearing on the issue of how persons deploy tactical actions to evade others' information-seeking attempts. We now consider the kinds of tactical maneuvers used by information seekers when their attempts to acquire social information are thwarted by targets. The data to be discussed here were collected as part of the Berger and Kellermann (1989) study just described. The design of this study enabled us to examine the effects of the various revealing conditions (High, Low, Normal) on the tactics of the High Seekers (Berger & Kellermann, 1986).

Analyses of these interactions showed, surprisingly, that High Seekers in incompatible dyads (High Seeker–Low Revealer) asked no more or fewer questions of their conversational partners than did High Seekers paired with High Revealers or Normals. However, the thwarted High Seekers did increase their disclosures in such content areas as their social relationships, attitudes concerning their well-being, and attitudes toward objects possessed by their evasive partners. High Seekers paired with Low Revealers also increased the frequency of statements they made about their partners. The High Seekers in the incompatible dyads showed cyclical fluctuations in their use of verbal backchannel responses during their interactions and they interrupted their partners less. In contrast to the tactical patterns shown by the High Seekers paired with Low Revealers, the High Seekers paired with High Revealers demonstrated fewer switching pauses, spent less time holding the floor, and were more responsive. In addition, these High Seekers also provided information that was judged to be more specific, informative, and elaborated. In general, the High Seeker–High Revealer dyads were judged to have higher levels of interaction coordination.

These findings were interpreted as support for the general notion that, at least in the domain of social information gathering, when persons' plans are thwarted, they do not necessarily abandon them and move to new ones. Rather, it appears that persons continue to do what they would normally do and try to augment their current tactics with potentially more effective ones. Thus, High Seekers who were thwarted did not alter their question-asking rates, but they did increase their disclosures of particular types of information to encourage their reticent partners to respond. Also, High Seekers tried to encourage their evasive partners to disclose information by varying their use of verbal back-channels over the course of their interactions. These tactical maneuvers may indicate that planning in this domain is not serial in the sense that failed plans are abandoned and new ones enacted, but that plans and their tactical instantiations accrete over time. How much plans and tactics accumulate is determined by the number of iterations one is willing to go through to reach a goal. Of course, there comes a time when no more plan options are available and there are no more tactical variations with which to pursue goals. However, there is evidence for considerable individual variation in plan sophistication and the domain specificity of these planning abilities (Berger, 1988a; Berger & Bell, 1988). Thus, in the case of failed goals, some persons might "run out of" planning options and unique tactical routines more rapidly than others, assuming that persons continue to pursue their goals.

FUTURE RESEARCH DIRECTIONS

The program of research discussed in this chapter focused on the tactical variations deployed by persons to achieve information-acquisition goals. We have also examined some disclosure-avoidance tactics. Although this research has been carried out within the broad categories of passive, active, and interactive strategies and tactics, it has lacked strong theoretical underpinnings. This lack of theoretical motivation is not limited to research on information-acquisition strategies, as the other chapters of the volume demonstrate. It is difficult to justify continuation of research programs that are limited to the description of strategies and tactics for reaching what are considered by researchers to be interesting or important social goals. Furthermore, research that goes beyond description to specify the conditions under which one or another strategy or tactic will be used has the appearance of theoretical motivation but not its substance.

What is needed to advance the study of strategic communication is an overarching theory that explains how social goals arise, how they are modified, how plans are developed and deployed, how strategies are selected, and how cognitive structures like plans and scripts are realized in action. Such a general theory would serve to integrate the extensive work done on the wide variety of social goals represented in the present volume. Berger (1988a) outlined several issues that such a theory must address, and artificial intelligence researchers

(Wilensky, 1983) developed and implemented planners that have begun to deal with such issues as how goals arise and how plans are modified interactively. Nevertheless, we are far from reaching the goal of an overarching theory of action production, at least from a planning perspective. If such a theory is not developed, we will see a continuation of a piecemeal approach to the study of communication strategies and little accumulation of knowledge.

In response to this line of argument, Berger (1988a) and Berger and Bell (1988) began to develop ways to index action plans. These measures have been found to be significantly related to performance in ongoing interactions (Berger, 1988a) and such long-term psychological states as shyness. In general, less sophisticated planners show more uneasiness during informal interactions and they tend to be more shy. Although the correlations observed in these studies have been modest (.34 to .49), they suggest the utility of this approach. The magnitudes of these correlations are not disappointing because, as we noted at the beginning of this chapter, competency in social action is not only the product of sophisticated plans but also of communication skills and such relatively fixed communication attributes as vocal quality. Measures of these latter attributes were not included in these studies. Furthermore, when persons have limited verbal access to their action plans, verbal reports about plans are likely to underrepresent their complexity (Berger, 1988a). Waldron (1990) demonstrated the usefulness of a cued-recall technique for determining the points at which individuals involved in strategic communication episodes engaged in planful thought. His results indicate that such thoughts are quite frequent during strategic interactions involving information seeking.

Additional research has explored the relationships among the complexity of plans, the degree to which alternative actions in plans are available to actors, and the fluency with which plans are enacted. Social actors attempting to achieve persuasion goals who have more ready access to alternative actions in their plans, as measured by response latencies, are more fluent when they carry out their plans in face-to-face interactions than are persons who show evidence of slower access to alternatives (Berger, 1988c). However, when persons with complex plans are subjected to questioning procedures that encourage them to develop even more action alternatives, their verbal fluency in enacting their plans is lowered relative to those whose plans are less complex. As a consequence, persons with complex plans may have more alternative actions from which to choose in the event of goal failure, but the increased number of alternative actions in their plans may act to debilitate their verbal fluency when their plan is realized in action (Berger, Karol, & Jordan, 1989).

Kellermann (1988) advanced a theory of strategy selection featuring the role played by the meta-goals of efficiency and appropriateness. Evidence suggests that these two meta-goals differentiate strategies from each other for a variety of different goals (Douglas, 1987b; Kellermann, 1992; Kellermann & Kim, 1991; Kellermann, Reynolds, & Chen, 1991). The theory posits that

situational, relational, and personal factors influence the levels of appropriateness and efficiency expected on particular occasions. In urgent situations, for
example, efficiency concerns may become paramount. Efficiency and appropriateness can be compatible, independent, or incompatible constraints influencing the selection of strategies. Compatibility is determined by the task
orientation and negative affect potential of the goal being pursued. Consequently, for some goals (e.g., having fun) appropriate strategies are also efficient,
but for other goals (e.g., information seeking), what is appropriate is independent of what is efficient (Kellermann, 1992; Kellermann & Kim, 1991;
Kellermann et al., 1991). Consequently, strategy selection is based on the goal
it is being used for and the extent to which it satisfies the levels of efficiency
and appropriateness expected on particular occasions.

Research on the conversation memory-organization packet (MOP) (Kellermann, 1991, in press; Kellermann et al., 1989; Kellermann & Lim, 1989,
1990) also provides a potential theoretical basis for understanding behavior
production. A MOP is a schema that organizes conversational tactics into plans
for the achievement of some goal(s). The conversation MOP is composed of
topic-centered scenes that contain tactics for their deployment. Furthermore,
evidence suggests a universal scene exists that can direct talk on any topic,
whether an individual is familiar with that topic or not. The universal scene
is composed of generalized "default" actions of (a) elicit/get facts, (b) discuss
facts, (c) evaluate facts, (d) discuss explanations, (e) discuss goals/intentions,
and discuss enabling conditions for the goals/intentions. For example, the topic-
based scene for hometowns involves finding out where someone is from (getting facts), discussing the hometown (e.g., what is done there, what restaurants or other objects are present there), evaluating the hometown (e.g.,
like/dislike of it), explaining the evaluation of the hometown, discussing plans
to return (i.e., goals/intentions), and discussing how those plans could be realized (e.g., how one could get a job there).

The research on the conversation MOP demonstrates that varying interaction goals affect the timing of deployment of scenes in the MOP though the
ordering of scenes remains similar regardless of one's interaction goal. For example, persons with elevated desires for information seeking, information revealing, and future interaction tend to move through the early, "nonpersonal"
scenes in the MOP more quickly than persons with depressed desires. Later,
however, more personal scenes in the MOP were reached more quickly by persons with these elevated desires; these persons spent more time on these topics.
By contrast, depressing these desires resulted in slow movement through the
early scenes in the MOP and fast movement (often skipping) the later more
personal scenes in the MOP. The extent to which persons "went down" the
universal scene for each topic in the MOP was the extent to which they went
"slow" or "fast" through scenes in the MOP. The most surprising finding
of this research was that the structure of conversations did not vary as

goals/desires changed and varied; rather, only the timing of deployment of scenes (i.e., topics of conversation) varied. Such a result suggests why and how the same behaviors can be multifunctional: Alterations in timing are used to influence goal attainment more than simple differences in actual behavior. Reported behavioral differences reflect variations in the timing of tactics (hence influencing the frequency of behaviors within any given time interval).

Such a perspective is consistent with the research on the interactive information-seeking strategies (interrogation, disclosure, relaxation). In that research, cyclicity was consistently demonstrated in the verbal behaviors of persons engaged in initial interaction. In other words, various verbal behaviors cycle over the course of conversations, waxing and waning as time progressed. For example, question-asking cycles over the course of conversation as do explanations for behavior and information about goals and intentions. Such cyclicity is to be expected from the deployment of the universal scene. As each topic is initiated, question asking would be expected to be high as per the question-driven nature of the get facts stage of the universal scene. However, as persons move toward discussion of evaluations, goals/intentions, and enabling conditions, interrogation sequences diminish while statement-based linguistic forms increase. Similarly, the universal scene suggests explanations (and other information) should exhibit cyclicity as a topic moves toward and then away from that part of the universal scene. In other words, the conversation MOP in conjunction with dynamic memory theory on which it is based provides one potential explanation of how plans are developed and manipulated to result in tactics to achieve various goals.

What we are advocating, then, is a turn from the study of communicative activity directed toward specific social goals to a more general focus on the production of strategic communication. Of course, any given investigation must use particular goals to study strategic communication processes; however, the crucial objective of such studies should be to understand the general processes involved in the production of goal-directed communicative action. Certainly, the contents of plans will vary in some ways from one social goal to the next; however, we believe the processes of plan retrieval, plan generation, and strategy selection are quite general. Moreover, there may be features of plans that are common across heterogeneous social goals. It is these general processes that should be the focus of future theory development and research efforts. Toward this end, some beginning steps have been made toward developing plan-based, selection-oriented, and flexibly adapted theories of strategic communication that address some of these issues (Berger, in press; Kellermann, 1988, in press), although considerably more work needs to be done in this direction.

REFERENCES

Abbott, V., & Black, J. B. (1986). Goal-related inferences in comprehension. In J. A. Galambos, R. P. Abelson, & J. B. Black (Eds.), *Knowledge structures* (pp. 123–142). Hillsdale, NJ: Lawrence Erlbaum Associates.

Archer, R. L. (1980). Self-disclosure. In D. M. Wegner & R. R. Vallacher (Eds.), *The self in social psychology* (pp. 183–205). New York: Oxford University Press.

Baxter, L. A., & Wilmot, W. W. (1984). "Secret tests": Social strategies for acquiring information about the state of the relationship. *Human Communication Research, 11,* 171–201.

Berger, C. R. (1973, December). *The acquaintance process revisited: Explorations in initial interaction.* Paper presented at the annual convention of the Speech Communication Association, New York.

Berger, C. R. (1975). Proactive and retroactive attribution processes in interpersonal communications. *Human Communication Research, 2,* 33–50.

Berger, C. R. (1979). Beyond initial interaction: Uncertainty, understanding, and the development of interpersonal relationships. In H. Giles & R. St. Clair (Eds.), *Language and social psychology* (pp. 122–144). Oxford: Basil Blackwell.

Berger, C. R. (1985). Social power and interpersonal communication. In M. L. Knapp & G. R. Miller (Eds.), *Handbook of interpersonal communication* (pp. 439–499). Newbury Park, CA: Sage.

Berger, C. R. (1988a). Planning, affect, and social action generation. In L. Donohew, H. Sypher, & E. T. Higgins (Eds.), *Communication, social cognition and affect* (pp. 93–116). Hillsdale, NJ: Lawrence Erlbaum Associates.

Berger, C. R. (1988b). Uncertainty and information exchange in developing relationships. In S. W. Duck (Ed.), *Handbook of personal relationships* (pp. 239–255). Chichester, England: Wiley.

Berger, C. R. (1988c, May). *Communication plans and communicative performance.* Paper presented at the annual convention of the International Communication Association, New Orleans, LA.

Berger, C. R. (in press). A plan-based approach to strategic communication. In D. E. Hewes (Ed.), *The cognitive bases of interpersonal communication.* Hillsdale, NJ: Lawrence Erlbaum Associates.

Berger, C. R., & Bell, R. A. (1988). Plans and the initiation of social relationships. *Human Communication Research, 15,* 217–235.

Berger, C. R., & Bradac, J. J. (1982). *Language and social knowledge: Uncertainty in interpersonal relations.* London: Edward Arnold.

Berger, C. R., & Douglas, W. (1981). Studies in interpersonal epistemology III: Anticipated interaction, self-monitoring, and observational context selection. *Communication Monographs, 48,* 183–196.

Berger, C. R., Karol, S. H., & Jordan, J. M. (1989). When a lot of knowledge is a dangerous thing: The debilitating effects of plan complexity on verbal fluency. *Human Communication Research, 16,* 91–119.

Berger, C. R., & Kellermann, K. A. (1983). To ask or not to ask: Is that a question? In R. N. Bostrom (Ed.), *Communication yearbook 7* (pp. 342–368). Newbury Park, CA: Sage.

Berger, C. R., & Kellermann, K. A. (1985, May). *Personal opacity and social information gathering: Seek, but ye may not find.* Paper presented at the annual convention of the International Communication Association, Honolulu, HI.

Berger, C. R., & Kellermann, K. A. (1986, May). *Goal incompatibility and social action: The best laid plans of mice and men often go astray.* Paper presented at the annual convention of the International Communication Association, Chicago, IL.

Berger, C. R., & Kellermann, K. A. (1989). Personal opacity and social information gathering: Explorations in strategic communication. *Communication Research, 16,* 314–351.

Berger, C. R., & Perkins, J. W. (1978). Studies in interpersonal epistemology I: Situational attributes in observational context selection. In B. D. Ruben (Ed.). *Communication yearbook 2* (pp. 171–184). New Brunswick, NJ: Transaction Press.

Berger, C. R., & Perkins, J. W. (1979, November). *Studies in interpersonal epistemology II: Self-monitoring, involvement, facial affect, similarity, and observational context selection.* Paper presented at the annual convention of the Speech Communication Association, San Antonio, TX.

Bernard, H. R., Killworth, P. D., & McCarty, C. (1982). INDEX: An informant-defined experiment in social structure. *Social Forces, 61,* 99–133.

Berscheid, E., Graziano, W., Monson, T., & Dermer, M. (1976). Outcome dependency: Attention, attribution, and attraction. *Journal of Personality and Social Psychology, 34,* 978–989.

Brand, M. (1984). *Intending and acting: Toward a naturalized action theory.* Cambridge, MA: MIT Press.

Bratman, M. E. (1987). *Intention, plans, and practical reason.* Cambridge, MA: Harvard University Press.

Brown, P., & Levinson, S. C. (1978). Universals in language usage: Politeness phenomena. In E. M. Goody (Ed.), *Questions and politeness: Strategies in social interaction* (pp. 56–289). Cambridge: Cambridge University Press.

Bruce, B. C. (1980). Plans and social actions. In R. J. Spiro, B. C. Bruce, & W. F. Brewer (Eds.), *Theoretical issues in reading comprehension* (pp. 367–384). Hillsdale, NJ: Lawrence Erlbaum Associates.

Bruce, B., & Newman, D. (1978). Interacting plans. *Cognitive Science, 2,* 195–233.

Byrne, D. (1971). *The attraction paradigm.* New York: Academic Press.

Calabrese, R. J. (1975). *The effects of privacy and probability of future interaction on initial interaction patterns.* Unpublished doctoral dissertation, Northwestern University, Evanston, IL.

Chaikin, A. L., & Derlega, V. J. (1974). *Self-disclosure.* Morristown, NJ: General Learning Press.

Dailey, W. O. (1985). *The effects of discussion on debiasing judgment: Two pilot studies.* Paper presented at the annual convention of the Speech Communication Association, Denver, CO.

Derlega, V. J., & Grzelak, J. (1979). Appropriateness of self-disclosure. In G. J. Chelune & Associates (Eds.), *Self-disclosure: Origins, patterns, and implications of openness in interpersonal relationships* (pp. 151–176). San Francisco: Jossey-Bass.

Dillon, J. T. (1982). The multidisciplinary study of questioning. *Journal of Educational Psychology, 74,* 147–165.

Dillon, J. T. (1986). Questioning. In O. Hargie (Ed.), *A handbook of communication skills* (pp. 95–127). London: Croom Helm.

Dindia, K. (1982). Reciprocity of self-disclosure: A sequential analysis. In M. Burgoon (Ed.), *Communication yearbook 6* (pp. 506–528). Newbury Park, CA: Sage.

Doelger, J. A., Hewes, D. E., & Graham, M. L. (1986). Knowing when to "second guess": The mindful analysis of messages. *Human Communication Research, 12,* 301–338.

Douglas, W. (1985). Anticipated interaction and information seeking. *Human Communication Research, 12,* 243–258.

Douglas, W. (1987a). Question-asking in same- and opposite-sex initial interactions: The effects of anticipated future interaction. *Human Communication Research, 14,* 230–245.

Douglas, W. (1987b). Affinity-testing in initial interactions. *Journal of Social and Personal Relationships, 4,* 3–15.

Ervin-Tripp, S. (1976). Is Sybil there? The structure of some American English directives. *Language in Society, 5,* 25–66.

Festinger, L. (1954). A theory of social comparison processes. *Human Relations, 7,* 114–140.

Gilbert, D. T. (1989). Thinking lightly about others: Automatic components of the social inference process. In J. S. Uleman & J. A. Bargh (Eds.), *Unintended thought* (pp. 189–211). New York: Guilford Press.

Gouldner, A. W. (1960). The norm of reciprocity: A preliminary statement. *American Sociological Review, 25,* 161–178.

Graham, J. A., Argyle, M., & Furnham, A. (1980). The goal structure of situations. *European Journal of Social Psychology, 10,* 345–366.

Hammond, K. J. (1989). *Case-based planning: Viewing planning as a memory task.* San Diego, CA: Academic Press.

Harvey, J. H., Yarkin, K. L., Lightner, J. M., & Towne, J. P. (1980). Unsolicited interpretation and recall of interpersonal events. *Journal of Personality and Social Psychology, 38,* 551–568.

Hastie, R., Ostrom, T. M., Ebbesen, E. B., Wyer, R. S., Jr., Hamilton, D. L., & Carlston, D. E. (Eds.). (1980). *Person memory: The cognitive basis of social perception.* Hillsdale, NJ: Lawrence Erlbaum Associates.

Hayes-Roth, B., & Hayes-Roth, F. (1979). A cognitive model of planning. *Cognitive Science, 3,* 275–310.

Hewes, D. E., & Graham, M. L. (1989). Second-guessing theory: Review and extension. In J. A. Anderson (Ed.), *Communication yearbook 12* (pp. 213–248). Newbury Park, CA: Sage.

Hewes, D. E., Graham, M. K., Doelger, J., & Pavitt, C. (1985). "Second guessing": Message interpretation in social networks. *Human Communication Research, 11,* 299–334.

Hewes, D. E., Graham, M. L., Monsour, M., & Doelger, J. A. (1989). Cognition and social information gathering strategies: Reinterpretation assessment in second-guessing. *Human Communication Research, 16,* 297–320.

Hewes, D. E., & Planalp, S. (1982). There is nothing as useful as a good theory . . . The influence of social knowledge on interpersonal communication. In M. E. Roloff & C. R. Berger (Eds.), *Social cognition and communication* (pp. 107–150). Newbury Park, CA: Sage.

Hobbs, J. R., & Evans, D. A. (1980). Conversation as planned behavior. *Cognitive Science, 4,* 349–377.

Hogarth, R. (1980). *Judgment and choice: The psychology of decision.* New York: Wiley.

Jones, E. E. (1964). *Ingratiation.* New York: Appleton-Century.

Jones, E. E., & Davis, K. E. (1965). From acts to dispositions: The attribution process in person perception. In L. Berkowitz (Ed.), *Advances in experimental social psychology* (Vol. 2, pp. 219–266). New York: Academic Press.

Jones, E. E., & Wortman, C. (1973). *Ingratiation: An attributional approach.* Morristown, NJ: General Learning Press.

Jourard, S. M. (1971). *Self-disclosure: An experimental analysis of the transparent self.* New York: Wiley Interscience.

Jourard, S. M., & Resnick, J. L. (1970). Some effects of self-disclosure among college women. *Journal of Humanistic Psychology, 10,* 84–93.

Kahneman, D., Slovic, P., & Tversky, A. (1982). *Judgment under uncertainty: Heuristics and biases.* Cambridge: Cambridge University Press.

Kellermann, K. A. (1984a). *A formal model of information exchange in initial interaction.* Unpublished doctoral dissertation, Northwestern University, Evanston, IL.

Kellermann, K. A. (1984b). The negativity effect and its implications for initial interaction. *Communication Monographs, 51,* 37–55.

Kellermann, K. A. (1986). Anticipation of future interaction and information exchange in initial interaction. *Human Communication Research, 13,* 41–75.

Kellermann, K. A. (1988). Understanding tactical choice: Metagoals in conversation. Paper presented at the Temple Discourse Conference, Philadelphia, PA.

Kellermann, K. A. (1991). The conversation MOP: II. Progression through the scenes of discourse. *Human Communication Research, 17,* 385–414.

Kellermann, K. A. (1992, November). *A goal-directed approach to gaining compliance: Differences in behavioral acceptability for different compliance-gaining goals.* Paper presented at the annual convention of the Speech Communication Association, Chicago, IL.

Kellermann, K. A. (in press). The conversation MOP: A model of patterned and pliable behavior. In D. Hewes (Ed.), *The cognitive bases of interpersonal communication.* Hillsdale, NJ: Lawrence Erlbaum Associates.

Kellermann, K. A., & Berger, C. R. (1984). Affect and the acquisition of social information: Sit back, relax, and tell me about yourself. In R. N. Bostrom (Ed.), *Communication yearbook 8* (pp. 412–445). Newbury Park, CA: Sage.

Kellermann, K. A., Broetzmann, S., Lim, T., & Kitao, K. (1989). The conversation MOP: Scenes in the stream of discourse. *Discourse Processes, 12,* 27–62.

Kellermann, K. A., Burrell, N., Mulcrone, J., Lim, T., & Kang, K. H. (1987). *Conditional inference and knowledge: If you don't tell, then we must know.* Paper presented at the annual convention of the Speech Communication Association, Boston, MA.

Kellermann, K. A., & Kim, M. S. (1991, May). *Working within constraints: Tactical choices in the pursuit of social goals.* Paper presented at the annual convention of the International Communication Association, Chicago, IL.

Kellermann, K. A., & Lim, T. (1989). Conversational acquaintance: The flexibility of routinized behaviors. In B. Dervin (Ed.), *Paradigm dialogues: Vol. 2* (pp. 172–187). Newbury Park, CA: Sage.

Kellermann, K. A., & Lim, T. (1990). The conversation MOP: III. Timing of scenes in discourse. *Journal of Personality and Social Psychology, 59,* 1163–1179.

Kellermann, K. A., Lim, T., Kang, K. H., Burrell, N., & Mulcrone, J. (1987). *Representativeness and the conjunction fallacy: It's Linda, Linda, and Linda.* Paper presented at the annual convention of the Speech Communication Association, Boston, MA.

Kellermann, K. A., Reynolds, R., & Chen, J. B. (1991). Strategies of conversational retreat: When parting is not sweet sorrow. *Communication Monographs, 58,* 362–383.

Killworth, P. D., Bernard, H. R., & McCarty, C. (1984). Measuring patterns of acquaintanceship. *Current Anthropology, 25,* 381–397.

Kunda, Z., & Nisbett, R. (1986). The psychometrics of everyday life. *Cognitive Psychology, 18,* 195–224.

Larsen, K. S., Martin, H. J., & Giles, H. (1977). Anticipated social cost and interpersonal accommodation. *Human Communication Research, 3,* 303–308.

Levin, F. M., & Gergen, K. J. (1969). Revealingness, ingratiation, and the disclosure of self. *Proceedings of the 77th Annual Convention of the American Psychological Association, 4,* 447–448.

Lichtenstein, E. H., & Brewer, W. F. (1980). Memory for goal-directed events. *Cognitive Psychology, 12,* 412–445.

McCann, C. D., & Higgins, E. T. (1988). Motivation and affect in interpersonal relations: The role of personal orientations and discrepancies. In L. Donohew, H. Sypher, & E. T. Higgins (Eds.), *Communication, social cognition, and affect* (pp. 53–79). Hillsdale, NJ: Lawrence Erlbaum Associates.

Merritt, M. (1976). On questions following questions in service encounters. *Language in Society, 5,* 315–357.

Miller, G. A., Galanter, E., & Pribram, K. H. (1960). *Plans and the structure of behavior.* New York: Holt, Rinehart, & Winston.

Miller, G. R. (1989). Second-guessing second-guessing: Yet another comment. In J. A. Anderson (Ed.), *Communication yearbook 12* (pp. 266–275). Newbury Park, CA: Sage.

Mishler, E. G. (1975). Studies in dialogue and discourse: II. Types of discourse initiated by and sustained through questioning. *Journal of Psycholinguistic Research, 4,* 99–121.

Nisbett, R. E., & Ross, L. (1980). *Human inference: Strategies and shortcomings of social judgment.* Englewood Cliffs, NJ: Prentice-Hall.

Parks, M. R., & Adelman, M. B. (1983). Communication networks and the development of romantic relationships. *Human Communication Research, 10,* 55–79.

Powell, W. J. (1968). Differential effectiveness of interviewer interventions in an experimenter interview. *Journal of Consulting and Clinical Psychology, 32,* 210–215.

Riesbeck, C. K., & Schank, R. C. (1989). *Inside case-based reasoning.* Hillsdale, NJ: Lawrence Erlbaum Associates.

Rogers, C. R. (1951). *Client-centered therapy: Its current practice, implications, and theory.* Boston: Houghton-Mifflin.

Roloff, M. E. (1989). On second-guessing the theory of second-guessing: A comment. In J. A. Anderson (Ed.), *Communication yearbook 12* (pp. 249–265). Newbury Park, CA: Sage.

Rosenbaum, M. E. (1986) The repulsion hypothesis: On the nondevelopment of relationships. *Journal of Personality and Social Psychology, 51,* 1156–1166.

Sacerdoti, E. D. (1977). *A structure for plans and behavior.* New York: Elsevier.

Schank, R. C. (1982). *Dynamic memory: A theory of reminding and learning in computers and people.* Cambridge: Cambridge University Press.

Schank, R. C., & Abelson, R. (1977). *Scripts, plans, goals, and understanding.* Hillsdale, NJ: Lawrence Erlbaum Associates.
Scherer, K. R. (1979). Voice and speech correlates of perceived social influence in simulated juries. In H. Giles & R. St. Clair (Eds.), *Language and social psychology* (pp. 88–120). Oxford: Basil Blackwell.
Schmidt, C. F. (1976). Understanding human action: Recognizing the plans and motives of other persons. In J. S. Carroll & J. W. Payne (Eds.), *Cognition and social behavior* (pp. 47–67). Hillsdale, NJ: Lawrence Erlbaum Associates.
Sermat, V., & Smyth, M. (1973). Content analysis of verbal communication in the development of a relationship: Conditions influencing self-disclosure. *Journal of Personality and Social Psychology, 26,* 332–346.
Snyder, M. (1981). Seek, and ye shall find: Testing hypotheses about other people. In E. T. Higgins, C. P. Herman, & M. P. Zanna (Eds.), *Social cognition: The Ontario symposium* (Vol. 1, pp. 277–303). Hillsdale, NJ: Lawrence Erlbaum Associates.
Suls, J. M., & Miller, R. L. (1977). *Social comparison processes.* New York: Halsted Press.
Taylor, S. E., & Crocker, J. (1981). Schematic bases of social information processing. In E. T. Higgins, C. P. Herman, & M. P. Zanna (Eds.), *Social cognition: The Ontario symposium* (Vol. 1, pp. 89–134). Hillsdale, NJ: Lawrence Erlbaum Associates.
Trope, Y., & Bassok, M. (1982). Confirmatory and diagnosing strategies in social information gathering. *Journal of Personality and Social Psychology, 43,* 22–34.
Van der Meij, H. (1986) *Questioning: A study on the questioning behavior of elementary school children.* Den Haag, The Netherlands: SVO.
Vondracek, F. W. (1969). The study of self-disclosure in experimental interviews. *Journal of Psychology, 72,* 55–59.
Waldron, V. R. (1990). Constrained rationality: Situational influences on information acquisition plans and tactics. *Communication Monographs, 57,* 184–201.
Webb, E. J., Campbell, D. T., Schwartz, R. D., & Sechrest, L. (1966). *Unobtrusive measures: Nonreactive research in the social sciences.* Chicago: Rand McNally.
Wilensky, R. (1983). *Planning and understanding: A computational approach to human reasoning.* Reading, MA: Addison-Wesley.
Worthy, M., Gary, A. L., & Kahn, G. M. (1969). Self-disclosure as an exchange process. *Journal of Personality and Social Psychology, 13,* 59–64.
Wyer, R. S., & Srull, T. K. (Eds.). (1984). *Handbook of social cognition* (Vols. 1–3). Hillsdale, NJ: Lawrence Erlbaum Associates.

Chapter 2

Compliance-Gaining Goals:
An Inductive Analysis of Actors'
Goal Types, Strategies, and Successes

Michael J. Cody
University of Southern California, Los Angeles

Daniel J. Canary
Ohio University

Sandi W. Smith
Michigan State University

The objective of compliance-gaining research is to increase our understanding of how social actors use messages to achieve goals. Whereas the research area focusing on "compliance-gaining message strategy selection" has been popular in the communication discipline in the last several years, research on dyadic social influence processes has a long history in social psychology (see reviews by Seibold, Cantrill, & Meyers, 1985; Wheeless, Barraclough, & Stewart, 1983). Three decades of research, for example, have focused on ingratiation tactics (Godfrey, Jones, & Lord, 1986; Jones, 1964; Jones & Wortman, 1973), bases of power (French & Raven, 1959; Raven, Centers, & Rodrigues, 1975; Raven & Kruglanski, 1970), and influence in the organization (Kipnis, 1972, 1976; Kipnis, Castell, Gergen, & March, 1976; Kipnis & Cosentino, 1969; Kipnis & Lane, 1962; Kipnis, Schmidt, & Braxton-Brown, 1990; Kipnis, Schmidt, & Wilkinson, 1980; Schmidt & Kipnis, 1984). Our contribution to the general area of influence processes began with an interest in how people perceive common influence situations (Cody & McLaughlin, 1980, 1985a; Cody, Woelfel, & Jordan, 1983), and extended to research attempting to uncover the types of strategies people use when influencing others (Cody, 1982; Cody, Greene, Marston, Baaske, O'Hair, & Schneider, 1986; Cody, McLaughlin, & Jordan, 1980; Cody, McLaughlin, & Schneider, 1981).

Recently, however, we have been more interested in how *goals* (rather than specific situation perceptions) direct strategies (Canary & Cody, in press;

Canary, Cody, & Marston, 1986; Canary, Cunningham, & Cody, 1988; Smith, Cody, LoVette, & Canary, 1990). Goals, we believe, have more to do with predicting the use of particular tactics than any specific perception of situations, but goals can be described in terms of situation perceptions, and can be differentiated from one another on the basis of situation perceptions. For instance, the goal of *Obtain Permission* (from one's parents) is perceived in terms of several salient features involving qualities of the target–agent relationship, rights and obligations, anticipated emotional reactions, and so on, whereas the goal of *De-escalate Relationship* is perceived in terms of different salient features.

In this chapter we discuss why we are now interested in goals. The second section of this chapter details how our research has progressed from relying on a dimensional model of situation perceptions to a categorical model of goal-types, addressing five topics: (a) why actors' goals should be studied; (b) conceptualization of goals; (c) categories of goals used in compliance-gaining research; (d) influence methods used in attaining goals; and (e) a general typology of influence goals. Two additional issues are addressed: First, we report the frequency by which various goals are pursued and examine how successful actors are when pursuing various goals. Thus, we present the results of a "nominating study" and a "diary study," each providing some evidence about how frequently college-age actors influence various targets. Second, we anticipate that males and females would pursue different types of goals; more specifically, females (vs. males) would more actively pursue goals pertaining to communal activities. To address this issue, we compared the responses of males and females in the nominating study, and we investigated gender differences in a study that examined reactions to 14 general goals (Canary et al., 1986). The last section of this chapter summarizes the studies, reviews what we currently know about how actors pursue goals, and proposes directions for further research.

First, however, we overview research conducted on influence methods and the developments that have been made in their study.

The Influence Literature: Typologies of Influence Methods

We know more about typologies of messages than we know of any other topic in the compliance-gaining literature (Bisanz & Rule, 1989, 1990; Cody et al., 1980; Craig, Tracy, & Spisak, 1986; Dillard & Fitzpatrick, 1985; Falbo, 1977a, 1977b; Falbo & Peplau, 1980; Goodchilds, Quadrado, & Raven, 1975; Kipnis, 1984; Kipnis et al., 1980; McLaughlin, Cody, & Robey, 1980; McQuillen, 1986; McQuillen, Higgenbotham, & Cummings, 1984; Rule & Bisanz, 1987; Tracy, Craig, Smith, & Spisak, 1984; Wiseman & Schenck-Hamlin, 1981; Witteman & Fitzpatrick, 1986). These studies suggest that there exists a finite set of message tactics, that actors have definite beliefs and expectations about the use of tactics, that actors have a distinct preference for using certain tactics, and that actors perceive and differentiate tactics on the basis of a few salient dimensions.

The first systematic approach of the study of influence processes was conducted by Raven and his colleagues (Raven & Kruglanski, 1970; French & Raven, 1959). Raven and Kruglanski argued that six sources of influence (expert, reward, coercive, legitimate, referent, and information) have predictable effects on four types of outcomes: the public behavior of the target, the private beliefs of the target, the target's future interaction with the agent, and the target's identification with the agent. Further, a substantial amount of work conducted in organizational settings (Bachman, Bowers, & Marcus, 1968; Student, 1968; see reviews in Bettinghaus & Cody, 1987, and Seibold et al., 1985) indicates that coercive influence results in negative consequences, that referent and expert sources of influence result in increased job satisfaction and higher levels of performance, that reward power was often effective in motivating others (if used consistently, etc.; see Bettinghaus & Cody), and that workers agreed that they are obligated to comply to requests that are legitimate.

Raven and his colleagues (Goodchilds et al., 1975) later addressed a fundamental issue—how does anyone, with or without power, go about influencing others? Few people have the ability to reward, coerce, claim to be an expert, and so on, when attempting to change others' behavior. A second issue concerned how actors, who have little power, go about influencing others. Goodchilds et al. analyzed essays students wrote on "How I Get My Way," and their report was followed by several multidimensional scaling studies that assessed influence methods (Cody et al., 1980; Falbo, 1977a; Falbo & Peplau, 1980; Wiseman & Schenck-Hamlin, 1981), and by studies that obtained factors of tactics by having actors rate tactics on likelihood-of-use rating scales (Kipnis et al., 1980). A third approach to the study of influence methods and the structure of such methods is the recent set of investigations into the validity of a persuasion schema (Bisanz & Rule, 1989, 1990; Greene, 1990; Greene, Smith, & Lindsey, 1988).

The results of the multidimensional scaling studies indicate that there exists a finite set of tactics actors employ and that the tactics are differentiated from one another on the basis of a few salient dimensions. Falbo (1977a) obtained two dimensions for 16 tactics, "indirect versus direct," and "rational versus nonrational," and Falbo and Peplau (1980) obtained two dimensions ("direct vs. indirect" and "bilateral vs. unilateral") for 13 tactics relevant to intimate relationships. Wiseman and Schenck-Hamlin (1981) identified 14 tactics; their multidimensional scaling solution yielded four dimensions: directness of tactics, manipulation of sanctions (punishing vs. rewarding), locus of control (pressure vs. freedom of choice), and explicitness of rationale. Cody

et al. (1980) assessed essays students wrote for three situations and obtained
two dimensions for each of the three situations: direct/rational versus coercive
and direct versus manipulative; cooperative versus negative consequences and
inaction versus direct/rational; and inaction versus manipulation and strong
versus weak. Generally speaking, direct methods include *simple statement* (or,
"direct request"), *persistence* and *assertion*, and indirect methods include *hinting, deceit,* and *emotionally oriented* tactics (flattery, other forms of ingratiation,
looking disappointed, etc.). Rational approaches include *reason, compromise, bargain, persuasion,* and *expertise*; less rational ones include *evasion, fait accompli,* and
threat.

One of the best examples of research aimed at assessing the factor structure
of influence strategies is the work by Kipnis and his colleagues. Kipnis et al.
(1980) had managers write essays on the influence methods they used on superiors, co-workers, and subordinates, and identified 14 categories of strategies: *clandestine* (8% of all essays), *personal negative actions* (8%), *administrative
sanctions* or negative actions (3%), *exchange* (8%), *persistence* (7%), *training* (6%),
reward (2%), *self-presentation* (5%), *direct requests* (10%), *weak ask* (6%), *demand*
(7%), *explanation* (17%), *gathering supporting data* (6%), and *coalitions* (7%). A
second group of managers rated 58 of the strategies on likelihood-of-use rating
scales, and eight factors were obtained: *assertiveness, ingratiation, rationality, administrative sanctions, exchange, upward appeals, blocking,* and *coalitions*. Later Kipnis and his colleagues created the POIS instrument (Profiles of Organizational
Influence Strategies), that included measures of *reason, friendliness, assertiveness,
coalitions, higher authority,* and *bargaining*. Status, goals, target resistance, and
organizational variables all play a role in affecting the frequency by which the
strategies are implemented (see following).

Fitzpatrick and Winke (1979) obtained five factors of conflict strategies:
manipulation, nonnegotiation, emotional appeals, personal rejection, and *empathetic understanding*. Similar types of messages have been obtained in research on
compliance-resisting (McLaughlin et al., 1980; McQuillen, 1986; McQuillen
et al., 1984). Shea and Pearson (1986) obtained three factors of relational maintenance tactics (balance, avoidance, and directness) and Baxter (1984) obtained
four factors of tactics that were interpreted in the framework of Brown and
Levinson's (1978) theory of politeness (but see Craig et al., 1986). Cody et
al. (1986) reviewed all proposed typologies and designed a questionnaire to
measure seven general methods (using multiple indicators of each factor). Their
confirmatory (LISREL) analyses indicated that the best-fitting solution (between model and data) was a model of seven correlated factors: *justification,
direct request, exchange, coercion, referent influence, manipulation of positive feelings,* and
manipulation of negative feelings. Finally, research in instructional communication also indicates that rewards, punishments, manipulation of negative feelings (i.e., guilt), manipulation of positive feelings, manipulation of positive
relations, exchange, coalitions (peer modeling), reasoning and rules, and ex-

pertise are commonly employed (e.g., see Barracalough, 1984; Kearney, Plax, Richmond, & McCroskey, 1984).

The latest approach is the cognitive approach used to assess the existence and operation of a persuasion schema. Schank and Abelson (1977) can be credited with developing a theory of "plan-based understanding" that assumes several fundamental propositions concerning the nature and organization of goals and methods for achieving goals (see also Rule & Bisanz, 1987):

1. Goals associated with the use of a persuasion schema constitute a small finite set.
2. There exists a standard set of methods that can be used to pursue goals.
3. If any of the standard methods fail, the actor may use additional ("auxiliary") methods.
4. The use of methods is ordered so that once an initial method is selected and fails, the individual will select a tactic further down in the sequence. Further, it is possible for the actor to skip over some methods.

Rule and Bisanz (1987; see also Bisanz & Rule, 1989, 1990; Rule, Bisanz, & Kohn, 1985) completed several analyses of the persuasion schema. First, their analyses of open-ended influence methods revealed 15 tactics that form five basic categories of message-types. Tactics are further ordered from the most preferred to the least preferred and these are listed in Table 2.1. The simple statement or direct request tactic, labeled *Ask*, represents the most preferred influence method. The second general category, *Self-Oriented*, includes "present information" and "mention personal benefits." Some tactics labeled "reason" or "rationality" in the multidimensional scaling and factor analytic work probably reflect this category, although tactics in the fourth category are also rational. Also included is the "butter-up" tactic (labeled "manipulation of positive feelings" in earlier work) because it involves manipulating the role or image of the actor. (Rule and Bisanz originally placed this tactic in the fifth category, *Negative Strategies*, because of its manipulative nature. The strategy was later moved to the second category because of how it was ranked, and because it deals with the self and the self-image.)

The third category, *Dyad Oriented* ("invoke role relationship," "bargain [favor]"), included tactics that appealed to the quality of the relationship (not completely unlike *referent* influence), and included the *exchange* tactics identified by Kipnis et al. (1980) (e.g., "I need to have Sunday night off, so can you do me a favor and switch shifts this weekend?"). The fourth category, appeals to *Social Principles*, included "norms," "altruism," and "moral principles." The fifth category, *Negative Strategies*, included two types of tactics: *manipulation* ("emotional appeals," "deception," and "bargain [object]"), in which case actors engage in impersonal bargaining, perhaps of a competitive nature, and *aggressive tactics* ("criticize," "threaten," and "force").

TABLE 2.1

Methods of Persuasion as Labeled and Described for Participants

Name	Description
Ask	Simply ask their friend to try to get cooperation. No particular reason is given.
Self-Oriented	
Present information (Invoke personal expertise)	The individual presents facts or evidence to try to get cooperation.
Mention personal benefits (Inform personal reason)[a]	The individual mentions how they personally would benefit to try to get cooperation. Or the individual mentions how their friend personally would benefit from cooperating.
Butter-Up[b]	The individual attempts to make their friend feel wonderful or important to try to get cooperation.
Dyad Oriented	
Mention relationship (Invoke role relationship)	The individual mentions an existing relationship to try to get cooperation. For example: "A good friend would do this."
Bargain (favor)	The individual offers to do a favor in exchange for cooperation.
Social Principles	
Mention similar behavior (Invoke norm)	The individual tells their friend about others who would do the same thing to try to get cooperation.
Mention benefit to others (Invoke altruism)	The individual mentions how their friend's cooperation will benefit others.
Make moral appeal (Invoke moral principle)	The individual makes an appeal to a moral value (e.g., it's the right thing to do) to try to get cooperation.
Bargain (object)	The individual offers a highly desired physical object (could be money) in exchange for cooperation.
Negative	
Emotional appeal	The individual cries, begs, throws a tantrum, sulks, or uses some other emotional display to try to get cooperation.
Criticize	The individual attacks their friend on a personal level, trying to make them feel personally inadequate if they do not cooperate.
Deceive	The individual misleads their friend to try to get cooperation.
Threaten	The individual informs their friend of negative things that will result from not cooperating.
Force	The individual physically assaults their friend or uses some other means of force to try to get cooperation.

[a]The names in parentheses after the labels provided for participants are the more technical labels used in the taxonomy developed by Rule, Bisanz, and Kohn, 1985.

[b]Bisanz and Rule originally placed "butter-up" in the category of *Negative* strategy, but later located the strategy as a *Self-Oriented* strategy, acknowledging the empirical data (see Rule & Bisanz, 1987).

Rule and Bisanz (1987) present three types of evidence concerning the validity of a persuasion schema. First, social actors are consistent in their rank ordering of the tactics and in their ratings of preference (and perceptions of social approval). Second, social actors acquire the strategies in a way consistent with the persuasion schema. Young children rely heavily on Ask, and decrease their reliance on Ask as they age. They increase reliance on Self-Oriented and Dyad-Oriented tactics (up until Grade 9) where frequency of use levels off, and they increase their reliance on appeals to Social Principles over the life cycle—children in the third grade did not generate any appeals to Social Principles, whereas 6.9% of all strategies generated by adults involved Social Principles. Adults generated far more negative tactics than children.

The strongest evidence in support of the validity of the persuasion schema stems from the several studies finding that the persuasion schema does in fact influence the processing of information. Rule and Bisanz (1987) constructed stories where an actor attempted to influence a target (e.g., to go out at night to see a play). In one version, the actor used tactics in a sequence identical to the expected, normative pattern (i.e., ask, followed by personal reason, bargain [favor], give altruistic reasons, and threaten). A second version was "mildly disordered," and a third version was "greatly disordered." Subjects read one of the versions and were asked 48 hours later to reconstruct the order by which the actor attempted the various tactics. If the persuasion schema is used in the processing of information, then subjects who were exposed to the normative "ordered list" would be correct more often than other subjects when reconstructing the sequence. This was what Rule and Bisanz (1987) found. Additional studies have been conducted by Greene et al. (1988).

We do not yet know how strongly the persuasion schema influences the processing of information, recall of strategy, or reactions to violations of the normative pattern. However, it is clear that the multidimensional scaling studies, the factor analytic studies, and the categories of tactics identified in Bisanz and Rule (1989, 1990) provide strong and consistent evidence concerning the types of tactics actors are likely to attempt. There is considerable evidence that actors prefer to use the tactics of Ask and "personal benefits" (see Cody et al., 1986; Witteman & Fitzpatrick, 1986). Also, it is clear that potential persuaders appeal to the quality of the relationship, use bargain (favor) or exchange, manipulate both positive feelings (ingratiation) and negative feelings (pout, sulk, criticize), and, occasionally, appeal to social principles and to force. The only major source of disagreement is the absence of some indirect strategies (e.g., hinting) from the Bisanz and Rule analyses, and from most of the factor analytic studies. However, hinting may be considered more of an information-gathering tactic than an actual influence method (see the discussion of hinting in Cody et al., 1980).

Not all studies using factor analytic approaches have obtained collaborative support for the existence of direct requests, rationality, assertiveness, exchange, and the like. Hunter and Boster (1986), for example, used a 20-year-old typology of tactics (Marwell & Schmitt, 1967) and found that the tactics were non-linearly related to one another and collapsed to form a single continuum. Although there is no doubt that tactics can be arrayed on a single continuum (see the preceding), problems stem from Hunter and Boster's recommendation that the ratings of likelihood-of-use for *all* tactics be summed together to provide one number reflecting "message selection" (also see Dillard & Burgoon, 1985). Aside from the theoretical problem (Hunter & Boster implicitly reject French & Raven's (1959) theoretical bases of power instead of an alternative—the items offered by Marwell & Schmitt (1967) were too poorly constructed to measure the underlying factors), there are three critical problems with using the Marwell–Schmitt typology:

1. The typology only offers 16 one-sentence statements, and 16 items are too few to measure any number of underlying factors or dimensions. Most inventories reviewed previously include 30 to 58 items, and include multiple indicators of underlying factors.

2. The statements were never validated. Obviously, how a statement is phrased has a significant impact on whether the utterance reflects bargain (object), bargain (favor), or some manipulation of negative feelings. A pure exchange item might be phrased, "George, I need to have Sunday night off. Can you do me a favor and switch shifts?", and another item might be contaminated because of an implication of guilt: "George, *you owe it to me* to switch this weekend." Also, evidence indicates that there are various forms by which an actor might attempt a type of tactic (i.e., there are several ways one can ingratiate), and successful forms of ingratiating and self-promoting involve indirect and subtle activities; unsuccessful methods are too blunt and direct (see Godfrey et al., 1986; McLaughlin et al., 1985). Substantially greater care has to be used in creating items in an inventory than what was done in Marwell and Schmitt.

3. The tactics offered by Marwell and Schmitt are obviously not exhaustive of relevant forms of tactics (see the preceding and Cody et al., 1980) as their list did not include direct requests (Ask), "presenting information," "mention personal benefits," some appeals to social principles, or major forms of ingratiation (Jones & Wortman, 1973).

A common assumption made in compliance-gaining literature is that there exists some standard set of tactics, phrased a particular way, that can be used universally in all influence goals and with all targets—with family, friends, and strangers, and when engaged in relational de-escalation, influencing strangers about conservation, and so on (Baglan, Lalumia, & Bayless, 1986; Miller et al., 1977). It is one thing to argue in favor of the existence of a persuasion schema that orders general types of tactics in preference, but it is misleading to assume or to argue that when actors generate tactics (a) there are no meaningful variations in how tactics are phrased, and (b) that the goals being pursued by actors do not have a significant impact on how the actors "skip down" the ordered list; actors might skip over Ask in some contexts to "present information," and in another context skip all the way down to negative strategies.

A number of studies indicate that actors produce a range of meaningful variations of the general types listed in Bisanz and Rule (1987). Cody et al. (1980) asked college students how they would convince a friend to repay a loan, and they found that 60% of the essays written were some variation on Ask (reason-giving, simple statement, question, disclaimer, plead—which they labeled 'altruism', and hint). Among bureaucrats, actors often skip over Ask and generate any number of oral arguments involving the presentation of information dealing with facts, the assignment of responsibility and consequences of an action (as in traffic court; see Cody & McLaughlin, 1988), or any number of variations on "present information," "dyad-oriented," and negative tactics (as in upward influence; see Schilit & Locke, 1982). Why actors skip over some methods and generate variations of types of tactics depends on the goals being pursued by the actor, the beliefs the actors have about interpersonal influence, and the actors' competence at implementing tactics.

Researchers should also be careful to distinguish among tactics, strategies, and plans. A *tactic* refers to a single act, a *strategy* refers to a behavioral sequence enacted to pursue some goal, and a *plan* refers to mental representations of states and transitions leading to accomplishments of goals (see Greene, 1990, for review). The vast majority of research on compliance-gaining deals only with tactics, although it is often the case that a tactic (a specific utterance used at one point in time) can only effect the desired change if used in particular sequence. For instance, a person cannot merely walk up to another and make the target feel guilty. A manipulation of guilt (one of the negative strategies in Bisanz and Rule's 1987 work), can only work as a tactic if the target has engaged in a line of behavior that makes a guilt induction plausible (the roommate didn't pay the phone bill on time, or if the actor can promote the idea in the mind of the target that he or she failed in some obligation). Only a few attempts have been made to study sequences of tactics, as in relational initiations (Berger, 1986, in press; Berger & Bell, 1988), selling used cars (Browne, 1973), and bargaining (see Chap. 11 in Bettinghaus & Cody, 1987) and power plays in organizations (Israeli, 1975).

TOWARD A CONCEPTUALIZATION
AND TYPOLOGY OF GOALS

Why Goals?

The 1970s witnessed a tremendous growth in research on how social actors perceive and categorize situations (see Cody & McLaughlin, 1985a). Researchers identified factors of role relationships (Marwell & Hage, 1970; Wish, Deutsch, & Kaplan, 1976; Wish & Kaplan, 1977), settings (Cantor, Mischel, & Schwartz, 1982a, 1982b; Craik, 1970, 1973; Russell & Ward, 1982; Stokols, 1978; Tversky & Hemenway, 1983), and activities in situations (Ekehammar, Schalling, & Magnusson, 1975; Krause, 1970; Magnusson, 1971; Magnusson & Ekehammar, 1973). Another expansive body of literature investigated the global structure underlying perceptions of situations (Biggers & Masterson, 1983; Cody & McLaughlin, 1980; Cody et al., 1983; Forgas, 1976, 1979, 1982, 1983a, 1983b; Hertzog & Bradac, 1984; Pervin, 1976, 1986). These studies provide support for the existence of at least seven factors: *Intimacy*; *Friendliness* (as opposed to resistance or hostility on the part of the target); *Pleasantness*; *Apprehension*; *Involvement* (in the situation); *Dominance*; and *Personal Benefits* (vs. "other benefit"). Other perceptions relevant to compliance-gaining include *Rights to Persuade* (Cody et al., 1983; Cody & McLaughlin, 1985a, 1985b) and *Relational Consequences* (Cody et al., 1983; Miller et al., 1977).

How do social actors use knowledge of situations to guide behavioral choices? After uncovering how actors perceive events, early studies (sampling few situations and relying on simple ANOVA designs) found some support for situation perception-tactic selection relationships (e.g., Clark, 1979; Cody et al., 1981), and interpreted these findings in terms of a cost/risk notion involving image, relational maintenance, and instrumental goals (Clark & Delia, 1979; McLaughlin et al., 1980). If an expansive and valid set of situation perception factors were identified, one would expect that studies that sampled a wide range of situations, precalibrated them on situation perception scales, and assessed both linear and interaction effects would advance our understanding of behavior. Unfortunately, recent tests have failed to support such an optimistic forecast. Using different methods, Cody, Greene et al., (1986) and Dillard and Burgoon (1985) found only weak relationships between situation perceptions and tactic selection.

Both of these studies relied on a *dimensional* model, one that posits that each influence situation has some loading on a set of dimensions or factors and that particular kinds of tactics are likely to be used in certain quadrants. Such a model implicitly assumes that each situation perception possesses some type of force or effect on behavior. In reality, a dimensional model hardly seems parsimonious, because there could be hundreds of linear, two-way interaction effects, three-way interaction effects, and so on. If we assume a minimum of seven factors, a 7 × 7 matrix would produce a complex set of "cells," most of which might be empty—a low rights to persuade situation involving low personal benefits to the actor, long-term relational consequences, a dominant, highly homophilous stranger, and so on. Also note that research that relies on a set of significant *interaction* terms (among situation perception factors) runs a risk of producing a number of findings that routinely fail to replicate. For example, studies might investigate the effects of Intimacy (High vs. Low) and Relational consequences (longer term vs. short term). In one study a situation is sampled where the intimate-long term consequences cell contains a relational escalation situation (engagement); in another study the cell contains a relational de-escalation situation; and in a third study a situation might be selected that involves advice giving (a loved one takes better care of his or her health, and relational qualities improve). Each of these situations is likely to involve different tactics, yet each fulfills the definition of an "intimate, long-term relational consequences" event.

An alternative and more parsimonious model assumes that situations are grouped together as goal categories that differ on the basis of a constellation of perceptions. For example, influencing a traffic court judge that one has been wrongly cited for an alleged offense involves a dominant target, high apprehension, anticipated resistance, low homophily, and high rights to persuade. Perceptions of relational consequences are irrelevant. A goal of escalating a casual relationship to an intimate one involves salient perceptions of intimacy, rights to persuade, homophily, little resistance, and low *personal* benefits (i.e., benefits are mutual). Anticipated situation apprehension may be low, but several alternate emotions are probably high (i.e., costs of rejection). However, target dominance is irrelevant. A typology of goals, then, would be more parsimonious than a matrix of "cells," and, perhaps more importantly, would specify a finite number of changes actors pursue in their social environments. Our purpose, therefore, is to identify a set of goals on the basis of various constellations of perceptions that reflect actors' cognitive representations of influence situations, and demonstrate that these representations influence tactical preferences.

Pervin (1986) similarly adopted the view that behavior in situations should be studied within a context of a theory of goals. He argued that the choice of situations and behavior is primarily directed toward obtaining goals, and that goals have properties that are *cognitive* (involving mental representations or images), *affective* (approach–avoidance) and *behavioral*; and he argued that goals vary in terms of content, time span, complexity, and importance. Pervin suggested that personality constructs can be viewed largely as goal systems; that we should study how people learn goals, and how they associate goals with specific people, objects, events, symbols, and processes; that we should study how people activate, select, maintain, and terminate goal-related actions; and that we should assess how incompatibilities between and/or among goals result in conflicts, depression, and the like. Indeed, actors' competence may be conceptualized as goal-specific motivation, knowledge, and skill in communicating (see also Spitzberg & Cupach, 1984).

Most research on goals and goal-directed behavior stems from work on goal-setting (Locke, 1986; Locke, Shaw, Saari, & Latham, 1981) and control theory (Carver & Scheier, 1982), and remarkably little is known about how people attempt to pursue interpersonal goals in daily life. By "influence goal" we mean a particular change in the actor's environment he or she intends to effect; for example, persuading one's parents to increase an allowance or to extend a curfew, and so on.

Goals can be hierarchically ordered at a minimum of three levels (see Dillard, 1990): motives, goals, and sub-goals. Motives exist at the highest level of the hierarchy and represent abstract intentional cause of behavior; for instance, an actor is motivated to have friendly, affiliative, and supportive relations with all members of his family, friends, and acquaintances. In our research, we have found that a "principled and honest" low self-monitor may decline from manipulating others and may refuse to pursue particular goals that involve strangers or that do not involve rights (but see Smith et al., 1990). Goals are more specific changes actors hope to achieve and reflect concrete operational definitions of motives (i.e., a friendly and sociable actor would be motivated to work together and cooperatively with a neighbor to resolve a dispute over a barking dog, etc., or a low self-monitor may decline to apply pressure on friends in order to gain compliance). Subgoals are specific actions that have to be conducted in order to fulfill goals. For instance, an actor who wants to sell his used car may have to (a) write and place an effective ad in the newspaper; (b) manage a particular image on the phone when targets call; (c) maintain or create an image of credibility when targets arrive to test drive the car; (d) create a sense of commitment (see Browne, 1973); (e) engage in actual bargaining and reach agreement; and, (f) finalize or terminate the interaction by discussing the service needs of the formerly owned automobile (the last step isn't actually necessary for the sale, but probably reflects a felt obligation to the new owner). According to Dillard (1990), goals are culturally viable explanations for behavior, they are often the focus of conscious awareness, they represent the level at which planning usually occurs, and they drive actions or sequences of actions.

O'Keefe and her colleagues (e.g., O'Keefe & McCornack, 1987; O'Keefe & Sheperd, 1987) argued that actors can pursue multiple conversational goals (e.g., regulatory and face-maintenance goals). O'Keefe's conception of conversational goals helps contextualize how persons might pursue their immediate influence goals. Consider a case of relational de-escalation. When communicating an intention to terminate or to de-escalate a relationship, additional conversational goals may be important to the actor: attempting not to hurt the feelings of the partner, being precise so that the target isn't misled, managing one's own image as a kind person, and so on. Hence, given these conditions, we can understand how the primary goal of relational de-escalation will be pursued. Nevertheless, conversational goals represent implicit standards of appropriateness that may be of secondary concern to the actor who is attempting to achieve a specific influence goal. In addition, Dillard, Segrin, and Harden (1987) argued that although multiple influence goals exist, strategic behaviors are best predicted by the actor's *primary* influence goal. Accordingly, we focus on actor's primary influence goals, although actors also attempt to accommodate conversational goals at the same time.

A second important feature of goal-directed behavior is that some goals are proactive and some are reactive. Proactive goals are ones that actors plan to achieve and direct their behaviors toward achieving. Reactive goals are ones where an actor is confronted with a problem (e.g., a violation of rights), the actor is less able to plan and is in less control of the sequence of events. We have found that reactive goals differ fundamentally from proactive goals in the tactics that are used and when escalation to conflict is probable (see following; Canary et al., 1988).

Our immediate aim is to distinguish categories of goals on the basis of situational features relevant to actors. Toward that end, the following subsections present (a) our framework for conceptualizing goal types, (b) a cluster analysis of compliance-gaining situations based on their perceptual similarities, (c) tactics used in various goal clusters, and (d) a typology of goal types.

Categories of Goals in Compliance-Gaining Situations

People develop categories of goals that contain relevant social knowledge about various aspects of situations. Knowledge of these goals is structured along horizontal and vertical dimensions. Rosch (1978) proposed that the vertical dimension of natural categories contains three basic classes: *superordinate*, *basic*, and *subordinate*, which are hierarchically organized according to levels of abstractness and inclusiveness. For example, one goal type might be categorized at the superordinate level as "cooperative," at the basic level as "asking a friend to go out," and at the subordinate as "asking a close friend to accompany you to the theater on a weekend night." Tversky and Hemenway (1983) noted that a decision that confronts researchers in their selection of levels for analysis concerns the degree of abstraction and inclusiveness. Instances of the superordinate level are quite abstract and do not share many features with one another. Instances of the subordinate level tend to overlap with other categories, so, although they are concrete, they do not differentiate well. Instances of the basic level are sufficiently abstract and share attributes in common with other category members but are differentiated from other category instances, offering distinctiveness and detail not found at other levels (Pavitt & Haight, 1985; Tversky, 1977).

In our view, each global dimension obtained through the multidimensional scaling studies already discussed reflects a superordinate level. This superordinate level analysis is too abstract to show profitably relationships between episode types and behaviors, as there can be several types of events at that level (e.g., for the relational consequences category we find relational initiations, relational escalations, and relational de-escalations). On the other extreme, specific episodes may be rich in detail, but they may not offer a parsimonious set of results that can be readily generalized. Accordingly, we adopt the basic level for our analysis.

The horizontal structure of categories contains a pattern of overlapping similarities (Tversky, 1977). There are no fixed set of features that determine category membership (Anderson, 1980). Thus, attributes may be shared among categories creating "fuzzy sets," or classes with continuous grades of membership (Zadeh, 1965). Category membership is probabilistic in nature as category instances vary from prototypical examples to ambiguous borderline cases at the overlapping, "fuzzy" boundaries (Broughton, 1984; Cantor & Mischel, 1977). Prototypes are hypothetical and are the most typical instances of a category that has all values filled in (Anderson, 1980). They are hypothetical in that they are abstract conceptions drawn from knowledge of particular category members (Cantor & Mischel, 1977, 1979a, 1979b; Cantor et al., 1982a, 1982b; Niedenthal, Cantor, & Kihlstrom, 1985). This implies that persons generalize from concrete influence situations to more generic ones.

Prototypes function as a standard by which information is compared and assimilated into the previously held social knowledge (Cantor & Mischel, 1977). New events are compared to the abstracted set of features comprising the prototype; when a sufficient degree of similarity exists between the target features and the prototype, the actor classifies the instance as a member of the category. Hence, an actor with a variety of past experiences within any particular compliance-gaining situation would have abstracted from these experiences a prototype of that situation, or a goal type.

Types of Goals in Compliance-Gaining Literature

Prototypes of goal categories contain different information, thus it is reasonable to expect that situational perceptions operate jointly to define various influence goals (Meyer, 1986). Further, describing goals in terms of situation perceptions can provide information about the salient differences among types of goals. That is, if there exists a finite set of goals actors pursue on a regular basis, then those goals ought to be distinguishable from one another on the basis of a constellation of different perceptions involving beliefs, affective states, and behavioral requirements. One type of goal, permission from parents, can be distinguished from another goal, giving advice to brothers and sisters, in terms of several salient differences in beliefs, roles, emotions, and so on. If this is true, then a cluster analysis of the 42 compliance-gaining events sampled in Cody et al. (1986) (most of which were sampled randomly from a population of events relevant to college-aged individuals; see Cody, 1978, Cody & McLaughlin, 1980) ought to reflect types of events that are similar in terms of (a) objectives or motives, (b) perceptual features that are relevant to the social actor (e.g., relational growth, rights to persuade, etc.), and (c) outcomes. Note that we do not argue that a cluster analysis of episodes creates a typology; rather, a cluster analysis of these events reveals distinctions that can be employed profitably in advancing a typology.

The cluster analysis of the Cody et al. (1986) events resulted in a clearly interpretable 12-cluster solution. Table 2.2 presents the cluster labels, example situations, and distinguishing features of each cluster.

Initiate Relationship reflects a common goal for college students, one comprising a large portion of "relational turning points" (Baxter & Bullis, 1986), and a goal for which actors' plans have been studied (Berger, 1986; Berger & Bell, 1988). Distinguishing features include target-receiver homophily, high intimacy, long-term relational consequences, personal benefits, and high apprehension. *Obtain Permission* (parent) involves events where college students seek permission from parents (e.g., to stay out late), and included several events where students sought assistance from parents (e.g., to buy a computer printer; see definitions of goals in the following). Distinguishing features involve short-term consequences, high intimacy, high-target dominance, and low apprehension. *Gain Assistance* (friend) concerns the common events in which a person seeks help from friends, and also, in this analysis, included several episodes in which friends shared activities (to go out together). Distinguishing features include low apprehension, low resistance, short-term consequences, high actor-target similarity, and high intimacy.

The fourth cluster, *Escalate Relationship*, represents events in which actors wanted to include the target in a wider range of situations with the actor (meet one's relatives, etc.) and increase intimacy. These events were perceived as involving high intimacy, high homophily, low resistance to compliance, low levels of personal benefits (both partners benefit), low situation apprehension, and high rights to persuade. *Give Advice* (friend) concerns events in which the actor attempts to give advice for the target's benefit (e.g., making career plans, who to date). They were perceived as involving low apprehension, low target dominance, low personal benefits (the target benefited), and homophilous relationships. The sixth cluster involves events in which the actor has to react to the behavior of others—one distinguishing feature in and of itself, as the majority of the events and clusters involve proactive goals. Barking dogs, smoking co-workers, and such, reflect episodes in which the actor feels compelled to *Protect* (a) *Right*. These episodes involve low intimacy, low homophily, high apprehension, and high rights to persuade.

A seventh cluster is *Gain Assistance* (stranger), and an eighth cluster involves

TABLE 2.2

Clusters and Distinguishing Features of Events Sampled in Cody et al. (1986)

Cluster Title	Example	Distinguishing Features
Initiate Relationship	There is a person in your Mass Communications class whom you would like to know better. You run into him or her after class and start a conversation. You want to ask him or her out (be asked).	—Long-term relational consequences —high situational apprehension —high personal benefits —high homophily —high intimacy
Obtain Permission (parent)	You want to persuade your parents to send some (more) money.	—high intimacy —high target dominance —short-term relational consequences —low situation apprehension
Gain Assistance (friend)	Your car is in the shop. You need a lift 5 miles to the dealership to pick up your car at 9 a.m. tomorrow.	—low target resistance —low situational apprehension —short-term consequences —high homophily —high intimacy
Escalate Relationship	You've just begun to date this particular boy or girl and you like him or her very much. You want to persuade your friend into coming home with you to meet relatives.	—high intimacy —high homophily —low resistance —low personal benefits —low situation apprehension —high rights to persuade
Give Advice (friend)	Your boy(girl) friend spends a good deal of time on his or her campus activities and neglects his or her grades. You want to persuade him or her to study more.	—low situation apprehension —low target dominance —low personal benefits —moderately high levels of homophily
Protect Right	Your neighbor frequently has friends over for get-togethers. Usually, someone turns up the stereo at 10:30 or 11:00 and the noise gets even louder as the evening progresses.	—low intimacy —low homophily —high situation apprehension —high rights to persuade

(Continued)

TABLE 2.2
(Continued)

Cluster Title	Example	Distinguishing Features
Gain Assistance (stranger)	For a class you are taking, you and other members must persuade a group of people with whom you are only faintly familiar to participate in an experiment.	—low intimacy —short-term consequences —low target dominance —high rights to persuade
Normative Request (superior; permission, gaining assistance)	You find out that one of the classes you desperately need to enroll in has been closed out. You want to persuade the professor into letting you enroll in the class.	—high target dominance —low intimacy —relatively high resistance
Selfish Request	You find that the math homework you need to have done for each class period absorbs a lot of time. You want someone in the class to help you.	—low rights to persuade —high resistance —low intimacy —long-term consequences
Enforce Obligation	One morning you wake up and find the plumbing dripping badly. You want the landlord to fix the plumbing.	—high rights to persuade —resistance —low target dominance
Give Advice (parent)	You notice that your father looks tired and overworked. You want to persuade him to take time off from work and find something relaxing to do.	—high intimacy —high target dominance —high resistance —low benefits —low apprehension
Normative Requests (bureaucrat)	On a recent trip back to school from vacation you are stopped by a police officer for speeding. You want to persuade him not to give you a ticket.	—low intimacy —short-term consequence —high resistance —high homophily —high apprehension

a *Normative Request* (superior). Both clusters depict events wherein the actor requests assistance from others. In Cluster 7 (help from someone during an emergency, gain assistance from strangers for a project), or, in Cluster 8, from a person in authority (enroll in a closed section of a course, permission to take a midterm late). *Gain Assistance* (stranger) involves somewhat higher levels of rights to persuade and lower levels of relational consequences than does *Normative Request* (superior), perhaps because assistance from strangers is sought when there is no alternative and one expects such assistance if needed. In fact, seeking assistance from a stranger is one of the least frequently pursued goals, yet it is one people are successful in achieving often (see following).

The last four categories reflect less common goals. *Selfish Request* (defined here as occurring when the actor argues that his or her goal attainment is superordinate to the target's goal-fulfillment) includes such events as trying to convince a co-worker to give up a preferable parking space, to convince a mother to keep a job she dislikes at a clothing store so that the teenager continues to get a discount, and so on. *Enforce Obligation* involves high rights to persuade, low target resistance, and low target dominance, and includes those events where the actor believes that the target should comply due to contractual agreements or a norm, such as a landlord's repairing plumbing, roommates' paying their share of the bills, and the like. *Give Advice* (parent) involves events in which the actor pursues altruistic motives, but with parents. Finally, *Normative Request* (bureaucrat) includes situations in which the actor tries to convince a traffic officer not to penalize him or her, or other episodes wherein the target occupies an official role. These events differ from *Normative Request* (superior) in perceived apprehension, resistance, and consequences. Only a few studies have examined how actors persuade bureaucrats (see following).

The cluster analysis results are important in developing a typology of goals for two reasons. First, it is obvious that social actors rely on both role relationships and motives to differentiate types of events. Motives, in this analysis, involve giving advice to others, gaining assistance from others, obtaining permission (at least from parents), changing relational definitions, and making "normative requests" (task-oriented goals). However, actors perceive and categorize events involving identical motives differently depending on the role relationship (e.g., advice-giving with parents vs. friends; gaining assistance from friends vs. strangers). This implies that there could be a standard set of motives such as *Obtain Permission*, *Give Advice*, and *Gain Assistance*, that exist across the range of possible role relationships in varying frequencies. For instance, a wider range of goals may occur with parents and friends than with strangers or superiors, and some motives may occur more frequently in some relationships than in others. Second, when categorizing episodes, actors apparently place some emphasis on rights, obligations, and perceptions of fairness—they perceive goals of *Protect Right*, *Enforce Obligation*, and *Selfish Request* as distinct goal types. These distinctions should be reflected in a typology of goals.

Tactics Used in Goal Types

Cody et al. (1986) had subjects write essays on "How I Get My Way" for each of their persuasion situations. They found significant, although weak, associations between situation perceptions and use of various arguments and tactics. However, if we are correct in arguing that assessing the impact of goal types is more informative than assessing situation perceptions, we should find that tactical selections are clearly related to types of goals. In fact, this was obtained. Further, Cody et al. only assessed "first attempt" tactics even though both "first attempt" and "second attempt" tactics were coded (there was no convenient way to assess Time 1 and Time 2 tactics for 42 events measured on multiple dimensions of situation perceptions).

Cody et al. (1986) labeled their categories a little differently than did Bisanz and Rule (1989, 1990), but found that 26% of first attempt tactics involved Ask and Self-Oriented tactics. These included direct requests and inform personal reason approaches. We refer to these attempts simply as *Direct Requests*. Thirty percent of the tactics involved supporting evidence, and we refer to this category as *Rationality*. Most of these involved explanations, logic, and reasons beyond merely mentioning a benefit to self, although some actors indicated that they would use supporting documents and rely on rules. The category closely parallels Kipnis' *Rationality* factor. Cody et al. also included a category of message type they labeled "Face maintenance," and included in it "butter-up," ingratiation, and small talk. We refer to this category simply as *Indirect* here. Six percent of the essays were indirect.

Three of the types of messages involved *Dyad-Oriented* tactics. *Exchange* (Bargain) represented 8% of the tactics, and "invoke role relationships" (*Referent* influence, generally speaking), represented 9% of the tactics (including "hold mutual talks without emotion to resolve the issue," "seeking understanding of how the target feels," etc.). A third category included attempts where the actor mentioned benefits that the target would derive from complying to the request ("Other benefit"). For instance, a *Direct Request* message ("I'm too tired to cook tonight. Let's order a pizza") might be followed by a second-attempt message where the actor lists a benefit to the target ("You won't have to clean up the kitchen, and you can get a salad as well"). *Other Benefit* approaches represent a *Dyad-Oriented* approach because they point out how the dyad jointly benefits from the proposed activity (although, sometimes, the benefit to the actor may be implicit). Seventeen percent of first-attempt tactics were Other Benefit. Bisanz and Rule's (1990) *Negative* tactics, including *Manipulation of Negative Feeling* (pout, sulk, show disappointment), and *Coerce*, represented only 4% of first attempt messages.

If Bisanz and Rule (1990) are correct that actors would use *Ask* first and then skip down the ordered list, we should witness fewer *Ask* behaviors among the second-attempt tactics, and an increase in *Dyad-Oriented*, *Rationality*, and *Negative* tactics. In fact, only 12% of second-attempt tactics used a "wait and ask again" approach. *Rationality* remained popular (31% of tactics), but did not increase substantially (from 30%). *Dyad-Oriented* tactics increased dramatically in popularity (39%; exchange, 15%, referent, 8%, and other benefit, 16%). As expected, *Negative strategies* increased in frequency as well, to represent 25% of the tactics. Sixteen percent of these involved manipulating *Negative Feelings*, and 9% involved *Coercive Influence*. (We distinguish between these two types when we discuss second-attempt tactics, because the two approaches are different from each other in intensity and are used in different goal types.) The only two exceptions to expected trends are that *Indirect* tactics were virtually never used as a second-attempt message, and that 27% of the actors selected not to use a second attempt at all—they withdrew. There were substantial differences in terms of the types of goals in which the actor escalated or withdrew. Table 2.3 reports the results.

A summary of the results are as follows:

1. Other-benefit tactics were used more often in *Give Advice* episodes and, to some extent, in *Escalate Relationship* and *Gain Assistance* (friend) situations. The tactic was used rarely, if ever, in *Protect Right* and *Enforce Obligation* categories. If subjects were not successful initially, they persisted in using other-benefit tactics in *Give Advice*, *Gain Assistance* (friend), and *Gain Assistance* (stranger) goal types (apparently trying to make assisting the actor seem like a benefit to the target; for example, "It is an interesting experiment and you'll learn something about yourself").

2. Referent influence (appeals to oneness, relational quality) were used more in *Initiate Relationship*, *De-escalate Relationship*, *Obtain Permission* (parent), *Escalate Relationship*, *Give Advice* (friend), and *Give Advice* (parent) goal types. They were used least in *Protect Right*. If not successful, actors used this emotionally based tactic in *Obtain Permission* (parent), *Give Advice* (parent), and *Enforce Obligation*.

3. Direct requests were used more often in *Gain Assistance* (friend), *Obtain Permission* (parent), *Enforce Obligation*, *Escalate Relationship*, and *Protect Right* goal types. They were rarely used in *Give Advice* or episodes involving bureaucrats. These tactics could hardly be used as a second attempt tactic immediately after a rejection, but several subjects indicated they would "wait and ask again." This approach was used in *Obtain Permission* (parent), *Escalate Relationship*, *Gain Assistance* (stranger), and *Protect Right* episodes.

4. Indirect tactics were used more often in *Obtain Permission* (parents), *Initiate Relationship*, *Gain Assistance* (friend, stranger), and with bureaucrats. In some cases, the tactics of small talk were used to "butter up" others (bureaucrats/parents), and at other times they were used possibly to assess the amount of resistance the target might display (i.e., information acquisition). The tactics were not used as second-attempt tactics, and were not used in *Give Advice*, *Enforce Obligation*, or *Selfish Request* episodes.

5. Rationality was popular, and it was used most often in *Obtain Permission* (parent), *Give Advice*, *Gain Assistance*, and *Selfish Request* episodes. Participants were most likely to use rationality in justifying a request to adults, asking for assistance from strangers, giving advice to peers, and when making selfish requests. As a second attempt tactic, rationality was used in *Obtain Permission* (parent), *Escalate Relationship*, and *Gain Assistance* (superior) goal types.

6. Exchange tactics were more likely to be used in *Enforce Obligation, Esca-*

TABLE 2.3
Use of Tactics in Pursuing Different Types of Goals*

Goal Type	First Attempt actic	Second Attempt Tactic
Gain Assistance (friend)	77% Direct request 41% Other benefit	29% Withdraw 25% Other benefit 18% Exchange
Obtain Permission (parent)	60% Direct request 53% Rationality 16% Referent/relational 13% Indirect	47% Rationality 20% Negative feelings 13% Referent/relational 13% Direct request (wait and ask again)
Enforce Obligation	58% Direct request 21% Exchange	55% Rationality 21% Coercive 16% Referent/relational
Give Advice (friend)	71% Other benefit 55% Rationality 19% Referent/relational 14% Distributive (warnings)	36% Other benefit 38% Withdraw 24% Negative feelings
Give Advice (parent)	97% Other benefit 67% Rationality 23% Referent/relational	51% Other benefit 38% Rationality 15% Referent/relational
Initiate Relationship	56% Referent/relational 26% Indirect	39% Withdraw 16% Direct request
Escalate Relationship	58% Direct requests 34% Other benefit 30% Exchange 16% Referent/relational	50% Rationality 25% Withdraw 24% Exchange 17% Negative feelings
Gain Assistance (stranger)	57% Rationality 25% Exchange 14% Indirectness 14% Distributive	23% Exchange 21% Other benefit 19% Direct request 15% Coercive
Normative Request (professor)	77% Rationality 32% Indirect	40% Rationality 26% Negative feelings
Normative Request (bureaucrat)	65% Rationality 30% Indirect 20% Distributive	50% Withdraw 20% Negative feelings
Selfish request	69% Rationality	54% Withdraw
Protect Right	72% Direct request 17% Exchange	22% Coercive 17% Negative feelings 17% Direct request (Wait and ask again) 16% Exchange

*Percentages can exceed 100% because respondents could use more than one type of message at a time.

late Relationship, *Gain Assistance* (stranger), and *Protect Right* goal types. Exchange was used as a means of activating a reciprocity rule (Cialdini, 1984) when overcoming habits (some habits in this data set), and when seeking assistance from peers or strangers. As a second-attempt tactic, subjects persisted in proposing exchange arrangements in *Escalate Relationship*, *Protect Right*, and *Gain Assistance* (friend) (e.g., "I'll go to your carnival on Sunday if you help me wash the car").

7. Negative tactics were used as a first attempt tactic with bureaucrats, as warnings to peers when giving advice, and as the manipulation of negative emotions when asking assistance from strangers. Nine percent of the sample used coercive influence as a second attempt tactic and these occurred largely in *Enforce Obligation*, *Protect Right*, and *Gain Assistance* episodes. Manipulation of negative feelings was used when peers failed to take advice, parents failed to comply to routine requests, professors failed to comply to normative requests, bureaucrats failed to comply, when the actors failed to stop annoyances or a violation of right, and when friends declined to escalate relationships.

8. A relatively large proportion of subjects withdrew from dyadic persuasion if they were not initially successful. They declined to try a second attempt in *Selfish Request*, *Initiate Relationship*, *Give Advice*, *Gain Assistance* (friend), and *Escalate Relationship* goal types. In some of these episodes the actor does not have a right to be persistent; in others, being persistent would only make matters worse, and some goals are not sufficiently important to demand persistent attempts. On the other hand, few subjects withdrew in *Enforce Obligation* or *Protect Right* episodes.

We argued earlier for the basic or intermediate level analysis of goal types, and we noted that there exists a superordinate level of organization. In fact, the 12 types of events appear to form 3 general types of episodes. First, *Initiate Relationship*, *Escalate Relationship*, *Give Advice*, and *Gain Assistance* (friend) merged to form a cluster of pro-relational or cooperative events. A second major category included Clusters 6, 7, and 8, events involving non-intimate relationships, where the actor is less in control of outcomes, but is preoccupied with various tasks (e.g., enrolling in closed sections of courses). Finally, a third set of events never merged together to form a single category, with Bureaucrats perceived as the one set of events most dissimilar to all others. Each of the last four categories, however, have something to do with the individual's role or sense of self. For example, the actor fights for his or her rights (*Enforce Obligation*) or displays a concern for self over the desires of others (*Selfish Request*) and confronts bureaucrats. This superordinate set parallels, but is not isomorphic to, the multidimensional solution cited in McCann and Higgins (1987) for 20 interpersonal goals (*We*, *task-orientation*, and *Me*), and it is also similar to the *relational*, *instrumental*, and *identity management* interaction goals offered by Clark and Delia (1979; Clark, 1979). But, relying on these more general categories provided weak links between type of goal and use of tactics. Different approaches were used in *Give Advice* than in *Change Relationship* goals, and different tactics were used in *Protect Right* than in *Gain Assistance*. Further, tactical selections differed among role relationships, even for the same goals. For instance, advice giving to parents elicited more other-benefit tactics and rationality tactics and fewer warnings (negative consequences of not complying) than did advice giving to friends (see Table 2.3). A more dramatic difference in tactical preferences occurred in the second-attempt essays. With friends, actors were likely to withdraw and use negative identity management along with rationality; with parents, they relied more on rationality and appeals to love. Clearly, compliance-gaining research should assess both role relationship and motive when examining actors' influence attempts.

A Typology of Goals

Clusters of situations similar to the ones in Table 2.2 are replicated in the situation perception literature (for instance, Cody & McLaughlin, 1980). For example, Dillard (1987) recently uncovered several clusters of "goal statements" similar to the ones obtained here and also found that rights and/or obligations and levels of personal benefits were important in distinguishing among types of goals. He labeled goals *Short-Term Activities*, *Self Interest*, *Target Health*, *Long-Term Activities*, *Family Matters*, and *Political Activities* (e.g., influencing others how to vote, etc.). However, cluster analyses of situations do not necessarily constitute a typology of goals. Rather, an integration of goal typologies with the knowledge of how actors perceive situations can help develop a meaningful typology of goals. First, Kipnis et al., (1980; see also Kipnis, 1984) identified several types of motives or goals organizational members pursued. When pursuing *self-interest* goals (e.g., seeking benefits from a supervisor), actors attempted to manage their impressions and to promote pleasant relationships. When attempting to *initiate change* by getting others to adopt new ideas, actors relied on rational tactics. When the compliance attempt involved the organizational objective of *improving the target's performance*, actors used more assertive approaches (e.g., administrative sanctions, simply demanding compliance); however, these tactics were not used when pursuing *personal objectives*. Finally, when attempting to *gain assistance* from others so that the actor could do his or her job, actors used direct requests. Kipnis (1984) also noted that the more reasons a manager has for influencing others, the range of tactics used increases.

   Schank and Abelson (1977) proposed that actors generally strive to achieve four goals: to *acquire information* or knowledge, to *acquire a physical object*, to *get power or authority to do something* (permission), or to *get someone to do something for you* (agency). Rule et al., (1985; Rule & Bisanz, 1987), however, found that participants also pursued other goals. They found only 23% of open-ended responses could be classified using the four goals suggested by Schank and Abelson; 95% of the responses, however, were coded into 12 types of goals. According to Rule and Bisanz (1987), the most common goals pursued by college-age students are *Opinion Change, Share Activity, Object, Gain Assistance*, and *Habits*.

The Rule and Bisanz (1987; Bisanz & Rule, 1989, 1990) typology is informative because it is quite expansive. In our view, however, two slight alterations are in order. First, some goals are similar to each other and merge on the basis of an overarching motive. For instance, *Gain Assistance* is a more general goal (relative to object, information, etc.) in which an actor wants help from the target to complete a task or to achieve another goal. Many episodes involving requests for information can be subsumed under the goal of *Gain Assistance* (e.g., gaining information on car loans), whereas others concern acquiring information to initiate relationships (e.g., asking a friend to find out about a particular individual's preferences). Similarly, obtaining an object from others often involves gaining assistance in order to complete some task (e.g., obtain money in order to buy a printer), but may also involve episodes in which actors selfishly try to secure an object from others. Thus, we subsumed several of the Rule and Bisanz goals under more inclusive categories. Second, we feel it is important to add several of the goal-types uncovered in the cluster analysis results discussed previously; that is, categories of *Enforce Obligation, Protect Right*, and *Selfish Request* (goal types that also parallel ones used in Kipnis et al., 1980). Selfish requests were included as a subgoal under *Gain Assistance* as actors in these episodes seek their goal at the target's cost.

Table 2.4, then, presents 11 general goal types, modifying the Rule and Bisanz (1987) typology but retaining all relevant features. *Obtain Permission* goals include several subcategories: single activities, ongoing activities, personal activities, and increased autonomy (requesting greater freedom from parents or superiors). *Gain Assistance* includes gaining information, help to fund activities, help to purchase goods, requests for financial assistance, requests for favors or consideration (to run an errand, etc.), and selfish requests. *Give Advice* episodes involve giving advice to others, such as relational advice (who should date whom, etc.), advice on health and habits, advice on social skills and appearance (what to wear, etiquette, etc.), and advice on financial and career planning. *Change Opinion* goals involve any attempts at getting targets to change opinions; *Share Activity* goals include mutual activities the actor-target shared (to eat out, etc.) and events in which the actor recommended to the target that he or she engage in an activity, and the recommendation did not appear to be advice on how the target can achieve a goal.

Elicit Support occurs when an actor seeks assistance from another to influence a third party. *Change Ownership* refers to material transactions, such as buying, selling, and contributing. *Violate Law* includes requests to do something that is personally destructive or otherwise antisocial (Rule and Bisanz' (1987) *Harm* category). *Enforce Obligation* situations are ones where there is a clear social contract to perform a behavior, but the behavior is not enacted. The goal of the actor in *Enforce Obligation* is similar to the goal in *Protect Right*, wherein targets

TABLE 2.4
A Typology of Compliance-Gaining Goals

Goal	Subcategories and Examples	
Obtain Permission	single activity:	to go to an all-night graduation party
	ongoing activity:	to have curfew extended
	personal activity:	to have ears pierced
	increased autonomy:	freedom from going to Church
Gain Assistance	information:	gain information about an object to purchase
	fund activity:	pay for airfare home
	purchase goods:	pay for a new printer for home computer
	financial assistance:	borrow money for new expenses
	favor/borrow object:	lend a car, borrow clothing
	favor/consideration:	run an errand for the actor
	selfish request:	keep job so actor can receive discount
Give Advice	relational:	give advice on who should date whom
	health/habit:	give advice on breaking habits
	social skills/appearance:	give advice on public behavior
	financial plan:	give advice on making plans, money
	career plan:	give advice on the target's career
Change Opinion	opinion change:	change opinion of film, Greek system
Share Activity	mutual activity:	shop together, walk together
	target's activity:	target should engage in a behavior
Elicit Support (Third Party)	family coalition:	seek aid in persuasion of another
	resolve conflict:	seek aid from a target to speak to a third person
	acquire information:	seek aid from a target to investigate a third person's attitudes
	relational initiation:	seek aid from a target to introduce actor to a potential dater
Change Ownership (Buying and Selling)	selling:	to sell something to others
	charity:	to sell raffle tickets, etc.
	buying:	to purchase materials from others
Violate Law	illegal activity:	propose an unlawful activity
Enforce Obligation	obligation:	target should fulfill contract or other obligation
Protect Right	annoyance:	a target's behavior infringes on the actor's rights, property, health
Change Relationship	initiation:	actor plans to begin or to initiate a relationship
	escalation/test of relationship:	actor plans to engage in an activity or persuade a dating partner to advance to a more intimate or personal level
	de-escalation:	actor plans to reduce the level of intimacy in an existing relationship

are perceived as violating personal rights. For example, a roommate who brings friends home for an unexpected late party violates a right to privacy. The final goal is *Change Relationship*, and there are three relevant subcategories: *Initiate*, *Escalate*, and *De-escalate*.

So far we have argued that there are compelling reasons to adapt a categorical representation of goal types, relative to a dimensional model of situation perceptions. The representational images of influence goals contain features of situation perceptions, as well as, we presume, additional perceptions (Dillard, 1987), affective responses, and behavioral expectations. Further, we are confident that both role relationship and type of motive are of critical importance in reactions to goals and in influencing behaviors. Finally, we offered a general typology of goals, one compatible with motives identified in Kipnis (1984), Rule and Bisanz (1987), and Dillard (1990, 1987). We now turn our attention to several studies conducted to assess how frequently individuals pursue various goals and with what success goals are achieved, and how males and females differ in pursuing goals.

THE NOMINATING STUDY

Three issues were addressed in the nominating study: How frequently do actors pursue various goals? When do they fail or succeed? What role does gender play in the pursuit of goals? This last issue is important because we have not yet developed a holistic view of how men and women differ in compliance-gaining activities. For example, the work by Johnson (1976) and Burgoon, Dillard, and Doran (1983) indicates that women are *expected* to rely on more indirect or personal tactics and rely less on coercion, expertise, or legitimate power.

However, demonstrating that women differ from men in their actual use of tactics has not proven an easy task. In conflict situations, women and men appear not to differ from one another in the use of tactics when in conflict with opposite-sex friends (Fitzpatrick & Winke, 1979). Instead, women use more personal rejection and emotional tactics when having conflict with other women, whereas males appear to use more "nonnegotiation" tactics (bluntly trying to get their way or refusing to discuss the matter) when in conflict with other males. Elsewhere, women reported greater use of personal criticism of their partner and shouting during a conflict, but use fewer denials (Canary et al., 1988). Females prefer rationality more than males do in many events, possibly using it to overcome lower initial credibility (see also Andrews, 1987; Falbo, 1977b; Warfel, 1984). Putnam and Wilson (1982) found that women, in organizations, were more indirect than men, but only during the first year on the job. More recently, Fairhurst (1986) concluded that few gender differences exist in measures of leadership style or ability in organizational settings.

In an organizational simulation, Instone, Major, and Bunker (1983) found that women used *more* coercive influence than males. Cody, Smith et al., (1986) found that females rated direct requests as less characteristic of self than did males, and that low self-monitoring males rated exchange tactics and referent power as less characteristic of self than did females (and high self-monitoring males); high self-monitoring males rated coercive influence as more characteristic of self than females (and low self-monitors; see Smith et al., 1990). However, when assigned specific hypothetical scenarios and asked to rate likelihood-of-use of tactics, respondents' gender differences largely disappeared.

Generally speaking, these studies suggest that gender differences are not pervasive. However, if we allow for the possibility that women pursue different goals and place emphasis on different motives than males do, then we can explain both (a) the persistence of gender-related stereotypes, and (b) the observation that females differ from males in terms of how tactics are characteristic of their usual way of influencing others. Females, at least in high school and in college, engage in more volunteer work than males, and display more social support and friendliness ("Students Try Volunteer Work . . ," 1987; Wood & Karten, 1986), thus we anticipate that women pursue more communal goals and strive to maintain more harmonious relationships with others. In fact, a few studies conducted over the years (Booth, 1972; Wheeler & Nezlek, 1977) indicate that females develop deeper, more affectively rich friendships than males, seeking more frequent contact, confiding more in, and engaging in more spontaneous activities with friends, especially the same-gender best friend. These results imply that females would pursue goals such as giving advice to others, volunteering for charity work, engaging in more mutual activities, and the like more frequently than males. Thus, pursuing communal goals would result in different tactics being rated as characteristic of typical influence methods. Further, females would be more persistent than males in pursuing particular goals (see following).

One hundred thirty-five females and 75 males listed their compliance-gaining events in 14 different categories, first by role relationship (e.g., parents, brothers/sisters) and then by motive (e.g., gain assistance, advice giving). For each episode, respondents indicated if they were successful, partially successful, or unsuccessful. Each episode was coded in terms of a role relationship and subdivided into different types of motives (see Tables 2.5 through 2.11). The episodes were readily recognized (intercoder reliability for these and other categories was satisfactory, with kappa $>$ .70; see Canary et al., 1988). Our method differed from the one used by Rule and Bisanz (1987) in two ways. First, we had more participants respond to a wider range of categories. Second, we did not include an "enemies" category. The 210 participants reconstructed 25 episodes each, on the average, generating over 5,000 episodes. The role relationships involved friends (39% of all episodes), family (29%), bureaucrats (12%), roommates (10%), and neighbors (8%).

TABLE 2.5
Compliance-Gaining Episodes Involving Parents

	Females				Males				
	S	PS	F	T	S	PS	F	T	Totals
1. Obtain Permission				170				71	
single activity	30	19	30	79	24	6	16	46	
ongoing activity	14	12	21	47	13	1	2	16	
personal activity	4	0	3	7	0	0	0	0	
increased activity	28	2	7	37	8	0	1	9	241
2. Gain Assistance				273				88	
information	3	2	1	6	0	0	0	0	
fund activities	23	5	9	37	2	0	0	2	
purchase goods	49	19	17	85	23	6	4	33	
financial assistance	54	20	4	78	20	3	5	28	
favor/borrow object	9	3	5	17	3	2	6	11	
favor/consideration	39	7	3	49	9	2	2	13	
selfish request	0	0	1	1	0	0	1	1	361
3. Give Advice				98				35	
relationship/third party	2	2	3	7	0	0	0	0	
financial plan	13	1	13	27	2	0	3	5	
health/habit	7	6	28	41	4	8	6	18	
social skills/appearance	2	4	9	15	0	1	1	2	
other	4	1	3	8	1	0	9	10	133
4. Change Opinion	10	12	8	30	4	8	7	19	49
5. Share (mutual) Activity	11	2	7	20	4	2	4	10	30
6. Elicit Support (coalition)	25	13	21	59	8	6	10	24	83
7. Change Ownership/charity	44	12	1	57	6	5	2	13	70

Note. S = Successful; PS = Partially Successful; F = Failed; T = Total.

Results

Tables 2.5 through 2.11 present the results of our analyses, Table 2.5 on episodes involving parents. Three goal types, *Obtain Permission*, *Gain Assistance*, and *Give Advice*, accounted for 76% of all of the episodes. As in most other role-relationship categories, success at influencing the target varied substantially from one motive to another. First, both males and females claimed to be more successful (65% for both males and females) in *Gain Assistance*, and to be least successful in *Give Advice* (29% females; 20% males) and in *Change Opinion* (33% females; 21% males) goals. Both males and females claimed modest success in *Share Activity* goals (55% females; 40% males), and when forming coalitions (42% females; 33% males) (*Elicit Support*). Females, however, were more effective in selling charity (coded here because most of the respondents sell raffle tickets, etc., to parents among other targets—selling is repeated again in Table 2.10, under ''selling'') (77% females; 46% males); however,

TABLE 2.6
Compliance-Gaining Episodes Involving Brothers/Sisters

	Females				Males				
	S	PS	F	T	S	PS	F	T	Totals
1. Gain Assistance				234				37	
borrow object	69	25	18	112	14	5	3	22	
obtain object (for free)	7	1	7	15	0	0	1	1	
favor/consideration	61	22	22	105	9	2	3	14	
selfish request	0	0	2	2	3	1	1	5	271
2. Give Advice				85				27	
relationship	6	3	29	38	1	3	6	10	
career/school	7	3	4	14	5	1	1	7	
health/habits	3	4	5	12	1	0	1	2	
social skills/appearance	5	2	5	12	2	1	0	3	
other	2	5	2	9	1	0	4	5	112
3. Change Opinion	8	8	9	25	4	5	4	13	38
4. Violate Law	0	0	0	0	3	1	1	5	5
5. Share Activity	59	14	15	88	10	11	7	28	116
6. Elicit Support	3	3	4	10	0	1	0	1	11
7. Enforce Obligation				16				10	
(household/chores	4	6	6	16	1	1	3	5	
agreements)	0	0	0	0	2	2	1	5	26
8. Protect Right				9				5	
possession	1	1	0	2	0	0	1	1	
nuisance	1	3	3	7	1	0	3	4	14
9. Change Ownership	0	0	0	0	2	0	7	9	9

Note. S = Successful; PS = Partially Successful; F = Failed; T = Total.

females appeared to be less effective in gaining permission from parents (45%
vs. 63%). Three gender differences were obtained in terms of frequency of
pursuing goals: females nominated (a) 2.0 episodes of *Gain Assistance* (vs. 1.2
per male respondent), (b) .73 episodes of *Give Advice* (vs. .47 per male respondent), and (c) .42 episodes of charity selling (vs. .17 per males). Thus, females
were more likely than males to seek assistance from, give advice to, and sell
raffle tickets, and so on, to parents. They claimed to be more successful than
males in most goals, except gaining permission.

Table 2.6 presents a breakdown of episodes involving brothers and sisters.
Females never engaged in *Violate Law* episodes, or events involving selling, and
males rarely attempted to elicit support from a brother or sister. For both males
and females, frequency of occurrence and percent of success were low for *Violate Law*, *Change Ownership*, *Elicit Support*, *Protect Right*, and *Enforce Obligation* (see
Table 2.6). As with parents, females and males were relatively ineffective at
giving advice (27% females; 37% males) and in changing opinions (32% females; 31% males). There were three observations concerning gender differences. The typical female (vs. male) was (a) twice as likely to try to give advice

TABLE 2.7
Compliance-Gaining Episodes Involving Roommates

	Females				Males				
	S	PS	F	T	S	PS	F	T	Totals
1. Gain Assistance				133				28	
borrow object	48	7	3	58	9	0	1	10	
favor/consideration	43	12	11	66	6	1	1	8	
selfish request	3	2	0	5	6	0	0	6	
other (permission to break rule)	4	0	0	4	3	0	0	3	161
2. Give Advice				34				15	
relationship	7	2	6	15	3	1	3	7	
health/habits	5	2	8	15	0	3	0	3	
social skills/appearance	1	1	2	4	3	0	0	3	
career/school	0	0	0	0	0	0	2	2	49
3. Share Activity	60	18	21	99	21	7	4	32	131
4. Change Opinion	2	4	1	7	2	2	2	6	13
5. Violate Law	0	0	0	0	0	0	1	1	1
6. Change Ownership	0	0	1	1	0	0	1	1	1
7. Elicit Support	3	0	0	3	4	0	1	5	8
8. Enforce Obligation				89				15	
household/chores	23	20	21	64	6	1	5	12	
routine (e.g., lights out)	2	6	4	12	0	0	0	0	
agreements (paying debts)	9	2	2	13	1	1	1	3	104
9. Protect Right				61				14	
possession	6	14	3	23	1	0	1	2	
nuisance	14	10	10	34	5	2	5	12	
lifestyle	3	0	1	4	0	0	0	0	75

Note. S = Successful; PS = Partially Successful; F = Failed; T = Total.

but usually ineffective when doing so, (b) more likely to seek assistance from brothers and sisters, but males were more successful (70% when they did ask for assistance, vs. 58% success for females), and (c) more likely to try to engage in mutual activities, and females were more successful in *Share Activity* goals (67%) than males (36%).

Goal types nominated for roommates are presented in Table 2.7. Participants gave less advice to roommates than they did to friends (see Table 2.7) or family. Instead, actors spent more time in *Gain Assistance*, *Share Activity*, *Enforce Obligation*, and *Protect Right* goals (87% of the 543 episodes involving roommates dealt with these four goals). A significant portion of compliance-gaining among roommates, then, merely dealt with maintaining living conditions. *Violate Law*, *Change Ownership*, *Elicit Support*, and *Change Opinion* goals were infrequent. Both females and males claimed to be successful in gaining assistance (74% females, 86% males), and to be fairly successful in *Share Activity* goal (61% females, 65% males). Both were only moderately successful in *Give Advice* (38% females, 40% males), *Enforce Obligation* (38% females, 47% males), and *Protect Right* goals

TABLE 2.8
Compliance-Gaining Episodes Involving Friends/Acquaintances

	Females				Males				
	S	PS	F	T	S	PS	F	T	Totals
1. Gain Assistance				408				189	
borrow school notes, supplies	68	11	9	88	22	2	0	24	
borrow objects (car, money)	55	6	8	69	42	0	5	47	
consideration/favor	42	5	4	51	53	0	2	55	
consideration/errand	21	3	5	29	14	1	1	16	
companionship	28	2	3	33	3	0	0	3	
school help	46	4	6	56	18	0	2	20	
help fix objects	28	0	3	31	5	1	0	6	
double/blind date	3	0	3	6	4	0	1	5	
sponsor, recommend	3	0	0	3	5	0	0	5	
keep secret	4	1	0	5	0	0	0	0	
help move	10	0	0	10	0	0	0	0	
help shop for particular item	6	1	0	7	0	0	0	0	
selfish request	13	0	7	20	4	2	2	8	597
2. Violate Law	0	0	1	1	1	0	0	1	2
3. Give Advice				319				158	
relationship	32	32	38	102	6	10	5	21	
social skills/appearance	42	31	2	75	10	18	7	35	
health/habits	2	1	2	5	0	1	2	3	
career/school	51	28	33	112	45	15	15	75	
personal/comforting	3	9	4	16	5	2	2	9	
other	3	2	4	9	13	2	0	15	477
4. Change Opinion	17	14	20	51	17	12	13	42	93
5. Share Activity	92	29	27	148	30	5	6	41	189
6. Elicit Support				120				51	
coalition	4	0	0	4	1	0	0	1	
relational initiation	64	7	10	81	21	9	4	34	
relational	16	4	2	22	1	0	1	2	
resolve conflict	11	1	1	13	10	3	1	14	171
7. Enforce Obligation	9	3	2	14	2	1	0	3	17
8. Change Relationship (confide)	16	1	4	21	2	2	0	4	25
9. Change Ownership	3	2	0	5	1	2	1	4	9

Note. S = Successful; PS = Partially Successful; F = Failed; T = Total.

(38% females, 43% males). Women were more likely than males to pursue goals involving assistance, activity, obligation, and rights.

Thirty-nine percent of all episodes nominated by respondents involved friends as targets (Table 2.8). No respondent listed an episode with a friend that involved protecting rights and there were infrequent *Violate Law*, *Enforce Obligation*, and *Change Ownership* goals. Of the few episodes focusing on the motive of relational changes (e.g., prompting friends to confide more), most were attempted by females. In comparison with other role relations, more *Share Activity* and *Elicit Support* goals were generated when friends were targets. Again,

TABLE 2.9
Compliance-Gaining Episodes Involving Bureaucrats

	Females				Males				
	S	PS	F	T	S	PS	F	T	Totals
1. Professor									
normative request				106				63	
grade change	19	4	6	29	17	5	14	36	
change exam date	5	2	6	13	1	2	1	4	
assistance in course	4	2	4	10	2	0	0	2	
permission to add course	20	4	3	27	10	2	3	15	
acquire grade information	14	4	2	20	2	0	0	2	
recommendation letter	4	0	0	4	3	0	0	3	
acquire facts on other	0	0	1	1	0	0	0	0	
illegal/buy a grade	0	0	1	1	0	0	0	0	
change opinion	1	0	0	1	1	0	0	1	169
2. Campus Guards									
considerations	12	1	2	15	2	0	2	4	19
3. University offices				35				14	
normative requests	8	0	6	14	9	0	1	10	
considerations	11	1	3	15	2	1	1	4	
selfish	0	2	2	4	0	0	0	0	
illegal	0	0	2	2	0	0	0	0	49
4. Police/Judge	52	1	33	86	26	7	40	73	159
5. Other officials				39				28	
normative requests	18	1	8	27	15	1	2	18	
considerations	5	2	3	10	2	2	6	10	
selfish	0	2	0	2	0	0	0	0	67
6. Employment settings				119				68	
normative requests									
permission	23	2	5	30	10	2	2	14	
raise/promotion	14	2	7	23	2	1	1	4	
advice giving	9	1	8	18	11	2	0	13	
get hired (no experience)	0	0	0	0	3	0	0	3	
opinion	1	0	0	1	1	0	0	1	
third person	7	7	2	16	7	2	5	14	
selfish	0	0	0	0	0	1	0	1	
co-workers/considerations	23	3	5	31	14	1	3	18	187

Note. S = Successful; PS = Partially Successful; F = Failed; T = Total.

both males and females were successful in *Gain Assistance* goals (80% females, 90% males), but less successful in *Give Advice* (42% females, 50% males) and *Change Opinion* categories (33% females, 40% males). Modest success was claimed in *Share Activity* (62% females, 73% males) and in *Elicit Support* goals (78% females, 65% males). Although females appear to generate more frequent episodes of *Gain Assistance* and *Elicit Support* (see Table 2.8), the most substantial difference between males and females dealt with *Share Activity* goals—females wanted friends to engage in mutual activities more than males; females

TABLE 2.10
Compliance-Gaining Episodes Involving Strangers/Neighbors

	Females				Males				
	S	PS	F	T	S	PS	F	T	Totals
1. Neighbors				6				5	
gain assistance	0	0	0	0	1	0	0	1	
considerations/borrow	1	0	0	1	1	0	0	1	
obligation	4	0	0	4	0	0	2	2	
considerations/errand	1	0	0	1	0	1	0	1	11
2. Landlord				1				5	
obligation	0	0	0	0	1	1	0	2	
considerations/favor	1	0	0	1	2	1	0	3	6
3. Strangers				40				23	
assistance (car trouble)	11	0	0	11	10	1	0	11	
assistance (physical help)	3	0	0	3	3	0	0	3	
considerations/favor	17	1	0	18	3	2	0	5	
illegal	1	0	0	1	1	0	0	1	
selfish	6	1	0	7	2	0	1	3	63
4. Selling				224				118	
expensive objects	16	1	5	22	39	4	2	45	
school supplies	4	2	0	6	3	4	1	8	
services	17	2	2	21	8	1	2	11	
equipment (camera, sports)	13	5	0	18	24	8	4	36	
clothing	43	24	8	75	3	0	0	3	
drugs	0	0	0	0	2	0	0	2	
charity	44	12	1	57	6	5	2	13	
handmade products	19	3	3	25	0	0	0	0	342

Note. S = Successful; PS = Partially Successful; F = Failed; T = Total.

generated 1.1 *Share Activity* episodes per person, versus .55 per male.

Table 2.9 presents the assessment of how frequently actors attempted to persuade bureaucrats. The most common subgoal we have labeled under the category of college professor is *Normative Requests*, and this involves both *Gain Assistance* and *Obtain Permission* goals. Both males and females claimed relative success in pursuing these goals (64% female, 56% males). When they did attempt to gain favors from campus guards (e.g., to secure parking in special lots), females were more successful than males (80% vs. 50%). Excluding selfish requests and illegal requests, both males and females achieved some success at making requests from university officials (79% males, 66% females). Regarding traffic problems, females claimed greater success than males (60% vs. 36%), and only two thirds of the females nominated such an episode (vs. 97% of the males). Excluding selfish requests, males and females claimed the same rates of success when persuading other officials (62% females, 61% males). Females and males reported similar success in employment settings (65% females, 70% males), although females reported less success at giving advice

TABLE 2.11
Compliance-Gaining Episodes Involving Romantic Partners

	Females				Males				
	S	PS	F	T	S	PS	F	T	Totals
Initiation				237				124	
directly ask him or her out	26	2	0	28	36	4	3	43	
joined desirable groups	35	0	1	36	18	0	2	20	
go to bars	6	1	1	8	8	7	2	17	
work/school environment	56	6	4	66	28	6	0	34	
have my own party	5	0	1	6	4	0	0	4	
third party (elicit support)	45	4	6	55	4	2	0	6	
switched schools	7	0	0	7	0	0	0	0	
old flame/friendship blossoms	12	0	1	13	0	0	0	0	
strategically showed interest	15	3	0	18	0	0	0	0	361
Escalation				80				31	
Test of trust	28	7	3	38	3	0	0	3	
do something special	13	1	2	16	10	2	0	12	
meet oldest friends	20	1	3	24	14	0	2	16	
live together	2	0	0	2	0	0	0	0	111

Note. S = Successful; PS = Partially Successful; F = Failed; T = Total.

to superiors (58% females, 85% males). Thus, females may be more successful than males in gaining assistance from some bureaucrats, but females may
experience less success in an advisory role with superiors.

Episodes involving strangers (i.e., landlords and neighbors) were infrequent
(Table 2.10). Both males (84%) and females (97%) achieved success in gaining assistance from strangers. Surprisingly, both males and females were successful in *Violate Law* and *Selfish Request* episodes (80%). Males and females
reported equal success rates in selling objects (70% females, 72% males).
However, males and females tended to sell different types of objects; 69% of
all objects males sold were expensive objects (e.g., cars, stereos) and equip-
ment (e.g., cameras), whereas 79% of the selling done by females involved
services (e.g., typing, babysitting), clothing, handmade products, and charity
selling.

A separate breakdown of episodes involving romantic partners is presented
in Table 2.11. Not surprisingly, both males (79%) and females (87%) claimed
to be successful in *Initiate Relationship* goals. However, only 28 of the 135 females reported directly asking males for a date, whereas 43 of the 75 males listed
direct requests. Instead, females relied more than males on third parties for in-
troductions, strategically showing interest and/or rekindling an old flame. Most
females (59%) reported an *Escalate Relationship* episode; 41% of the males did so.
A key difference was that females were substantially more likely to devise a
test of trust than were males—48% versus 10%, respectively. Baxter and Wilmot (1984) also found that females propose more relational tests than do males.

Summary

This study lends insights into how both role relationships and motives are relevant in characterizing compliance-gaining events. For instance, requests for permission were common with parents, but were rare in other role relationships. Gaining assistance and advice giving are common motives among intimates, but actors were typically unsuccessful at giving advice. Respondents were generally less successful in influencing brothers/sisters (49%), parents (52%), and roommates (56%), than in influencing bureaucrats (60%), friends (66%), and neighbors/strangers (73%), possibly because targets are more likely to comply with a request for assistance than for other motives. When we assess levels of success by goal type, respondents claimed to be successful in *Gain Assistance* (73%), *Change Relationship* (83%), *Change Ownership* (70%), *Share Activity* (62%), *Elicit Support* (61%), and *Obtain Permission* and *Normative Request* episodes (57%). They appear to be relatively ineffective in *Protect Right* (32%), *Change Opinion* (34%), *Violate Law* (36%), *Give Advice* (40%), and *Enforce Obligation* (41%) goals.

In addition, females more frequently than males pursued the following:

1. Activities with brothers/sisters, roommates, and friends.
2. Gaining assistance from parents, brothers/sisters, and roommates.
3. Advice giving to parents and brothers/sisters.
4. Charity selling (subgoal).
5. Relational changes with friends: prompting friends to comply more, planning a relational escalation, and devising tests of trust; to be more indirect in devising relational initiations.
6. Protecting rights and enforcing obligation goals with roommates.
7. Selling qualitatively different objects and services.

In terms of reported success, females (as opposed to males):

1. Sold charity more effectively, and with parents, were somewhat more successful in *Share Activity* and *Change Opinion* goals, but were less effective in gaining permission from parents.
2. Were more effective in gaining the compliance of brothers and sisters to engage in activities, but were less effective in gaining assistance from brothers/sisters and less effective in giving advice to brothers/sisters.
3. Were more effective in pursuing *Elicit Support* goals, but less effective in *Share Activity* goals with friends.
4. Were more effective in securing special favors from some types of bureaucrats, especially guards and police, but less successful in giving advice to superiors.

THE RATING SCALE STUDY

We would be more confident in our findings about gender differences if they were replicated using alternative subjects and methods. This is one reason for conducting the rating scale study reported here. A second purpose was to assess how people use tactics to achieve each goal type. For these purposes, we analyzed the Canary et al. (1986) data in terms of gender and goal-type differences. There were 125 males and 224 females. Canary et al. provided 14 common goals (see Table 2.12) to respondents and had them rate the extent they found each of the goals easy to imagine, how confident they would be in entering into the events, the probability that they would enter into the goal events actively, the likelihood that they would be persistent, and the frequency with which they experience the goal. Next, respondents indicated the likelihood of using each of several representative tactics: direct requests, manipulation of positive feelings (ingratiation), exchange, manipulation of negative feelings (act hurt, sulk, etc.), rationality, coercive influence, referent influence, and avoidance. The data were analyzed by two MANOVAs, which were followed with separate repeated measures analysis for each variable found to be significant for the general multivariate tests. Table 2.13 presents the means for how respondents reacted to the goals; Table 2.14 presents the means for likelihood of tactic use.

Briefly, the data indicate that *Share Activity* was reacted to with much ease, confidence, and frequency, and involved selection of direct requests, but not rationality. *Enforce Obligation* goals were entered into actively and persistently, and prompted the selection of coercive influence (relative to other goals). *Protect Right* and *Initiate Relationship* goals were reacted to with least-expected persistence, and received lower ratings of expected use of rationality. *Escalate Relationship* was entered into confidently, actively, and with persistence, and actors selected positive manipulation of feelings and referent influence more here than in most other goals. *De-escalate Relationship* was easy to imagine, and involved the selection of rationality, referent appeal, and compromise. *Elicit Support* and *Gain Assistance* (stranger) goals were more difficult to imagine and less frequently experienced than most other goals. *Initiate Relationship* and *Share Activity* involved the least likelihood of rationality (see Table 2.14).

This study and the findings reported in Table 2.3 evidenced a number of similarities concerning compliance-gaining strategies:

> *Rationality.*   First, both studies indicate that rationality was generally preferred in most goals, except in *Initiate Relationship* and *Share Activity*. And rationality was used most popularly on adults (professors, parents), when giving advice, and when proposing relational changes.

TABLE 2.12
Fourteen Goal Types and Exemplars

Share Activity (friend)

Please imagine the following situation: *You want to have a routine night out with your friends.*

Example: You and your friends haven't gone out for a night on the town in some time and you want to persuade them into going with you this Friday evening.

Bureaucrats

Please imagine the following situation: *You want to persuade a person in authority or in a bureaucracy to do something.*

Example: On a recent trip back to school from vacation, you are going ''about'' 60 mph when you are stopped by a police officer for speeding. You want to persuade the officer not to give you a ticket.

Give Advice (friend)

Please imagine the following situation: *You are giving advice to someone about whom you care.*

Example: A close friend of yours at college has been spending a good deal of time on his or her non-academic activities and has neglected his or her grades. You want to persuade him or her to study more and, generally speaking, to set some career goals.

De-escalate Relationship

Please imagine the following situation: *You want to break off a dating relationship with a person you have dated for a few months.*

Example: Although you first liked dating a particular person, you now realize that the two of you really do not have a lot in common. You want to persuade him or her that you only want to be friends, nothing more.

Gain Assistance (friend)

Please imagine the following situation: *You want to persuade an acquaintance to help you do something.*

Example: You find that the math homework you need to have for class each period absorbs a good deal of your time—time that you really do not have since you started working 3 days a week. You want to persuade someone you know in class to help you with the homework.

Enforce Obligation

Please imagine the following situation: *You want to persuade a person to fulfill his or her obligation to you.*

Example: You have lived in your apartment complex for some months. One Saturday evening you wake up late and find the kitchen plumbing dripping very badly. You want to persuade the landlord to fix the plumbing promptly.

Initiate Relationship

Please imagine the following situation: *You want to initiate a relationship with a person of the opposite sex or to increase the intimacy in a relationship.*

Example: There is a person of the opposite sex in your Mass Communication class whom you would like to know better. You run into him or her after class and start a conversation. You want to persuade him or her to get together again and get to know each other.

(Continued)

TABLE 2.12
(Continued)

Gain Assistance (professor)

Please imagine the following situation: *You want a professor to do you a special favor.*
Example: You find that one of the classes you desperately need to enroll in has been closed out. You want to persuade the professor into letting you enroll in this class.

Elicit Support (Third Person)

Please imagine the following situation: *You want to persuade an acquaintance to help a third party.*
Example: You believe that a friend of yours is drinking (alcoholic beverages) too much, and you also believe that the drinking problem has become quite apparent to many people over the last several weeks. You want to persuade this person's closest friend to talk about the problem with him or her so that he or she might stop drinking.

Give Advice (parent)

Please imagine the following situation: *You want to give advice to your parents about some long-term goal of theirs.*
Example: On a visit home recently you see that your father looks tired and overworked. You want to persuade him to take time off from work and find something relaxing to do.

Escalate Relationship

Please imagine the following situation: *You want to include someone special to you into your social world by including him or her in activities with your friends and family.*
Example: You have dated your boyfriend or girlfriend for some time and the two of you really get along well. You want to persuade him or her into coming home for the weekend to meet your relatives.

Protect Right

Please imagine the following situation: *You want to persuade someone from engaging in an annoying habit.*
Example: Your neighbor frequently has friends over for small parties. Usually, about 10:30 or 11:00 at night someone will turn on the stereo, and it will get louder as the guests get louder. You want to persuade your neighbor to keep the noise down when it gets late.

Gain Assistance (stranger)

Please imagine the following situation: *You want a stranger to do a special favor for you.*
Example: For a social science class that you are taking, you (and your group members) need to have a group of students participate in your experiment. The project counts as a large percentage of your grade. You want to persuade a group of people in the cafeteria to participate in your project.

Obtain Permission (parent)

Please imagine the following situation: *You want to gain permission from your parents to do something.*
Example: You want to persuade your parents to send (or loan) you more money for college.

Note. From Canary, Cody, and Marston (1986).

TABLE 2.13
Mean Reactions to Goal Types

Goal Type	Easy to Imagine	Confident	Actively Enter	Persistent	Frequent
Share Activity (Friend)	1.67	1.93	1.87	2.62	2.68
Bureaucrats	2.03	3.73	3.10	3.75	4.27
Give Advice (friend)	1.91	2.72	2.40	2.76	3.31
De-escalate Relationship	1.80	2.63	2.61	2.42	3.04
Gain Assistance (friend)	2.28	2.60	2.61	3.62	3.89
Enforce Obligation	2.03	2.02	1.86	1.74	3.76
Initiate Relationship	1.97	2.84	2.85	4.51	3.68
Gain Assistance (Professor)	1.68	2.48	2.05	2.48	3.04
Elicit Support	2.55	2.81	2.81	2.72	4.41
Give Advice (Parent)	2.53	3.25	2.49	2.65	3.95
Escalate Relationship	1.95	1.92	1.83	2.40	3.22
Protect Rights	2.08	2.75	2.69	2.51	3.64
Gain Assistance (Stranger)	2.81	2.86	2.89	3.61	4.54
Obtain Permission (parent)	1.91	2.17	2.24	2.89	2.93

Note. The smaller the number, the greater the confidence, persistence, frequency, and so on. From Canary, Cody, and Marston (1986).

TABLE 2.14
Mean Likelihood of Using Strategies in Goal Types

Goal Type	Direct	+ Feel	Comp	− Feel	Ration	Coerce	Refer	Avoid
Share Activities (friend)	3.98	2.96	3.26	4.85	2.57	6.28	3.99	4.42
Bureaucrat	5.10	2.63	3.74	4.37	2.13	6.29	5.25	4.58
Give Advice (friend)	4.69	3.26	2.92	3.88	1.79	5.86	3.24	5.17
De-escalate Relationship	4.95	3.39	2.96	4.72	1.85	5.88	2.70	5.48
Gain Assistance (friend)	4.36	2.59	2.68	4.93	2.04	6.18	3.71	4.26
Enforce Obligation	3.78	3.08	3.43	3.94	1.89	4.25	3.99	5.88
Initiate Relationship	4.26	2.25	3.99	5.30	3.47	6.45	3.86	3.73
Gain Assistance (professor)	4.76	2.38	2.82	4.33	1.57	6.27	4.59	5.32
Elicit Support (Third Person)	4.86	3.61	3.06	3.79	1.74	5.81	3.01	5.07
Give Advice (Parent)	4.79	2.96	2.92	4.14	1.75	6.11	2.71	5.11
Escalate Relationship	4.17	2.41	2.76	3.61	1.87	5.85	2.11	5.06
Protect Rights	3.84	3.48	2.91	4.22	1.98	4.08	3.78	5.30
Gain Assistance (stranger)	4.49	2.38	3.49	5.20	1.95	6.36	4.95	4.32
Gain Permission (parent)	4.91	2.70	2.23	4.42	1.67	6.29	3.35	4.92

Note. Smaller numbers reflect greater likelihood of use. Direct = Direct Request; + Feel = Manipulation of Positive Feelings; Comp = Compromise; − Feel = Manipulation of Negative Feelings; Ration = Rationality; Coerce = Coercion; Refer = Referent Power; Avoid = Avoidance. From Canary, Cody, and Marston (1986).

Coercive Influence.   Both studies indicate that coercive influence is least preferred (among all influence tactics), but that the tactic may be used as a viable method in *Protect Right* and *Enforce Obligation* goals. The rating scale study, however, indicated that coercive influence would not be used in a situation involving a bureaucrat. The event sampled here dealt with police officers giving tickets, and it is unlikely that warnings, threats, or aggression would occur in such events (see Cody & McLaughlin, 1985b). However, 8% of people who appear in traffic court adopt the approach of attacking the credibility of fairness of the ticketing officer (Cody & McLaughlin, 1988). Perhaps episodes involving bureaucrats should be divided into smaller units based on perceptions and anticipated affective states.

Persistence.   Our studies also indicate that respondents are most likely to be persistent in *Protect Right* and *Enforce Obligation* goals, and least persistent in *Initiate Relationship*, when confronting some bureaucrats, and in some types of *Gain Assistance* goals.

Manipulation of Negative Feelings.   The results of the cluster analysis previously described indicated that manipulation of negative feelings was not a popular first-attempt tactic, but that the approach would be used as either a first- or second-attempt tactic in *Give Advice, Share Activity, Obtain Permission* (parent), *Escalate Relationship,* or *Gain Assistance* goal types, and when dealing with bureaucrats. The results of the rating scale study also indicated that manipulation of negative feelings is fairly infrequent and is a viable tactic in *Give Advice* (friend), and *Escalate Relationship* episodes. The rating scale study also indicated that negative feelings would be manipulated in *Elicit Support* goals (M = 3.79) (prompting a friend to help another friend). The approach was least used in *Initiate Relationship* and *Gain Assistance* (stranger), according to the rating scale study.

Referent Appeal.   Both studies indicated that *Relational Escalation* and *Relational De-escalation* episodes prompted the highest ratings of referent tactics, and that referent appeal was also considered useful in *Give Advice* episodes, and when influencing parents (permission; see Table 2.14). The rating scale study also indicated that referent influence is preferred in *Elicit Support* episodes (M = 3.01), and is rarely used on bureaucrats and on strangers.

Direct Request.   Both studies also indicated that the simply worded direct request was more likely to be used in *Share Activity* (friend), *Protect Right,* and *Enforce Obligation* episodes, but is rarely used in *Give Advice* goals, or when influencing bureaucrats. The rating scale study further indicated that this simple influence approach was not preferred in relational change goals (Ms = 4.17 to 4.95).

Manipulation of Positive Feelings.   In the essay-writing project we coded essays as "face maintenance" or "indirect" if the respondent used small talk, hinted, or put on a "happy face" (i.e., tried to invoke liking). These tactics were more commonly used in *Obtain Permission* (parent), *Gain Assistance,* and *Escalate Rela-*

tionship goals, and with bureaucrats. In the rating scale study, manipulation of positive feelings received higher ratings in several of the same episodes: *Bureaucrats* (*M* = 2.63), *Initiate Relationship* (*M* = 2.25), *Gain Assistance* (professor) (*M* = 2.38), *Gain Assistance* (stranger) (*M* = 2.38), and *Obtain Permission* (parent) (*M* = 2.70). According to the rating scale study, *Escalate Relationship* also prompted high ratings of preference of positive manipulation of feelings (*M* = 2.41).

Exchange. Exchange occurred often in *Enforce Obligation, Escalate Relationship, Gain Assistance,* and *Protect Right* goal types. Most of these trends were replicated in the rating scale study. Exchange was rated as a preferred tactic in *Escalate Relationship* (*M* = 2.76), *Gain Assistance* (professor) (*M* = 2.18), *Protect Right* (*M* = 2.91), and *Gain Assistance* (friend) goals (*M* = 2.68). The rating scale study, however, indicated that respondents were not more likely to use exchange in *Gain Assistance* (stranger) requests than in other goals, although the rating scale study only sampled one event. Under conditions of a pressing need or an actual emergency, an agent may still propose an exchange in order to gain assistance.

In terms of reactions to goals, females differed from males in a number of ways (all mean differences are significant at the .01 alpha level). Females:

1. Rated *Escalate Relationship* easier to imagine than males did (*Ms* = 1.77, 2.17) and claimed they would be more likely to enter actively into such events (*Ms* = 1.74, 2.02).
2. Rated *De-escalate Relationship* easier to imagine (*Ms* = 1.65, 2.08), indicated they would be more persistent (*Ms* = 2.31, 2.66), and claimed to more frequently experience *De-escalate Relationship* (*Ms* = 2.87, 3.37).
3. Indicated less confidence in *Initiate Relationship* (*Ms* = 3.05, 2.50), less persistence (*Ms* = 4.94, 3.81), less willingness to enter the events (*Ms* = 3.11, 2.40), and less frequency of experience in initiations (*Ms* = 4.05, 3.03).
4. Rated *Give Advice* (friend) as easier to imagine (*Ms* = 1.77, 2.17), expected more persistence (*Ms* = 2.52, 3.21), and indicated a greater willingness to enter into the events (*Ms* = 2.27, 2.67).
5. Rated *Give Advice* (parent) as a goal they would more actively enter into (*Ms* = 2.32, 2.81) and claimed greater persistence (*Ms* = 2.46, 2.99).
6. Rated *Share Activity* (friend) as a goal they more frequently experienced (*Ms* = 2.58, 2.90).
7. Rated *Elicit Support* easier to imagine (*Ms* = 2.40, 2.83), indicated a greater willingness to pursue the goals (*Ms* = 2.57, 3.26), claimed greater persistence (*Ms* = 2.48, 3.17), and rated themselves higher in confidence (*Ms* = 2.67, 3.09).
8. Rated *Gain Assistance* (professor) (asking for a special favor) as a goal that is easier to imagine than did males (*Ms* = 1.57, 2.27).

9. Indicated they would be more persistent in pursuing *Protect Right* goals
   (Ms = 2.35, 2.83).
10. Rated persistence higher in *Enforce Obligation* (Ms = 1.57, 2.05), but
    males claimed to be more frequently involved in confronting others about
    obligations (Ms = 3.51, 3.92).
11. Reported less frequently experience encountering bureaucrats (here,
    traffic officers) than did males (Ms = 4.57, 3.78).

Further, males and females differed from one another in a number of ways
when attempting to influence the target. Females:

1. Were less likely to use direct requests across all goal types (Ms = 4.64,
   4.26), and were more likely to use coercive influence across all goal types
   (Ms = 6.13, 5.42).
2. Rated manipulation of negative feelings lower in preference in four goal
   types: *Gain Assistance* (friend) (Ms = 5.22, 4.40), *Share Activity* (friend)
   (Ms = 5.02, 4.53), *Gain Assistance* (stranger) (Ms = 5.36, 4.89), and
   Initiate Relationship (Ms = 5.64, 4.66).
3. Rated manipulation of positive feelings higher in preference in 11 goals:
   Share Activity (friend) (Ms = 2.79, 3.26), *Bureaucrats* (Ms = 2.48, 2.92),
   De-escalate Relationship (Ms = 3.20, 3.78), *Gain Assistance* (friend) (Ms =
   2.39, 2.97), *Enforce Obligation* (Ms = 2.84, 3.54), *Gain Assistance* (professor) (Ms = 2.10, 2.89), *Elicit Support* (Ms = 3.40, 3.98), *Give Advice* (parent) (Ms = 2.67, 3.52), *Escalate Relationship* (Ms = 2.03, 3.08), *Protect
   Right* (Ms = 3.27, 3.90), and *Obtain Permission* (parent) (Ms = 2.46, 3.14).
4. Rated exchange higher in seven of the goals: *Share Activity* (friend) (Ms
   = 3.08, 3.62), *Give Advice* (friend) (Ms = 2.74, 3.22), *Escalate Relationship* (Ms = 2.60, 3.03), *De-escalate Relationship* (Ms = 2.78, 3.30), *Enforce Obligation* (Ms = 3.17, 3.92), *Protect Right* (Ms = 2.62, 3.38), and
   Obtain Permission (parent) (Ms = 2.03, 2.61).
5. Rated rationality higher in preference in 11 of the goals: *Share Activity*
   (friend) (Ms = 2.37, 2.87), *Give Advice* (friend) (Ms = 1.58, 2.15), *De-
   escalate Relationship* (Ms = 1.68, 2.09), *Gain Assistance* (friend) (Ms = 1.89,
   2.23), *Gain Assistance* (professor) (Ms = 1.39, 1.88), *Elicit Support* (Ms
   = 1.42, 2.28), *Give Advice* (parent) (Ms = 1.53, 2.16), *Escalate Relationship* (Ms = 1.17, 2.14), *Protect Right* (Ms = 1.66, 2.50), *Gain Assistance*
   (stranger) (Ms = 1.70, 2.32), and *Obtain Permission* (parent) (Ms = 1.55,
   1.86).
6. Rated referent power higher in preference in four goals: *Elicit Support*
   (Ms = 2.79, 3.34), *Escalate Relationship* (Ms = 1.98, 2.38), *Protect Right*
   (Ms = 3.63, 4.10), and *De-escalate Relationship* (Ms = 2.50, 3.08).

7. Rated avoidance lower in *Enforce Obligation* (*Ms* = 6.08, 5.60) and *Elicit Support* goals (*Ms* = 5.30, 4.65).

Both the nominating and rating scale studies indicated that females pursue more communal goals than males: females pursued more *Give Advice, Share Activity,* and *Elicit Support* episodes, displayed more interest and stronger reactions to relational escalation and de-escalation goals, and expected to be more persistent in *Protect Right* and *Enforce Obligation* episodes. Men, on the other hand, more often had to confront bureaucrats, related more to *Enforce Obligation* goals, and experienced greater control in *Initiate Relationship* goals. As expected, males were more likely to use a blunt direct request when seeking assistance or activity from peers and negative manipulation of feelings when influencing others. (Males also preferred avoidance more in 2 of 14 goal types.) Females relied more on manipulation of positive feelings, referent influence, and, with familiar targets, exchange. Some literature suggests that females might rely on rationality as a means of overcoming expectations of lower credibility. Females did in fact rate rationality higher in preference than did males in most goals. Men and women rated rationality equally high, however, when dealing with bureaucrats and when enforcing obligations, and rated rationality equally low when initiating relationships.

THE DIARY STUDY: A COMPARISON TO THE NOMINATING STUDY

Sixty college students kept diaries of whom they tried to influence during a 12-week period, noting the circumstances surrounding the request, and whether they were successful or unsuccessful. The diaries were used as part of a junior-level course in persuasion and the students wrote a paper concerning how they influenced others. The diaries were brought to class and examined by the teaching assistant every 2 weeks. The students generated over 3,000 episodes. Table 2.15 presents a summary of the nominating and diary studies.

The diary study revealed somewhat higher levels of reported success by the respondents, suggesting that recalled data is not particularly flawed by overestimating success. In fact, in only two areas did we find evidence that recalled data is associated with pervasive biases. First, when recalling episodes of relational changes, actors claimed extremely high rates of success (83%; compared to 62% in diary data), indicating that in hindsight actors claimed to have more control of changes in relational definitions than might be the case. (The results of Hill, Rubin, & Peplau, 1976, similarly suggest that dating partners prefer not to be the *target* of disengagement, but wish to control relational definitions.) Second, the 210 respondents in the nominating study recalled only 65 cases of making selfish requests, but the 60 respondents in the diary study generated

TABLE 2.15
Compliance-Gaining Goals and Claimed Success
by Role Relationship and Motive

	Recalled Data		Diary Data	
	% Frequency	% Success	% Frequency	% Success
Roles				
Parents	18	52	14	65
Sisters/Brothers	11	49	7	67
Friends	39	66	49	72
Roommates	10	56	11	70
Neighbors/Strangers	8	73	3	76
Bureaucrats	12	60	16	64
Goals				
Obtain Permission	7	57	2	57
Normative Request (bureaucrats)	8	57	7	66
Gain Assistance	30	73	47	75
Give Advice	16	40	13	59
Change Opinion	4	34	3	54
Share Activity	9	62	16	69
Elicit Support (Third Party)	6	61	2	74
Change Ownership	7	70	0	72
Violate Law	0	36	0	0
Enforce Obligation	3	41	3	68
Protect Right	2	32	0	66
Change Relationship	8	83	4	62

Note. Zero percentage means that less than 1% of the total number of episodes could be categorized into the goal type.

105 selfish requests. Selfish requests may be fairly routine behaviors that are conveniently forgotten or redefined over time.

On the other hand, the data demonstrate that (a) the two methods are in agreement in terms of levels of success for most of the goals being studied; and (b) students construct a somewhat modified and restricted social environment at college (compared to the general picture we get from recalled data). Both methods indicate that *Gain Assistance*, selling, and *Elicit Support* (episodes were generally regarded as more successfully pursued than *Obtain Permission, Change Opinion, Give Advice*, and other goals. Most of the differences between the two methods, we believe, could be attributable to changes in the students' global environment or to changes in age and status. The recalled data produced a sizable number of requests involving family members (29% of all episodes), where *Permission* and *Assistance* (from parent) and *Assistance, Advice Giving*, and *Activity* (with brothers/sisters) are frequent. However, once at college, students made fewer requests of family members (21% of all requests), made fewer requests involving *Permission* (7% vs. 2%), made more requests involving *Assistance* (30% vs. 47%), and more requests involving *Activity* (9% vs. 16%). College students claimed greater success in influencing family members in the diaries, in part because different kinds of requests were made, and were more successful in *Gain Assistance* than in other goals.

The college students' compliance-gaining world changes outside the family as well when we rely on the diary method. Students made more requests of friends (39% vs. 49%), fewer requests of strangers (8% vs. 3%), and more requests of bureaucrats (12% vs. 16%). In terms of motives, college students spent little time (in the midst of a semester) selling, protecting rights, and eliciting support (i.e., involving themselves in third-party episodes to help another). However, participants did recall episodes of each type (7%, 2%, and 6%, respectively, in the nominating study). Perhaps episodes like *Protect Right* and *Elicit Support* are vivid or involve cognitive work, and thus are easily recalled.

The two methods each have advantages and disadvantages. The recalled data sampled a wider range of episodes, a number of memorable episodes (e.g., permission from parents to extend curfew, annoyances that were problematic), and episodes that might occur seasonally (e.g., travel in mutual activities), but produced several biases in responding. On the other hand, a diary method may tap into current events that should be easy to recall and report on, but produce a restricted range—the single most typical case of compliance gaining among college students is to ask a friend for a favor (e.g., for a ride, to take notes in class). Such episodes are hardly likely to prompt actors to use verbally assertive tactics (as Dillard & Burgoon, 1985, tried to study), and are not the types of episodes one considers socially significant.

WHAT WE KNOW AND NEED TO KNOW ABOUT INFLUENCE GOALS

Our primary purpose was to offer a preliminary typology of goals. We wanted to assess how goal types are perceived, to describe goals social actors report they pursue with varying degrees of success/failure, and to provide preliminary evidence as to *how* people attempt to gain compliance from others. Our second purpose was to investigate how males and females differ in their orientations toward and in their pursuit of goals.

Regarding the Nature of Goals

What we've learned is that social actors (here, college students) relied heavily on parents, brothers/sisters, and friends for assistance (one fourth of the episodes in the nominating study were of this nature), and gave considerable advice to the same set of role relations. Additionally, goals involving parents and routine activities were frequently experienced. Actors sought permission from parents and activities and support from friends. With roommates they frequently experienced *Protect Right, Enforce Obligation*, and *Shared Activity* goals, but, relative to other relationships involving interdependence, they spent little time in *Give Advice* and *Gain Assistance* episodes. Considerably different types of motives were involved when influencing bureaucrats, strangers, and neighbors, who were infrequently influenced. Both the nominating study and the rating scale study indicated that the least frequently experienced episodes involved *Gain Assistance* (stranger), episodes with bureaucrats, and *Elicit Support* goals.

Preliminary evidence also can be offered concerning tactical decisions. Coercive influence was regarded as a viable option in *Enforce Obligation* and *Protect Right* goals, and direct requests were rated as useful in *Share Activity, Enforce Obligation*, and *Protect Right* goals, in which, presumably, the actor doesn't have to justify a request (again) and in which the actor perceives that rights and obligations are clearly defined. Referent influence was used when giving advice, when trying to make relational changes, and when eliciting support from others. Manipulation of positive feelings was similarly used when changing relational definitions, gaining assistance from others, and influencing parents. Manipulation of negative feelings was rated much lower in preference than was manipulation of positive feelings, but was rated as a possible option in relational escalation (one would act disappointed if a friend rejected such a move), in *Elicit Support* (one would act disappointed if a friend refused to help another), and when giving advice. Exchange tactics were used on friends and parents, to negotiate relational definitions, in *Protect Right* and *Enforce Obligation* goals, and (with less frequency) when giving advice and gaining assistance from others. Some form of rationality was used on adults, such as bureaucrats and parents, and when actors gave advice—although the precise nature of rationality was different in advice-giving episodes than when influencing bureaucrats.

One of the most important implications of these studies concerns the need to examine both role relationships and motives when studying social influence processes. Qualitatively different types of goals are pursued with parents, brothers/sisters, friends, roommates, bureaucrats, and strangers. We would similarly expect that some goals generate considerably different approaches and arguments than do other goals. For instance, the set of approaches used to obtain a date or to initiate a relationship (Berger, 1986; Berger & Bell, 1988) has little correspondence to the set of tactics used to alter relational definitions (Banks, Altendorf, Greene, & Cody, 1987; Baxter, 1982, 1985; Braaten, 1987; Cody, 1982; Wilmot, Carbaugh, & Baxter, 1985), or tactics used purposefully to induce jealousy to alter the allocation of rewards between partners (White, 1980), or when influencing bureaucrats, either in upward influence attempts (Kipnis, 1984; Krone, 1986; Schilit & Locke, 1982) or in traffic court (Cody & McLaughlin, 1988). Some illicit modes of influencing others vary in perceived appropriateness from one goal or relational type to another. For example, Lindskold and Walters (1983) reported that actors rate lies to bureaucrats as less offensive and less inappropriate than other types of lies.

Further, it appears that tactics that are effective in pursuing one goal are not effective when pursuing a different one. For instance, Schilit and Locke (1982) found that "logically presenting ideas" was the most popular method for influencing superiors, but that the tactic was not significantly related to effectiveness. Instead, using the superior as a platform to present ideas and trading job benefits were associated with effective compliance, and threats, challenges, and the use of external pressure on the superior were significantly associated with increased failure. In traffic court, however, Cody and McLaughlin (1988) found that challenges, denials, excuses, and justifications were not related to reducing penalties for traffic violations (although previous research on accounts offered to family, friends, and acquaintances indicates that apologies and excuses were likely to lead to honoring; see Cody & McLaughlin, 1985b). However, only the use of "logical proofs" resulted in success (e.g., "I have a letter here from the City Planner's office indicating that this intersection is under investigation (for change) because of the confusing road signs . . ."). Thus, when dealing with an official who is charged with making a determination of guilt beyond "reasonable doubt," rationality and evidence were the only effective forms of oral argument, whereas in organizational contexts successful compliance depends on a host of other variables (Kipnis, 1984; Krone, 1986; Schilit & Locke, 1982).

Regarding Gender Differences and Goals

Studies in recent years have obtained the full range of gender-based outcomes. Part of the inconsistency in this literature stems from career and age differences, as career-oriented women may differ little from males once they have been socialized into the organization and have achieved certain levels of status. And we also know that career-oriented women elicit fewer gender-role stereotypical responses from others and that the career-oriented female constitutes a different type of consumer, as opposed to the "stay at home" or "working just for the job" female (see, for instance, Barak & Stern, 1986; Barry, Gilly, & Doran, 1985; Bellante & Foster, 1984; Eagly & Steffen, 1984; Eagly & Wood, 1982; Fairhurst, 1986; Jackson, McDaniel, & Rao, 1985; Putnam & Wilson, 1982).

Our results, however, indicate that college-age females (vs. males) show a marked preference for communal goals. But our results also indicate that females might be very direct and aggressive when pursuing particular outcomes. First, females pursued more goals with family and friends that involved mutual activities, giving advice, seeking support for others, and gaining assistance.

They were also more concerned than males with protecting rights and making relational changes (escalations and de-escalations). Compatible with stereotypes (Burgoon et al., 1983; Johnson, 1976; Pearson, 1985), males claimed to rely more on direct requests and coercive influence (as far as ratings of likelihood-of-use are concerned), whereas females relied more on referent power, compromise, and manipulation of positive feelings (for certain goals; see preceding). However, females also claimed to think more about attaining certain goals and rated certain goals as more salient (i.e., easier to imagine, etc., in *Give Advice, Change Relationship, Protect Right*), and females rated expected persistence higher for certain types of important goals (*De-escalate Relationship, Give Advice, Elicit Support, Protect Right*, and *Enforce Obligation*). Other projects conducted recently argue that females may be quite direct, persistent, assertive, and even manipulative in pursuing goals involving relational changes, protecting rights, and when establishing or reestablishing fairness and equity in social relations (de Turck, 1985; Shea & Pearson, 1986; White, 1980). Finally, there is growing evidence that gender differences play a small and perhaps insignificant role in marital conflicts, because partners tend to reciprocate tactics (Burggraf & Sillars, 1987); that is, females will use more assertive tactics if their partners use them.

Implications for Influence Contexts: The Example of Organizational Goals

The evidence presented in this paper focused on college students. Although this focus is warranted given our desire to rethink much of the literature on influence that has been developed utilizing this population, specific contexts probably involve a different set of goals. We anticipate, however, that the fundamental nature of influence goals does not change; that is, goals have the content characteristics described earlier in this chapter. Still other unique situational characteristics would imply alternative sets of goals. For example, Jablin (1987) noted that the organization is comprised of various situational factors such as span-of-control, hierarchy position, organizational size, and sub-unit size. Erez and Rim (1982), Kipnis et al. (1980), and Rim and Erez (1980) reported five common influence topics: assistance on the job, getting others to do their job, self-interest, initiating change, and improving performance.

The picture that emerges from these studies is that organizational members pursue a set of common motives but do so through different methods, depending on their position in the organization. Moreover, the motive of improving performance was cited as the primary reason that middle managers sought compliance from superiors and subordinates (61% and 21%, respectively). Superiors were shown to be less flexible in one study, primarily relying on assertive tactics, whereas superiors and subordinates used a high degree of emotionally laden clandestine tactics in another study. Future research should examine a more exhaustive list of common organizational goals in order to assess the impact of situational features on influence attempts. In addition, future research should attempt to discern personal and organizational factors that might mediate the process of goal satisfaction through compliance gaining. Erez and Rim (1982), for example, found that ownership, size, number of subordinates, and professional discipline were related to motives and choice of influence tactics.

Implications Concerning Compliance Resisting and Conflict

If goal types and role relationships jointly provide a parsimonious scheme for accounting for strategic choices in compliance *gaining*, then it is reasonable to assume that the same types of motives and role relationships will influence the selection of compliance-*resisting* tactics (McLaughlin et al., 1980; McQuillen, 1986; McQuillen et al., 1984). McLaughlin et al. (1980) assessed compliance-resisting tactics in terms of three situation perceptions, and interpreted complex three-way interaction effects in an effort to show how situations impact different types of influence tactics. However, three-way interactions are difficult to interpret, lack parsimony, and lack stability. The results of McLaughlin et al. are quite straightforward if we reinterpret them in terms of goals. For instance, the negotiation tactics were used to resist proposed *Relational Change* (i.e., move together to a new town), and when rights were being violated (neighbor with a loud stereo); justification for noncompliance was used more often with neighbors and roommates when resisting *Enforce Obligation* (clean up one's room), and when making a selfish request (the Shade tree situation utilized in Miller et al., 1977); and nonnegotiation tactics were used least to resist selfish requests and when resisting advice given by others.

Whereas compliance resisting reflects a desire not to comply to another's goal, conflict entails communication about two or more incompatible goals (see Sillars, Wilmot, & Hocker, this volume). Recently, we extended our typology of influence goals to include conflict episodes (Canary et al., 1988). In that study, the most common goals in conflict were *Enforce Obligation* (23.2%), *Maintain Relationship* (i.e., where romantic partners disagree about the relationship's current level of intimacy, 12.9%), and *Share Activity* (i.e., if and/or where to go someplace, 12.1%). In addition, Canary et al. (1988) found that conflict goals accounted for 18% of the variation of self-reported *integrative* (cooperative) and *distributive* (competitive) tactics. It appears clear to us that we can conceptualize profitably compliance-resisting and conflict situations using the mechanisms we have proposed here. Yet, much more research is needed to examine the processes entailed in initial goal proposal, resistance, conflict, and goal emergence and re-definition.

Implications for a Theory of Strategic Message Generation

A cognitive-based theory of compliance-gaining message selection seeks to explain behavior in terms of cognitive structures and processes (Greene, 1990; Bisanz & Rule, 1990a; Smith, 1982, 1984; Smith et al., 1990). Berger (1985), for example, argued that a minimum of seven factors should be included in a schema of strategy selection (e.g., intimacy, relative power, etc.). Smith (1982, 1984) argued that tactics are generated (and responded to) largely on the basis of a set of rules involving self-identity, image maintenance, and relationship rules. Smith argued that some rules are more important in some situations than in others, which is similar to our argument that actors have primary influence goals that direct tactical choices (see also Dillard et al., 1987).

Literature reviewed previously suggests that influence goals are pursued according to persuasion schema that organizes tactics along a preferred order, influences memory, and affects the frequency by which the tactics are used. When generating tactics in particular goals, however, actors "skip down" the ordered list and generate any number of variations of "present information," and so on. It is clear that different strategies and arguments are used in the pursuit of different goals, and that different sequences of actions are probable (compare how one secures a date vs. selling a car). In this chapter, we have argued that constellations of perceptions can be combined to inform an understanding of the content characteristics of goals. Others have made similar arguments (e.g., Dillard, 1990; Meyer, 1986), although our own formulation stems from our previous concern with perceptions of compliance-gaining strategies derived from MDS studies (Cody & McLaughlin, 1980). Issues remain concerning the content characteristics of goals as they are perceived by actors, including the hierarchical nature of goals (i.e., superordinate, basic, subordinate), primary *versus* secondary multiple goals, influence and conversational goal distinctions, and goal emergence during conflict. Finally, there are goals in which the self-image is activated.

Persons with different personalities (e.g., self-monitors) differ in terms of motives. Smith et al. (1990) found that high self-monitors rated all goals as easier to imagine and rated persistence as more probable than did low self-monitors. High self-monitors also rated anticipated success, willingness to enter, and familiarity higher in several goals involving interpersonal relations and outcomes. Low self-monitors were less likely to use emotionally oriented strategies (i.e., manipulating positive or negative feelings) and relationally oriented strategies (i.e., referent influence, exchange), and presumably rejecting the notion of "manipulating" others (see Smith et al., 1990). These results support the notion that the "principled and honest" low self-monitor (see Snyder, 1987) adopts a different set of rules about appropriate behaviors, rejecting "manipulation," and seemingly expecting a world where friends share common rules of obligations and commitments (see Smith et al., 1990). Future research should examine how salient personality features such as self-monitoring and locus of control (Canary et al., 1986, 1988) operate within different goals. The evidence to date indicates that goals and personality factors interact in clear ways to affect strategic behaviors.

Conclusion

This chapter presents a typology of goals that depicts particular motives discussed in the fields of cognitive social psychology, communication, and organizational behavior, integrating definitions of motives with situation perceptions to account for distinctions relevant to actors. There is no doubt that actors frequently pursue certain goal types with varying degrees of confidence and anticipated persistence, and there is no doubt that actors adapt their messages for particular targets and particular motives. Further, we found that the basic or intermediate level of analysis was more profitable for examining tactical choices than the superordinate level analysis. Thus, we believe that the efforts by Dillard, Rule and Bisanz, Kipnis, as well as our own and others', have resulted in a viable typology of goals that clearly reflects how social actors think about influencing others, and one that is strongly associated with behaviors. In the next phase of this research, we want to assess more fully the content of cognitive representations of goal types and examine actors' behavioral expectations for compliance. Targets are expected to comply to certain requests due to reciprocity constraints, relational commitment, values or principles, and the like (Cialdini, 1984; Dillard & Fitzpatrick, 1985). We further want to analyze how actors' goals are linked to *process*; that is, how actors usually plan interactions; how other person variables are related to goal pursuit and motives; how communication transforms actors' perceptions of the situation (Giles & Hewstone, 1982); and how actors reinterpret their goals during and following strategic communication.

ACKNOWLEDGMENTS

We wish to thank the following individuals for their important contributions: Joan Cashion, Shannon LoVette, Margaret L. McLaughlin, and John Wiemann. We also wish to thank Nancy Baker for assistance in typing the manuscript.

REFERENCES

Anderson, J. R. (1980). *Cognitive psychology and its implications*. San Francisco: Freeman.
Andrews, P. H. (1987). Gender differences in persuasive communication and attribution of success. *Human Communication Research, 13*, 372–385.

Bachman, J. G., Bowers, D. G., & Marcus, P. M. (1968). Bases of supervisory power: A comparative study in five organizational settings. In A. S. Tannenbaum (Ed.), *Control in organizations* (pp. 229–238). New York: McGraw-Hill.

Baglan, T., Lalumia, J., & Bayless, O. L. (1986). Utilization of compliance-gaining strategies: A research note. *Communication Monographs, 53,* 289–293.

Banks, S. P., Altendorf, D. M., Greene, J. D., & Cody, M. J. (1987). An examination of relationship disengagement: Perception of break-up strategies and outcomes. *Western Journal of Speech Communication, 51,* 19–41.

Barak, B., & Stern, B. (1986). Women's age in advertising: An examination of two consumer age profiles. *Journal of Advertising Research, 25,* 8–47.

Barraclough, R. A. (1984). *A multidimensional scaling analysis of teacher's perceptions of the bases of interpersonal power in the classroom.* Unpublished doctoral dissertation, West Virginia University.

Barry, T. E., Gilly, M. C., & Doran, L. E. (1985). Advertising to women with different career orientations. *Journal of Advertising Research, 25,* 26–35.

Baxter, L. A. (1982). Strategies for ending relationships: Two studies. *Western Journal of Speech Communication, 46,* 223–241.

Baxter, L. A. (1984). An investigation of compliance-gaining as politeness. *Human Communication Research, 10,* 427–456.

Baxter, L. A. (1985). Accomplishing relational disengagement. In S. Duck & D. Perlman (Eds.), *Understanding personal relationships* (pp. 243–265). Beverly Hills, CA: Sage.

Baxter, L. A., & Bullis, C. (1986). Turning points in developing romantic relationships. *Human Communication Research, 12,* 469–493.

Baxter, L. A., & Wilmot, W. W. (1984). "Secret test": Social strategies for requiring information about the state of the relationship. *Human Communication Research, 11,* 171–202.

Bellante, D., & Foster, A. C. (1984). Working wives and expenditure on services. *Journal of Consumer Research, 11,* 700–707.

Berger, C. R. (1985). Social power and interpersonal communication. In M. L. Knapp & G. R. Miller (Eds.), *Handbook of interpersonal communication* (pp. 439–499). Beverly Hills, CA: Sage.

Berger, C. R. (1986). Planning, affect, and social action generation. In R. L. Donohew, H. Sypher, & E. T. Higgins (Eds.), *Communication, social cognition, and affect* (pp. 6–87). Hillsdale, NJ: Lawrence Erlbaum Associates.

Berger, C. R. (in press). Planning and scheming: Strategies for initiating relationships. In P. McGhee, R. Burnett, & D. Clarke (Eds.), *Accounting for relationships: Social representation of interpersonal links.* London: Methuen.

Berger, C. R., & Bell, R. A. (1988). Plans and the initiation of social relationships. *Human Communication Research, 15,* 217–235.

Bettinghaus, E. P., & Cody, M. J. (1987). *Persuasive communication* (4th ed.). New York: Holt, Rinehart, & Winston.

Biggers, T., & Masterson, J. T. (1983). *Emotion-eliciting qualities of interpersonal situations as the basis for a typology.* Unpublished manuscript, University of Miami.

Bisanz, G. L., & Rule, B. G. (1989). Gender and persuasion schema: A search for cognitive invariants. *Personality and Social Psychology Bulletin, 15,* 4–18.

Bisanz, G. L., & Rule, B. G. (1990). Childrens' and adults' comprehension of narratives about persuasion. In M. J. Cody & M. L. McLaughlin (Eds.), *Psychology of tactical communication* (pp. 48–69). Clevedon, England: Multilingual Matters.

Booth, A. (1972). Sex and social participation. *American Sociological Review, 37,* 183–192.

Braaten, D. (1987). *The impact of attribution of responsibility, dependence/independence, and gender on the selection of relational conflict tactics.* Unpublished doctoral dissertation, University of Southern California.

Broughton, R. (1984). A prototype strategy for the construction of personality scales. *Journal of Personality and Social Psychology, 47,* 1134–1146.

Brown, P., & Levinson, S. (1978). Universals in language usage: Politeness phenomena. In E. Gordy (Ed.), *Questions and politeness: Strategies in social interaction* (pp. 56–289). Cambridge: Cambridge University Press.

Browne, J. (1973). *The used-car game: A sociology of the bargain.* Lexington, MA: Lexington Books.

Burggraf, C. S., & Sillars, A. L. (1987). A critical examination of sex differences in marital communication. *Communication Monographs, 54,* 276–294.

Burgoon, M. J., Dillard, J. P., & Doran, N. E. (1983). Friendly or unfriendly persuasion: The effects of violations of expectations by males and females. *Human Communication Research, 10,* 283–294.

Canary, D. J., & Cody, M. J. (in press). *Interpersonal communication: A goals-based approach.* New York: St. Martin's Press.

Canary, D. J., Cody, M. J., & Marston, P. (1986). Goal types, compliance-gaining, and locus of control. *Journal of Language and Social Psychology, 5,* 249–269.

Canary, D. J., Cunningham, E. M., & Cody, M. J. (1988). An examination of locus of control and goal types in managing interpersonal conflict. *Communication Research, 15,* 426–446.

Cantor, N., & Mischel, W. (1977). Traits as prototypes: Effects on recognition memory. *Journal of Personality and Social Psychology, 35,* 38–48.

Cantor, N., & Mischel, W. (1979a). Prototypes in person perception. In L. Berkowitz (Ed.), *Advances in experimental social psychology* (Vol. 12, pp. 3–52). New York: Academic Press.

Cantor, N., & Mischel, W. (1979b). Prototypicality and personality: Effects on free recall and personality impressions. *Journal of Research in Personality, 13,* 187–205.

Cantor, N., Mischel, W., & Schwartz, J. (1982a). Social knowledge: Structure, content, use, and abuse. In A. H. Hastorf & A. M. Isen (Eds.), *Cognitive social psychology* (pp. 33–72). New York: Elsevier/North-Holland.

Cantor, N., Mischel, W., & Schwartz, J. (1982b). A prototype analysis of situations. *Cognitive Psychology, 14,* 45–77.

Carver, C. S., & Scheier, M. F. (1982). Control theory: A useful conceptual framework for personality—Social, clinical and health psychology. *Psychological Bulletin, 92,* 111–135.

Cialdini, R. (1984). *Influence.* New York: Quill.

Clark, R. A. (1979). The impact of self-interest and desire for liking in the selection of communicative strategies. *Communication Monographs, 46,* 257–273.

Clark, R. A., & Delia, J. (1979). Topoi and rhetorical competence. *Quarterly Journal of Speech, 65,* 187–206.

Cody, M. J. (1978, November). *A multidimensional scaling of naturalistic situations.* Paper presented to the Speech Communication Association, Minneapolis, MN.

Cody, M. J. (1982). A typology of disengagement strategies and an examination of the role intimacy, reactions to inequity, and relational problems play in strategy selection. *Communication Monographs, 49,* 148–170.

Cody, M. J., Greene, J. O., Marston, P., Baaske, K., O'Hair, H. D., & Schneider, M. J. (1986). Situation perception and the selection of message strategies. In M. L. McLaughlin (Ed.), *Communication yearbook 8* (pp. 390–420). Beverly Hills, CA: Sage.

Cody, M. J., & McLaughlin, M. L. (1980). Perceptions of compliance-gaining situations: A dimensional analysis. *Communication Monographs, 47,* 132–148.

Cody, M. J., & McLaughlin, M. L. (1985a). The situation as a construct in interpersonal communication research. In M. L. Knapp & G. R. Miller (Eds.), *Handbook of interpersonal communication* (pp. 263–312). Beverly Hills, CA: Sage.

Cody, M. J., & McLaughlin, M. L. (1985b). Models for sequential construction of accounting episodes: Situational and interactional constraints on message selection and interaction. In R. L. Street, Jr. and J. N. Cappella (Eds.), *Sequence and pattern in communication behavior* (pp. 50–69). London: Edward Arnold.

Cody, M. J., & McLaughlin, M. L. (1988). Accounts on trial: Oral arguments in traffic court. In C. Antaki (Ed.), *Analyzing lay explanations: A casebook of methods* (pp. 113–126). London: Sage.

Cody, M. J., McLaughlin, M. L., & Jordan, W. J. (1980). A multidimensional scaling of three sets of compliance-gaining strategies. *Communication Quarterly, 28*, 34–46.

Cody, M. J., McLaughlin, M. L., & Schneider, M. J. (1981). The impact of relational consequences and intimacy on the selection of interpersonal persuasion tactics: A reanalysis. *Communication Quarterly, 29*, 91–106.

Cody, M. J., Woelfel, M. L., & Jordan, W. J. (1983). Dimensions of compliance-gaining situations. *Human Communication Research, 9*, 99–113.

Craig, R. T., Tracy, K., & Spisak, F. (1986). The discourse of requests: Assessment of a politeness approach. *Human Communication Research, 12*, 437–468.

Craik, K. H. (1970). Environmental psychology. In K. H. Craik, B. Kleinmutz, R. L. Rosnow, R. Rosenthal, J. A. Cheyne, & R. H. Walters (Eds.), *New directions in psychology* (Vol. 4, pp. 1–22). New York: Holt, Rinehart, & Winston.

Craik, K. H. (1973). Environmental psychology. *Annual Review of Psychology, 24*, 403–421.

deTurck, M. A. (1985). A transactional analysis of compliance-gaining behavior: Effects of non-compliance, relational contexts, and actors' gender. *Human Communication Research, 12*, 54–78.

Dillard, J. P. (1987). *Influence goals in close relationships*. Unpublished manuscript, University of Wisconsin, Department of Communication Arts, Madison, WI.

Dillard, J. P. (1990). Primary and secondary goals in interpersonal influence. In M. J. Cody & M. L. McLaughlin (Eds.), *Psychology of tactical communication* (pp. 70–90). Clevedon, England: Multilingual Matters.

Dillard, J. P., & Burgoon, M. (1985). Situational influences on the selection of compliance-gaining messages: Two tests of the predictive utility of the Cody–McLaughlin typology. *Communication Monographs, 52*, 289–304.

Dillard, J. P., & Fitzpatrick, M. A. (1985). Compliance-gaining in marital interaction. *Personality and Social Psychology Bulletin, 11*, 419–433.

Dillard, J. P., & Segrin, C., & Harden, J. M. (1987, July). *Goals and interpersonal influence*. Paper presented to the Third International Conference on Language and Social Psychology, Bristol, England.

Eagly, A. H., & Steffen, V. L. (1984). Gender stereotypes stem from the distribution of men and women into social roles. *Journal of Personality and Social Psychology, 46*, 735–754.

Eagly, A. H., & Wood, W. (1982). Inferred sex differences in status as a determinant of gender stereotypes about social influence. *Journal of Personality and Social Psychology, 43*, 915–928.

Ekehammar, B., Schalling, D., & Magnusson, D. (1975). Dimensions of stressful situations: A comparison between response analytic and stimulus analytic approaches. *Multivariate Behavioral Research, 10*, 155–164.

Erez, M., & Rim, Y. (1982). The relationship between goals, influence tactics, and personal and organizational variables. *Human Relations, 35*, 871–878.

Fairhurst, G. T. (1986). Male–female communication on the job: Literature review and commentary. In M. L. McLaughlin (Ed.), *Communication yearbook 9* (pp. 83–116). Newbury Park, CA: Sage.

Falbo, T. (1977a). A multidimensional scaling of power strategies. *Journal of Personality and Social Psychology, 35*, 537–547.

Falbo, T. (1977b). Relationships between sex, sex role, and social influence. *Psychology of Women Quarterly, 1*, 62–72.

Falbo, T., & Peplau, L. A. (1980). Power strategies in intimate relationships. *Journal of Personality and Social Psychology, 38*, 618–628.

Fitzpatrick, M. A., & Winke, J. (1979). You always hurt the one you love: Strategies and tactics in interpersonal conflict. *Communication Quarterly, 26*, 3–11.

Forgas, J. P. (1976). The perceptions of social episodes: Categorical and dimensional representations of two different social milieus. *Journal of Personality and Social Psychology, 34*, 199–209.

Forgas, J. P. (1979). *Social episodes: The study of interaction routines*. London: Academic.

Forgas, J. P. (1982). Episode cognition: Internal representations of interaction routines. In L. Berkowitz (Ed.), *Advances in experimental social psychology* (Vol. 15, pp. 59–101). New York: Academic Press.

Forgas, J. P. (1983a). Social skills and the perception of interaction episodes. *British Journal of Clinical Psychology, 22*, 195–207.

Forgas, J. P. (1983b). Language, goals, and situation. *Journal of Language and Social Psychology, 2*, 267–293.

French, J. R. P., & Raven, B. (1959). The bases of social power. In D. Cartwright (Ed.), *Studies in social power* (pp. 150–167). Ann Arbor, MI: Institute for Social Research.

Giles, H., & Hewstone, M. (1982). Cognitive structures, speech, and social situations: Two integrative models. *Language Science, 4*, 187–219.

Godfrey, D. K., Jones, E. E., & Lord, C. G. (1986). Self-promotion is not ingratiating. *Journal of Personality and Social Psychology, 50*, 106–115.

Goodchilds, J. D., Quadrado, C., & Raven, B. H. (1975, April). *Getting one's way.* Paper presented to the Western Psychological Association, Sacramento, CA.

Greene, J. O. (1990). Tactical social action: Toward some strategies for theory. In M. J. Cody & M. L. McLaughlin (Eds.), *Psychology of tactical communication* (pp. 31–47). Clevedon, England: Multilingual Matters.

Greene, J. D., Smith, S. W., & Lindsey, A. E. (1988, May). *Of things unseen: Searching for cognitive representations of compliance-gaining acts.* Paper presented to the International Communication Association, New Orleans.

Hertzog, R. L., & Bradac, J. J. (1984). Perceptions of compliance-gaining situations: An extended analysis. *Communication Research, 11*, 363–391.

Hill, C. T., Rubin, Z., & Peplau, L. (1976). Breakups before marriage: The end of 103 affairs. *Journal of Social Issues, 32*, 147–168.

Hunter, J. E., & Boster, F. J. (1986). A model of compliance-gaining message selection. *Communication Monographs, 54*, 63–84.

Instone, D., Major, B., & Bunker, B. B. (1983). Gender, self confidence, and social influence strategies: An organizational simulation. *Journal of Personality and Social Psychology, 44*, 322–333.

Israeli, D. (1975). The middle manager and the tactics of power expansion: A case study. *Sloan Management Review, 16*, 57–70.

Jablin, F. M. (1987). Organizational entry, assimilation, and exit. In F. M. Jablin, L. L. Putnam, K. H. Roberts, & L. W. Porter (Eds.), *Handbook of organizational communication* (pp. 679–740). Newbury Park, CA: Sage.

Jackson, R. W., McDaniel, S. W., & Rao, C. P. (1985). Food shopping and preparation: Psychographic differences of working wives and housewives. *Journal of Consumer Research, 12*, 110–113.

Johnson, P. (1976). Women and power: Toward a theory of effectiveness. *Journal of Social Issues, 32*, 99–110.

Jones, E. E. (1964). *Ingratiation: A social-psychological analysis.* New York: Appleton-Century-Crofts.

Jones, E. E., & Wortman, C. (1973). *Ingratiation: An attributional approach.* Morristown, NJ: General Learning Press.

Kearney, P., Plax, T. G., Richmond, V. P., & McCroskey, J. C. (1984). Power in the classroom IV: Alternatives to discipline. In R. Bostrom (Ed.), *Communication yearbook 8* (pp. 724–746). Beverly Hills, CA: Sage.

Kipnis, D. (1972). Does power corrupt? *Journal of Personality and Social Psychology, 24*, 33–41.

Kipnis, D. (1976). *The powerholders.* Chicago: University of Chicago Press.

Kipnis, D. (1984). The use of power in organizations and in interpersonal settings. In S. Oskamp (Ed.), *Applied Social Psychology Annual No. 5* (pp. 179–210). Beverly Hills, CA: Sage.

Kipnis, D., Castell, P. J., Gergen, M., & March, D. (1976). Metamorphic effects of power. *Journal of Applied Psychology, 61*, 127–135.

Kipnis, D., & Cosentino, J. (1969). Use of leadership powers in industry. *Journal of Applied Psychology, 53*, 460–466.

Kipnis, D., & Lane, W. (1962). Self-confidence and leadership. *Journal of Applied Psychology, 46*, 291–295.

Kipnis, D., Schmidt, S. M., & Braxton-Brown, G. (1990). The hidden costs of persistence. In M. J. Cody & M. L. McLaughlin (Eds.), *Psychology of tactical communication* (pp. 160–174). Clevedon, England: Multilingual Matters.

Kipnis, D., Schmidt, S. M., & Wilkinson, J. (1980). Intraorganizational influence tactics: Explorations in getting one's way. *Journal of Applied Psychology, 65*, 44–452.

Krause, M. (1970). The use of social situations for research purposes. *American Psychologist, 25*, 748–753.

Krone, K. J. (1986, May). *The effects of decision type, message initiation, and perceptions of centralization of authority on subordinates' use of upward influence message types.* Paper presented to the International Communication Association, Chicago.

Linkskold, S., & Walters, P. S. (1983). Categories for acceptability of lies. *Journal of Social Psychology, 120*, 129–136.

Locke, E. A. (1986). *Generalizing from laboratory to field settings.* Lexington, MA: Lexington Press.

Locke, E. A., Shaw, K. N., Saari, L. M., & Latham, G. P. (1981). Goal setting and task performance: 1969–1980). *Psychological Bulletin, 90*, 125–152.

Magnusson, D. (1971). An analysis of situational dimensions. *Perceptual and Motor Skills, 32*, 851–867.

Magnusson, D., & Ekehammar, B. (1973). An analysis of situational dimensions: A replication. *Multivariate Behavioral Research, 8*, 331–339.

Marwell, G., & Hage, J. (1970). The organization of role-relationships: A systematic description. *American Sociological Review, 35*, 884–900.

Marwell, G., & Schmitt, D. R. (1967). Dimensions of compliance-gaining behavior: An empirical analysis. *Sociometry, 30*, 350–364.

McCann, C. D., & Higgins, E. T. (1987, May). *Goals and orientations in interpersonal relations: How intrapersonal discrepancies produce negative affect.* Paper presented to Interpersonal Communication Association, Montreal.

McLaughlin, M. L., Cody, M. J., & Robey, C. S. (1980). Situational influences on the selection of strategies to resist compliance-gaining attempts. *Human Communication Research, 7*, 14–36.

McQuillen, J. S. (1986). The development of listener-adapted compliance-resisting strategies. *Human Communication Research, 12*, 359–375.

McQuillen, J. S., Higgenbotham, D. C., & Cummings, M. C. (1984). Compliance-resisting behaviors. In R. N. Bostrom (Ed.), *Communication yearbook 8* (pp. 747–762). Beverly Hills, CA: Sage.

Meyer, J. R. (1986, November). *Interpersonal situation schemata and message design.* Paper presented to the Speech Communication Association, Chicago.

Neidenthal, P. M., Cantor, N., & Kihlstrom, J. F. (1985). Prototype matching: A strategy for social decision making. *Journal of Personality and Social Psychology, 48*, 575–584.

O'Keefe, B. J., & McCornack, S. A. (1987). Message design logic and message goal structure: Effects on perceptions of message quality in regulative communicative situations. *Human Communication Research, 14*, 68–92.

O'Keefe, B. J., & Shepherd, G. J. (1987). The pursuit of multiple objectives in face-to-face persuasive interactions: Effects of construct differentiation on message organization. *Communication Monographs, 54*, 396–419.

Pavitt, C., & Haight, L. (1985). The "competent" communicator as a cognitive prototype. *Human Communication Research, 12*, 225–241.

Pearson, J. C. (1985). *Gender and communication.* Dubuque, IA: William C. Brown.

Pervin, L. A. (1976). A free-response description approach to the analysis of person–situation interaction. *Journal of Personality and Social Psychology, 34*, 465–474.

Pervin, L. A. (1986). Personal and social determinants of behavior in situations. In A. Furham (Ed.), *Social behavior in context* (pp. 81–102). Boston: Allyn & Bacon.

Putnam, L. L., & Wilson, C. E. (1982). Communicative strategies in organizational conflicts: Reliability and validity of a measurement scale. In M. Burgoon (Ed.), *Communication yearbook 6* (pp. 629–652). Beverly Hills, CA: Sage.

Raven, B. H., Centers, R., & Rodrigues, A. (1975). The bases of conjugal power. In R. E. Cromwell & D. H. Olson (Eds.), *Power in families* (pp. 217–231). New York: Wiley.

Raven, B. H., & Kruglanski, A. W. (1970). Conflict and power. In P. Swingle (Ed.), *The structure of conflict* (pp. 69–109). New York: Academic Press.

Rim, Y., & Erez, M. (1980). A note about tactics used to influence superiors, co-workers, and subordinates. *Journal of Occupational Psychology, 53*, 39–321.

Rosch, E. (1978). Principles of categorization. In E. Rosch & B. B. Lloyd (Eds.), *Cognition and categorization* (pp. 27–48). Hillsdale, NJ: Lawrence Erlbaum Associates.

Rule, B. G., & Bisanz, G. L. (1987). Goals and strategies of persuasion: A cognitive schema for understanding social events. In M. Zanna, P. Herman, & J. Olson (Eds.), *Social influence: The Fifth Ontario Symposium in Personality and Social Psychology* (pp. 185–206). Hillsdale, NJ: Lawrence Erlbaum Associates.

Rule, B. G., Bisanz, G. L., & Kohn, M. (1985). Anatomy of a persuasion schema: Targets, goals, and strategies. *Journal of Personality and Social Psychology, 48*, 1127–1140.

Russell, J. A., & Ward, L. M. (1982). Environmental psychology. *Annual Review of Psychology, 33*, 651–688.

Schank, R. C., & Abelson, R. (1977). *Scripts, plans, goals, and understanding.* Hillsdale, NJ: Lawrence Erlbaum Associates.

Schilit, N. K., & Locke, E. A. (1982). A study of upward influence in organizations. *Administrative Science Quarterly, 27*, 304–316.

Schmidt, J. M., & Kipnis, D. (1984). Managers pursuit of individual and organizational goals. *Human Relations, 37*, 781–794.

Seibold, D. R., Cantrill, J. G., & Meyers, R. A. (1985). Communication and interpersonal influence. In M. L. Knapp & G. R. Miller (Eds.), *Handbook of interpersonal communication* (pp. 551–614). Beverly Hills, CA: Sage.

Shea, B. C., & Pearson, J. C. (1986). The effects of relationship type, partner intent, and gender on the selection of relationship maintenance strategies. *Communication Monographs, 53*, 352–364.

Smith, M. J. (1982). Cognitive schemata and persuasive communication: Toward a contingency rules theory. In M. Burgoon (Ed.), *Communication yearbook 6* (pp. 330–362). Beverly Hills, CA: Sage.

Smith, M. J. (1984). Contingency rules theory, context, and compliance behaviors. *Human Communication Research, 10*, 489–512.

Smith, S. W., Cody, M. J., LoVette, S., & Canary, D. J. (1990). Self-monitoring, gender, and compliance-gaining goals. In M. J. Cody & M. L. McLaughlin (Eds.), *Psychology of tactical communication* (pp. 91–137). Clevedon, England: Multilingual Matters.

Snyder, M. (1987). *Public appearances, private realities: The psychology of self-monitoring.* New York: Freeman.

Spitzberg, B. H., & Cupach, W. R. (1984). *Interpersonal communication competence.* Beverly Hills, CA: Sage.

Stokols, D. (1978). Environmental psychology. *Annual Review of Psychology, 29*, 253–295.

Student, K. P. (1968). Supervisory influence and work-group performance. *Journal of Applied Psychology, 52*, 188–194.

Students try volunteer work. (1987, February 23). *Los Angeles Times*, p. 8.

Tracy, K., Craig, R. T., Smith, M., & Spisak, F. (1984). The discourse of requests: An assessment of compliance-gaining requests. *Human Communication Research, 10*, 513–538.

Tversky, A. (1977). Features of similarity. *Psychological Review, 84*, 327–352.

Tversky, A., & Hemenway, K. (1983). Categories of environmental scenes. *Cognitive Psychology, 15*, 121–149.

Warfel, K. A. (1984). Gender schemas and perceptions of speech style. *Communication Monographs, 51*, 253–267.

Wheeler, L., & Nezlek, J. (1977). Sex differences in social participation. *Journal of Personality and Social Psychology, 35*, 742–754.

Wheeless, L. R., Barraclough, R., & Stewart, R. (1983). Compliance-gaining and power in persuasion. In R. N. Bostrom (Ed.), *Communication yearbook 7* (pp. 105–145). Beverly Hills, CA: Sage.

White, G. L. (1980). Inducing jealousy: A power perspective. *Personality and Social Psychology Bulletin, 6,* 222–227.

Wilmot, W. W., Carbaugh, D. A., & Baxter, L. A. (1985). Communicative strategies used to terminate romantic relationships. *Western Journal of Speech Communication, 49,* 204–216.

Wiseman, R. L., & Schenck-Hamlin, W. (1981). A multidimensional scaling validation of an inductively derived set of compliance-gaining strategies. *Communication Monographs, 48,* 251–270.

Wish, M., Deutsch, M., & Kaplan, S. (1976). Perceived dimensions of interpersonal relations. *Journal of Personality and Social Psychology, 33,* 409–420.

Wish, M., & Kaplan, S. (1977). Toward an implicit theory of interpersonal communication. *Sociometry, 40,* 234–246.

Witteman, H., & Fitzpatrick, M. A. (1986). Compliance-gaining in marital interaction: Power bases, processes, and outcomes. *Communication Monographs, 53,* 130–143.

Wood, W., & Karten, S. J. (1986). Sex differences in interaction style as a product of perceived sex differences in competence. *Journal of Personality and Social Psychology, 50,* 341–347.

Zadeh, L. (1965). Fuzzy sets. *Information and Control, 3,* 338–353.

Chapter 3

The Language of Control in Interpersonal Communication

James J. Bradac
John M. Wiemann
Kathleen Schaefer
University of California, Santa Barbara

In everyday discussions of intepersonal behavior, people say things like: "He's at the very top of the heap"; "She always seems to get her way"; "He's bossy"; "She's very demanding"; and "I really lost my temper when he laughed at me." These claims (and hundreds of others that we could produce) show that untutored persons (i.e., persons who are not social scientists) both think and talk about the concept of *control*. And a good deal of research has been done that is at least indirectly related to naive conceptions of control, although relatively few studies have focused on communication variables related to these conceptions. A much larger body of research has ignored naive conceptions of control altogether (not inappropriately), examining instead outcomes and processes defined as "controlling" by specialists or technical experts, that is, social scientists. In this chapter, we discuss research from both traditions, focusing on communication variables that are important in interpersonal contexts; but the largest (and we think most interesting and novel) part of the chapter focuses on naive conceptions, perceptions, and evaluations of control. We attempt to systematize where possible, and we also attempt to offer some novel insights and possibilities along the way.

CONTROL AS AN INTERACTIONAL OUTCOME

The study of social power or interpersonal influence is one of the oldest and largest topics in social psychology, with many subareas embracing such well-known topics as social comparison, social facilitation, conformity, and leadership. The key concern with this sort of study is the specification of conditions that are associated with one or another person achieving dominance, "getting his (or her) way," or in some way affecting the responses of another, however minimally; for example, causing him or her to utter relatively well-learned nonsense syllables when performing a false recognition task (Henchy & Glass, 1968). Much of the classic work in this area has used research situations that are minimally interactive or communicative in nature; for example, studies exploiting the "Asch paradigm" (Asch, 1951) or investigating the consequences of "mere presence" of organisms (Zajonc, 1965). In the former case, confederates simply announce decisions regarding a perceptual judgment task in an attempt to affect the decision of a target respondent. In the latter case, a confederate who is simply physically present in a nonevaluative role constitutes a stimulus that may or may not affect a respondent's motor performance on a well learned or poorly learned task.

More in line with our interests, a smaller body of research has investigated the achievement of control in fully interactive contexts, where one or more persons are communicating face-to-face. Both laboratory and naturalistic settings have been examined in this regard. One program of research has emerged from the work of Gregory Bateson, and a representative study here examined the evolution of mutual control in newly acquainted pairs of naval recruits by examining the sequencing of "one-up," "one-down," and "one-across" messages (Fisher & Drecksel, 1983).

A number of studies have examined various conversational phenomena, for example, interruptions and turn-taking behaviors, and these have been related to both conversational control and, more generally, control in relationships (Dindia, 1987; Wiemann, 1985). For example, in many situations a person who interrupts another in order to call attention to some aspect of the environment whenever an unpleasant issue is raised achieves dominance, at least of a localized sort: A: "Have you forgotten the money you owe me? I mean"— B: "Excuse me! Look! There is a flea on the wall!" If the interrupter typically succeeds over time to switch the topical flow in a favorable (from his or her perspective) direction, this person's pattern of interruption gives him or her a degree of relational control. The repeated interruption–acceptance of interruption sequence is both an indicant and a cause of this control. Communication is a resource for the regulation of one's own and other's behavior, and the appropriate use of this resource constitutes an aspect of communicative competence (Wiemann, 1977).

Other studies have examined the effects of various interpersonal communication strategies on the achievement of control, usually defined as one person's obtaining something from another, for example, compliance to a request. So, for example, the "foot-in-the-door" technique (gradually escalated requests; Dillard, 1990; Freedman & Fraser, 1966), the "door-in-the-face" technique (moderated requests following large initial requests; Cialdini et al., 1975), and ingratiation (Jones, 1964) can, under some circumstances, produce high levels of compliance, a measure of communicator control.

CONTROL AS SITUATIONALLY BASED STRATEGIC BEHAVIOR

One can put people in hypothetical situations where their goal is to get something from other people (i.e., compliance-gaining situations), one can ask these would-be compliance gainers what they would say or do to get their way, and subsequently one can examine their verbal and nonverbal messages. Here "control" is not an achievement, an obtained goal, or an outcome (e.g., the movement of an individual in the direction of a majority opinion), but rather one or another type of *message* or *message strategy* designed to meet the demands of a particular kind of situation. So, in a sense, one can talk of "controlling messages," or messages that are high or low in control.

Thus, Courtright, Millar, and Rogers-Millar (1979) distinguished "dominance" from "domineeringness" on empirical grounds. Domineeringness is "a characteristic of an individual's message behavior " (p. 190), specifically the ratio of "one-up" messages to total messages produced in a given message sample. On the other hand, dominance is "a relational outcome of the communication processes" (p. 190), specifically the ratio of "one-up"/"one-down" message sequences between two persons to total message sequences in a given sample of message sequences. Courtright et al. provided some evidence that in marital dyads, husbands' domineeringness is negatively related to the satisfaction of both relational partners.

From a different perspective, that of attribution theory (Heider, 1958), Sillars (1980) investigated the kinds of strategies used by roommates experiencing conflict. His results can be interpreted as indicating that situations involving blame directed toward others elicit "passive-indirect" strategies (e.g., avoidance and hinting) and distributive strategies (e.g., demanding and threatening), whereas situations involving blame to self elicit "integrative" strategies (e.g., self-disclosure and problem solving). The connections between other situational dimensions and compliance-gaining message production have been explored also. For example, Miller, Boster, Roloff, and Seibold (1977) found that for intimate situations with short-term effects, altruism, altercasting, and liking were highly probable strategies, whereas for intimate situations with long-term effects, threatening, promising, liking, and use of expertise were strategies with a high probability of occurrence.

The Miller et al. (1977) study and most other studies have assumed the subjective validity of certain situational distinctions, distinctions imposed on respondents by researchers. A small number of studies have examined the distinctions that are, in fact, salient to compliance-gainers (e.g., Cody & McLaughlin, 1980;

Cody, Woelfel, & Jordan, 1983; Hertzog & Bradac, 1984). For example, it appears that anticipated resistance to persuasion on the part of the target of compliance gaining is a highly salient component of the situation for many would-be compliance gainers. A useful summary of research on compliance-gaining messages can be found in Bettinghaus and Cody (1987).

CONTROL AS AN ASPECT
OF COMMUNICATOR PERSONALITY

It appears that some individuals have a strong need to control their physical and social environment; these persons may be described as being high in pow-er motivation (Ng, 1980). Other persons do not need high levels of control. Apart from need or motivation, some individuals believe that they have high levels of control over their environment, whereas others believe that their lev-els of control are quite low (Rotter, 1966). These general suggestions can be extended to the more specific domain of communication. For example, a plau-sible construal of the results of many studies of communication apprehension is that some persons (high CAs) fear that they have little control over commu-nication situations, whereas others believe that they exert a great deal of communication-relevant control (McCroskey, 1977). Thus, one might expect high CAs to attempt to control or structure their communication environment whenever possible in order to simplify or reduce communicative demands (and thereby reduce subjective uncertainty), and there is some evidence that sup-ports this expectation (e.g., Daly & McCroskey, 1975).

With regard to power motivation in communication, Norton's (1983) research on communicator style revealed a cluster of responses to self-report measures of communication tendencies that he labeled "dominant and con-tentious." Representative items are: In most social situations I tend to come on strong; I have a tendency to dominate informal conversations with other people; Very often I insist that other people document or present some kind of proof for what they are arguing; and, I am very argumentative. Presum-ably, persons scoring high on these items see themselves as dominant and con-tentious across a variety of situations; this is a relatively stable disposition to respond in a highly controlling way. To the extent that this disposition exists (or at least to the extent that it is important compared to other dispositions), it may be useful to examine communication patterns in families, focusing on children to get a picture of the genesis of power motivation for communication (Bradac, Tardy, & Hosman, 1980). The recent work in this area is rooted in the tradition of research on leadership motivation and the search for personal-ity correlates of leadership behavior (see Steinfatt, 1987, for a review of classic approaches to personality traits and communication).

SIMILARITIES AND DIFFERENCES
AMONG THE THREE APPROACHES

At one level the approaches to the study of communication and control as outlined differ considerably: They locate control in different places. For the "interactional outcome" position, control is inferred when something is obtained, for example, when a petition is (or is not) signed, or when the floor is (or is not) held. For the "situationally elicited message" position, control is inferred when a certain type of message is produced in a certain type of situation, for example, when a self-blaming roommate generates an "integrative" message (Sillars, 1980). For the "communicator personality" position, control is inferred when some behavior or behavior trace is seen as an index of a trait or stable disposition to exert influence, not as a situationally coerced event. Of course, these different loci for control could be examined simultaneously in ambitious validation studies: Do communicators high in motivation to control produce certain kinds of compliance-gaining messages in certain kinds of situations and do these messages achieve high levels of interactional control, in fact?

At another level, the three approaches just sketched are identical: Each relies on special instruments, procedures, measures, and logics designed by technical experts with special theories, and on the basis of data obtained with these special devices the expert renders a judgment of high or low control. The determination of control is in the hands of the researcher, and on the basis of this determination hypotheses rise and fall in favor. Thus, on the basis of a machine-assisted coding system, the researcher may define a turn as "the instant one participant . . . starts talking alone and end[ing] immediately prior to the instant another participant starts talking alone" (Feldstein & Welkowitz, 1978, p. 335, quoted in Cappella & Street, 1985, p. 6). Or loadings of items generated by a multidimensional scaling analysis dictate the structure of a compliance-gaining message type. Or responses to Norton's Communicator Style Measure specify via smallest space analysis whether persons are high or low in contentiousness and communication dominance.

These researcher-generated constructs of control in interpersonal communication are potentially useful and powerful. Indeed their utility and validity have been demonstrated repeatedly. But there is another approach that can supplement the three approaches described, and this might be labeled the "naive-construal-of-control" approach or the "perceptual" approach, to use a shorter and more general label. Thus, naive judgments of control can be compared with those of technical experts for the purpose of discovering theoretically productive similarities and differences. Essential questions for those interested in the "perceptual" approach are: How do untutored persons in everyday life think about, conceptualize, and dimensionalize communicator control? And what communicative and contextual factors affect their perceptions (and evaluations) of control? A growing body of pertinent research exists that addresses these questions, especially the second one, albeit rather oblique- ly. Before squarely addressing issues pertaining to naive construals of control, we discuss analogues from other areas of endeavor to provide some context.

NAIVE AND TECHNICAL JUDGMENTS

Naive judgments have been routinely used by social scientists throughout this century, although they have been less frequently studied as objects of special interest. To be sure, there is an old tradition of research on "social judgment" (reflecting a still older tradition of research on psychophysical judgments), but until the advent of attribution theory (Heider, 1958), the judgments of naive persons typically constituted raw data with no inherent interest, data that were meaningless until refined and interpreted by persons with special devices. Classic cases are linguists' reliance on the reports of native speakers to construct gram- mars of a language, and factor analytic studies of attitudes, including research on the "authoritarian personality" (Adorno, Frenkel-Brunswik, Levinson, & Sanford, 1950). Methodologically, the latter case is related to the study of control as a communicator personality dimension that we previously discussed.

The example of linguists' use of native speaker judgments is worth developing here because it provides a clear contrast with some recent research on naive construals of language, which we discuss later. In standard descriptive linguis- tics, phonetic analyses of speech are made initially that reveal co-occurrence patterns of sounds; the extent to which differences in sounds are used to con- vey differences in meaning are assessed by confronting native speakers with hypothetical "minimal pairs" and asking the speakers if the members of the pair mean different things: Is a "pin" different than a "bin?" If yes, then the /b/-/p/ distinction is phonemic in the language (as it is in English). The discovery of phonemes provides the basis for establishing rules for higher or- der constructions, eventually for a grammar of the language. Other assessment procedures are used along the way, but this is enough to make the point that the native speaker's judgment of difference or identity is used to formulate a technical grammar of the language, including morphophonemic rules and syn- tactic rules, rules of which most native speakers are unaware.

A technical grammar can be compared to and contrasted with a "naive gram- mar," which is a tacit theory regarding (among other things) principles of sen- tence well-formedness that are used by native speakers when processing putative sentences of the language and rendering judgments of acceptability and gram- maticality. Some linguistic combinations that are impermissible for linguists may be permissible for "naive grammarians," and vice versa (Bradac, Mar- tin, Elliott, & Tardy, 1980). In the case of constructing a naive grammar, the native speaker's perception of well-formedness, grammaticality, and the like is the object to be explained, and linguistic and nonlinguistic factors that influence this perception merit investigation. More generally, one may attempt to explain the "coherence judgments" that persons make when processing spoken messages (Kellermann & Sleight, 1989).

Along the same line, Preston (1986) had native informants from five geographical areas (Hawaii, southeastern Michigan, southern Indiana, western New York, and New York City) respond to the instruction: "Outline and label the different speech areas of the United States." The responses of these persons constituted dialect maps reflecting in each case a naive dialectal typology. Preston then created composite maps for each of the five groups of respondents. There were areas of agreement and disagreement across groups; for example, the majority of the respondents in each group described a speech area as existing in the south, whereas 64% of the western New York respondents described a New England speech area and 0% of the southern Indiana respondents did so. There are some areas of agreement, but many of disagreement between the naive respondents' maps and a technical "production" dialect map of the United States. For example, Preston noted that one "striking contrast between this [technical] map and any of the perceptual maps . . . is the degree of detail speakers from every area seem to have about regional distribution of speech in the western half of the country. The production dialectologists' boundaries run out near the Mississippi River, but the linguistically naive go right on drawing lines" (p. 234).

The contrasting of naive and technical judgments has been undertaken in other areas as well. For example, Sternberg, Conway, Ketron, and Bernstein (1981) compared psychologists' and laypersons' understandings of the concept of *intelligence*, and White (1983) compared laypersons conceptions of physical motion with the predictions of modern physical theory (Newtonian dynamics). In both of these cases, once again, there were both similarities and differences between the conceptions of naive persons and technical experts.

To return to the main focus of this chapter, the types of judgments of interpersonal control made by technical experts that were described previously can be supplemented with the judgments of untutored persons. It may be that some forms of control described by specialists are not noticed by nonspecialists, and vice versa. The antecedents and consequences of the forms of control that are perceived by untutored persons can be (and are being) examined by researchers. Implicit models of control may guide persons' interpretations of and reactions to control attempts of partners in interpersonal contexts. Such interpretations and reactions cannot be fully understood until these models are explicated.

NAIVE MODELS OF INTERPERSONAL CONTROL

How do persons in everyday life think about interpersonal control and how does this thinking affect their reactions to others? There has been very little research undertaken to examine explicitly the kinds of models that persons use when thinking and talking about interpersonal control. To be sure, one can extrapolate from the large body of research and theory on attribution processes in order to make some general predictions; for example, persons will distinguish between dispositional and situational causes of controlling behavior, and persons are likely to see their own attempts to exert control as being situationally caused, whereas the control attempts of others will be viewed as indicating a dispositional tendency (Nisbett & Ross, 1980). But what is needed is a more detailed examination of the kinds of schemata, plans, scripts, or models that persons have for interpersonal control and the circumstances that make these knowledge structures salient (Cappella & Street, 1989). Also, it would be useful to explore systematically the lexicon of control: What sorts of terms do people use when they talk about control? How are these terms interpreted or understood by others in various contexts? We speculate about these questions, touching base here and there with the scanty data that are available.

First, in support of the claim made at the beginning of this chapter, it is worth noting that there is a good deal of evidence that untutored persons think about control when they conceptualize interpersonal communication and relationships. For example, in a multidimensional scaling study of interpersonal perceptions, Wish, Deutsch, and Kaplan (1976) found *Dominance* to be one of four major dimensions of construal, along with *Solidarity*, *Task Orientation*, and *Arousal*. The dominance–solidarity distinction is interesting because it parallels a finding emerging in many studies of speech evaluation: Two factors that are obtained consistently when naive respondents evaluate communicators and their messages are dominance (or power or status) and solidarity (or sociability or attractiveness) (Bradac, 1990; Zahn & Hopper, 1985). A study examining the correlations among various speech act types and the *Dominance* and *Solidarity* dimensions of interpersonal perception found that *evaluates hearer negatively, disapproval reaction, forceful assertion,* and *forceful request* are negatively associated with solidarity but positively associated with dominance (D'Andrade & Wish, 1985). In a cluster analysis, three of these speech acts constituted a cluster (along with *request commitment*) labeled *Hostile Statements* by the researchers.

The latter findings are suggestive. They may indicate that in some contexts when people think about interpersonal control, they think in negatively valenced terms. Indeed, it seems to us that there is a generally pejorative lexicon for discussing issues of control. In conjunction with this possibility, the reader should do a thought experiment at this point: Evaluate along a positive–negative dimension the following synonyms for the noun ''control'' taken from Roget's *Thesaurus* (Lewis, 1961, p. 85): determination, manipulation, regulation, command, domination, predomination, sway, ascendancy, upper hand, whip hand, mastery, rule, subjection, subjugation, subordination, check, bridle, rein, curb, restraint, restriction, containment, corner, monopoly, wirepulling, address, and strategy. If the reader's linguistic intuitions are similar to ours, the majority of these terms will be seen as having a negative connotation. To the extent that there is a negative cast to terms for "control," the discussion of problems of control in relationships, say, between spouses or parent and child, may have a built-in difficulty. To the extent that talk about control constitutes a part of how persons define their relationships, relational definitions may have a negative tinge (Bradac, 1983). Certain kinds of relationships seem especially likely to produce negative conceptions based on control, for example, relationships between peers exhibiting mutual dislike (Wiemann & Krueger, 1980).

That there may be a negative cast to thoughts about interpersonal control seems plausible in light of suggestions that individuals resist threats to their personal freedom (Brehm, 1966). Bowers (1974) argued that explicit threats, for example, are rarely used in interpersonal communication because they directly deny interpersonal independence, an important value in our culture (also see Gibbons, Bradac, & Busch, 1992). Instead, communicators may use indirect means to get their way in order to adhere to politeness norms (Lim & Bowers, 1991). On the other hand, there is evidence that argues for a qualification of this rule: At least some untutored persons believe that direct and even impolite forms may be used with impunity by persons who are relatively high in power or status (Steffen & Eagly, 1985).

Negative connotations for control may not extend to the realm of *self*-control in interpersonal contexts. We may expect communicators to control their communicative behaviors in the sense of self-regulation and may evaluate them negatively when our expectations are violated; for example, high levels of repetition produced by a communicator may lead observers to perceive low control of communicative behavior and to evaluate the communicator as being low in intellectual competence (Bradac & Wisegarver, 1984). The distinction between "She (or he) is the kind of person who does not control others" versus "She (or he) is out of control" may be an important and basic one for persons thinking about or perceiving control in interpersonal situations (Hosman & Siltanen, 1991).

Perhaps consistent with some of the preceding suggestions are results of a study by Pavitt and Haight (1985). These researchers attempted to discover whether a prototype for the "competent communicator" exists that is distinct from prototypes of other skilled performers, say, "the artistically talented person." A distinct prototype for communication competence did emerge, and associated with this prototype were a number of frequently listed attributes (obtained from respondents in free elicitation): intelligent, articulate, confident, outgoing, well-dressed, gets ideas across, and listens well. None of these attributes pertains to control of others, but *confident* and perhaps *intelligent* (Bradac & Wisegarver, 1984) can be viewed as indicants of self-control.

For specific communication contexts (verbal disagreement, meeting strangers, and an interview), the attributes associated with prototypically competent communicators differed somewhat from the general across-context prototype; specifically, the relatively frequently listed attributes were for verbal disagreement: listens carefully and gestures often; for meeting strangers: dresses well, friendly, smiles nicely, articulate, confident, has drink in hand, and starts conversation; for interview: confident, relaxed, well-dressed, talkative, alert, friendly, articulate, intelligent, and gestures often. Only *starts conversation* and perhaps *talkative* seem to represent the concept of *controls other person*. Self-control again emerges in these specific contexts, for example, confident, relaxed, and intelligent. The *verbal disagreement* context can be seen as a context where interpersonal control is highly salient (D'Andrade & Wish, 1985) and importantly in this case attributes associated with overt control of other are not listed as being prototypically competent; rather the two attributes listed frequently indicate that according to naive models of these respondents the competent communicator in this context of control is empathic and expressive.

The models, plans, or folk theories that constitute naive persons' knowledge of interpersonal control are greatly in need of further explication. To the extent that naive knowledge structures guide communication performance and the interpretation of performance, this is an important kind of research to be undertaking. The surface has barely been scratched. It will be necessary to examine the role that representations of control play in message production and interpretation. At some point it will be necessary also to attempt to characterize the form that representations regarding control actually take: Are they general relational dimensions, expectations regarding classes of appropriate behavior, or expectations regarding concrete behaviors reflecting beliefs about rights and obligations? Planalp (1985) provided a hint that the latter option may be viable, whereas language expectancy theory might be construed as supporting the viability of the second option (Burgoon, 1990).

ANTECEDENTS AND CONSEQUENCES
OF PERCEIVED CONTROL

What factors lead untutored persons to attribute high or low control to communicators? And what are the consequences of these attributions? At a general level, various perceived communicator characteristics will affect judgments of the extent to which a communicator's utterances are likely to achieve control in the sense of gaining compliance. For example, a communicator's perceived reward or punishment power appears linearly related to the extent to which both implicit and explicit messages will be taken as threats or promises likely to secure a message recipient's compliance (Murdock, Bradac, & Bowers, 1984, 1986). Factors such as communicator status seem likely to affect perceptions of message control, perhaps by virtue of the reward and punishment power that is attached to status attributions: The messages of high-status persons will be perceived as higher in control potential than the messages of their lower-status counterparts (Bradac & Wisegarver, 1984; Steffen & Eagly,

1985). More globally, it seems likely that in situations where controlling messages are expected, there will be a tendency to perceive messages as relatively
controlling in fact; that is, in many situations perceptions will be warped in
the direction of communication expectancies regarding control (Bradac & Street,
1989/1990).

Apart from perceptions of communicator role or communication situations,
certain aspects of the messages that communicators produce have been shown
to affect naive perceptions of control. Much of the work that is relevant here
has been conducted under the rubric "powerful or powerless" styles of talk,
so the aspect of control being examined here is perceived power. Initially on
the basis of descriptive data obtained in courtrooms during jury trials, O'Barr
(1982) suggested that there are certain linguistic features that cluster in the
utterances of persons low in social power (e.g., inexpert witnesses) and that
these features are largely absent in the utterances of high-power persons (e.g.,
lawyers and judges). The powerless style included a relatively high number
of hedges ("and, well, I sort of like that"), tag questions ("It is true, isn't
it?"), intensifiers ("I really didn't want to"), polite forms ("Yes, sir"), hesitations ("My father . . . uh . . . lied"), and deictic phrases ("That man over
there hit me"). By contrast, the powerful style was comparatively fluent, terse,
and direct. The linguistic indicators of the low-power style are similar to features that characterize Lakoff's (1973) "female register." It has been suggested that the powerless style reflects a feeling of uncertainty on the part of the
communicator, that it is not merely an attribute that a certain class of speakers carry around with them (Berger & Bradac, 1982). An implication of this
is that in some unfamiliar situations even judges and lawyers may appear powerless linguistically.

After describing the features characterizing powerful and powerless styles,
O'Barr and his associates explored some perceptual consequences of this distinction. In one study, powerful and powerless versions of witness testimony
were created and manipulated in an experimental design using a male and female speaker—gender X power of style (Erickson, Johnson, Lind, & O'Barr,
1978). For both genders, the versions exhibiting the powerful style were perceived as more credible. Subsequently, Bradac, Hemphill, and Tardy (1981)
replicated this basic pattern in two studies: The powerful style produced relatively positive ratings of communicator competence and attractiveness. Bradac
and Mulac (1984b) created high- and low-power versions of both counselor
and client remarks in a hypothetical crisis-intervention context. The powerful
style produced more positive ratings of sociointellectual status and attractiveness for both counselor and client.

Which linguistic features are responsible for these rather consistent effects?
Bradac et al. (1981) suggested that the powerless style construct includes several
subvariables that are potentially orthogonal; for example, in some situations
a speaker may become more hesitant but may maintain a constant level of

politeness. This suggested the desirability of examining the effects of each of the six subcomponents of the powerless style in comparison with the effects of ostensibly powerful messages, which Bradac and Mulac did (1984a). Among other things these investigators found that messages exhibiting the ostensibly powerful style were indeed rated as relatively powerful and effective. Messages exhibiting polite forms and intensifiers were also rated highly on these measures. On the other hand, messages exhibiting hesitations, hedges, and tag questions were judged as relatively low in effectiveness and power. Messages exhibiting deictic phrases were perceived to reside at a neutral point.

Related to these outcomes are the results of a study by Hosman and Wright (1987). These researchers found that a relatively low incidence of both hedges and hesitations in messages resulted in positive ratings of communicator authoritativeness and attractiveness. Also, both hedges and hesitations were directly related to attributions of guilt in a hypothetical court case. In the most recent study of the separate effects of the components of powerless speech, Hosman and Siltanen (1991) found that fewer hedges and hesitations again resulted in higher ratings of authoritativeness, as did fewer tag questions. On the other hand, fewer intensifiers resulted in lower authoritativeness ratings.

Especially interesting from the standpoint of this chapter, Hosman and Siltanen (1991) found that an ostensibly powerful message and a message containing a high number of intensifiers produced attributions of high communicator self-control and high control over others. On the other hand, hedges, hesitations, and tag questions produced attributions of relatively low self- and other-control. A second study, comparing the effects of messages combining high or low levels of hedging, hesitation, and intensification, replicated the previously described findings for hedges and hesitations. Intensifiers, on the other hand, produced no significant effect when combined with high or low levels of hedging and hesitation, a finding that replicates a result of an earlier study by Hosman (1989). Apparently, the solitary appearance of intensifiers in a message increases ratings of communicator power, self-control, and so on, whereas the joint appearance of intensifiers and hedges or hesitations results in a reduction of the effects of intensification. Thus, the effects of intensifiers can be described as being "context dependent" in this particular sense.

So, it appears that hedges, hesitations, and tag questions are perceived by naive respondents as being low in power and effectiveness in a variety of contexts. Using a rather different research paradigm, Brooke and Ng (1986) failed to find a connection between the use of tag questions and hedges by discussants in a small group and evaluations of competence and attractiveness by fellow discussants. Tag questions and hedges were also not related to influence ratings of fellow discussants, although number of words and number of successful turns were. There are a number of possibilities regarding the negative results for tags and hedges. For example, and not very interestingly, the number of respondents in the study was small (23) and possibly the variance of these linguistic forms was small also. More interestingly, the respondents in this study were involved participants rather than third-party observers of other persons' interactions as in the studies discussed previously. Perhaps what counts as power or influence is different for these different kinds of respondents; indeed, there is some evidence that observers of and participants in interaction may rate the same verbal and nonverbal behaviors (e.g., fast or slow speech rate) dissimilarly (Street, 1985; Street, Mulac, & Wiemann, 1988).

The consistent outcomes of research on powerful and powerless styles using the third-party observer paradigm in conjunction with our earlier suggestion that "control" is connotatively negative for many people suggests what might seem to be a paradox on the face on it: If control is evaluated negatively, why does the powerful style yield consistently positive judgments of communicator attractiveness and competence? There are a number of possibilities here, which previous studies for the most part have not addressed.

Perhaps powerful speakers are seen as having a high potential for controlling others, which is negative, but are also seen as having positive attributes such as strength and high intelligence; perhaps the positive associations outweigh the negative connotations of control. Or perhaps powerful communicators who control others but not "me," the respondent in a typical experiment, are indeed attractive, and perhaps this attractiveness increases as others are controlled more while "I" am controlled less. This differential between communicator's control of others and communicator's control of "me" may give to "me" (the respondent) positive feelings of autonomy. If this hypothesis is viable, it would seem likely that the respondent's locus of control (Rotter, 1966) may interact with the communicator's powerful or powerless style; perhaps "high externals" (persons who perceive themselves to be controlled by others and the environment) would be especially sensitive to feelings of decreased autonomy and would therefore evaluate the powerful style less favorably than would "high internals." When people say "power is sexy," they may find attractive the powerful person's ability to control others coupled with the *nonuse* of this ability vis-à-vis themselves.

Or perhaps the high-power style does not make salient the communicator's ability to control others but rather his or her high level of self-control, including the ability to regulate communicative behaviors. (The Hosman and Siltanen study, 1991, suggests that both aspects of control may be made salient by power of style.) As we already suggested, self-control may be associated with high levels of attributed communicative competence (Pavitt & Haight, 1985). There is evidence that persons in our culture generally value the trait of being in control of self (Stern & Manifold, 1977); accordingly, being "out of control" or controlled by others is regarded negatively. Bradac and Wisegarver (1984) found that persons apparently can perceive variations in self-control of communication behavior: "control of communication style" emerged as a separate dimension in a factor analysis of evaluative responses. They also found

that this dimension was correlated with a dimension of "intellectual competence" in that both were affected by variations in the communicator's level
of lexical diversity—the higher the diversity level, the higher the ratings for
"competence" and "control." Relatedly, Gibbons, Busch, and Bradac (1991)
found that several evaluative items merged in a general "competence/control"
factor, which was positively related to a communicator's power of style.

The distinction between perceived control of others and perceived ability
to control self suggests a final topic to be broached briefly: self-perceptions of
communication control. Not only do persons perceive and evaluate others along
a dimension (or dimensions) of communication control, they perceive and evaluate themselves as well. They have beliefs and feelings about the extent to which
they are generally in control communicatively; that is, they make dispositional attributions regarding self and they have beliefs and feelings about communicative control in specific situations—they make situational self-attributions.
It is worth noting that these self-attributions may or may not correspond to
the determinations of, for example, high or low communication apprehension
rendered by a researcher using PRCA (McCroskey, 1977). For one thing,
researcher-generated items regarding self-perceptions of communication control may not correspond highly to dimensions of control that are salient to a
particular "self." Also, for self-presentational reasons (Baumeister, 1982) a
person who experiences a feeling of low control may respond in such a way
as to indicate that he or she feels strongly in control; in other situations the
reverse may be true.

FINAL REMARKS

The preceding discussion suggests an important implication regarding the assessment and determination of levels of communicator control: Perceptions and
evaluations of control may vary radically depending on the source of the data
and the type of control being examined. Specifically, researcher judgments
regarding who is in control in an interpersonal episode may differ from the
judgments of participants, because observers and participants may attach
differential weights to particular behaviors; they may evaluate these behaviors
differently as a result of dissimilar demands or responsibilities being placed
on them (Street, 1985); and they may have different models or theories that
may lead them to attend selectively to dissimilar phenomena.

An interesting case in point is the determination of level or degree of self-
control in communication. A communicator may perceive himself or herself
to be highly anxious and almost out of control as a result of attending closely
to his or her unusually rapid heartbeat, a cue that is usually not available to
observers of communicative performance who may accordingly judge his or
her level of self-control to be average or even high. There is evidence of this

sort of observer–performer discrepancy in assessments of communication anxiety or arousal (Sparks & Greene, 1992; but see Burgoon & LePoire, 1992). And attached to these dissimilar assessments of self-control are other important assessments, for example, level of communicative or intellectual competence. Thus, in the situation just described, the communicator may judge himself or herself as low in competence, whereas the observers of his or her performance may believe that he or she performed competently and may even infer that he or she has a ''competent'' personality.

An important implication is that researchers and theorists should be clear about the kind of control that is of interest to them. The data source for testing hypotheses regarding communication control does not present itself neutrally for examination. Predictions about relationships between communication and control that hold for one data source may not generalize to others.

REFERENCES

Adorno, T. W., Frenkel-Brunswik, E., Levinson, D. J., & Sanford, R. N. (1950). *The authoritarian personality*. New York: Harper & Row.

Asch, S. (1951). Effects of group pressure upon the modification and distortion of judgment. In M. H. Guetzkow (Ed.), *Groups, leadership, and men* (pp. 117–190). Pittsburgh, PA: Carnegie.

Baumeister, R. F. (1982). A self-presentational view of social phenomena. *Psychological Bulletin, 91*, 3–26.

Berger, C. R., & Bradac, J. J. (1982). *Language and social knowledge: Uncertainty in interpersonal relations*. London: Edward Arnold.

Bettinghaus, E. P., & Cody, M. J. (1987). *Persuasive communication* (4th ed.). New York: Holt, Rinehart, & Winston.

Bowers, J. W. (1974). Guest editor's introduction: Beyond threats and promises. *Communication Monographs, 41*, iv–vi.

Bradac, J. J. (1983). The language of lovers, flovers, and friends: Communication in social and personal relationships. *Journal of Language and Social Psychology, 2*, 141–163.

Bradac, J. J. (1990). Language attitudes and impression formation. In H. Giles & W. P. Robinson (Eds.), *Handbook of language and social psychology* (pp. 387–412). Chichester, England: Wiley.

Bradac, J. J., Hemphill, M. R., & Tardy, C. H. (1981). Language style on trial: Effects of ''powerful'' and ''powerless'' speech upon judgments of victims and villains. *Western Journal of Speech Communication, 45*, 327–341.

Bradac, J. J., Martin, L. W., Elliott, N. D., & Tardy, C. H. (1980). On the neglected side of linguistic science: Multivariate studies of sentence judgment. *Linguistics: An Interdisciplinary Journal of the Language Sciences, 18*, 967–995.

Bradac, J. J., & Mulac, A. (1984a). A molecular view of powerful and powerless speech styles: Attributional consequences of specific language features and communicator intentions. *Communication Monographs, 51*, 306–319.

Bradac, J. J., & Mulac, A. (1984b). Attributional consequences of powerful and powerless speech styles in a crisis-intervention context. *Journal of Language and Social Psychology, 3*, 1–19.

Bradac, J. J., & Street, R. L., Jr. (1989/1990). Powerful and powerless styles of talk: A theoretical analysis of language and impression formation. *Research on Language and Social Interaction, 23*, 195–242.

Bradac, J. J., Tardy, C. H., & Hosman, L. A. (1980). Disclosure styles and a hint at their genesis. *Human Communication Research, 6*, 228–238.

Bradac, J. J., & Wisegarver, R. (1984). Ascribed status, lexical diversity, and accent: Determinants of perceived status, solidarity, and control of speech style. *Journal of Language and Social Psychology, 3*, 239-255.

Brehm, J. W. (1966). *A theory of psychological reactance.* New York: Academic Press.

Brooke, M. E., & Ng, S. H. (1986). Language and social influence in small conversational groups. *Journal of Language and Social Psychology, 5*, 201-210.

Burgoon, J. K., & LePoire, B. A. (1992). A reply from the heart: Who are Sparks and Greene and why are they saying all these horrible things? *Human Communication Research, 18*, 472-482.

Burgoon, M. (1990). Language and social influence. In H. Giles & W. P. Robinson (Eds.), *Handbook of language and social psychology* (pp. 51-72). Chichester, England: Wiley.

Cappella, J. N., & Street, R. L., Jr. (1985). Introduction: A functional approach to the structure of communication behavior. In J. N. Cappella & R. N. Street (Eds.), *Sequence and pattern in communicative behavior* (pp. 1-29). London: Edward Arnold.

Cappella, J. N., & Street, R. L., Jr. (1989). Message effects: Theory and research on mental models of messages. In J. J. Bradac (Ed.), *Message effects in communication science* (pp. 24-51). Newbury Park, CA: Sage.

Cialdini, R. B., Vincent, J. E., Lewis, S. K., Catalan, J., Wheeler, D., & Darby, B. L. (1975). Reciprocal concessions procedure for inducing compliance: The door-in-the-face technique. *Journal of Personality and Social Psychology, 31*, 206-215.

Cody, M. J., & McLaughlin, M. L. (1980). Perceptions of compliance-gaining situations: A dimensional analysis. *Communication Monographs, 47*, 132-148.

Cody, M. J., Woelfel, M. L., & Jordan, W. J. (1983). Dimensions of compliance-gaining situations. *Human Communication Research, 9*, 181-187.

Courtright, J. A., Millar, F. E., & Rogers-Millar, L. E. (1979). Domineeringness and dominance: Replication and extension. *Communication Monographs, 46*, 179-192.

Daly, J. A., & McCroskey, J. C. (1975). Occupational choice and desirability as a function of communication apprehension. *Journal of Counseling Psychology, 22*, 309-313.

D'Andrade, R. G., & Wish, M. (1985). Speech act theory in quantitative research on interpersonal behavior. *Discourse Processes, 8*, 229-259.

Dillard, J. P. (1990). Self-inference and the foot-in-the-door technique: Quantity of behavior and attitudinal mediation. *Human Communication Research, 16*, 422-447.

Dindia, K. (1987). The effects of sex of subject and sex of partner on interruptions. *Human Communication Research, 13*, 345-371.

Erickson, B., Johnson, B. C., Lind, A. E., & O'Barr, W. M. (1978). Speech style and impression formation in a court setting: The effects of ''powerful'' and ''powerless'' speech. *Journal of Experimental Social Psychology, 14*, 266-279.

Feldstein, S., & Welkowitz, J. (1978). A chronography of conversation: In defence of an objective approach. In A. W. Siegman & S. Feldstein (Eds.), *Nonverbal behavior and communication* (pp. 329-378). Hillsdale, NJ: Lawrence Erlbaum Associates.

Fisher, B. A., & Drecksel, G. L. (1983). A cyclical model of developing relationships: A study of relational control interaction. *Communication Monographs, 50*, 66-78.

Freedman, J. L., & Fraser, S. C. (1966). Compliance without pressure: The foot-in-the-door technique. *Journal of Personality and Social Psychology, 4*, 195-202.

Gibbons, P., Bradac, J. J., & Busch, J. (1992). The role of language in negotiations: Threats and promises. In L. Putnam & M. Roloff (Eds.), *Communication and negotiation* (pp. 156-175). Newbury Park, CA: Sage.

Gibbons, P., Busch, J., & Bradac, J. J. (1991). Powerful versus powerless language: Consequences for persuasion, impression formation, and cognitive response. *Journal of Language and Social Psychology, 10*, 115-133.

Heider, F. (1958). *The psychology of interpersonal relations.* New York: Wiley.

Henchy, T., & Glass, D. C. (1968). Evaluation apprehension and the social facilitation of dominant and subordinate responses. *Journal of Personality and Social Psychology, 10*, 446-454.

Hertzog, R. L., & Bradac, J. J. (1984). Perceptions of compliance-gaining situations: An extended analysis. *Communication Research, 11*, 363–391.

Hosman, L. A. (1989). The evaluative consequences of hedges, hesitations, and intensifiers: Powerful and powerless speech styles. *Human Communication Research, 15*, 383–406.

Hosman, L. A., & Siltanen, S. A. (1991, November). *The attributional and evaluative consequences of powerful and powerless speech styles: An examination of the "control of others" and "control of self" explanations.* Paper presented at the meeting of the Speech Communication Association, Atlanta.

Hosman, L. A., & Wright, J. W., II. (1987). The effects of hedges and hesitations on impression formation in a simulated courtroom context. *Western Journal of Speech Communication, 51*, 173–188.

Jones, E. E. (1964). *Ingratiation: A social analysis.* New York: Appleton-Century-Crofts.

Kellermann, K., & Sleight, C. (1989). Coherence: A meaningful adhesive for discourse. *Communication Yearbook, 12*, 95–129.

Lakoff, R. (1973). Language and woman's place. *Language and Society, 2*, 45–81.

Lewis, N. (1961). *The new Roget's thesaurus in dictionary form.* New York: G. P. Putnam's Sons.

Lim, T. S., & Bowers, J. W. (1991). Facework: Solidarity, approbation, and tact. *Human Communication Research, 17*, 415–450.

McCroskey, J. C. (1977). Oral communication apprehension: A summary of recent theory and research. *Human Communication Research, 4*, 78–96.

Miller, G. R., Boster, F., Roloff, M., & Seibold, D. (1977). Compliance-gaining message strategies: A typology and some findings concerning effects of situational differences. *Communication Monographs, 44*, 37–51.

Murdock, J. I., Bradac, J. J., & Bowers, J. W. (1984). Effects of power on the perception of explicit threats, promises, and thromises: A rule-governed perspective. *Western Journal of Speech Communication, 48*, 344–361.

Murdock, J. I., Bradac, J. J., & Bowers, J. W. (1986). On the "equivalency assumption" and other tangential matters: A reply to Schenck-Hamlin and Georgacarakos. *Western Journal of Speech Communication, 50*, 208–213.

Ng, S. (1980). *The social psychology of power.* London: Academic Press.

Nisbett, R. E., & Ross, L. (1980). *Human inference: Strategies and shortcomings of social judgment.* Englewood Cliffs, NJ: Prentice-Hall.

Norton, R. (1983). *Communicator style.* Newbury Park, CA: Sage.

O'Barr, W. M. (1982). *Linguistic evidence: Language, power, and strategy in the courtroom.* New York: Academic Press.

Pavitt, C., & Haight, L. (1985). The "competent communicator" as a cognitive prototype. *Human Communication Research, 12*, 225–242.

Planalp, S. (1985). Relational schemata: A test of alternative forms of relational knowledge as guides to communication. *Human Communication Research, 12*, 3–29.

Preston, D. R. (1986). Five visions of America. *Language in Society, 15*, 221–240.

Rotter, J. B. (1966). Generalized expectancies for internal versus external control. *Psychological Monographs, 80*, 1–28.

Sillars, A. L. (1980). Attributions and communication in roommate conflicts. *Communication Monographs, 47*, 180–200.

Sparks, G. G., & Greene, J. O. (1992). On the validity of nonverbal indicators as measures of physiological arousal: A response to Burgoon, Kelly, Newton, and Keeley-Dyreson. *Human Communication Research, 18*, 445–471.

Steffen, V. J., & Eagly, A. H. (1985). Implicit theories about influence style: The effects of status and sex. *Personality and Social Psychology Bulletin, 11*, 191–205.

Steinfatt, T. M. (1987). Personality and communication: Classic approaches. In J. C. McCroskey & J. A. Daly (Eds.), *Personality and interpersonal communication* (pp. 42–126). Newbury Park, CA: Sage.

Stern, G. S., & Manifold, B. (1977). Internal locus of control as a value. *Journal of Research in Personality, 11*, 237–242.

Sternberg, R. J., Conway, B. E., Ketron, J. L., & Bernstein, M. (1981). People's conceptions of intelligence. *Journal of Personality and Social Psychology, 33*, 409-420.

Street, R. L., Jr. (1985). Participant-observer differences in speech evaluation. *Journal of Language and Social Psychology, 4*, 125-130.

Street, R. L., Jr., Mulac, A., & Wiemann, J. M. (1988). Speech evaluation differences as a function of perspective (participant versus observer) and presentational medium. *Human Communication Research, 14*, 333-363.

White, B. Y. (1983). Sources of difficulty in understanding Newtonian dynamics. *Cognitive Science, 7*, 41-65.

Wiemann, J. M. (1977). Explication and test of a model of communicative competence. *Human Communication Research, 3*, 195-213.

Wiemann, J. M. (1985). Power, status and dominance: Interpersonal control and regulation in conversation. In R. L. Street, Jr., & J. N. Cappella (Eds.), *Sequence and pattern in communicative behavior* (pp. 85-102). London: Edward Arnold.

Wiemann, J. M., & Krueger, D. L. (1980). The language of relationships. I. Description. In H. Giles, W. P. Robinson, & P. M. Smith (Eds.), *Language: Social psychology perspectives* (pp. 55-62). Oxford: Pergamon.

Wish, M., Deutsch, M., & Kaplan, S. J. (1976). Perceived dimensions of interpersonal relations. *Journal of Personality and Social Psychology, 33*, 409-420.

Zahn, C., & Hopper, R. (1985). Measuring language attitudes: The Speech Evaluation Instrument. *Journal of Language and Social Psychology, 4*, 113-123.

Zajonc, R. B. (1965). Social facilitation. *Science, 149*, 269-274.

Chapter 4

Affinity Seeking

John A. Daly
Pamela O. Kreiser
University of Texas

People want others to like them. This desire is a basic, perhaps even defining, characteristic of humans. But, people also know they have to do certain things, act certain ways, to get others to like them. From early childhood on, people learn ways to develop and socially maintain relationships. What they do to accomplish these objectives is the focus of research on affinity seeking and maintenance. To understand how important affinity is, one only needs to imagine a person who lacks any skill at affinity seeking or maintenance: Would he or she have friends? Perhaps. But the more likely consequences are not so positive—loneliness, social powerlessness, and low self-esteem. In this chapter we review work done on the related constructs of affinity seeking and affinity maintenance. To forecast briefly the directions this chapter takes: First, we define *affinity seeking* and *maintenance* as active social processes that have at their heart communication. Then we describe a conceptual model of affinity seeking that provides a theoretic framework for understanding research on the topic. Third, we provide a brief review of the research on the various strategies that are incorporated into the construct of affinity. Finally we discuss potential directions for future research on affinity.

CONCEPTUALIZING AFFINITY SEEKING

It is important to understand the nature of affinity research. For many years, scholars in a variety of disciplines have examined affinity seeking, but not under that label. Instead, researchers explored many of the components of affinity seeking under rubrics such as attractiveness, altruism, responsiveness, and so on. But the piecemeal nature of this work failed to reflect any integrative conceptualization. Bell and Daly's (1984) effort was in that direction—to discover a conceptual scheme that integrated diverse lines of scholarship within one realm. Since that time many scholars have recognized that affinity seeking, as an integrated concept, is an important aspect of the interpersonal communication process (Bell & Daly, 1984; Bell, Tremblay, & Buerkel-Rothfuss, 1987; Douglas, 1987; Richmond & Furio, 1985; Richmond, Gorham, and Furio, 1987; Tolhuizen, 1989a; Woltjen & Zakahi, 1987). Research on the topic of affinity has been conducted in a variety of communication settings: initial interactions (Douglas, 1987), same-sex friendships (Gendrin, 1990), developing relationships (Tolhuizen, 1989a), mixed-gender relationships (Richmond & Furio, 1985; Richmond et al., 1987), marriage (Bell, Daly, & Gonzales, 1987), supervisor/subordinate relationships (Richmond, McCroskey, & Davis, 1986), and in the classroom (Gorham, Kelley, & McCroskey, 1989; McCroskey & McCroskey, 1986; Richmond, 1990; Roach, 1991).

Affinity seeking is defined as ''the active social-communicative process by which individuals attempt to get others to like and to feel positive toward them'' (Bell & Daly, 1984, p. 91). A careful look at this definition is instructive: First, research on the affinity construct highlights *active* rather than passive activity. This is critical, for most research related to the construct traditionally focuses on passive behaviors. For instance, there is a plethora of research on physical attractiveness and its relationship to liking (Berscheid & Walster, 1974). But the vast majority of that scholarship assumes attractiveness—it is not something people manipulate, it is not something that can be ''used'' to accomplish liking. It is instead, a property of a person (one exception, reviewed later, are inducements for dating found in actions such as preening and in advertisements found in newspapers). Realistically, we know this isn't always so. People dress better when on first dates, when they think they may meet someone important, and when they go to job interviews. Why? Because they recognize that attractiveness has consequences. Similarly, research has consistently found links between propinquity and the development of friendships. People who, by chance, live closer to each other have a greater likelihood of initiating relationships with each other (Festinger, Schachter, & Back, 1950; Menne & Sinnett, 1971). But sometimes people actively seek to place themselves close to others in order to create opportunities for interaction. This active, strategic move represents the direction affinity research takes. A third case are studies linking personality and demographic characteristics to relationship development (e.g., Kerckhoff & Davis, 1962; Neimeyer & Mitchell, 1988). Again, this research, although quite interesting, assumes passivity rather than active manipulation to achieve affinity. The same bias toward nonactive, nonstrategic enactments is true in communication scholarship. For instance, there is a large body of research linking self-disclosure propensities to liking (e.g.,

Sprecher, 1989; but see Parks, 1982). But very little research conceptualizes disclosure as a manipulative tactic that is sometimes used to enhance affinity. Research programs on affinity-related topics such as these are not alone in their tendencies to explore passive rather than active behaviors. Critiques of social support research, for example, offer the same sort of argument. Although people sometimes actively seek out support from others, research seldom examines how they do this (Conn & Peterson, 1989).

Second, the construct emphasizes the *strategic* nature of the different behaviors incorporated in the typology. People actively and intentionally engage in the behaviors described by the typology to obtain predicted outcomes. For example, listening, another part of the affinity typology, is seldom viewed as a strategic activity—something someone does to affect others' impressions of them. But people do listen strategically. Suppose you meet an attractive stranger who winds on endlessly about a topic for which you have not the slightest interest. Assuming the attraction is strong enough you may feign listening simply to maintain, in that person's eyes, a positive impression.

Third, research on affinity seeking and maintenance assumes that at any one point in time there are various affinity strategies available to individuals, and that people have the capacity to *choose* among different strategies to accomplish different goals. There is a strong assumption that people are, to varying degrees, cognizant of their choices. Certainly people differ in the number of strategies that come to mind at any one point in time and certainly there are situational limits to strategy selection. But even given these limitations, the presumption is that people can generally make choices to engage, or not engage, in certain affinity strategies in some settings.

Fourth, affinity is centrally a communication construct. We "make" people like us through our communication, verbal and nonverbal. The behaviors described in the typology are accomplished interactively. Finally, affinity research has a well-defined measure of its success: liking. The goal of affinity is to generate, maintain, or enhance liking of one person by another. Certainly, in some cases that liking may be transformed into persuasion or learning. But at its core, the construct's focus is straightforward: liking is critical and affinity strategies are the ways people attempt to generate that feeling in others.

Bell and Daly (1984) presented a four-stage model describing affinity seeking in terms of antecedent factors, constraints, strategic activity, and target responses. The model appears in Fig. 4.1.

Antecedent Factors. There are three main antecedent factors in affinity-seeking behavior: interaction goals, motives for seeking affinity, and level of consciousness. Interaction goals are the aims the interactants have in a social exchange. People may have only one goal in some conversations—to generate or maintain affinity. But often, they have multiple goals that must be juggled successfully for a competent performance. Conceptually, the importance of goals

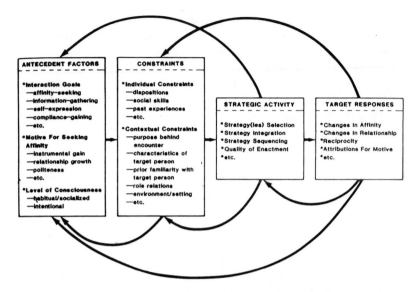

FIG. 4.1.   A model of the affinity-seeking process.

varies even as a single interaction proceeds. One might imagine a vector of
weights associated with different goals at different points in time (see Fig. 4.2).
Consider a sales call. A salesperson has any number of goals she or he must
juggle throughout the call, goals such as affinity, persuasion, information giving, and information acquisition. At the start of the sales call the primary goal
of the salesperson may be affinity—getting the customer to like her or him.
The weight associated with affinity is large; the weights associated with the
other goals are smaller. But quickly the call moves to an information exchange.
Qualifying the customer, discovering the customer's interests, and so on requires that the information component receive a stronger weight. And although
affinity is still important, the weight assigned to it may be less now than at
Time 1. As the exchange moves to Time 3, persuasion may become the
predominant goal—it is weighted more than the other goals. Yet affinity and
information are still relevant. The point of this example is that in any interaction there are multiple goals that an interactant must juggle. Affinity is so

GOALS	TIME 1	TIME 2		TIME X
K_1	$W_{1.1}$	$W_{2.1}$	. . . .	
K_2	$W_{1.2}$	$W_{2.2}$	. . . .	
K_3	$W_{1.3}$	$W_{2.3}$	. . . .	
K_n	$W_{1.n}$	$W_{2.n}$	. . . .	

FIG. 4.2.   Weighting goals as a function of time.

central it will almost always be a component in any interaction. However, the relative weight associated with it may change both among interactions and within an individual exchange. In some cases, affinity may be the entire goal of the interactants. But in many other cases, there are multiple goals, one of which is affinity. More importantly, the general goals established by the interactants for an exchange may shape the choice of affinity strategies a person uses. Certain goals (e.g., infatuated-romantic goals vs. manipulative, impression-management goals) may affect the choices people make among the different strategies. Further, there are conceptual weights associated with each affinity strategy at any point in time. In a typical exchange, various affinity strategies may be enacted simultaneously and sequentially. The context of the interaction, the purposes at hand, and the people involved may shape those weights. At the start of a romantic "pick-up" certain affinity strategies may play predominant roles (e.g., physical attractiveness, dynamism) but as the relationship develops, others may become more, or just as, central to affinity seeking (e.g., openness, listening). Parenthetically, the psychological weights interactants place on these goals and strategies may, in fact, serve as interesting cognitive measures of competency. It may well be that one could identify highly competent individuals, ask them to provide relative weights for different interaction goals at different phases of a conversation, and then use their estimates as a baseline for conversational expertise. Furthermore, it might be that competency in interaction may be defined in terms of timing. Highly competent interactants know when to initiate a particular strategy, when to shift weights associated with various strategies and goals, and when to avoid using some strategy. The capacity to time one's moves well may be a useful meter of competence. Zanna and Pack (1975) provided an example of this choicemaking process. Female college students anticipated they were going to meet an attractive male who held either traditional or nontraditional views of the "ideal" woman. When anticipating a meeting with a traditional man, women tended to be described as more feminine and less intelligent; when the purported meeting was with a nontraditional man, women tended to highlight intelligence over femininity.

Bell and Daly (1984) also suggested that there are multiple motives for affinity. Indeed, it is interesting that when we examine research in the field of communication there appears to be a tendency to assume simple outcome measures—persuasion means attitude change, affinity means liking. But why do people want to persuade one another? Why do people want others to like them? We haven't, as a discipline, done careful analyses of the motives for those outcome measures. In affinity, one can suppose a very basic motive is the seemingly innate sociability of human beings; relationships demand affinity. But there are other potential motives as well. To accomplish persuasion, affinity is important; to accomplish instruction, liking for a teacher may be critical; to get others to listen and remember information, affinity may be key.

In addition to the concern for the broad nature of people's communication goals, the motives involved in a specific interaction (Hilton & Darley, 1985) must also be considered. Taking this information into consideration brings to the fore the numerous studies of preinteraction expectancies (e.g., Honeycutt, 1989; Ickes, Patterson, Rajecki, & Tanford, 1982). Some of the issues related to preinteraction expectancies and affinity have been explored by Gendrin and Honeycutt (1988).

The issue of consciousness is a third antecedent. Clearly there are times when people consciously decide that they want to generate affinity in others and then make clear choices among the strategies to accomplish that goal. But at other times, there may be less awareness. Indeed, some affinity strategies may be so overlearned that conscious awareness of them is quite limited. When examining awareness we need to think not only of the awareness of the initiator but also of the potential target. There may be cases when the initiator is quite conscious of an affinity move that is beyond the conscious awareness of the target, and vice versa. For instance, suppose a person has a first date with someone. The person, seeking to impress the other, dresses quite well. But to the other, this person's appearance may not seem a consciously chosen alternative at all. He or she may suppose that this is how the individual always appears. Perhaps the most sophisticated interactant knows how to both manipulate affinity strategies and manage the awareness of the other.

Constraints.   Both personal and contextual characteristics operate as constraints in Bell and Daly's (1984) model. Personal characteristics include ''people's dispositions, social skills, and past experiences'' (p. 94). Certain personality characteristics such as affiliation needs, loneliness, shyness, and self-monitoring, to name but a few, may impact the decision to initiate affinity, the choice of affinity strategies used by the individual, and the effectiveness of the implementation. Interactants' social skills may similarly impinge on affinity attempts. Highly skilled individuals may select different strategies and engage in them at different levels of effectiveness than their less-skilled counterparts. Finally, people's attempts at any communication move are not ahistorical. What has worked before will probably be used again; what has failed miserably in the past will probably be studiously avoided. The aforementioned allusion to overlearning may be relevant here. People who have successfully used a certain affinity strategy with great regularity in the past may come to be unaware that they use it at all. Indeed, the habitual nature of many communication behaviors, although perhaps efficient, may also be problematic. People get in trouble when they cease attending to specific situational cues, assuming that what worked in the past will work well now.

Contextual characteristics can also impinge on affinity behavior. Obviously, where and when the encounter takes place is important. Certain environments are more conducive to certain strategy moves than other environments.

The purpose(s) of an interaction affect choices as well. Certain interactions may, by the nature of their purpose, preclude certain strategies. There are implicit, and sometimes explicit, requirements placed on interactants by the reasons for an exchange. But perhaps the most important of contextual characteristics are those having to do with the others involved in the interaction. What works with one person may not work with another. When people interact with strangers they may choose different strategies than when conversing with well-known friends; people may opt for some strategies when dealing with subordinates, other strategies when dealing with superiors; what is effective with children may not be effective with adults; people who are lonely may be more susceptible to certain moves than people who feel almost overwhelmed by the number and quality of their relationships. The point is that affinity is truly an interactional variable. To study affinity, as have many researchers, as something associated with only one interactant, misses perhaps the most interesting and basic question that scholars in communication need to examine: the inherent jointness of social interaction. It takes at least two people to make an interaction, and each person involved influences what happens. Space limitations preclude a full exposition of this issue. Suffice to say that if we ever want to truly understand affinity processes we need to focus on the inherently interactive nature of the phenomena.

Strategic Activities. Four clusters of strategic activities in affinity seeking are identified by Bell and Daly (1984): strategy, length of enactment, sequencing, and quality of enactment. First, "individuals seeking affinity must decide on an optimal strategy or strategies in a given situation" (p. 94). People decide what they think works best in a situation. This assumption needs to be treated with caution. There are many times when interactants do not make the effort to enact optimal choices—they perhaps don't find the particular exchange important enough to maximize the likelihood of success. In some exchanges people even opt for minimally acceptable strategies, ones that will probably achieve, at best, only minimally satisfactory results, even when knowing that there is the potential for better results with greater effort. Communication scholarship has not spent a good deal of time exploring the mundaneness of satisfactory communication outcomes (one exception is Gendrin & Honeycutt, 1988). Everything doesn't always have to go perfectly and people know this in their day-to-day lives. At other times, an exchange has an optimal outcome that is vitally important to the person. Communicators may behave very differently depending on the degree to which an optimal outcome is desired.

Bell and Daly (1984) also emphasized the combinatory processes involved in affinity. Typologies describe various strategies available to an interactant; but in most actual interactions, these strategies are combined in many different ways. They are not independent of one another. When trying to generate affinity people may integrate 5 or 6 or even 10 of the strategies in their attempt. The ways in which the different strategies are combined and the decision processes behind these combinations represent interesting avenues for future work. None has been done to date. In all fairness, affinity research is not alone in operationally assuming independence among strategies. Research on compliance, for example, shares that problem.

Affinity-seeking strategies not only need to be integrated, they must also be sequenced. Sequencing supposes that there are better and worse patterns for arranging different strategies. In one sense, the issue of sequencing of strategies is similar to the vector model previously presented to describing multiple-interaction goals. It is interesting how little attention has been paid to sequencing in communication research focusing on effectiveness. Aside from some limited attention in the persuasion literature (e.g., foot in door, primacy) little has been done. Yet sequencing may be a very basic component of communication effectiveness—some moves work better when they follow others; some moves make little sense unless others have preceded them. Finally, there is the issue of the quality with which affinity-seeking strategies are enacted. There are better and worse enactments of each strategy. This is important and it is something that hasn't been carefully examined by researchers. Most research simply asks people whether someone does or does not engage in a strategy. But that begs the question because if a person engages in a strategy but does it badly, then the outcome may not be the one anticipated. The quality of the enactment is as important as the fact that the strategy was enacted at all. It may well be that in some cases, deciding not to enact a strategy because of the actor's inability to do it well, may be a strategy itself, as well as the hallmark of highly competent communicators.

Target Responses.   Bell and Daly (1984) suggested that the response of the other interactants must be carefully considered in affinity research. They suggest three sorts of responses: affective, behavioral, and cognitive ones. Affective responses include changes in the affinity that the target person feels toward the actor enacting an affinity move. Behavioral responses include the physical and verbal actions elicited by the affinity-seeking activities. Cognitive responses include judgments, perceptual changes, and learning.

DEVELOPING THE TYPOLOGY OF AFFINITY SEEKING: ITS NATURE AND CORRELATES

The typology of affinity-seeking strategies was initially devised through an analysis of the responses of 22 small brainstorming groups, comprised of adults enrolled in workshops and undergraduate students. Group members were asked to "produce a list of things people can say or do to get others to like them," or to "produce a list of things people can say or do to get others to dislike them."

Responses were content analyzed, categories were developed, and a typology of 25 strategies was constructed. In a series of studies following that initial one, the typology was refined. It is presented in Table 4.1. One should note that when Bell, Daly, and Gonzales (1987) examined affinity-maintenance strategies of adult married women they found eight additional strategies. They are included at the bottom of Table 4.1.

We make two important disclaimers from the start. First, we limit ourselves to research emphasizing the active enactment of each strategy. We exclude cases where scholars have simply correlated a behavior that falls within a strategy category with some outcome without concern for whether the behavior is an intentional activity to generate affinity. An example here might help: There has been an enormous body of research on the relationship of physical attractiveness and similarity on liking. Much of this research assumes a passive person who is either attractive (or unattractive) or similar (or dissimilar) from another. That sort of research is excluded in this review. On the other hand, there is research relating, for example, the degree of attractiveness of a defendant to sentencing severity in trial situations. The presumption of studies like those is that attractiveness is something a person manipulates to affect an outcome. That sort of research is of interest in this review.

Second, we do not intend to be encyclopedic in this review. We highlight examples of research falling within each category, recognizing from the start that there are many projects that would deservedly fall in each strategy class but that are not mentioned. Space restrictions and limited knowledge of many areas preclude such coverage.

To organize this review we use areas where current research has been conducted. These are: gender, personality correlates, affinity in relationships, affinity maintenance in marriage, affinity in organizational settings, affinity in instructional settings, the affinity-seeking competency instrument, and affinity testing.

Gender

One strand of research in affinity focuses on gender differences in the utilization of different strategies. In their initial study of affinity seeking, Bell and Daly (1984) compared male and female respondents' self-reported tendencies to use each strategy. Females preferred strategies of conversational rule-keeping, eliciting other's disclosures, listening, sensitivity, and similarity significantly more than males. Richmond et al. (1987) also discovered gender differences in self-reported use of strategies. Females report using strategies of eliciting other's disclosure, including other, listening, physical attractiveness, sensitivity, trustworthiness, assuming equality, and conceding control significantly more than males report engaging in those strategies. Alternatively, males

TABLE 4.1
A Typology of Affinity-Seeking Strategies

1. *Altruism.* The affinity seeker strives to be of assistance to the target in whatever she or he is currently doing. Example: The affinity seeker is generally available to run errands for the target.
2. *Assume Control.* The affinity seeker presents himself or herself as a person who has control over whatever is going on. Example: The affinity seeker takes charge of the activities engaged in by the target and herself or himself.
3. *Assume Equality.* The affinity seeker strikes a posture of social equality with the target. Example: The affinity seeker avoids one-up games and behaving snobbishly.
4. *Comfortable Self.* The affinity seeker acts comfortable and relaxed in settings shared with the target. Example: The affinity seeker ignores annoying environmental distractions, seeking to convey a "nothing bothers me" impression.
5. *Concede Control.* The affinity seeker allows the target to assume control over relational activities. Example: The affinity seeker permits the target to plan a weekend that the two will share.
6. *Conversational Rule-Keeping.* The affinity seeker adheres closely to cultural rules for polite, cooperative interaction with the target. Example: The affinity seeker acts interested and involved in conversations with the target.
7. *Dynamism.* The affinity seeker presents herself or himself as an active, enthusiastic person. Example: The affinity seeker is lively and animated in the presence of the target.
8. *Elicit Other's Disclosures.* The affinity seeker encourages the target to talk by reinforcing the target's conversational contributions. Example: The affinity seeker queries the target about the target's opinions regarding a significant personal issue.
9. *Facilitates Enjoyment.* The affinity seeker tries to maximize the positiveness of relational encounters with the target. Example: The affinity seeker tries to maximize the positiveness of relational encounters with the target.
10. *Inclusion of Other.* The affinity seeker includes the target in the affinity seeker's social groups. Example: The affinity seeker plans a party for the target, which numbers friends of the affinity seeker as guests.
11. *Influence Perceptions of Closeness.* The affinity seeker engages in behaviors that cause the targets to perceive the relationship as closer than it has actually been. Example: The affinity seeker uses nicknames and talks about "we," rather than "you and I," when discussing their relationship with the target.
12. *Listening.* The affinity seeker listens actively and attentively to the target. Example: The affinity seeker asks the target for frequent clarification and elaboration, and verbally recalls things the target has said.
13. *Nonverbal Immediacy.* The affinity seeker signals interest in the target through various nonverbal cues. Example: The affinity seeker smiles frequently at the target.
14. *Openness.* The affinity seeker discloses personal information to the target. Example: The affinity seeker reveals some social insecurity or fear to the target.
15. *Optimism.* The affinity seeker presents himself or herself to the target as a positive person. Example: The affinity seeker focuses on positive comments and favorable evaluations when discussing mutual acquaintances with the target.
16. *Personal Autonomy.* The affinity seeker presents herself or himself to the target as an independent, free-thinking person. Example: The affinity seeker demonstrates a willingness to express disagreement with the target about personal and social studies.
17. *Physical Attractiveness.* Affinity seeker tries to look and dress attractively as possible in the presence of the target. Example: The affinity seeker always engages in careful grooming before interacting with the target.
18. *Present Interesting Self.* The affinity seeker presents herself or himself to the target as someone who would be interesting to know. Example: The affinity seeker discreetly drops the names of impressive or interesting acquaintances in the presence of the target.
19. *Reward Association.* The affinity seeker presents himself or herself in such a way that the target perceives the affinity seeker can reward the target for associating with him or her. Example: The affinity seeker showers the target with gifts.

(Continued)

118

TABLE 4.1
(Continued)

20. Self-Concept Confirmation. The affinity seeker demonstrates respect for the target and helps the target to "feel good" about herself or himself. Example: The affinity seeker compliments the target frequently.
21. *Self-Inclusion.* The affinity seeker arranges the environment so as to come into frequent contact with the target. Example: The affinity seeker plans to have afternoon cocktails at the same time and place as the target.
22. *Sensitivity.* The affinity seeker acts in a warm, empathetic manner toward the target. Example: The affinity seeker sympathizes with the target regarding a personal problem the target is experiencing.
23. *Similarity.* The affinity seeker seeks to convince the target that the two of them share many similar tastes and attitudes. Example: The affinity seeker often points out things to the target that the two of them have in common.
24. *Supportiveness.* The affinity seeker supports the target in the latter's social encounters. Example: The affinity seeker sides with the target in a disagreement the target is having with a third party.
25. *Trustworthiness.* The affinity seeker presents herself or himself to the target as an honest, reliable person. Example: The affinity seeker consistently fulfills commitments made to the target.

Affinity-Maintenance Strategies*

1. *Faithfulness.* Spouse is faithful to partner. Example: She or he does not engage in extramarital sexual relationships.
2. *Honesty.* Spouse is honest and sincere in interactions with partner. Example: She or he does not lie, cheat, or engage in pretense.
3. *Physical Affection.* Spouse is physically affectionate with partner. Example: She or he frequently engages in sexual relations with partner.
4. *Reliability.* Spouse is dependable in carrying out his or her responsibilities to partner and family. Example: She or he promptly completes household duties.
5. *Self-Improvement.* Spouse tries to improve self to please partner. Example: She or he takes classes to become more knowledgeable about world affairs.
6. *Shared Spirituality.* Spouse and partner share spiritual activities. Example: They pray together and attend religious services as a couple.
7. *Third-Party Relations.* Spouse demonstrates positive feelings toward the partner's friends and family. Example: She or he is friendly with the partner's mother even though the woman is obnoxious.
8. *Verbal Affection.* Spouse is verbally affectionate with partner. Example: She or he expresses great love for the partner.

*Note: These are eight additional strategies reported by subjects in Bell, Daly, and Gonzales (1987) study of affinity maintenance in marriage.

describe themselves as using strategies of assuming control, altruism, presenting an interesting self, rewarding association, and self-concept confirmation significantly more than females. Tolhuizen (1989a) found that females were significantly more likely than males to report using strategies of listening, nonverbal immediacy, sensitivity, similarity, and trustworthiness whereas males were significantly more likely than females to report using the assume control strategy. Interestingly, when Tolhuizen summed across all affinity strategies he found no overall differences due to gender. Gendrin (1990) found that females, with same-sex friends, were more likely to use strategies of sensitivity, nonverbal immediacy, assuming equality, listening, openness, physical attractiveness, eliciting other's disclosure, and rewarding association whereas males were more likely to use personal autonomy, self-inclusion, dynamism, influencing perceptions of closeness, facilitating enjoyment, presenting an interesting self, and supportiveness with other males.

In the Richmond et al. study (1987) respondents also predicted which gender would use each of the affinity-seeking strategies more in cross-gender dyads. When compared to what males thought females would use, females believed males would be more likely to use strategies of eliciting other's disclosure, including others, assuming control, altruism, optimism, dynamism, personal autonomy, and facilitating enjoyment. However, for one strategy, conceding control, females' use as predicted by males was significantly greater than males' use as predicted by females.

Bell, Daly, and Gonzales (1987) discovered differences in wives' perceptions of what affinity-maintenance strategies they, and their spouses, used in their marriage. Wives reported greater likelihood of using the following 20 of 28 affinity-maintenance strategies identified in the study than they perceived their husbands did. Wives felt they were more likely to use altruism, dynamism, eliciting other's disclosures, facilitating enjoyment, honesty, including other, influencing perceptions of closeness, listening, openness, physical attractiveness, presenting an interesting self, reliability, reward association, self-concept confirmation, self-improvement, self-inclusion, sensitivity, sharing spirituality, similarity, and supportiveness than their husbands. Wives' perceive more frequent use of only one strategy by their husbands, physical affection.

Richmond et al. (1987) also compared predictions about the opposite gender to self-reported use. Females thought males would use strategies of including others, listening, physical attractiveness, trustworthiness, conceding control, presenting a comfortable self, influencing perceptions of closeness, assuming control, and dynamism more than males said they actually used those strategies. On the other hand, males felt they used the strategy of facilitating enjoyment significantly more than females thought they did. The strategies of concede control, comfortable self, influence perceptions of closeness, assume control, present interesting self, reward association, self-concept confirmation, self-inclusion, similarity, and supportiveness were predicted by males to be used by females significantly more than what females reported they actually did. Yet, females' self-reported use of strategies such as eliciting other's disclosure, including other, listening, physical attractiveness, sensitivity, trustworthiness, assuming equality, optimism, and facilitating enjoyment were found to be significantly greater than what males predicted.

This last set of findings is of particular interest. It hints that members of each gender may not be highly accurate in their judgments of what the opposite gender does to elicit affinity. This can obviously create any number of relational problems because people enter a relationship with certain expectations and those expectations affect their satisfaction. To the extent that people's expectations don't match their partner's self-expectations, problems may emerge. For instance, if one person in the relationship, say the female, believes that males generally show affinity by taking control, she may not perceive an individual male who chooses not to take control as being particularly interested in developing a relationship with her.

Clearly, the results on gender differences are mixed. The bulk of the literature suggests some difference. When people are asked to report what they do in terms of affinity seeking (e.g., Bell & Daly, 1984; Tolhuizen, 1989a), males and females highlight different strategies. When people are asked to offer their stereotypes of what males and females do (e.g., Richmond et al., 1987), there are also notable gender differences. Wives see significant differences between what they do and what their husbands do in terms of affinity maintenance (Bell, Daly, & Gonzales, 1987). Men and women differ in ways they attempt to intensify their relationships as well (Tolhuizen, 1989b). Men are significantly more likely than women to report directly asking their partners to go to a deeper relational level and directly telling the other person of their love and affection. Females reported they discussed intensification and strategically accepted the other's attempt to intensify more than males.

On the other hand, there are two cases where no differences were observed. The first is Tolhuizen's (1989a) finding of no gender differences when using a summed measure of affinity. This finding is easily explained: His decision to use a summed measure may have easily masked differences in specific strategy differences. Clearly, this is the case, as he did find gender differences on six individual strategies. The second case (Roach, 1991) asked undergraduates to rate their teachers on affinity, and revealed no differences in the perceived affinity behaviors of male and female teachers. The Roach findings are more difficult to interpret. A possible explanation lies in the methods used in the various studies. If we limit ourselves to investigations where people rated others on affinity (Bell, Daly, & Gonzales, 1987; Richmond et al. 1987; Roach, 1991) we find an interesting difference. In the first two studies, subjects were either directly or indirectly cued to make comparisons between males and females. Wives in the Bell, Daly, and Gonzales (1987) study rated both themselves and their spouses. Females and males, in the Richmond et al. study (1987) were asked to evaluate both themselves and members of the opposite sex. But, in the Roach (1991) study, no comparison was even hinted at. Students chose one teacher and rated him or her. Gender was not presented as a salient dimension. It may well be that people believe that there are gender differences in affinity seeking and maintenance and that belief is elicited when making ratings where gender differences are highlighted. But when gender is not a salient dimension, no differences emerge.

Personality Correlates

Bell and Daly (1984) investigated correlations among the 25 affinity-seeking strategies and nine personality construct measures: communication apprehension (McCroskey, 1977); social anxiety, public and private self-consciousness (Fenigstein, Scheier, & Buss, 1975); Machiavellianism (Christie & Geis, 1970); interaction involvement (Cegala, 1980); self-monitoring (Snyder, 1974, 1979); assertiveness (Lorr & More, 1980); and communicator style (Norton, 1978). Bell, Tremblay, and Buerkel-Rothfuss (1987) used self-report questionnaires of affinity seeking along with similar personality measures. Results of both of these studies showed numerous statistically significant correlations that were in the directions one would typically expect.

Communication apprehension and its close cousin, social anxiety, were negatively related to the use of various affinity-seeking strategies that included active communication (e.g., assuming control, dynamism) while positively related to more passive strategy such as conceding control. When affinity seeking is conceptualized as a dispositional tendency, there is an inverse relationship between apprehension and the tendency to seek affinity. This pattern is reflected in related variables such as loneliness, assertiveness, and interaction involvement. Bell, Tremblay, and Buerkel-Rothfuss (1987) found an inverse relationship between loneliness and affinity-seeking tendencies; Bell and Daly (1984) found positive relationships between assertiveness and respondents reports' of their likelihood of using active affinity strategies such as assuming control, dynamism, and personal autonomy, while finding inverse relationships between assertiveness and more passive strategies such as supportiveness and conceding control. Bell, Tremblay, and Buerkel-Rothfuss (1987) found that assertiveness was positively related to tendencies to seek affinity, when that construct is considered as a dispositional characteristic. They also found positive relationships between both affinity-seeking competence and strategy performance of affinity and interaction involvement.

Overall, the pattern of results suggests that personality variables reflecting high levels of communication activity are positively related to affinity: People who seek out and enjoy social interaction tend to report greater affinity-seeking behavior. The exceptions are interesting: Passive affinity strategies such as conceding control and supportiveness were inversely related to these personality measures of communicative propensity.

Affinity in Relationships

Creating a relationship is often a strategic, active move. Davis (1973), for instance, looked at the "pick-up" move designed to create affinity. He noted six stages that pick-ups often go through. Daly, Hogg, Sacks, Smith, and Zimring (1983) examined nonverbal preening in bars and restaurants. They found that people were most likely to preen when attempting to meet potential dating partners or when on a first or second date. Studies of personal advertisements provide interesting insight into people's beliefs of what is successful in attracting potential relational partners. One finding that seems somewhat consistent across investigations is that women tend to emphasize attractiveness more than men, who instead emphasize status moves (Buss, 1989; Deaux & Hanna, 1984; Koestner & Wheeler, 1988). On the other hand, when describing their own personalities men tend to emphasize their expressive trait, whereas women highlight their instrumental traits (Koestner & Wheeler, 1988) perhaps as a reflection of what they believe the opposite sex is seeking.

A central concern of research on affinity seeking is its association with various aspects of relationship development. Such an interest seems quite reasonable: One assumes that affinity seeking is one means by which people create relationships, and affinity-maintenance strategies incorporate many of the ways people encourage the continuation of their relationships.

One direction research takes focuses on the impact of relational states on the selection of affinity strategies. Tolhuizen (1989a) asked respondents to consider four levels of relationship development: "1) new acquaintance, 2) fully developed, stable friendship, 3) deteriorating friendship in which the desire is to save and continue the relationship, and 4) deteriorating friendship in which the desire is to terminate the relationship" (p. 86). The sort of relationship respondents imagined themselves to be in affected their choices of affinity strategies. For example, people felt they were more likely to use strategies of comfortable self, influencing perceptions of closeness, openness, rewarding association, and self-inclusion in fully developed relationships than in any of the other three levels of relationship development. They felt more likely to use two strategies, facilitating enjoyment and supportiveness, in fully developed friendships than in relationships with new acquaintances; more likely to use strategies of listening, presenting interesting self, sensitivity, similarity, and supportiveness in developed relationships than in deteriorating relationships they do not wish to save; and more likely to use strategies of facilitating enjoyment, listening, presenting interesting self, sensitivity, and similarity in developed relationships than in deteriorating relationships they wished to terminate.

In initial interactions people seek not only to create affinity in others but to test the degree of affinity others feel for them. "How much does the other person like me?" "Does he or she like me at all?" These sorts of questions are ones that may arise in an interactant's mind as an initial conversation continues. Douglas (1987) proposed, for instance, that people use eight strategies to assess how well liked they are in initial interactions: (a) confronting, "actions that required a partner to provide immediate and generally public evidence of his or her liking" (e.g., I asked her if she like me); (b) withdrawing, "actions that require a partner to sustain the interaction" (e.g., saying you're leaving with the hope the other would say "stay"); (c) sustaining, "actions

designed to maintain the interaction without affecting its apparent intimacy"
(e.g., keep asking questions); (d) hazing, "actions that required a partner to
provide a commodity or service to the actor at some cost to him or herself"
(e.g., asking the other to drive you home when home is a far distance away);
(e) diminishing self, "actions that lowered the value of self; either directly by
self-deprecation or indirectly by identifying alternative reward sources for a
partner" (e.g., saying you're not very interesting but hoping the other person
would say you are); (f) approaching, "actions that implied increased intimacy
to which the only disconfirming partner response is compensatory activity"
(e.g., moving closer to the other and he or she doesn't move away); (g) offering, "actions that generate conditions favourable for approach by a partner"
(e.g., putting yourself in a position that makes it quite possible, if the other
person wishes, for him or her to ask you out); and (h) networking, "actions
that included third parties, either to acquire or transmit information" (e.g.,
letting the other's friends know you are interested in him or her).

Using dimensions of efficiency and social appropriateness, Douglas (1987)
found that testing strategies of confronting, approaching, sustaining, and networking are seen by people as significantly more efficient than strategies of
diminishing self, hazing, and withdrawing. One strategy, sustaining, is judged
as significantly more socially appropriate than any other strategy, and strategies of offering, approaching, and networking are viewed as significantly more
socially appropriate than strategies of confronting, withdrawing, hazing, and
diminishing self. Three strategies (withdrawing, hazing, and diminishing self)
are considered both inefficient and inappropriate. Arguing that people, in initial exchanges, like to reduce their uncertainty (and like those who reduce their
uncertainty), Douglas suggested that the three are likely to induce negative
affect, which in turn will increase uncertainty—a dispreferred state.

The decision to try to move a relationship to a deeper, more intense stage
is an interesting one. It sometimes may happen naturally, but often it is something one partner or both try to "make" happen. Tolhuizen (1989a) examined
how people strategically attempt to intensify their romantic relationships. He
suggested four major clusters of strategies. The first cluster emphasizes *social
rewards and attraction*, which incorporates strategies such as increasing reward
for the partner, giving partner tokens of affection, adapting one's own behaviors
in order to impress the other, increasing physical attractiveness through manipulation of appearance, and systematically attempting to enmesh oneself in the
other's social milieu. The second cluster highlights *intimacy* moves and includes
strategies where one person, in an attempt to intensify the relationship, makes
suggestive moves such as hinting and flirting, initiates or engages in sexual
intimacy, and demonstrates affection through nonverbal behaviors such as gaze
and touch. The third cluster includes *passive and indirect* strategies such as asking the other for assistance and support and agreeing to the other's request
for a deeper relationship. The final group of strategies, labeled *verbal directness*

and intimacy, incorporates techniques such as increasing contact with the other person, directly discussing with the other the possibility of intensifying the relationship, making a direct request for a more intense relationship, verbally expressing love and affection, and using language that assumes a deeper relationship.

Affinity Maintenance

Affinity *seeking* is obviously important for establishing relationships. But just as important are people's ability to maintain relationships through various affinity strategies. What do people do to keep others liking them? Hays (1984) examined correlates of friendship development among college students. Quantity of interaction tended to increase over the first 6 weeks for friendships that were growing whereas it decreased for friendships that were fading. As time went on, the amount of interaction decreased for all relationships, but the degree of intimacy (affection) became more important. Marston, Hecht, and Robers (1987) as part of a larger study asked a number of people how they communicated love to their partners. The most frequently mentioned techniques included directly telling the other that they loved them, doing special things for their lovers, being supportive and attentive, physical expressiveness, and just being together. When asked how their partners demonstrated love, respondents' most frequent descriptions included directly telling the other, physical contact, being supportive, having things done for them, being together, and communicating feeling.

Bell, Daly, and Gonzales (1987) examined affinity maintenance in marriage in three studies. In their first study, respondents who had been married for an average of 11 years were asked open-ended questions about the strategies they use to maintain liking and solidarity in their marriage relationships. Responses were coded and a typology of 28 strategies was devised. Most of these strategies were easily classified into Bell and Daly's (1984) 25-strategy typology. However, a few additional clusters were uncovered and a few of Bell and Daly's categories failed to arise among married respondents. Four of Bell and Daly's affinity-seeking strategies, assuming control, personal autonomy, comfortable self, and nonverbal immediacy, were not identified as affinity-maintenance strategies. Participants identified eight additional strategies: faithfulness, honesty, physical affection, reliability, self-improvement, sharing spirituality, third-party relations, and verbal affection.

In the next study, Bell, Daly, and Gonzales (1987) asked wives what they wanted, in terms of affinity behaviors, from their husbands as well as what they thought their husbands wanted from them. The affinity behaviors most desired in husbands included being faithful, honest, physically attractive, sensitive, and confirming of the wife's self-concept. Wives believed that their husbands most wanted them to be faithful, honest, physically affectionate, sensitive, and physically attractive. Far less important to wives were strategies of conceding control, dynamism, equality, and self-improvement. When these ratings of importance were correlated with perceived marital quality, a number of strategies (honesty, including other, influencing perceptions of closeness, listening, openness, physical affection, sensitivity, shared spirituality, verbal affection) were positively related to marital quality. Interestingly, wives' perceptions that their husbands desired them to concede control to maintain affinity was associated with lower marital quality.

A third study (Bell, Daly, & Gonzales, 1987), correlated marital quality with wives' perceptions of their own and their husband's frequency of strategy use. Wives reported the most frequently used strategies by both themselves and their husbands were faithfulness, honesty, physical attractiveness, self-concept confirmation, supportiveness, and verbal affection. Least frequently used strategies were altruism, conceding control, conversational rule-keeping, dynamism, equality, shared spirituality, and similarity. Wives felt they engaged in almost every affinity behavior more than their husbands. The only exception was for physical affection—wives felt their husbands engaged in this more frequently as a way of maintaining affinity. When frequency judgments were correlated with marital quality there were numerous positive and significant relationships. Wives' perceptions of marital quality was related to the frequency with which wives reported engaging in 18 of the strategies and the frequency with which wives felt their husbands engaged in 24 of the strategies.

Finally, Bell, Daly, and Gonzales (1987) investigated predictors of wives' perceived marital quality. Because the frequency of husbands' use of five particular strategies had accounted for more than half of the variance related to the marital quality measure, wives' perceptions of marital quality were regressed on these particular strategies. The stepwise regression revealed the following results in order: sensitivity, spirituality, physical affection, self-inclusion, and honesty.

Taken together, the research on affinity seeking and maintenance in developing established relationships supports the proposition that successful relationships are marked by positive affinity moves. Affinity is a critical part of intimacy. Clearly, the pattern of results suggest that the ways affinity seeking and maintenance are enacted impinges on relational quality. Gender, relationship length, and relationship goals all effect choices among strategies that in turn lead to greater or less affinity.

Affinity in Organizational Settings

Richmond et al. (1986) explored affinity-seeking strategies in organizational settings. They probed the relationship of supervisor use of power and affinity-seeking strategies with subordinate satisfaction. In their study they found that 17 of the 25 affinity-seeking strategies identified by Bell and Daly (1984) are seen as commonly used by supervisors. These strategies are assuming control, assuming equality, comfortable self, conversational rule-keeping, dynamism, eliciting other's disclosures, facilitating enjoyment, listening, nonverbal immediacy, openness, optimism, personal autonomy, physical attractiveness, self-concept confirmation, sensitivity, supportiveness, and trustworthiness. Two different ways of measuring affinity-seeking behaviors were created for this study. The first was a binary choice when subordinates were asked whether or not their supervisors used each strategy. The second measure asked respondents to indicate the degree to which their supervisors used each strategy they had marked "yes" to previously.

Significant and positive correlations were found between subordinate satisfaction with supervision and the supervisor's perceived use (measured in a binary fashion) of assuming equality, comfortable self, conversational rule-keeping, eliciting other's disclosures, facilitating enjoyment, including other, listening, nonverbal immediacy, openness, optimism, physical attractiveness, self-concept confirmation, sensitivity and trustworthiness. Additionally, significant and positive relationships were found between the perceived frequency of use of most of the affinity-seeking strategies just noted and perceived supervisor satisfaction by the subordinate. Overall, the data suggest that subordinates' satisfaction with their supervisors is positively and significantly related to the perception that their supervisors use a variety of affinity strategies. Finally, there were two significant negative correlations among perceived supervisor satisfaction by the subordinate and the use of two affinity-seeking strategies: assuming control and presenting an interesting self.

Affinity in Instructional Settings

One setting where affinity seeking appears especially important is the classroom. A number of scholars have examined the relationships of affinity-seeking behaviors to various instructional outcomes. McCroskey and McCroskey (1986) completed the first classroom-focused study on affinity seeking. They asked experienced elementary and high school teachers how often they thought other teachers engaged in each of the 25 strategies identified by Bell and Daly (1984). They found good consistency in the rank ordering of strategies used by teachers and those reported by college students in the Bell and Daly study. Table 4.2 includes a summary of the rank ordering of strategy use.

Gorham et al. (1989) extended the McCroskey and McCroskey (1986) study in two ways. First, they clustered responding teachers into groups based on the grade levels they taught. Second, they used open-ended questions (e.g., "Please provide five specific examples from the past year of what you have done to get a student to like you"). Responses were then independently coded into categories. The coding of affinity-seeking strategies fit nicely with the Bell and Daly category system yielding very high intercoder agreement (98.9%)

with the original typology. The most common strategies were facilitating enjoyment and conceding control. Table 4.2 includes the rank ordering of strategy use by teachers. When responses were clustered by grade level some interesting findings emerged. For example, four strategies (trustworthiness, sensitivity, self-inclusion, and elicit disclosure) were used more as grade level rose. Conceding control was used the least in middle grades and more often in lower and higher grade levels. Facilitating enjoyment, nonverbal immediacy, and self-concept confirmation were used less in higher grades than in lower grades. Altruism was found mostly in the senior high grades.

When Gorham et al. (1989) compared the rank ordering of strategies they obtained from teachers with the results of studies by Bell and Daly (1984) and McCroskey and McCroskey (1986), they discovered relatively little similarity. McCroskey and McCroskey found a rank order correlation of .80 between

TABLE 4.2
Rank Order of Teacher Affinity-Seeking Strategies

Strategy	McCroskey & McCroskey	Gorham et al.	Roach
Altruism	14.5	12	8
Assume Control	12.5	22	6.5
Assume Equality	14.5	22	10
Comfortable Self	12.5	17.5	1
Concede Control	22	5	17
Conversational Rule-Keeping	7	22	6.5
Dynamism	7	17.5	4
Elicit Other's Disclosure	3.5	5	12.5
Facilitate Enjoyment	9	1.5	11
Inclusion of Other	25	22	24
Influence Perceptions of Closeness	21	16	25
Listening	7	14	5
Nonverbal Immediacy	5	8.5	18
Openness	19.5	10.5	23
Optimism	10	14	9
Personal Autonomy	16	22	3
Physical Attractiveness	1	22	12.5
Present Interesting Self	18	22	14
Reward Association	23	10.5	21
Self-Concept Confirmation	11	1.5	16
Self-Inclusion	24	7	20
Sensitivity	2	5	15
Similarity	19.5	14	19
Supportiveness	17	8.5	22
Trustworthiness	3.5	3	2

Note: The above rank-ordered comparisons illustrate perceptions of different strategy use. McCroskey and McCroskey (1986) asked teachers how often affinity strategies had been observed in the classroom. Gorham et al. (1989) asked teachers what strategies they used to generate affinity. Roach (1991) asked students how often their teachers used each strategy.

their rank ordering and the rank ordering Bell and Daly discovered. Gorham et al. found much smaller rank order correlations (.21 with McCroskey & McCroskey; .17 with Bell & Daly). They interpreted these low correlations as artifactual tied to the method of data collection. McCroskey and McCroskey had teachers check off frequently used behaviors; Gorham et al. had teachers respond by listing responses to an open-ended question about their teaching in a particular subject area. The explanation may be only partially correct as Bell and Daly's rank ordering was drawn from open-ended responses as well. What is more likely (and Gorham et al. noted this) is the specificity of the Gorham et al. question and technique for coding responses. Many teachers, when answering the Gorham et al. question, listed very specific behaviors they would use in their classrooms. Thus, a math teacher might list five or six different "facilitate enjoyment" behaviors (e.g., make fractions interesting, show movies, take a pie and cut it into sections), each of which were counted individually. This might artificially increase the numbers associated with some strategies.

Richmond (1990) related perceived teacher affinity-seeking strategies to students' motivation to study, self-reported learning, attitudes toward course, instructor, and the behaviors recommended in the courses, and intentions to continue enrollment in courses such as the one the teacher taught as well as other courses taught by the teacher.

There was a significant and positive correlation between students' perceptions that their teachers used affinity-seeking strategies and students' motivation to study course materials. In addition, the multiple correlations between perceived teacher affinity-seeking and every other outcome variable (e.g., perceived learning, affect towards course material and instructor, intention to take future courses in area and taught by instructor) were all large and positive. Richmond (1990) also collected data on students' perceptions of their instructors' use of behavior alteration techniques and immediacy behaviors. She found that in predicting the various outcomes, affinity-seeking behaviors were more powerful than behavioral alteration techniques. Affinity seeking seems to count more in students' feeling about course material and instructors than behavioral alteration techniques.

Roach (1991) had undergraduate students rate college instructors on affinity-seeking behavior as well as rate themselves on how much they thought they learned in the instructor's class, how much they liked the class and the instructor, and how likely they would be to use the behaviors suggested by the instructor (these ratings were virtually the same as those used by Richmond, 1990). Roach found that overall, students felt professors used affinity-seeking strategies more than teaching assistants did. In a strategy-by-strategy analysis, he found that teaching assistants were perceived to use strategies of assuming control, comfortable self, personal autonomy, and trustworthiness less than faculty members while more often using (in a perceived sense) assuming equality, conceding control, eliciting other's disclosure, and self-inclusion than faculty. Ignoring these differences, Roach found that perceived affinity seeking by instructors was positively and significantly related to liking for instructors, perceived learning, and liking for the subject matter, replicating nicely the findings of Richmond (1990).

Most recently, Thompson and Frymier (1991) provided another replication of the findings of Richmond. They found positive correlations between perceptions of teachers' use of various affinity strategies and various self-reported instructional outcomes. Taken together these three investigations make a clear point: Students who think their instructors engage in high levels of affinity seeking also have positive evaluation of the instructors, the course material, and how much they learned in the course. The consistency of these findings is impressive. Two cautions are in order about these findings. One has to do with causality. It may be that when students like a teacher, a subject area, or feel like they are motivated to learn, they come to also see the instructor as being both more likable and more interested in making them like the course. In correlational work this is always a problem but it needs to be highlighted when findings such as these are reported. The second has to do with methods bias. It may well be that many of the correlations obtained by these researchers are due to the self-report nature of the questions. The various measures may, in a sense, all be seen as tapping the same general factor in respondents' minds: liking for the teacher. It would be quite useful to obtain independent measures of learning or re-enrollment, for instance, to discover whether affinity seeking has relationships, independent of self-report data, with these outcomes.

Affinity-Seeking Instrument

Bell, Tremblay, and Buerkel-Rothfuss (1987) conducted a series of five studies in order to examine affinity-seeking competence. In the first study, these researchers developed and refined the Affinity-Seeking Instrument (ASI), which is made up of two underlying dimensions: affinity-seeking competence (ASC) and strategic performance (SP). In the second study, Bell, Tremblay, and Buerkel-Rothfuss assess the factor structure of the instrument and found it to be stable. In the third study, responses using the instrument were correlated with various personality constructs. A stepwise regression was conducted to investigate these constructs further. Three variables, dyadic communication apprehension, loneliness, and social assertiveness, accounted for 36% of the variance in the ASC dimension of the scale, and four variables, acting, other-directedness, dyadic communication apprehension, and independence, accounted for 31% of the variance on the SP dimension of the instrument. Study 4 examined affinity-seeking skills and perceptions of abilities according to friends. Results suggested only moderate correlations. In the fifth and final study, outcomes of affinity-seeking strategies were examined. Results suggest that "affinity-seeking skills facilitate the obtainment of positive social outcomes" (p. 14).

Buerkel-Rothfuss and Bell (1987) extended research on the Affinity-Seeking Instrument by further exploring questions of the measure's validity. Evidence of validity of the ASC scale was obtained. People's reports of affinity-seeking competence were significantly and positively correlated with partners' liking for both female and male targets. In addition, females' reported competence was significantly and positively correlated with perceptions that they were effective, open, and precise communicators according to their male partners. Buerkel-Rothfuss and Bell also reported a significant relationship between self-evaluations of affinity-seeking competence and people's reports of how well they felt they knew their partner.

The same study found no evidence to support the validity of the Strategic Performance dimension of the Affinity-Seeking Instrument. They suggested that there is a critical difference between affinity obtained by those who wish to "get along" and those who wish to "get ahead." Buerkel-Rothfuss and Bell (1987) concluded that situational differences may account for differences in the salience of affinity-seeking ability.

In an extensive study using the ASI, Gendrin and Honeycutt (1988) found few behavioral correlates for the personality variable. Among strangers who were interacting, affinity-seeking competence was positively and significantly related to smiling, and the strategic performance scale was, among acquainted interactants, positively and significantly related to a composite behavior measure tapping involvement in the interaction.

CONCLUSIONS

This catalog of findings tied to the affinity-seeking construct presents a number of difficult issues for anyone trying to briefly summarize what is known today. One general, and unarguable, conclusion is that more research needs to be done on the construct. We address some of these "to do's" later. But beyond a call for more work, what can we usefully conclude at this point? First, introducing the notion of affinity as a strategic, intentional, and social activity has had some valuable consequences. At the very least, the theoretical presumptions have shifted attention toward a strategic framework that encompasses affinity. Second, we know that there are some reliable differences associated with affinity in a variety of contexts including classrooms, organizations, and relationships with a variety of different social roles (wife, husband; supervisor, subordinate) and personality predispositions.

There are a number of obvious limitations in the existing research that ought to be mentioned. First, and foremost, scholars have not yet focused on the actual behavioral enactments associated with affinity. We have, at this time, almost no investigations (except Gendrin & Honeycutt, 1988) that have empirically tapped behaviors associated with affinity. Instead, the research relies almost exclusively on self-reports and general ratings of others. It is time we examine the behavioral ways people go about getting others to like them. Second, scholars need to start explicating, and testing, the various theoretic issues involved in affinity. Research reviewed in this chapter is almost entirely descriptive, detailing correlates of affinity. But what of the process involved in affinity? We know far less about these aspects, and all the demographics of affinity one wishes to explore will not replace solid studies of the underlying dynamics of the process. Third, the existing research on topics tied to the affinity construct needs to be integrated within the model and within the typology. For reasons of space we limit the bulk of our discussion to studies that used, or started with, the Bell and Daly (1984) typology. But the construct is far more than the typology. Future scholarship should attempt to integrate the vast literatures associated with both the model and the individual categories composing the typology. In addition, the methods used in many of these studies are questionable on both logical and measurement theory grounds. For instance, when people are presented with checklists of alternatives, responses are suspect because people may mark off things that have little to do with what actually would come to mind if they were unprompted. More importantly, what people say they do, and what they actually do (behaviorally), doesn't always match. Affinity scholars need to deal with issues such as these. Finally, future scholarship needs to better delineate the outcome measure—what liking is and how it is measured. Surprisingly little scholarship has considered the definitional, measurement, and methodological issues involved in clearly explicating what liking means to people. People often decide to "make" others like them. How they go about doing this is what affinity is all about. The beginnings are there.

REFERENCES

Bell, R. A., & Daly, J. A. (1984). The affinity-seeking function of communication. *Communication Monographs, 51*, 91–115.

Bell, R. A., Daly, J. A., & Gonzales, C. (1987). Affinity-maintenance strategies in marital relations. *Journal of Marriage and the Family, 49*, 445–454.

Bell, R. A., Tremblay, S. W., & Buerkel-Rothfuss, N. L. (1987). Interpersonal attraction as a communication accomplishment: Development of a measure of affinity-seeking competence. *Western Journal of Speech Communication, 51*, 1–18.

Berscheid, E., & Walster, E. (1974). Physical attractiveness. In L. Berkowitz (Ed.), *Advances in experimental social psychology* (Vol. 7, pp. 157–215). New York: Academic Press.

Buerkel-Rothfuss, N. L. & Bell, R. A. (1987). Validity of the affinity-seeking instrument. *Communication Research Reports, 4*, 24–30.

Buss, D. M. (1989). Sex differences in human mate preferences: Evolutionary hypotheses tested in 37 cultures. *Behavioral and Brain Sciences, 12*, 1–14.

Cegala, D. J. (1980). Interaction involvement: A cognitive dimension of communicative competence. *Communication Education*, *30*, 109–121.

Christie, R., & Geis, F. L. (1970). *Studies in Machiavellianism*. New York: Academic.

Conn, M. K., & Peterson, C. (1989). Social support: Seek and ye shall find. *Journal of Social and Personal Relationships*, *6*, 345–358.

Daly, J. A., Hogg, E., Sacks, D., Smith, M., & Zimring, L. (1983). Sex and relationship affect social self-grooming. *Journal of Nonverbal Behavior*, *7*, 183–189.

Davis, M. (1973). *Intimate relations*. New York: Free Press.

Deaux, K., & Hanna, R. (1984). Courtship in the personal column: The influence of gender and sex role orientation. *Sex Roles*, *1*, 363–375.

Douglas, W. (1987). Affinity-testing in initial interactions. *Journal of Social and Personal Relationships*, *4*, 3–15.

Fenigstein, A., Scheier, M. F., & Buss, A. H. (1975). Public and private self-consciousness: Assessment and theory. *Journal of Consulting and Clinical Psychology*, *43*, 522–527.

Festinger, J., Schachter, S., & Back, K. W. (1950). *Social pressure in informal groups: A study of human factors in housing*. New York: Harper.

Gendrin, D. (1990). *Affinity competence in relationships*. Unpublished doctoral dissertation, Louisiana State University, Baton Rouge.

Gendrin, D., & Honeycutt, J. M. (1988). *The relationship between self-reported affinity-seeking competence and nonverbal immediacy behaviors among strangers and acquaintances*. Paper presented at the annual convention of the Speech Communication Association, New Orleans, LA.

Gorham, J., Kelley, D. H., & McCroskey, J. C. (1989). The affinity-seeking of classroom teachers: A second perspective. *Communication Quarterly*, *37*, 16–26.

Hays, R. B. (1984). The development and maintenance of friendship. *Journal of Social and Personal Relationships*, *1*, 75–98.

Hilton, J. L., & Darley, J. M. (1985). Constructing other persons: A limit on the effect. *Journal of Experimental Social Psychology*, *21*, 1–18.

Honeycutt, J. M. (1989). Effects of preinteraction expectancies on interaction involvement and behavioral responses in initial interaction. *Journal of Nonverbal Behavior*, *13*, 25–36.

Ickes, W., Patterson, M., Rajecki, D. W., & Tanford, S. (1982). Behavioral and cognitive consequences of reciprocal versus compensatory responses to preinteraction expectancies. *Social Cognition*, *1*, 160–190.

Kerckhoff, A. C., & Davis, D. E. (1962). Value consensus and need complementarity in mate selection. *American Sociological Review*, *27*, 295–303.

Koestner, R., & Wheeler, L. (1988). Self-presentation in personal advertisements: The influence of implicit notions of attraction and role expectations. *Journal of Social and Personal Relationships*, *5*, 149–160.

Lorr, M., & More, W. W. (1980). Four dimensions of assertiveness. *Multivariate Behavioral Research*, *15*, 127–138.

Marston, P. J., Hecht, M. L., & Robers, T. (1987). 'True love ways': The subjective experience and communication of romantic love. *Journal of Social and Personal Relationships*, *4*, 387–407.

McCroskey, J. C. (1977). Oral communication apprehension: A summary of recent theory and research. *Human Communication Research*, *4*, 78–96.

McCroskey, J. C., & McCroskey, L. L. (1986). The affinity-seeking of classroom teachers. *Communication Research Reports*, *3*, 158–167.

Menne, J. M. C., & Sinnett, R. E. (1971). Proximity and social interaction in residence halls. *Journal of College Student Personnel*, *12*, 26–31.

Neimeyer, R. A., & Mitchell, K. A. (1988). Similarity and attraction: A longitudinal study. *Journal of Social and Personal Relationships*, *5*, 131–148.

Norton, R. W. (1978). Foundation of a communicator style construct. *Human Communication Research*, *4*, 99–112.

Parks, M. (1982). Ideology in interpersonal communication: Off the couch and into the world. In M. Burgoon (Ed.), *Communication yearbook 5* (pp. 79–108). New Brunswick, NJ: Transaction.

Richmond, V. P. (1990). Communication in the classroom: Power and motivation. *Communication Education, 39*, 181–195.

Richmond, V. P., & Furio, B. J. (1985). *Affinity seeking in cross-gender dyads.* Paper presented at the annual convention of Speech Communication Association, Denver, CO.

Richmond, V. P., Gorham, J. S., & Furio, B. J. (1987). Affinity-seeking communication in collegiate female–male relationships. *Communication Quarterly, 35*, 334–348.

Richmond, V. P., McCroskey, J. C., & Davis, L. (1986). The relationship of supervisor use of power and affinity-seeking strategies with subordinate satisfaction. *Communication Quarterly, 34*, 178–193.

Roach, D. K. (1991). The influence and effects of gender and status on university instructor affinity-seeking. *Southern Communication Journal, 57*, 73–80.

Snyder, M. (1974). The self-monitoring of expression behavior. *Journal of Personality and Social Psychology, 30*, 526–537.

Snyder, M. (1979). Self-monitoring processes. In L. Berkowitz (Ed.), *Advances in experimental social psychology* (Vol. 12, pp. 85–128). New York: Academic.

Sprecher, S. (1987). The effects of self-disclosure given and received on affection for an intimate partner and stability of the relationship. *Journal of Social and Personal Relations, 4*, 115–127.

Thompson, C. A., & Frymier, A. B. (1991). *Affinity seeking in the classroom: Its impact on teacher credibility, student motivation, and learning.* Paper presented to the International Communication Association Convention, Chicago, IL.

Tolhuizen, J. H. (1989a). Affinity seeking in developing relationships. *Communication Reports, 2*, 83–91.

Tolhuizen, J. H. (1989b). Communication strategies for intensifying dating relationships: Identification, use, and structure. *Journal of Social and Personal Relationships, 6*, 413–434.

Woltjen, L. M., & Zakahi, W. R. (1987). *The assessment of the relationship among loneliness, affinity-seeking competence, and communication apprehension.* Paper presented at the Eastern Communication Association Convention, Syracuse, NY.

Zanna, M. P., & Pack, S. U. (1975). On the self-fulfilling nature of apparent sex differences in behavior. *Journal of Experimental Social Psychology, 11*, 583–591.

Chapter 5

Comforting Messages: Features, Functions, and Outcomes

Brant R. Burleson
Purdue University

During the last 10 years, considerable research has focused on the cognitive and motivational factors underlying the production of *comforting behaviors*, those actions directed at managing the emotional distress of others (e.g., Applegate, 1980; Applegate, Burke, Burleson, Delia, & Kline, 1985; Bar-Tal, Raviv, & Goldberg, 1982; Burleson, 1982, 1983a, 1984a; Eisenberg-Berg & Lennon, 1980; Samter & Burleson, 1984; Strayer, 1981; Yarrow & Waxler, 1976; Zahn-Waxler, Iannotti, & Chapman, 1982). The aim of this research has been to (a) identify the types of knowledge needed to generate highly sophisticated, sensitive comforting strategies, and (b) understand how personality and situational factors affect the motivation to construct such strategies. This research has led to a better understanding of how demographic factors, social cognition, value orientations, and features of interpersonal relationships affect the use of sensitive comforting messages (for reviews, see Burleson, 1984b, 1985). It has also contributed to an improved understanding of message production processes in general (see Burleson, 1987).

Although a good deal of attention has been given to factors underlying the production of comforting messages, only recently have researchers begun to examine outcomes associated with the use of these messages. There is a certain irony in this because a primary motive for research on the production of comforting messages has been the belief that "sophisticated" comforting strategies do a better job of relieving distress than less-sophisticated strategies.

Clearly, identifying effective or successful comforting strategies would have both theoretical and practical import. Theoretically, understanding which messages reliably yield certain outcomes should suggest much about how messages are interpreted, processed, and accorded particular meanings. Further, knowing which messages generally do the best job of relieving emotional distress would have significant implications for practice in therapy, counseling, and everyday helping.

Unfortunately, assessing the effects of comforting messages is no simple matter. Comforting has often not been adequately distinguished from other forms of communication. The features of effective comforting strategies have sometimes been specified only vaguely. Further, the nature of the outcomes supposedly produced by "effective" comforting strategies has not been sufficiently detailed. Indeed, as argued in the following, what effectiveness or success means in the context of comforting itself turns out to be a complex matter.

In an effort to build a foundation for more detailed and focused work, this chapter synthesizes and integrates much of the current literature on the effects of comforting messages. I begin by defining comforting and discussing schemes for representing qualitative differences in comforting messages. The chapter then articulates a framework for evaluating the effects comforting messages, arguing for a multidimensional approach to the assessment of message effects. The core of the chapter reviews studies conducted by my colleagues and me, as well as other researchers, that have assessed how people perceive and are affected by different comforting messages. The review also integrates work on comforting conducted by communication researchers with related work carried out in clinical and social psychology.

COMFORTING IN THE WORLD OF EVERYDAY LIFE

Definition

In our research, we have defined comforting strategies as messages having the goal of alleviating or lessening the emotional distresses experienced by others (Burleson, 1985). These distressed states are seen as arising from a variety of everyday hurts and disappointments. Several features and implications of this definition merit comment.

First, we view comforting as an activity directed at managing or modifying the *psychological* states of others. Although physical or material problems can contribute to a state of emotional distress, we have assumed that comforting activity focuses on the management of *feelings* rather than the treatment of physical or material conditions.

Second, we have focused our attention on comforting activity addressing the moderate feelings of disappointment or sadness that arise from everyday events. We have not dealt with the behavioral strategies used to cope with extreme feelings of depression or grief arising from extraordinary events (such as the loss of a spouse). Some research (e.g., Brockoop, 1973; Lindemann, 1965) suggests that these more intense emotional experiences require responses qualitatively different from those used to manage everyday emotional upsets. Although we have restricted ourselves to examining the more moderate and ordinary forms of emotional distress, research (e.g., DeLongis, Coyne, Dakof, Folkman, & Lazarus, 1982; Eckenrode, 1984; Kanner, Coyne, Schaefer, & Lazarus, 1981) suggests that success in coping with everyday upsets is one of the best predictors of mood, psychological well-being, and physical health.

Third, our research has focused on the *verbal* strategies through which people attempt to comfort distressed others. Clearly, empathy, understanding, and support can be conveyed through nonverbal channels (e.g., D'Augelli, 1974; Haase & Tepper, 1972; Shapiro, 1968; Shapiro, Foster, & Powell, 1968; Tepper & Haase, 1978), especially through warm touches (e.g., Brammer, 1985; Pattison, 1973). However, our efforts have focused on understanding the verbal means through which comfort is conveyed.

Fourth, as comfort is usually provided with the primary intention of benefiting another, we have viewed comforting as a form of altruistic behavior. This means that although providers of comfort may experience some benefit or self-gain as a result of their efforts (e.g., heightened self-esteem, an enhanced relationship with the other), these are secondary outcomes and not primary goals sought by the comforter (see Bar-Tal, 1976; Krebs, 1970).

Properties of Sophisticated Comforting Strategies

The Rogerian Approach to Comforting.   Several writers have offered analyses of sophisticated, good, or sensitive comforting strategies. Obviously, comforting is an activity in which counselors and psychotherapists regularly engage. In psychology, one popular analysis of comforting behavior has been forwarded by Rogers (1957, 1975) and his associates (Aspy, 1975; Carkhuff & Berenson, 1977; Truax & Carkhuff, 1967).

Rogers (1957) maintained that for a counselor to bring about improvement in a client, it was necessary and sufficient that the counselor express empathy, nonpossessive warmth (or unconditional positive regard), and genuineness (or congruence). *Empathy* refers to the degree to which therapists are successful in communicating their awareness and understanding of the client's feelings in language that is attuned to the client. *Respect* or *nonpossessive warmth* refers to the extent to which the therapist communicates nonevaluative caring and positive regard for the client, respecting the client as a person. *Genuineness* is the extent to which therapists are nondefensive, real, and authentic in their interactions with clients; whatever the therapist expresses is a real and significant part of himself or herself.

Empathy, warmth, and genuineness (often referred to collectively as the *therapeutic conditions*) supposedly bring about improvement because the climate fostered by these conditions maximizes the client's self-exploration, self-understanding, and development of appropriate plans of action (see Carkhuff & Berenson, 1977). Emotional hurt often stems from the invalidation of the self, either directly (e.g., rejection by a valued other) or indirectly (e.g., failing at something connected to one's self-concept). The therapeutic conditions convey to distressed others that their feelings are recognized and appreciated, that they are valued as persons, and that they are accepted by another (the helper) in the context of an honest relationship.

Although the therapeutic conditions do not by themselves remove the source of distressed others' hurts (e.g., personal rejections, task failures), they do provide the context in which people can explore and seek understanding of their feelings. The insights attained through guided exploration provide a basis for the development of plans that move distressed persons from where they are to where they want to be (see Carkhuff & Berenson, 1977). Thus, mental and emotional health is signaled not by how well people control external events (for, after all, many events are not within the direct control of the individual), but rather by how well one *responds* to events—cognitively, affectively, and behaviorally. In summary, Rogers' therapeutic conditions are held to facilitate exploration, insight, and understanding by distressed others that, in turn, facilitates the development of appropriate actions.

Although Rogers' work has been influential both within and outside clinical psychology, it also has been the target of frequent criticism. For example, some scholars (e.g., Lambert, DeJulio, & Stein, 1978) challenge Rogers' claim that therapist empathy, genuineness, and warmth are necessary and sufficient for client improvement. In addition, the reliability and validity of the instruments developed to assess empathy, genuineness, and warmth have been severely criticized (e.g., Beutler, Johnson, Neville, & Workman, 1973; Caracena & Vicory, 1969; Chinsky & Rappaport, 1970; Rappaport & Chinsky, 1972).

At least part of these methodological problems stem from the three therapeutic conditions having been assessed primarily through global ratings of taped or transcribed interactions (see Carkhuff, 1969; Truax & Carkhuff, 1967). Specific message features that might convey empathy, genuineness, and warmth have not been identified and used in assessing the provision of these qualities. Failure to identify specific message features for conveying the therapeutic conditions also has created problems in training efforts. Too often, instructions regarding the expression of empathy, genuineness, and warmth have been disappointingly general and vague, and few studies have detailed the crucial components of training programs that supposedly lead to enhanced effectiveness of helpers (see Lambert & DeJulio, 1977).

In spite of the conceptual and methodological problems in the Rogerian framework, it has enjoyed considerable popularity in the communication discipline. Although Rogers' work focuses on the contexts of counseling and psychotherapy, his principles have been generalized and applied to a variety of everyday interpersonal communication events, including supporting, sympathizing, and comforting (e.g., see Howell, 1982; Patton & Giffin, 1981; Stewart, 1986). Indeed, Rogers' principles are an integral part of the "ideology of intimacy" (Parks, 1982) that continues to characterize textbooks in interpersonal communication.

Unfortunately, most applications of Rogers' work in communication suffer from the same problems evident in counseling and clinical contexts. That is, message features through which empathy, genuineness, and warmth can be conveyed are usually not specified, so recommendations regarding the expression of these qualities are often disappointingly global and vague. The polar opposite also occurs: representing empathy as something conveyed through fixed verbal formulas (such as "what I hear you saying is . . ."). Actualizing imperatives to be empathic, genuine, and warm requires concrete specification of how these qualities can be expressed without reducing them to a few static phrases. Some progress in this regard has been made in the communication discipline by Applegate (1978, 1980) and his co-workers.

The Study of Comforting Messages in the Communication Discipline.   Drawing from the sociolinguistic theory of Bernstein (1975) and the structural-developmental theories of Werner (1957) and Piaget (1970), Applegate (1978; also see Applegate & Delia, 1980) proposed that comforting messages could be evaluated for the extent to which the feelings and perspective of a distressed other are explicitly acknowledged, elaborated, and granted legitimacy. Although parallels in the dimensions discussed by Rogers and Applegate are apparent, Applegate (1978, 1980) went further than most Rogerians in suggesting that messages intended to convey comfort could be coded for the extent to which they accepted, acknowledged, elaborated, and legitimized the feelings and perspective of a distressed other. Toward this end, Applegate developed a coding system composed of nine hierarchically organized categories; messages are assigned to levels of the hierarchy based on the presence or absence of specific features.

Applegate's coding system is composed of three major levels with three sublevels within each major level. Comforting messages scored within the lowest major level of the hierarchy either implicitly or explicitly deny the feelings and perspective of the distressed other (e.g., "You shouldn't be so upset about losing your boyfriend. After all, there are a lot of fish in the sea. So forget him and go catch yourself another one"). Messages providing an implicit recognition of the feelings and perspective of the distressed other are scored within the second major level of the hierarchy (e.g., "Gee, I'm sorry you guys broke up. I guess things like this happen though. Breaking up just seems to be a part of relationships"). Messages providing an explicit acknowledgment and elaboration of the other's feelings and perspective are scored within the highest major level of the hierarchy (e.g., "I know it must hurt. I know you're feeling a lot of pain and anger right now. And that's OK, 'cause I know you were really involved; you guys were together a long time and you expected things to work out differently'').

Several modifications and refinements of Applegate's original coding system have been presented (e.g., Applegate et al., 1985; Burleson, 1982; Ritter, 1979). Versions of this coding system have been applied in analyses of comforting messages produced by children, adolescents, and several different adult populations. Table 5.1 presents a detailed description of this coding system.

The hierarchically ordered categories of this system generally reflect the extent to which the feelings and perspective of a distressed other receive explicit acknowledgement, elaboration, and legitimation. However, there are several more specific ways in which highly sophisticated comforting strategies (as defined by this system) differ from unsophisticated strategies.

First, sophisticated comforting strategies project a greater degree of involvement with distressed others and their problems. Such strategies are more listener-centered (i.e., discover and explicate the *other's* feelings and perspective), whereas less sophisticated strategies are more speaker-centered (i.e., tell the other what the speaker thinks about the situation or how the speaker thinks the other should feel or act).

Second, sophisticated comforting strategies are evaluatively neutral. That is, these strategies generally describe and explicate feelings and the situations producing these feelings. Less sophisticated strategies often contain direct evaluations of feelings, persons, and actions connected with the distressful situation.

Third, sophisticated comforting strategies are more feeling centered. Sophisticated strategies tend to focus on the proximate causes of another's distressed state (i.e., the psychological and affective *reactions* to certain events), whereas less sophisticated strategies focus more on the distal causes of distress (i.e., the events themselves).

Fourth, sophisticated comforting strategies are generally more accepting of the distressed other. These strategies legitimize the feelings and point of view of the other rather than imposing the speaker's point of view.

Fifth, sophisticated strategies often contain a cognitively oriented explanation of the feelings being experienced by a distressed other. Due to the intensity and immediacy of their feelings, distressed persons may lack understanding of these feelings. The sensitive explication of these feelings may lead to insight and understanding by the distressed other, and thereby contribute to the other gaining distance from and a perspective on his or her feelings.

In summary, Applegate's hierarchical coding system conceptually and operationally defines sophisticated comforting strategies as those messages that explicitly acknowledge, elaborate, and legitimize the feelings and perspective of a distressed other. In addition, sophisticated comforting strategies contain

TABLE 5.1
Hierarchical Coding System for Sensitivity of Comforting Strategies

"What would you say to make a friend feel better about not receiving an invitation to another child's party?"

0. No response (subject is unable to think of anything to say).

I. *Denial of Individual Perspectivity*

The speaker condemns or ignores the specific feelings that exist in the situation for the person addressed. This denial may be either explicit or implicit.

  1. Speaker condemns the feelings of the other.

    "I'd tell her she had no reason to feel that way about not getting invited, and if she felt that way, she was no friend of mine."

  2. Speaker challenges the legitimacy of the other's feelings.

    "There's nothing to be upset about—it's just an old party."

  3. Speaker ignores the other's feelings.

    "I'd tell her there've been other parties, and she should be happy about going to them."

II. *Implicit Recognition of Individual Perspectivity*

The speaker provides some implicit acceptance of and/or positive response to the feelings of the other, but does not explicitly mention, elaborate, or legitimize those feelings.

  4. Speaker attempts to divert the other's attention from the distressful situation and the feelings arising from that situation.

    "When it's my party I'll invite you."

  5. Speaker acknowledges the other's feelings, but does not attempt to help the other understand why those feelings are being experienced or how to cope with them.

    "I'm sorry you didn't get invited to the party."

  6. Speaker provides a nonfeeling-centered explanation of the situation intended to reduce the other's distressed emotional state.

    "Maybe your invitation to the party got lost in the mail. Or maybe there just wasn't enough room to invite everybody in the whole class."

III. *Explicit Recognition and Elaboration of Individual Perspectivity*

The speaker explicitly acknowledges, elaborates, and legitimizes the feelings of the other. These strategies may include attempts to provide a general understanding of the situation. Coping strategies may be suggested in conjunction with an explication of the other's feelings.

  7. Speaker explicitly recognizes and acknowledges the other's feelings, but provides only truncated explanations of these feelings (often coupled with attempts to "remedy" the situation).

    "I know you feel bad about not going to the party, but you're my friend—lots of people like you. When my party comes up, I'll invite you."

  8. Speaker provides an elaborated acknowledgement and explanation of the other's feelings.

    "Gee, I'm really sorry about the party. I didn't mean to make you feel bad by mentioning it, but I know I did. It's not fun being left out. Maybe it's a mistake. I'll talk to Sharon. OK?"

  9. Speaker helps the other to gain a perspective on his or her feelings and attempts to help the other see these feelings in relation to a broader context or the feelings of other.

    "Well, I'd tell her that I really understand how she feels, that I haven't been invited to a special party sometimes and I know it hurts—you can feel rejected. But I'd say maybe Jean really wanted to have you but her parents wouldn't let her invite everybody. And that I've had parties where I couldn't invite everybody I wanted, and she probably has too. So it doesn't mean that Jean doesn't like her or anything, just maybe her mom was letting her have like only a few people."

Note. Adapted from Applegate (1980) and Burleson (1982). Roman numerals correspond to major levels of the coding system and Arabic numerals correspond to the sublevels at which specific message strategies are scored.

features that express receiver focus, evaluative neutrality, feeling centeredness, interpersonal acceptance, and insight or understanding.

The theoretical framework from which Applegate derived this hierarchical analysis of comforting strategies is that of *constructivism* (see Delia, O'Keefe, & O'Keefe, 1982), a perspective maintaining that the structure of behavior reflects the underlying structure of thought. Thus, comforting messages scored in the higher levels of this hierarchy are regarded as structurally and developmentally more sophisticated because explicitly acknowledging, elaborating, and legitimizing the other's feelings requires advanced cognitive abilities through which the other's perspective can be recognized, internally represented, coordinated with other relevant perspectives, and integrated with the speaker's own understanding of the situation. In other words, messages scored in the higher levels of the hierarchy are regarded as more sophisticated and advanced because they reflect greater complexity in thinking about people, feelings, social situations, and the process of communication.

A growing body of evidence supports the claim that higher level comforting strategies constitute more sophisticated and developmentally advanced modes of functioning. The analysis of message production developed within the constructivist perspective views the competence to produce sensitive comforting strategies as a developmental achievement (see Burleson, 1987; Delia et al., 1982). In particular, the ability to produce sophisticated message forms such as sensitive comforting strategies has been hypothesized to be a function of developmentally related differences in the complexity of persons' *interpersonal constructs*, the cognitive structures through which individuals interpret, evaluate, and anticipate the thoughts and behaviors of others. Consistent with these notions, several studies have found that the use of highly sensitive comforting strategies increases with age throughout childhood and adolescence (e.g., Burleson, 1982; Ritter, 1979). More important, studies employing samples of both children and adults have consistently found the use of sensitive comforting strategies positively associated with the complexity of persons' interpersonal constructs (e.g., Applegate, 1980; Burleson, 1983a, 1984a; see the reviews by Burleson, 1984b, 1985, 1987).

There is support, then, for the idea that comforting strategies coded in the higher levels of Applegate's hierarchy constitute more sophisticated and advanced forms of behavior. However, showing that higher level comforting strategies are more sophisticated is not equivalent to showing that these strategies are more *effective*. That is, without supporting evidence, it cannot be concluded that formally better strategies (i.e., cognitively more sophisticated forms of behavior) also are functionally better strategies (i.e., more effective at achieving their intended objective). Recently, several studies have examined whether the use of sophisticated comforting strategies is associated with desirable social outcomes. The remainder of this chapter reviews these studies and related work.

CONCEPTUAL AND METHODOLOGICAL ISSUES IN THE ASSESSMENT OF COMFORTING STRATEGY OUTCOMES

Problems in Assessing the Effects of Comforting Messages

Research assessing the effectiveness of different comforting strategies faces problems not encountered by work focusing on other communicative goals. For example, studies assessing the effectiveness of different informative or persuasive strategies can randomly assign subjects to different message treatments; the effects of message variables can then be assessed by looking at differences in knowledge or attitudes. However, both ethical and practical problems prevent the use of such experimental methods in studies of comforting.

Experimentally assessing the effectiveness of comforting messages requires samples of emotionally distressed persons. Obviously, one would not want to do anything to create such samples. Moreover, if confronted with persons experiencing "naturally induced" emotional distress, there is an obligation to do what one can to help such people. Randomly assigning distressed people to different message treatments might be viewed as ethically suspect, especially if it is possible that some message treatments might exacerbate, rather than relieve, the distressed condition. Further, there is no objective measure for determining the degree of emotional distress experienced by people. This makes it difficult (if not impossible) to assess levels of emotional distress either before or after exposure to comforting messages.

These practical and ethical concerns have led to the use of alternative research designs in the study of comforting. For example, some studies (e.g., Elliott, 1985) have examined how "naturally upset" people respond to the different comforting messages uttered spontaneously in clinical contexts. Other studies (e.g., Burleson & Samter, 1985a, Study 1) have used confederates trained to feign emotional distress and then evaluate the effectiveness of responses to their distress cues. Still other work (e.g., Samter, Burleson, & Murphy, 1987) has employed experimental designs asking subjects to rate the effectiveness of alternative comforting strategies. Although each of these designs has flaws, the triangulation achieved with multiple designs can yield reasonably sound conclusions about the effects of different comforting strategies.

A Framework for Examining the Effects of Comforting Messages

Too often, studies of comforting have been limited by reliance on a unidimensional conception of message effect. That is, researchers have frequently focused exclusively on the comparative utility of different strategies for relieving emotional distress in an immediately present context. Although this is surely an important outcome on which to focus, it is not the only significant outcome of comforting behavior. A bit of reflection suggests there are at least four classes of effects that should be considered when assessing outcomes of different comforting strategies.

The first and most obvious effect is whether sophisticated comforting strategies are successful in achieving their primary instrumental goal. That is, do sophisticated strategies generally do a better job of reducing distress than less sophisticated strategies? Are people suffering from emotional upsets likely to feel better after hearing sophisticated comforting strategies? These questions reflect concern with the immediate, instrumental outcome of comforting messages.

Ideally, though, the successful comforting interaction not only leads the distressed other to feel better in the immediate situation, but also leaves the other in a better position to cope with distressful events in the future. In other words, it is possible that over time, exposure to sophisticated comforting strategies helps people attain deeper understandings of their emotional dynamics and how they are likely to react in potentially distressful situations. These understandings may aid them in managing future situations more effectively. Thus, we should consider whether exposure to sophisticated comforting strategies enhances the recipient's long-term ability to cope with distressful situations.

Many theorists (e.g., Clark & Delia, 1979; Watzlawick, Beavin, & Jackson, 1967) suggested that, besides instrumental outcomes, virtually all messages have effects on the relationship between and identities of the interactants. This seems especially likely in the emotionally charged atmosphere of comforting encounters. For example, the quality of a helper's message may influence how the distressed other feels about the helper; more sophisticated strategies may result in greater liking for the helper. Observers of the comforting encounter also can use the helper's behavior as a source of information in making interpersonal evaluations. Less obviously, the quality of helpers' messages might exert some influence on how they feel about themselves and distressed others: A sophisticated strategy leading to some visible improvement in the other might enhance the helper's self-esteem and positive self-feeling as well as contribute to the helper's liking for the other. Thus, the comforting strategies used by a person may have rather immediate effects on interpersonal relationships and social identities.

The messages used also may have a cumulative effect on the quality of a helper's relationship with others. That is, persons who consistently use sophisticated comforting strategies may become more liked and have more friends than those who regularly use less sophisticated messages. Thus, the comforting strategies used by a person may have long-term effects on such matters as the maintenance and enhancement of interpersonal relationships.

In summary, there are at least four types of outcomes associated with the use of comforting strategies. Messages may be more or less effective in immediately easing the other's distress; messages also may be more or less useful in helping the other learn to cope with later instances of distress. The messages employed by a helper may further have both short-term and long-term effects on the quality of the helper's relationship with the distressed other, as well as on the helper's self-concept. The next section reviews research on different comforting strategies with respect to these outcomes.

RESEARCH ON THE EFFECTS
OF COMFORTING MESSAGES

Research on the Immediate, Instrumental Effects
of the Therapeutic Conditions

A tradition of research in clinical psychology devoted itself to establishing the effectiveness—even superiority—of the Rogerian therapeutic conditions as means of managing human distress. Summarized in several sources (Carkhuff & Berenson, 1977; Truax & Carkhuff, 1967; Truax & Mitchell, 1971), this research supposedly demonstrated that helpers expressing high levels of empathy, genuineness, and warmth brought about greater improvement in distressed others than helpers expressing lesser degrees of the therapeutic conditions. Although many of these studies were conducted with clinical populations (even patients of psychiatric hospitals), the conclusions drawn were expressed in quite general terms: High levels of the therapeutic conditions would relieve distress and improve functioning.

Unfortunately, many of the results reported in this research have not been widely replicated (e.g., Kurtz & Grummon, 1972). Moreover, many of the studies have been subjected to trenchant criticism (see the reviews of Lambert et al., 1978; Mitchell, Bozarth, & Krauft, 1977; Parloff, Waskow, & Wolfe, 1978). In particular, studies have been indicted for vague and ambiguous conceptual definitions of the skills examined, reliance on instruments of dubious reliability and validity, and numerous technical problems (e.g., small sample sizes, interpretation of marginally significant results, lack of randomization, failure to use control groups, use of raters not blind to experimental treatments, etc.).

Even those studies employing more rigorous research designs and specific conceptual and operational definitions of the therapeutic conditions have not yielded consistent support for the notion that high levels of the conditions ease emotional distresses associated with everyday hurts and disappointments. For example, Reisman and Yamokoski (1974) found that "empathic" responses (exemplified in scripted dialogues) were neither expected nor desired when college students sought help with personal problems from friends. In a follow-up, study, Venzor, Gillis, and Beal (1976) found that neither clients in counseling nor college students preferred empathic responses from friends or counselors when these responses were demonstrated in scripted discussions of personal problems. Replicating these latter findings, Barnett and Harris (1984) found that college students preferred supportive messages containing instrumental advice over those exhibiting the therapeutic conditions.

Similar results have been obtained in studies examining the utility of different response styles by telephone counselors. For example, Libow and Doty (1976) reported two studies comparing empathic-listening and active advice-giving styles of telephone counseling. In neither study was the empathic-listening style preferred by the college student participants. McWhirter and Marks (1972) found the rated empathy of telephone counselors' interactions with clients unrelated to either peer or supervisor ratings of counselor effectiveness. Stein and Lambert (1984) extensively reviewed the telephone counseling literature and concluded that it is "questionable whether receiving high versus low levels of these therapist conditions truly relates to client satisfaction" (p. 110).

At best, then, there is limited support for the claim that clients in therapy, seekers of help from telephone hotlines, or nonclinical populations seeking help from peers prefer helpers who behave in a fashion consistent with the therapeutic conditions. Moreover, there is little replicated work showing that the therapeutic conditions facilitate the solving of problems or the reduction of emotional distress. Several factors may account for these somewhat surprising conclusions.

First, as previously suggested, the therapeutic conditions often have not been clearly defined either conceptually or operationally. This means that there has been confusion about just what constitutes, for example, "empathic" responses (see Lambert et al., 1978). At an empirical level, such confusion raises the possibility that the operationalizations of the therapeutic conditions employed in some studies may not have been valid. Thus, preferences for and effects of the therapeutic conditions may not have been adequately tested.

Second, the therapeutic conditions may be useful for aiding the resolution of only some problems and emotional upsets. Even if insight and understanding are prerequisite for planning appropriate actions, it is not clear that the self-exploration facilitated by the therapeutic conditions is invariably the best route to insight and understanding. For example, some research (e.g., Barnett & Harris, 1984; Russell, Slaikeu, Tapp, Tulkin, & Walfisch, 1978) suggests that more directive approaches (i.e., advice giving, exposition, problem solving) are preferred by helpees and result in more favorable outcomes. D'Augelli, Danish, and Brock (1976) argued that the appropriateness of empathy and related responses depend on characteristics of the problem and the distressed other.

Third, views of the role and function of the therapeutic conditions need to be integrated with a broader understanding of the helping process. It may be, for example, that some problems and emotional upsets are best treated initially

with empathy, genuineness, and warmth. The therapeutic conditions may calm
the other, help the other get a grasp on the problem, and build motivation
to take appropriate action. Following this, however, other techniques (e.g.,
advice giving, problem solving, skill training) may best aid the resolution of
the situation.

From a communication perspective, the most severe problems in research
on the therapeutic conditions stem from (a) failure to distinguish between
characteristics of the communicator and characteristics of the messages employed by the communicator, (b) failure to distinguish between the verbal and
nonverbal features of message behavior, and (c) failure to identify the specific
features constituting and defining messages exhibiting high levels of the therapeutic conditions. This latter inadequacy is, perhaps, the most serious: Without
precise and unambiguous specification of the "effective ingredients" of empathic, warm, and genuine messages (i.e., specification of the components giving these messages their distinctive character and power), it is impossible to
design and conduct studies assessing whether such messages help people more
than alternatives. To serve both theoretical and pragmatic interests, researchers must be able to identify specific features of messages and determine if messages with these features help attain desired outcomes such as the provision
of emotional support and comfort.

Constructivist Research on the Immediate, Instrumental
Effects of Sophisticated Comforting Strategies

A major objective in the research on comforting conducted by my colleagues
and me has concerned whether those messages defined as sophisticated by constructivist theory do a better job of relieving emotional distress. This research
has been facilitated by the conceptual analysis of comforting messages developed in constructivist theory, as well as by related systems of message representation (such as Applegate's) that specify the features of strategies having different
degrees of sophistication. Several research designs have been employed in our
effort to assess whether comparatively sophisticated strategies are superior at
helping distressed others feel better.

Our initial investigation (Burleson & Samter, 1985a, Study 1) employed
confederates trained both to feign emotional distress and to evaluate the sensitivity of subjects' responses to their distress cues. Participants (73 college wom-
en) interacted with a confederate who pretended to be upset over having been
"dumped" by her boyfriend the prior evening. Immediately after this episode,
both the confederate and a concealed observer rated participants' behaviors
for involvement, concern, responsiveness, sympathy, and support. In addition, the interactions were videotaped and subsequently content analyzed. We
scored the sophistication of all comforting efforts using a modified form of Applegate's hierarchical coding system. Ratings of participant involvement, con-

cern, responsiveness, sympathy, and support were positively related to the number of comforting acts exhibited by participants. More important, rated sensitivity of the participant's behavior was strongly associated ($r = .53$) with the proportion of highly sophisticated comforting acts produced by the participant, but was unassociated ($r = -.12$) with the proportion of unsophisticated comforting acts (i.e., those scored in the lowest major level of the hierarchy). These results suggest that persons employing a high proportion of sophisticated comforting strategies are experienced (by the confederate) and perceived (by the observer) as offering more help, support, sympathy, and so on.

Although the findings of this study are intriguing, they do not unambiguously establish that perceptions of another's support and sensitivity are a function of the comforting strategies employed. For example, it is possible that participants using many sophisticated comforting strategies also systematically exhibited other nonverbal, paraverbal, or uncoded verbal behaviors that may have been responsible for the raters' impressions. This possibility suggested the need to examine people's perceptions of comforting strategies in isolation from potentially confounding factors. Consequently, we undertook an investigation aimed at obtaining unconfounded judgments of the sensitivity and effectiveness of different comforting strategies.

In this latter study (Burleson & Samter, 1985a, Study 2), participants (148 college students) read several hypothetical situations depicting a friend experiencing some form of emotional distress, examined a list of nine messages (one corresponding to each category in Applegate's hierarchy) that might be used to comfort the distressed friend, and then rated each message for effectiveness and sensitivity. In addition, participants ranked the nine messages for overall quality. Impressively, we found that mean effectiveness ratings, mean sensitivity ratings, and mean quality rankings of the messages corresponded exactly with the hierarchical ordering defined by Applegate's coding system. These results suggest that the theoretically based ordering of strategies represented in Applegate's hierarchical coding system closely corresponds with people's everyday intuitions about the content of effective and sensitive comforting messages. These findings were subsequently replicated in two other investigations (Samter et al., 1987, Studies 1 & 2).

An important question is whether comforting strategies are evaluated uniformly. That is, are judgments about what constitutes effective and sensitive comforting consensual, or are there individual differences in these judgments? We have addressed this question in two studies.

In the first investigation (Burleson & Samter, 1985b), participants (117 college students) read and ranked for overall quality several sets of comforting messages. As in our other work, one message within each set exemplified each of the nine levels in Applegate's coding system. Difference scores were computed for discrepancies between the ranks participants assigned the strategies and the theoretical order to the strategies. A low difference score meant that the participant evaluated the strategies in a manner highly consistent with the order specified by theory, and a high difference score indicated little agreement between the participant's ordering and the theoretical ordering. Also, because average rankings of the comforting strategies were found to correspond exactly with the theoretical ordering of these strategies (Burleson & Samter, 1985a, Study 2), a high difference score suggested a nonnormative or idiosyncratic evaluation of the comforting messages. Generally, these difference scores were only weakly and nonsignificantly correlated with several individual-difference variables, including biological gender, interpersonal construct differentiation, interpersonal construct abstractness, emotional empathy, and two aspects of communication apprehension. Moreover, the average difference score was low, indicating that evaluations of the comforting messages closely comformed with those specified by theory.

These findings were replicated and extended by Samter et al. (1987) in a study of comforting dialogues. Participants read conversations containing comforting strategies instantiating one of the three major levels of Applegate's hierarchy; subsequently, they made predictions about the effectiveness of the comforting effort and the desirability of the episode's outcome. Results indicated that the perceived value of different comforting strategies did not vary as a function of either individual or situational differences.

This series of studies demonstrates that comforting strategies identified by constructivist theory as more sophisticated are generally perceived as more sensitive and effective means of managing emotional upsets. Moreover, the perceived effectiveness and sensitivity of highly sophisticated strategies (as well as the perceived ineffectiveness and insensitivity of less sophisticated strategies) do not vary as a function of several individual-difference and situational factors. The consistency of these results is impressive, especially when contrasted with the ambiguous and contradictory findings populating the literature on the effects of the therapeutic conditions. Thus, there appear to be consensual notions (at least within the populations examined) about what constitutes "good" comforting messages, and these notions seem well captured by the constructivist analysis of message sophistication.

Recent research by Elliott and his colleagues in clinical and quasi-clinical contexts substantiates many of the findings of our studies on the effects of sophisticated comforting strategies. In an impressively detailed study, Elliott (1985) had college students discuss a problem of their choosing with counselors; these interactions were tape recorded. Subsequently, the tape of the interaction was played back for the students and they identified the four most helpful and the four least helpful comments made by the counselors. Analyses of the helpful comments identified both "task" and "interpersonal" clusters of comments. Within the task cluster, students perceived as most helpful those comments aiding them in getting a new perspective on their problem. These comments provided new information or new viewpoints contributing to increased insight, awareness, and cognitive restructuring. Within the interpersonal cluster, students perceived as most helpful those comments displaying appreciation of their feelings and sympathy with their situation. Also of interest, objective coders classified the comments students perceived most helpful as *interpretations, reflections,* or *reassurances*—all types of statements in which the helper articulates and legitimizes the other's feelings (see Elliott, Barker, Caskey, & Pistrang, 1982; Elliott, Stiles, et al., 1982; Goodman & Dooley, 1976).

Elliott's (1985) results provide further support for the notion that sophisticated comforting strategies—those acknowledging, elaborating, and legitimizing the feelings of the other while contextualizing the distress-producing situation—represent effective means of handling emotional upsets. Moreover, these finding are particularly significant because they provide insight about the utterances people subjectively experience as helpful. Importantly, Elliott's results have been replicated with both clinical and nonclinical populations (see Barkham & Shapiro, 1986; Elliott, James, Reimschuessel, Cislo, & Sack, 1985).

Research on the immediate, instrumental effects of comforting messages thus shows that people generally perceive theoretically sophisticated strategies as the most effective and sensitive means of responding to another's distress. Moreover, these perceptions do not vary as a function of several individual-difference and situational variables. More important, recent research by Elliott (1985) suggests that messages similar in structure to those regarded here as sophisticated are experienced by distressed others as particularly helpful. Converging bodies of evidence thus support the value of sophisticated comforting strategies for managing the emotional states of others.

Although it appears that sophisticated comforting strategies are useful ways of managing the distressed states of others, it should not be assumed that such strategies are invariably the best or most effective responses. In developing a specific comforting response, helpers need to consider individual characteristics of the distressed other, the relationship shared with the other, features of the social situation, and the cultural milieu in which comforting occurs. It is quite conceivable that relatively unsophisticated strategies might do the best job of comforting another in a specific situation. Presumably, the advanced cognitive processes of those able to produce sophisticated strategies enable them to determine the specific strategy most likely to comfort another in a particular situation. This, however, is a hypothesis that remains to be tested.

Research on the Long-Term, Instrumental Effects of Sophisticated Comforting Strategies

Studies of peer social support consistently find that persons receiving large amounts of support or having large support networks are better adjusted and better able to cope with stress than those receiving little support or having small support networks (see Albrecht & Adelman, 1987; Sarason & Sarason,

1985). Although important, these findings only show that the presence or amount of support from peers predicts coping and adjustment. Virtually no research has examined how differences in the quality of supportive or comforting messages affects the long-term ability of persons to cope with distressful events.

There are, however, several ways in which regular exposure to sophisticated comforting strategies might help recipients develop the resources necessary for the self-management of distressful situations. For example, message recipients might derive rules for the functional management of their emotions by analyzing comforting strategies to which they have been exposed. Such analyses could yield several rules for managing emotional distress, including: (a) don't suppress or ignore feelings, but rather work to explore, recognize, and articulate them, (b) view feelings as responses to specific situations (rather than as chronic conditions), (c) try to understand how particular features of situations, and their effects on hopes and goals, cause particular feelings, and (d) view distressful situations in the context of broader goals, ambitions, and hopes.

If such rules are internalized, practiced, and used, they may help people manage the disappointments and hurts they are sure to encounter. Relevant questions for empirical study thus include whether people have sets of rules for managing their own affective states (i.e., whether they have implicit theories of affect management); whether these rules are derived, at least in part, from the comforting strategies to which they have been exposed; and whether exposure to sophisticated comforting strategies provides people with a better basis for the self-management of their affective states than exposure to less-sophisticated strategies.

It is also possible that regular exposure to sophisticated comforting strategies enhances the social–cognitive development of message recipients. This may equip them with refined cognitive tools for understanding themselves, others, and affectively charged situations. Social–cognitive development (indexed by the degree of depth and detail exhibited in thinking about people and social situations) is one important factor underlying the ability to produce sophisticated comforting strategies (see the reviews by Burleson, 1985, 1987). It seems reasonable, then, to suppose that persons with advanced levels of social–cognitive development do a better job at self-comforting. However, the question remains whether regular exposure to sophisticated comforting strategies actually enhances the social–cognitive development of message recipients.

Some evidence suggests that sophisticated comforting messages serve such a function. For example, Applegate, Burleson, and Delia (1992; see also Delia, Burleson, & Kline, 1979) found that mothers capable of producing sophisticated comforting strategies had children with higher levels of social–cognitive development than mothers capable of producing only less sophisticated comforting strategies. However, these correlational results are far from definitive because (a) it was not directly shown that mothers capable of producing sophisticated comforting strategies used such strategies when interacting with their children, and (b) mothers capable of producing sophisticated comforting strategies also were capable of producing other sophisticated messages (such as advanced disciplinary strategies) known to be associated with higher levels of social–cognitive development in children (see Burleson, 1983b).

Samter, Burleson, and Basden (1989) reported some experimental evidence suggesting that exposure to sophisticated comforting strategies affects the social-cognitive abilities of message recipients. Applying theoretical concepts developed by O'Keefe and Delia (1982), Samter et al. argued that sophisticated comforting messages constitute more complex forms of behavior. Participants in this study read comforting messages at one of three levels of complexity and then wrote impressions of the source of the messages. The researchers reasoned that persons exposed to more sophisticated (or complex) messages would, in the effort to accommodate their representation of the environment to the degree of structural complexity in that environment, form more differentiated impressions of the message source than persons exposed to less sophisticated messages. Confirming this hypothesis, there was a significant effect for level of message sophistication on impression differentiation. However, this effect was qualified by an interaction with the perceiver's level of interpersonal cognitive complexity—an interaction showing the effect of message sophistication on the cognitions of recipients was strongest for those with complex cognitive systems. Although this study provides support for the idea that level of message sophistication influences persons' cognitive structuring of events, it does not establish that *continued* exposure to sophisticated comforting strategies affects level of social–cognitive development. Longitudinal research is needed to acquire more direct evidence.

In summary, it is possible that regular exposure to sophisticated comforting strategies facilitates the ability to self-manage emotional distress. Two mechanisms through which exposure to sophisticated comforting messages might influence the ability to self-manage distress have received some attention. As yet, however, no empirical evidence has conclusively shown that persons regularly exposed to sophisticated comforting strategies either derive rules for the functional management of affect from these strategies or develop advanced social–cognitive abilities.

Research on the Immediate, Relational Effects of Sophisticated Comforting Strategies

A small, but growing body of literature suggests that the users of sophisticated comforting strategies are perceived more positively than the users of less sophisticated strategies. For example, Burleson and Samter (1985a, Study 1) found that confederates trained to feign emotional distress in the presence of experimental participants better liked those participants employing a high proportion of sophisticated comforting strategies. In a study employing more rigorous, but less life-like procedures, Samter et al. (1987) found that participants reading conversations containing sophisticated comforting strategies rated the fictional source of the messages more positively than subjects reading conversations containing less-sophisticated strategies.

There is an obvious explanation for these results: People tend to like those who make them feel good (or, at least, make them feel less bad), and research surveyed previously indicates that sophisticated comforting strategies are more effective at reducing emotional distress than their less sophisticated counterparts. Indeed, it is conceivable that clumsy or insensitive comforting efforts may make distressed others feel worse, and thereby contribute to a negative evaluation of the comforter. The evaluations of uninvolved observers (such as those in the Samter et al., 1987, investigation) suggest that people use comforting behavior they observe as a basis for evaluating the social competence and likability of message producers. Comforting may be a salient activity in the world of everyday life, and people who comfort well thus may be better liked and viewed as more competent than those less skilled in this activity.

Interestingly, the results of a recent study by Notarius and Herrick (1988) show that the users of sophisticated comforting strategies feel better about themselves than do the users of less sensitive strategies. Participants interacted with a confederate who feigned distress about having been dumped by her boyfriend. Mood of the participants was assessed both before and after interacting with the confederate. Those using unsophisticated strategies were more anxious and depressed following the interaction than those using sophisticated strategies. In addition, users of less sophisticated strategies were more rejecting of the confederate following the episode than users of sophisticated strategies.

Perhaps users of unsophisticated strategies recognize their messages lack efficacy, and thus become frustrated with both their lack of success and the person they ineffectually seek to help (see DePaulo, 1982; Wortman & Lehman, 1985). If these outcomes are regularly experienced by the users of unsophisticated strategies, it wouldn't be surprising if they came to ignore or avoid comforting situations (thereby, of course, eliminating the possibility of improving their comforting skills). In contrast, users of sophisticated strategies probably experience higher levels of success, enjoy the feelings of accomplishment consistent with effective behavioral performance, and may receive expressions of appreciation from those they help. These positive experiences may lead users of sophisticated strategies to seek out situations in which they can practice and further develop their comforting skills.

In summary, the available evidence suggests that users of sophisticated comforting strategies are better liked, more positively evaluated, and feel better about both themselves and the distressed other. Users of highly sophisticated strategies thus not only benefit those experiencing distress, they also benefit themselves by leading others to form positive impressions of them and by building their own self-esteem.

Research on the Long-term Relational Consequences of Sophisticated Comforting Strategies

Given the findings just discussed, it is reasonable to suppose that the regular use of sophisticated comforting strategies is associated with positive, long-term relational consequences. Although this conclusion hasn't been firmly established, some evidence suggests that the use of unsophisticated comforting strategies is associated with relational difficulties.

Burleson, Applegate, Burke, Clark, Delia, and Kline (1986) had 75 grade school children complete a battery of six communication skills assessments, including the ability to produce sophisticated comforting strategies. Sociometric methods were employed with the participants to classify them into groups of popular, average, neglected, and rejected children. The researchers found that comforting skill best discriminated the groups of children, with those in the rejected group having significantly poorer comforting skills than children in any of the other groups. Children in the rejected group were those whom peers said they least liked to play with and found to be mean or nasty.

Although the correlational data of this study will not support strong causal inferences, much other research has found children's social and communicative skills causally related to their acceptance by peers (see the reviews by Burleson, 1986; Renshaw & Asher, 1982). Thus, it is reasonable to suggest that one factor contributing to the poor peer relationships of the rejected children was their inferior comforting skills. A child with poor comforting skills, even if well motivated, may make distressed peers feel worse rather than better, and many children have sharp memories for emotional hurts inflicted by peers.

Burleson and Waltman (1987) attempted to replicate the results of Burleson et al. (1986) with a group of preadolescents. Unfortunately, the task used by Burleson and Waltman to assess comforting skill failed to yield a meaningful range of scores (virtually all participants responded to the comforting situations with stereotypic strategies); thus, no relationship was found between comforting skills and peer acceptance. However, Burleson and Waltman did find that both peer- and teacher-based measures of the emotional support offered by preadolescents to classmates were positively associated with interpersonal cognitive complexity, a known correlate of comforting skill. These latter results are consistent with several studies (Kurdek & Krile, 1982; Marcus, 1980; McGuire & Weisz, 1982; Rothenberg, 1970) finding acceptance by peers positively related to children's affective and social role-taking abilities—abilities instrumental in the production of sophisticated comforting strategies (e.g., Burleson, 1984a).

The relationship between comforting skill and peer acceptance in adult populations was examined by Samter and Burleson (1990). These researchers had college students living in fraternities and sororities complete a battery of communication skill assessments and provide both positive and negative sociometric nominations for all members of their houses. There were significant negative correlations between comforting skill and the number of negative nominations received by an individual. That is, persons with poor comforting skills had more house members nominate them as someone they disliked. Although these correlational findings are open to several interpretations, they replicate Burleson et al.'s (1986) results with children, and are consistent with the hypothesis that poor comforting skills contribute to peer rejection.

In summary, limited evidence suggests that the ability to produce sophisticated comforting strategies may have long-term effects on the quality of people's interpersonal relationships. However, the potential long-term relational effects of comforting styles need much more extensive investigation.

CONCLUSION

Comforting strategies designated sophisticated by constructivist theory are perceived as more effective than unsophisticated strategies, and some evidence suggests that these strategies do a better job of relieving the emotional hurts of others. Moreover, regular exposure to sophisticated comforting messages may help recipients develop skills for the self-management of potentially distressful situations. Compared to persons using less-sophisticated comforting strategies, users of sophisticated strategies are better liked and more positively evaluated by both message recipients and observers. Further, users of sophisticated comforting strategies report feeling better both about themselves and those they try to help. Finally, there is some evidence suggesting that persons able to produce sophisticated comforting strategies have better relationships with peers than those less able to produce such strategies. In summary, the use of sophisticated comforting messages appears associated with several desirable outcomes.

Studies of message outcomes take on added significance in light of evidence suggesting that comforting is a highly consequential activity in the world of everyday life. Research indicates that the events prompting comforting efforts, though less intense than life crises, have serious implications for psychological and physical well-being (see DeLongis et al., 1982; Eckenrode, 1984; Kanner et al., 1981). Fortunately, sophisticated comforting strategies aid recipients in coping with stressful events, and thus improve the quality of people's lives. Consistent with these findings, people view comforting as a significant activity and place high value on the comforting skills of their friends (for a detailed discussion of the social significance of comforting activity, see Burleson, 1990).

Although existing findings about the effects of sophisticated comforting strategies are encouraging, there are many gaps in our knowledge that need filling. The results of most studies assessing the instrumental and relational effects of different comforting strategies are only suggestive and, therefore, need to be supplemented by more detailed empirical work. Carrying out such work will not be easy, for, as suggested, there are special problems associated with assessing the effects of comforting messages. Research designs such as those employed by Elliott (1985) offer promise of providing more valid, *in situ* assessments of the effects of different messages.

A primary goal for future research should be increasing the precision of our understanding about *how* comforting messages affect the emotional states of others. Knowing that a certain message is generally the most effective means of managing distress has some scientific value. However, such knowledge has limited practical utility because people need to know, not what generally works best, but rather what will work best in the particular situations they face. Giving useful advice about the provision of comfort in specific situations requires research on the factors leading to different forms of emotional distress. We also need more detailed knowledge about how a variety of contextual variables influences the interpretation and, hence, effects of comforting efforts. In particular, we need to know how aspects of the distressful event, features of the setting in which comforting occurs, and the character of the relationship between the helper and helpee influence the reception, processing, and effects of comforting messages.

Research examining how contextual factors mediate the influence of comforting messages, although motivated by the desire to provide practical advice about relieving emotional distress, also holds promise of deepening our theoretical understanding about how the human affective system works—about why certain events lead to pain, and about how certain cognitive experiences (i.e., hearing certain things said) can lessen this pain. For example, theorists writing from the perspective of attribution theory (e.g., Abramson, Seligman, & Teasdale, 1978; Brickman et al., 1982; Garber & Seligman, 1980; Rehm & O'Hara, 1979) suggested it is the cognitive appraisal of events, particularly their perceived controllability, that leads to experiences of depression or loss. This implies that comforting messages may bring relief to others by getting them to reappraise the situation and modify their attributions (see Valins & Nisbett, 1972). Indeed, some research indicates that emotions such as fear (e.g., Ross, Rodin, & Zimbardo, 1969) and anxiety (e.g., Wilson & Linville, 1982) can be modified through messages directed at modifying the attributions of recipients. Other researchers (see Albrecht & Adelman, 1987) suggested that effective comforting messages encourage catharsis or the venting of pent-up emotions.

These ideas signal that understanding the comforting process will require developing detailed models of the human affective system and the relation between affect and cognition. Studies examining how and why comforting messages work thus promise to tell us much about ourselves and our emotional lives.

REFERENCES

Abramson, L. Y., Seligman, M. E. P., & Teasdale, J. D. (1978). Learned helplessness in humans: Critique and reformulation. *Journal of Abnormal Psychology, 87*, 49–74.

Albrecht, T. L., & Adelman, M. B. (Eds.). (1987). *Communicating social support.* Newbury Park, CA: Sage.

Applegate, J. L. (1978). *Four investigations of the relationship between social cognitive development and person-centered regulative and interpersonal communication.* Unpublished doctoral dissertation, University of Illinois at Urbana-Champaign.

Applegate, J. L. (1980). Adaptive communication in educational contexts. *Communication Education, 29*, 158–170.

Applegate, J. L., Burke, J. A., Burleson, B. R., Delia, J. G., & Kline, S. L. (1985). Reflection-enhancing parental communication. In I. E. Sigel (Ed.), *Parental belief systems: The psychological consequences for children* (pp. 107–142). Hillsdale, NJ: Lawrence Erlbaum Associates.

Applegate, J. L., Burleson, B. R., & Delia, J. G. (1992). Reflection-enhancing parenting as antecedent to children's social-cognitive and communicative development. In I. E. Sigel, A. McGillicuddy-Delisi, & J. Goodnow (Eds.), *Parental belief systems: The psychological consequences for children* (Vol. 2, pp. 3–39). Hillsdale, NJ: Lawrence Erlbaum Associates.

Applegate, J. L., & Delia, J. G. (1980). Person-centered speech, psychological development, and the contexts of language usage. In R. St. Clair & H. Giles (Eds.), *The social and psychological contexts of language* (pp. 245–282). Hillsdale, NJ: Lawrence Erlbaum Associates.

Aspy, D. N. (1975). Empathy: Let's get the hell on with it. *Counseling Psychologist, 5*, 10–14.

Barnett, M. A., & Harris, R. J. (1984). Peer counselors and friends: Expected and preferred responses. *Journal of Counseling Psychology, 31*, 258–261.

Bar-Tal, D. (1976). *Prosocial behavior: Theory and research.* New York: Wiley.

Bar-Tal, D., Raviv, A., & Goldberg, M. (1982). Helping behavior among preschool children: An observational study. *Child Development, 53*, 396–402.

Barkham, M., & Shapiro, D. A. (1986). Counselor verbal response modes and experienced empathy. *Journal of Counseling Psychology, 33*, 3–10.

Bernstein, B. (1975). *Class, codes, and control: Theoretical studies towards a sociology of language* (Rev. ed.). New York: Schocken Books.

Beutler, L. E., Johnson, D. T., Neville, C. W., & Workman, S. N. (1973). Some sources of variance in accurate empathy ratings. *Journal of Consulting and Clinical Psychology, 40*, 167–169.

Brammer, L. M. (1985). *The helping relationship: Processes and skills* (3rd ed.). Englewood Cliffs, NJ: Prentice-Hall.

Brickman, P., Rabinowitz, V. C., Karuza, J., Jr., Coates, D., Cohn, E., & Kidder, L. (1982). Models of helping and coping. *American Psychologist, 37*, 368–384.

Brockoop, G. W. (1973). Crisis intervention: Theory, process, and practice. In D. Lester & G. W. Brockoop (Eds.), *Crisis intervention and counseling by telephone.* Springfield, IL: C. C. Thomas.

Burleson, B. R. (1982). The development of comforting communication skills in childhood and adolescence. *Child Development, 53*, 1578–1588.

Burleson, B. R. (1983a). Social cognition, empathic motivation, and adults' comforting strategies. *Human Communication Research, 10*, 295–304.

Burleson, B. R. (1983b). Interactional antecedents of social reasoning development: Interpreting the effects of parent discipline on children. In D. Zarefsky, M. O. Sillars, & J. R. Rhodes (Eds.), *Argument in transition: Proceedings of the Third Summer Conference on Argumentation* (pp. 597–610). Annandale, VA: Speech Communication Association.

Burleson, B. R. (1984a). Age, social–cognitive development, and the use of comforting strategies. *Communication Monographs, 51,* 140–153.

Burleson, B. R. (1984b). Comforting communication. In H. E. Sypher & J. L. Applegate (Eds.), *Communication by children and adults: Social cognitive and strategic processes* (pp. 63–104). Beverly Hills, CA: Sage.

Burleson, B. R. (1985). The production of comforting messages: Social–cognitive foundations. *Journal of Language and Social Psychology, 4,* 253–273.

Burleson, B. R. (1986). Communication skills and childhood peer relationships: An overview. In M. L. McLaughlin (Ed.), *Communication yearbook 9* (pp. 143–180). Beverly Hills, CA: Sage.

Burleson, B. R. (1987). Cognitive complexity. In J. C. McCroskey & J. A. Daly (Eds.), *Personality and interpersonal communication* (pp. 305–349). Newbury Park, CA: Sage.

Burleson, B. R. (1990). Comforting as everyday social support: Relational consequences of supportive behaviors. In S. Duck (Ed.), *Personal relationships and social support* (pp. 66–82). London: Sage.

Burleson, B. R., Applegate, J. L., Burke, J. A., Clark, R. A., Delia, J. G., & Kline, S. L. (1986). Communicative correlates of peer acceptance in childhood. *Communication Education, 35,* 349–361.

Burleson, B. R., & Samter, W. (1985a). Consistencies in theoretical and naive evaluations of comforting messages. *Communication Monographs, 52,* 103–123.

Burleson, B. R., & Samter, W. (1985b). Individual differences in the perception of comforting messages: An exploratory investigation. *Central States Speech Journal, 36,* 39–50.

Burleson, B. R., & Waltman, P. A. (1987). Popular, rejected, and supportive preadolescents: Social–cognitive and communicative characteristics. In M. L. McLaughlin (Ed.), *Communication yearbook 10* (pp. 533–552). Newbury Park, CA: Sage.

Caracena, P. F., & Vicory, J. R. (1969). Correlates of phenomenological and judged empathy. *Journal of Counseling Psychology, 16,* 510–515.

Carkhuff, R. R. (1969). *Helping and human relations.* New York: Holt, Rinehart & Winston.

Carkhuff, R. R., & Berenson, B. G. (1977). *Beyond counseling and therapy* (2nd ed.). New York: Holt, Rinehart & Winston.

Chinsky, J. M., & Rappaport, J. (1970). Brief critique of the meaning and reliability of "accurate empathy" ratings. *Psychological Bulletin, 73,* 379–382.

Clark, R. A., & Delia, J. G. (1979). *Topoi* and rhetorical competence. *Quarterly Journal of Speech, 65,* 187–206.

D'Augelli, A. R. (1974). Nonverbal behavior of helpers in initial helping interactions. *Journal of Consulting and Clinical Psychology, 21,* 360–363.

D'Augelli, A. R., Danish, S., & Brock, G. W. (1976). Untrained paraprofessionals' verbal helping behavior: Description and implications for training. *American Journal of Community Psychology, 4,* 275–282.

Delia, J. G., Burleson, B. R., & Kline, S. L. (1979, April). *Person-centered parental communication and the development of social–cognitive and communicative abilities: A preliminary longitudinal analysis.* Paper presented at the Central States Speech Association convention, St. Louis, MO.

Delia, J. G., O'Keefe, B. J., & O'Keefe, D. J. (1982). The constructivist approach to communication. In F. E. X. Dance (Ed.), *Human communication theory* (pp. 147–191). New York: Harper & Row.

DeLongis, A., Coyne, J. C., Dakof, G., Folkman, S., & Lazarus, R. S. (1982). Relation of daily hassles, uplifts, and major life events to health status. *Health Psychology, 1,* 119–136.

DePaulo, B. M. (1982). Social-psychological processes in informal help seeking. In T. A. Willis (Ed.), *Basic processes in helping relationships* (pp. 255–279). New York: Academic Press.

Eckenrode, J. (1984). Impact of chronic and acute stressors on daily reports of mood. *Journal of Personality and Social Psychology, 46,* 907–918.

Eisenberg-Berg, N., & Lennon, R. (1980). Altruism and the assessment of empathy in the preschool years. *Child Development, 51,* 552–557.

Elliott, R. (1985). Helpful and nonhelpful events in brief counseling interviews: An empirical taxonomy. *Journal of Counseling Psychology, 32,* 307–322.

Elliott, R., Barker, C. B., Caskey, N., & Pistrang, N. (1982). Differential helpfulness of counselor verbal response modes. *Journal of Counseling Psychology, 29,* 354–361.

Elliott, R., James, E., Reimschuessel, C., Cislo, D., & Sack, N. (1985). Significant events and the analysis of immediate therapeutic impacts. *Psychotherapy, 22,* 620–630.

Elliott, R., Stiles, W. B., Shiffman, S., Barker, C. B., Burstine, B., & Goodman, G. (1982). The empirical analysis of help-intended communications: Conceptual framework and recent research. In T. A. Wills (Ed.), *Basic processes in helping relationships* (pp. 333–356). New York: Academic Press.

Garber, J., & Seligman, M. E. P. (1980). *Human helplessness: Theory and applications.* New York: Academic Press.

Goodman, G., & Dooley, D. (1976). A framework for help-intended communication. *Psychotherapy: Theory, Research, and Practice, 13,* 106–117.

Haase, R. F., & Tepper, D. T., Jr. (1972). Nonverbal components of empathic communication. *Journal of Counseling Psychology, 19,* 417–424.

Howell, W. S. (1982). *The empathic communicator.* Belmont, CA: Wadsworth.

Kanner, A. D., Coyne, J. C., Schaefer, C., & Lazarus, R. S. (1981). Comparison of two modes of stress measurement: Daily hassles and uplifts versus major life events. *Journal of Behavioral Medicine, 4,* 1–39.

Krebs, D. L. (1970). Altruism: An examination of the concept and a review of the literature. *Psychological Bulletin, 73,* 258–302.

Kurdek, L. A., & Krile, C. (1982). A developmental analysis of the relation between peer acceptance and both interpersonal understanding and perceived social self-competence. *Child Development, 53,* 1485–1491.

Kurtz, R. R., & Grummon, D. L. (1972). Different approaches to the measurement of therapist empathy and their relationship to therapy outcomes. *Journal of Consulting and Clinical Psychology, 39,* 106–115.

Lambert, M. J., & DeJulio, S. S. (1977). Outcomes in Carkhuff's human resource development: Where's the donut? *Counseling Psychologist, 6,* 79–86.

Lambert, M. J., DeJulio, S. S., & Stein, D. M. (1978). Therapist interpersonal skills: Process, outcome, methodological considerations, and recommendations for future research. *Psychological Bulletin, 85,* 467–489.

Libow, J. A., & Doty, D. W. (1976). An evaluation of empathic listening in telephone counseling. *Journal of Counseling Psychology, 23,* 532–537.

Lindemann, E. (1965). Symptomatology and management of acute grief. In H. J. Parad (Ed.), *Crisis intervention: Selected readings* (pp. 7–21). New York: Family Service Association of America.

Marcus, R. F. (1980). Empathy and popularity of preschool children. *Child Study Journal, 10,* 133–145.

McGuire, K. D., & Weisz, J. R. (1982). Social cognition and behavior correlates of preadolescent chumship. *Child Development, 53,* 1478–1484.

McWhirter, J. J., & Marks, S. E. (1972). An investigation of the relationship between the facilitative conditions and peer and group leader ratings of perceived counselor effectiveness. *Journal of Clinical Psychology, 28,* 116–117.

Mitchell, K. M., Bozarth, J. D., & Krauft, C. C. (1977). A reappraisal of the therapeutic effectiveness of accurate empathy, non-possessive warmth, and genuineness. In A. S. Gurman & A. M. Razin (Eds.), *Effective psychotherapy: A handbook of research* (pp. 482–502). New York: Pergamon Press.

Notarius, C. I., & Herrick, L. R. (1988). Listener response strategies to a distressed other. *Journal of Social and Personal Relationships, 5,* 97–108.

O'Keefe, B. J., & Delia, J. G. (1982). Impression formation and message production. In M. E. Roloff & C. R. Berger (Eds.), *Social cognition and communication* (pp. 33–72). Beverly Hills, CA: Sage.

Parks, M. R. (1982). Ideology of interpersonal communication: Off the couch and into the world. In M. Burgoon (Ed.), *Communication yearbook 5* (pp. 79–108). New Brunswick, NJ: Transaction.

Parloff, M. B., Waskow, I., & Wolfe, B. (1978). Research on therapist variables in relation to process and outcome. In S. L. Garfield & A. E. Bergin (Eds.), *Handbook of psychotherapy and behavior change: An empirical analysis* (2nd ed., pp. 233–282). New York: Wiley.

Pattison, J. E. (1973). Effects of touch on self-exploration and the therapeutic relationship. *Journal of Consulting and Clinical Psychology, 40,* 170–175.

Patton, B. R., & Giffin, K. (1981). *Interpersonal communication in action: Basic text and readings* (3rd ed.). New York: Harper & Row.

Piaget, J. (1970). Piaget's theory. In P. H. Mussen (Ed.), *Carmichael's handbook of child psychology* (3rd ed., pp. 703–732). New York: Wiley.

Rappaport, J., & Chinsky, J. M. (1972). Accurate empathy. Confusion of a construct. *Psychological Bulletin, 77,* 400–404.

Rehm, L. P., & O'Hara, M. W. (1979). Understanding depression. In I. H. Frieze, D. Bar-Tal, & J. S. Carroll (Eds.), *New approaches to social problems* (pp. 209–236). San Francisco: Jossey-Bass.

Reisman, J. M., & Yamokoski, T. (1974). Psychotherapy and friendship: An analysis of the communications of friends. *Journal of Counseling Psychology, 21,* 269–273.

Renshaw, P. D., & Asher, S. R. (1982). Social competence and peer status: The distinction between goals and strategies. In K. H. Rubin & H. D. Ross (Eds.), *Peer relationships and social skills in childhood* (pp. 375–395). New York: Springer-Verlag.

Ritter, E. M. (1979). Social perspective-taking ability, cognitive complexity, and listener-adapted communication in early and late adolescence. *Communication Monographs, 46,* 40–51.

Rogers, C. R. (1957). The necessary and sufficient conditions of therapeutic personality change. *Journal of Consulting Psychology, 21,* 95–103.

Rogers, C. R. (1975). Empathic: An unappreciated way of being. *Counseling Psychologist, 5,* 2–10.

Ross, L., Rodin, J., & Zimbardo, P. G. (1969). The reduction of fear through induced cognitive-emotional misattribution. *Journal of Personality and Social Psychology, 12,* 279–288.

Rothenberg, B. B. (1970). Children's social sensitivity and the relationship to interpersonal competence, intrapersonal comfort, and intellectual level. *Developmental Psychology, 2,* 335–350.

Russell, M., Slaikeu, K. A., Tapp, J. T., Tulkin, S. R., & Walfisch, S. (1978). The relationship between technical effectiveness and task-oriented work in telephone counseling. *Crisis Intervention, 9,* 96–101.

Samter, W., & Burleson, B. R. (1984). Cognitive and motivational influences on spontaneous comforting behavior. *Human Communication Research, 11,* 231–260.

Samter, W., & Burleson, B. R. (1990, June). *The role of affectively oriented communication skills in the friendships of young adults: A sociometric study.* Paper presented at the International Communication Association convention, Dublin.

Samter, W., Burleson, B. R., & Basden, L. (1989). Behavioral complexity is in the eye of the beholder: Effects of cognitive complexity and message complexity on impressions of the source of comforting messages. *Human Communication Research, 15,* 612–629.

Samter, W., Burleson, B. R., & Murphy, L. (1987). Comforting conversations: Effects of strategy type on evaluations of messages and message producers. *Southern Speech Communication Journal, 52,* 263–284.

Sarason, I. G., & Sarason, B. R. (Eds.). (1985). *Social support: Theory, research, and applications.* Dordrecht, Netherlands: Martinus Nijhoff.

Shapiro, J. G. (1968). Relationships between visual and auditory cues of therapeutic effectiveness. *Journal of Clinical Psychology, 34,* 236–269.

Shapiro, J. G., Foster, C. P., & Powell, T. (1968). Facial and bodily cues of genuineness, empathy, and warmth. *Journal of Clinical Psychology, 34,* 233–236.

Stein, D. M., & Lambert, M. J. (1984). Telephone counseling and crisis intervention: A review. *American Journal of Community Psychology, 12,* 101–126.

Stewart, J. (Ed.). (1986). *Bridges not walls* (4th ed.). New York: Random House.

Strayer, F. F. (1981). The nature and organization of altruistic behavior among preschool children. In J. P. Rushton & R. M. Sorrentino (Eds.), *Altruism and helping behavior: Social, personality, and developmental perspectives*. Hillsdale, NJ: Lawrence Erlbaum Associates.

Tepper, D. T., & Haase, R. F. (1978). Verbal and nonverbal communication of facilitative conditions. *Journal of Counseling Psychology*, *25*, 35–44.

Truax, C. B., & Carkhuff, R. R. (1967). *Toward effective counseling and psychotherapy*. Chicago: Aldine.

Truax, C. B., & Mitchell, K. (1971). Research on certain therapist characteristics. In A. Bergin & S. Garfield (Eds.), *Handbook of psychotherapy and behavior change* (pp. 193–214). New York: Wiley.

Valins, S., & Nisbett, R. E. (1972). Attribution processes in the development and treatment of emotional disorders. In E. E. Jones, D. E. Kanouse, H. H. Kelley, R. E. Nisbett, S. Valins, & B. Weiner (Eds.), *Attribution: Perceiving the causes of behavior* (pp. 270–299). Morristown, NJ: General Learning Press.

Venzor, E., Gillis, J. S., & Beal, D. G. (1976). Preference for counselor response styles. *Journal of Counseling Psychology*, *23*, 538–542.

Watzlawick, P. H., Beavin, J. B., & Jackson, D. (1967). *The pragmatics of human communication*. New York: Norton.

Werner, H. (1957). The concept of development from a comparative and organismic point of view. In D. B. Harris (Ed.), *The concept of development* (pp. 125–146). Minneapolis: University of Minnesota Press.

Wilson, T. D., & Linville, P. W. (1982). Improving the academic performance of college freshman. Attribution therapy revisited. *Journal of Personality and Social Psychology*, *42*, 367–376.

Wortman, C. B., & Lehman, D. R. (1985). Reactions to victims of life crises. Support attempts that fail. In I. G. Sarason & B. R. Sarason (Eds.), *Social support: Theory, research, and application* (pp. 463–489). Dordrecht, Netherlands: Martinus Nijhoff.

Yarrow, M. R., & Waxler, C. Z. (1976). Dimensions and correlates of prosocial behavior in young children. *Child Development*, *47*, 118–125.

Zahn-Waxler, C., Iannotti, R., & Chapman, M. (1982). Peers and prosocial development. In K. H. Rubin & H. S. Ross (Eds.), *Peer relationships and social skills in childhood* (pp. 133–162). New York: Springer-Verlag.

Chapter 6

Communication Strategies in Conflict and Mediation

Alan L. Sillars
William W. Wilmot
University of Montana

Conflict is an affliction common to all of us, however, the ways that people "struggle" with one another are quite diverse. One married couple might not ever discuss important issues, yet the next will argue incessantly over minutia. Of interest to most students, researchers, and practitioners in the area of dispute resolution is how the process of conflict, with its many idiosyncratic elements, relates to conflict and relationship outcomes. There is a touch of idealism revealed in our belief that appropriate control over the process of communication may lead to more equitable, humane, and satisfying forms of conflict than are often experienced. Still, the relationship between communication and conflict is not straightforward. Sometimes the ostensibly "best" forms of communication lead to the worst consequences and vice versa.

In this chapter, we consider how dispute resolution is shaped by styles and strategies of communication. To narrow the topic slightly we have focused mostly on marital and intimate dyads, although we believe that most of the points raised in this chapter extend to other contexts as well. Our description of communication in conflict entails a logical sequence of steps. First, one must be able to describe what people do when they have conflict; for example, they may lash out, apologize, sulk, laugh, or disclose. Toward this end, we present a descriptive taxonomy of conflict styles and discuss the implications of each style. The taxonomy was developed and refined from repeated observations of interpersonal and marital conflict. Different versions of the taxonomy have been used to analyze conversations of married couples (Burggraf & Sillars, 1987; Fitzpatrick, Fallis, & Vance, 1982; Pike & Sillars, 1985; Zietlow & Sillars,

1988), college roommates (Sillars, 1981), and decision-making groups (Holmes & Poole, 1991).

The second step in our analysis is to describe the characteristics of communication systems. This involves a shift in the level of analysis from individual messages to recurring patterns of communication. System characteristics are potentially more revealing than individual styles. A particular form of communication, say a single angry outburst or even a series of outbursts, may reveal little about the interpersonal relationship that is observed until the recurring events that elicit the outbursts are understood. This is hardly a new idea but it is difficult to put into practice. It is simply easier to describe individual conflict styles than it is to describe patterns of interaction. Our discussion focuses on five properties of conflict patterns: variety, symmetry, continuity, stationarity, and spontaneity.

The third step is to consider communication strategies used by third parties to alter conflict within the primary dyad. We are specifically concerned with conflict mediation, an intervention process in which a neutral third party helps conflicting individuals come to a voluntary settlement. There is a natural connection between mediation and basic research on communication in conflict, as mediation is fundamentally a communication activity (see Donohue, 1991). The most effective mediator strategies grow from an informed analysis of the communication strategies of the conflict parties. A mediator's role is often to disrupt noncollaborative strategizing by the principal parties and to temporarily alter communication patterns that block collaborative agreements.

As the titles of this chapter and book suggest, the organization of conflict is to some extent strategic, meaning that people attempt to carry out planned sequences of conflict in order to achieve their goals. The language of strategies and tactics is familiar in the conflict literature, partly due to the militaristic origins and overtones of much conflict research (e.g., Bartos, 1970; Etzioni, 1967; Hocker & Wilmot, 1991; Shelling, 1960). However, the implication that conflict is a strategic event is only partly correct. Although individuals behave strategically at times, at other times conflicts proceed without clear goals and plans. Much conflict behavior is experienced as ''just happening.'' The spouse who is criticized by the other may automatically respond with a counter complaint and not make a reflective choice about those behaviors (Baxter & Philpott, 1983; Gottman, 1982). In order to avoid confusing such reflex behaviors with planned sequences of conflict, we use the term *style* to describe types of communicative acts and the term *pattern* to describe the larger sequence of acts. The terms *strategy* and *strategizing* refer explicitly to particular goal-directed acts and to the activity of planning.

In the next section of this chapter we discuss individual communication styles used in interpersonal conflict. The subsequent section describes organizational properties of communication patterns that seem related to compatibility and management of conflict. The third and final section of the chapter considers how third-party mediators strategize in order to restructure individualistic communication patterns.

A DESCRIPTIVE TAXONOMY OF COMMUNICATION IN CONFLICT

Most research on communication and conflict has focused on directness (i.e., the decision to confront or avoid), affect (hostility vs. affiliation), or a combination of these two dimensions (Sillars, Colletti, Parry, & Rogers, 1982; Sillars & Weisberg, 1987). The most basic decision in any conflict is whether to confront or avoid an issue (Raush, Barry, Hertel, & Swain, 1974). However, this is not strictly speaking an either–or matter, as people may partly acknowledge their grievances and, at the same time, partly obscure or deny them. Conflict styles range on a continuum from maximally direct (i.e., threats and insults) to maximally indirect (i.e., outright denial of conflict), with several in-between styles that are only partially explicit (e.g., joking or intellectualizing about conflict). Further, there does not appear to be an absolute relationship between the directness of the style and the effects it has on interpersonal conflicts. Studies have observed that some harmonious couples communicate about conflicts very directly, whereas other harmonious couples avoid conflicts (Raush et al., 1974; Sillars & Weisberg, 1987).

Affect is a second important dimension of conflict styles. Some styles are hostile (e.g., confrontation), others are neutral or friendly (e.g., conciliatory behavior and humor), and still other styles, such as conflict avoidance, are inconsistent or unclear in the sort of emotion expressed. The implications of affect are reasonably straightforward. Generally, people who are more compatible (i.e., satisfied, well-adjusted, and the like) are more friendly to one another. For example, they make fewer confrontational statements, speak in a more positive vocal tone, sit closer together, touch one another more, and so forth (see Sillars & Weisberg, 1987). The main point of doubt about affect is whether negative communication is more a symptom or cause of incompatibility in relationships.

The following section describes seven styles of communication that are the basis of an analytic scheme used to study interpersonal and marital conflicts. The categories are revised from an earlier analytic scheme (see Sillars et al., 1982). The complete category system is illustrated in Table 6.1. In this scheme, "confrontive" and "analytic" remarks represent clear examples of engagement styles of conflict, whereas "denial and equivocation," "topic management," and "noncommittal" remarks represent nonengagement styles. "Irreverent" and "conciliatory" remarks fall in between the clear examples of engagement and non-engagement styles. Affect separates confrontive remarks, which are hostile, from conciliatory, analytic, irreverent, and non-

TABLE 6.1
Summary of Conflict Codes

Conflict Codes	*Illustrations*
A. *Denial and Equivocation*	
1. *Direct denial.* Statements that deny that a conflict is present.	"That's not a problem."
2. *Implicit denial.* Statements that imply denial by providing a rationale for a denial statement, although the denial is not explicit.	"We've never had enough money to disagree over." (In response to a question about disagreements over money.)
3. *Evasive remarks.* Failure to acknowledge or deny the presence of a conflict following a statement or inquiry about the conflict by the partner.	"That could be something that a person might resent but I don't know."
B. *Topic Management*	
4. *Topic shifts.* Statements that terminate discussion of a conflict issue before each person has fully expressed an opinion or before the discussion has reached a sense of completion.	"Okay, the next issue is. . . ." (The preceding statement occurs before each person has disclosed his or her opinion on the topic.)
5. *Topic avoidance.* Statements that explicitly terminate discussion of a conflict issue before it has been fully discussed.	"I don't want to talk about that." "This isn't getting us anywhere. Let's move on."
C. *Noncommittal Remarks*	
6. *Noncommittal statements.* Statements that neither affirm nor deny the presence of conflict and which are not evasive replies or topic shifts.	"The kids are growing up so fast I can't believe it."
7. *Noncommittal questions.* Unfocused and conflict-irrelevant questions.	"What do you think?" "Was it last summer we went to Maine?"
8. *Abstract remarks.* Abstract principles, generalizations, or hypothetical statements which are not evasive remarks.	"All people are irritable sometimes."
9. *Procedural remarks.* Procedural statements that supplant discussion of conflict.	"It's your turn to talk." "You aren't speaking loud enough."
D. *Irreverent Remarks*	
10. *Friendly joking.* Friendly joking or laughter.	"We need to clean the house or torch it [stated in a friendly tone of voice]."
E. *Conciliatory Remarks*	
11. *Supportive remarks.* Statements that refer to understanding, support, acceptance, positive regard for the partner, shared interests and goals, compatibilities with the partner, or strengths of the relationship.	"I can see why you would be upset." "You don't stay irritable long."
12. *Concessions.* Statements that express a willingness to change, show flexibility, make concessions or consider mutually acceptable solutions to conflicts.	"I think I could work on that more." "I think we have a good chance of working this out."
13. *Acceptance of responsibility.* Statements that attribute responsibility for conflict to self or to both parties.	"I think we've both contributed to the problem." "Okay. That one's my fault, I guess."

(Continued)

166

TABLE 6.1
(Continued)

Conflict Codes	Illustrations
F. Analytic Remarks	
14. *Descriptive statements.* Nonevaluative statements about observable events related to conflict.	"I criticized you yesterday for getting angry with the kids."
15. *Disclosive statements.* Nonevaluative statements about events related to conflict which the partner cannot observe, such as thoughts, feelings, intentions, motivations, and past history.	"I swear I never had such a bad week as that week." "I didn't think we'd be able to talk about the kids without yelling."
16. *Qualifying statements.* Statements that explicitly qualify the nature and extent of conflict.	"Communication is mainly a problem when we're tired."
17. *Soliciting disclosure.* Nonhostile questions about events related to conflict that cannot be observed (thoughts, feelings, intentions, motives, or past history).	"What were you thinking when you said. . . .''
18. *Soliciting criticism.* Nonhostile questions soliciting criticism of oneself.	"Does it bother you when I stay up late?"
G. Confrontative Remarks	
19. *Personal criticism.* Remarks that directly criticize the personal characteristics or behaviors of the partner.	"Sometimes you leave and you don't say goodbye or anything. You just walk right out." "I can't believe you let that one incident ruin our whole evening."
20. *Rejection.* Statements in response to the partner's previous statements that imply personal antagonism toward the partner as well as disagreement.	"Oh come on." "You're exaggerating."
21. *Hostile imperatives.* Requests, demands, arguments, threats, or other prescriptive statements that implicitly blame the partner and seek change in the partner's behavior.	"If you're not willing to look for a new job then don't complain to me about it."
22. *Hostile jokes.* Joking, teasing or sarcasm at the expense of the partner.	"It's very easy to say 'Gee I *really* appreciate you' [said mockingly]."
23. *Hostile questions.* Directive or leading questions that fault the partner.	"Who does most of the cleaning around here?"
24. *Presumptive remarks.* Statements that attribute thoughts, feelings, motivations or behaviors to the partner that the partner does not acknowledge.	"You're purposefully making yourself miserable."
25. *Denial of responsibility.* Statements that minimize or deny personal responsibility for conflict.	"That's not my fault." "You can't blame me for everything."

committal remarks, which are friendly or neutral. The styles are considered here roughly in the order of increasing directness.

Denial and Equivocation

Denial and equivocation refer to statements that either directly deny the existence of a conflict, imply that there is no conflict, or that present an evasive, self-invalidating response. Denial, really a form of lying, is the most blatant instance of conflict avoidance. In the research that Sillars and colleagues reported (Burggraf & Sillars, 1987; Pike & Sillars, 1985; Sillars, 1981), instances of denial were identified by comparing what people privately reported in questionnaires to what they said in a conversation with their partner. In the conversations, people were given a list of relationship conflicts (e.g., lack of time spent together, disagreements about cleaning or caring for the house or apartment) and were asked to discuss whether these topics were a problem in the relationship. If a person reported on the questionnaire that an issue represented a relationship problem but denied it to the partner, the statement was coded as an instance of denial.

Evasive remarks occur when one person asks a question or makes a statement about conflict and the other person responds ambiguously. Evasive remarks are related to the concept of "disqualification." Disqualification is the creation of a message that invalidates itself through obscurity (Bavelas, Black, Chovil, & Mullett, 1992; Watzlawick, Beavin, & Jackson, 1967). The message may be vague, ambiguous, or paradoxical, thus providing an unclear statement about the interpersonal relationship. Disqualifying remarks mostly occur when people see themselves in a "bind" (i.e., an approach–avoidance conflict). When given a choice between the awkward truth (e.g., "I don't like the gift you gave me and I am going to return it"), an outright lie (e.g., "The gift is perfect, I really love it"), and a disqualifying response (e.g., "I appreciate your thoughtfulness"), people usually say that they would choose the latter (Bavelas et al., 1992).

The most prolific avoiders we have observed have been college roommates. Over one fifth of the statements made by roommates during conversations about their relationship were some form of denial or equivocal remark (Sillars, 1980). Some of these statements represented a schizophrenic form of equivocation where the speaker first acknowledged a conflict and then tried to take it back, often in the same sentence (e.g., "I get pretty ticked off sometimes but it's not really a problem"). The heavy use of denial by roommates is to be expected, given the awkward and unprecedented social arrangement that roommates have. The fact that they live in the same house and sometimes in the same room guarantees conflict. However, because the decision to live together is for financial, not personal reasons, many roommates are strangers both before and after they decide to do dishes together. Because of the "intimate but not intimate'' nature of the relationship, the conflicts of roommates tend to be characterized by much brooding, nervous tension, and denial.

Married couples express conflict more freely than college roommates but they still use denial and equivocation frequently. This is particularly the case with more traditional couples (Sillars, Pike, Jones, & Redmon, 1983), as well as middle-aged and elderly couples (Zietlow & Sillars, 1988), who are presumably more traditional than young couples. Although traditional couples do not think of themselves as conflict avoiders (Fitzpatrick, 1988), their recorded conversations demonstrate avoidance (Burggraf & Sillars, 1987), probably because of an overriding concern for tactfulness and discretion in communication (Fitzpatrick, 1988). Nontraditional couples are less apt to censor themselves because they believe open communication to be of fundamental importance.

Topic Management

The second most obvious way of avoiding conflict is to change the subject of conversation. Again, the roommates studied by Sillars (1981) were skilled at this form of conflict avoidance. Given a choice of talking about the conflict between themselves, the conflict between two roommates down the hall, or the faults of a third roommate, individuals seemed much more at ease with the latter two options. Among married couples, middle-aged, traditional, and ''separate'' couples (i.e., those who prefer high autonomy in the relationship) are more apt to terminate the discussion of conflict using topic shifts (Sillars et al., 1983; Zietlow & Sillars, 1988), thus suggesting their discomfort with direct communication about conflict.

Topic management can itself be a source of conflict, as the other party may resist a topic shift. The party who controls the topic is able to set the agenda for the relationship by implicitly deciding which issues are important to address and when they can be considered. Topic management can become overtly confrontive as in the case of ''cross complaining'' (Gottman, 1979). Cross complaining occurs when couples alternate in expressing their feelings about unrelated problems, rather than acknowledging and discussing problems one at a time. When instances of topic control become overtly competitive, as in the case of cross complaining, they cease to represent a form of conflict avoidance and are more descriptive of the confrontive style of conflict.

Noncommittal Styles

Somewhere in between clear examples of avoidance and engagement are remarks that neither deny nor acknowledge conflict issues. Noncommittal styles may take a variety of forms, including unfocused questions (e.g., ''What do you think?''), abstract or vague generalities (e.g., ''Nothing in life that is worthwhile comes easily''), ''intellectualizing'' (''The deeper the issue the more your self is threatened''), discussion of friends, acquaintances, and relatives (''Mom always said that marriage is hard work''), procedural comments about the process of discussion (''You'll have to speak up so that I can hear you''), and other forms of abstract, vague, or tangential discussion. The common denominator in these examples is that they put psychological and emotional distance between the person and the conflict issue without actually denying or directly evading it. In some contexts, noncommittal remarks may be seen as acts of conflict avoidance. Shifting the level of abstraction, for example, is one way that individuals can avoid conflict without seeming to ignore an issue altogether. However, noncommittal remarks may also be used to express conflict cautiously and indirectly. In other instances, noncommittal remarks reflect particular ways of seeing conflict.

We have observed two prototypes of the noncommittal style; the ''congenial'' couple and the ''intellectual'' couple. In the first case, discussion seems to be much more like polite small talk than conflict, because conflict issues are never actually discussed. Instead, the conversation will center on topically relevant but conflict-irrelevant issues. For example, if the original issue has to do with disagreements about leisure time, the discussion might involve a story about children and television in the newspaper, where the neighbors are going for their summer vacation, or how the last Christmas party went. Although the discussion is topically relevant to areas of potential conflict, it does not address actual conflict. Rather, the discussion takes the form of a low risk, low disclosure ''chat.'' The equanimity of the discussion seems to coincide with a blasé or stoic perception of marital conflicts.

The second prototypic way of remaining noncommittal is to intellectualize about conflicts, such that the issues, although ostensibly the topic of conversation, are not discussed concretely. One couple we observed was strongly convinced of the central role played by communication in marriage and they related virtually every potential source of marital conflict to the need for open communication. They did so, ironically, without saying anything definite about their own marriage. The discussion was constantly characterized by abstract, third-person language. Potentially, couples such as this might find greater meaning in abstract principles than in the operational details of marriage.

Irreverence

Humor is not within the traditional focus of research on conflict and related topics (e.g., decision making or problem solving). Generally we assume that these topics are serious matters. Weick (1971) wryly noted that the subjects in conflict or problem-solving studies occasionally fail to grasp the seriousness of the situation and play with the researcher's well-designed instructions. One interpretation is that these individuals have gone outside the boundaries of the research and are performing something other than conflict. On the other hand, humor can also be construed as a basic conflict-management strategy. As Weick pointed out, levity enables individuals to redefine "problems" as "annoyances" that are dealt with more easily and with less fretting. Recognizing the absurd element in an absurd situation improves one's response to it, whereas taking the situation too seriously produces a maladaptive response (Weick, 1971).

Humor is not a clear instance of avoidance or engagement because it potentially serves several roles. Some individuals use humor to manage tension and to work through conflicts in a less threatening way. On the other hand, lampooning an idea is one form of tangential response, so humor is sometimes linked to conflict avoidance. Sarcastic humor results from a paradoxical message where the speaker at once declares something and at another level denies it (i.e., "I'm only kidding"), which potentially serves as an evasive style of conflict.

Humor can also be verbally competitive and abusive, as in the case of the biting sort of humor that we identify under the confrontive style (i.e., hostile joking). Perhaps the most abusive form of humor is to refuse to take seriously what another person does, for example, to laugh at another's heartfelt disclosures. However, determining whether sarcastic humor is good natured or hostile is not always easy, particularly for someone outside the relationship who cannot know the full context. The intent of sarcastic jokes cannot be determined from the words alone and even nonverbal cues such as intonation can mislead ("dry" humor being the most misleading). One borderline form of conflict could be described as "play fighting," where individuals trade sarcastic but playful insults. Rather than representing a destructive form of conflict, play fighting may indicate that the partners are cohesive and trusting. What seems to separate play fighting from the real thing is that the individuals understand and encourage one another's humor, that is, the partner willingly "takes the bait." For example, one highly satisfied couple we observed had the following to say after a long, candid, and "straight" discussion of their marriage:

W: As far as the television is concerned, you dominate the TV. That is like your domain. You do like television more than I do *but* I will say that is one of our areas of thin ice there because . . .

H: You always want to watch like *The Brady Bunch*. Now I like *I Love Lucy*.

W: The *Brady Bunch*! You shit! I could name a few things I didn't put on there [the questionnaire]. Like as far as duties around the house, I could run you into the ground!

H: [speaking dramatically to the tape recorder] That's the way it's really like around here.

W: [laughing] We sure enjoy it but it's one hell of a fight!

H: Well you do, you do watch *The Brady Bunch*!

W: Oh I *never* watch *The Brady Bunch*!

H: Oh you watch . . . Alright, what are some of the other good ones you watch?

W: I like *I Love Lucy.*

H: Now I like *I Love Lucy* but there's a couple other ones . . .

W: [interrupting] You always want to watch . . . the intellectual ones like *Masterpiece Theater* and all the ones on history. But occasionally we could watch something I wanted to watch.

H: Well I agree with that but . . .

W: [laughing] Bullshit! You never want to watch what I want to watch! [The argument continues for another 5 minutes.]

Conciliation

Conciliatory remarks are statements that seek reconciliation, for example, through concessions, compliments, statements empathizing with the partner's feelings or point of view, or statements acknowledging the speaker's own contributions to conflict. These are essentially relationship-repair messages, which are the direct counterpart of demands, criticism, ridicule, and accusations. Conciliatory behavior by one party may lead to a softening of another person's stance or halt an escalatory spiral, as it allows the other person to maintain or restore face (see Folger & Poole, 1984). Thus, more-satisfied spouses make more conciliatory remarks than less-satisfied spouses (Sillars et al., 1983), and conciliatory moves in bargaining often lead to greater cooperation in return (see Putnam, 1985).

Conciliatory remarks clearly represent a more direct style of conflict than other styles considered thus far, as conciliatory behavior generally implies that the existence of a conflict has been acknowledged. Still, conciliation is primarily aimed at relationship repair. It does not necessarily lead to a direct discussion of the content issues at hand, particularly if a person concedes simply to end further consideration of the conflict. Kilmann and Thomas (1975) described conciliatory behavior (i.e., "accommodation") as a cooperative but nonassertive style of conflict, which is similar in the latter respect to conflict avoidance. Conciliatory messages can also be a form of "passive resistance," as in the case when one partner admits guilt without any commitment to change (i.e., "You're right, I'm no damn good"). This occurred with one couple we observed in which the husband might be characterized as a "sports-a-holic." The husband readily admitted that he was rarely home, sometimes being gone seven nights a week, as he was continually either refereeing or participating in some sports activity. He infrequently interacted with his children or wife at home, spending much of his time watching sports on television. The husband admitted guilt and empathized with his wife's situation at every turn in the conversation but, like a compulsive gambler or alcoholic who refuses treatment, there was no implication of change forthcoming in any of his statements. The conciliatory messages were evidently an attempt to sooth but not address the problem.

The Analytic Style

The obvious alternative to avoidance and confrontation is to "analyze" the conflict from a collaborative standpoint. Behaviors affiliated with this style include self-disclosure and descriptive statements of a nonevaluative nature, nonhostile questions soliciting information, opinions, or confirmation from the other party, statements that explain, "document," or qualify general feelings and observations, and suggestions that are presented for mutual consideration without the speaker assuming a strong advocacy role. Of course, people also disclose feelings, describe behaviors, and ask questions when they use the confrontive style but they add insulting and demeaning implications to their comments. The affective tone of analytic comments is neutral or positive. A further distinguishing attribute of the analytic style is concreteness. Whereas confrontive remarks tend to expand the conversational focus by raising abstract issues of blame or personal character, analytic remarks tend to narrow the focus by describing specific behaviors, feelings, perceptions, and situations relevant to a conflict. Behaviorally and situationally specific disclosure and description is seen by some family therapists as a needed antidote to the vague and overgeneralized terms that spouses often use to refer to one another (e.g., "You *never* think of anyone but yourself." See Thomas, 1977; Weiss, Hops, & Patterson, 1973). As the term *analytic* implies, the essence of this style is to give and seek information in the interests of coming to a better understanding of the issues. The analytic style is naturally aligned with the cultural metaphor of communication as "work" (as in "working on one's relationship" or "working out difficulties"), which represents a prominent contemporary view of relationships (Katriel & Phillipsen, 1981). Individuals who blend this style with conciliatory behaviors are seen as more competent social actors than individuals who confront or avoid (Canary & Cupach, 1988; Cupach, 1982).

Virtually all communication texts and training programs encourage individuals to practice some version of the analytic style, under the assumption that it is the most underdeveloped and underutilized style. In the conflict studies of Sillars and his colleagues, married couples utilized this style as much as 43% of the time in one study and as little as 16% in another. Across four samples of married couples, the rate of analytic (sometimes called "informational") remarks has averaged 25%, which compares to an average of 25% confrontive remarks (also called "distributive"), 8% conciliatory remarks (also called "supportive"), and 42% for the combination of various forms of avoidance, indirect or noncommittal statements, and humor (Burggraf & Sillars, 1987; Pike & Sillars, 1985; Sillars et al., 1983; Zietlow & Sillars, 1988). These figures testify that, although couples use the analytic style of communication frequently, it is far from the primary style in most cases.

A further assumption of texts and training programs is that conflicts are most effectively managed to both parties' satisfaction if information about the interests of both parties is made explicit. Once the interests of each party are mutually understood then it may be possible to devise "integrative" solutions that satisfy the key interests of both parties (Fisher & Ury, 1981; Walton & McKersie, 1965). Thus, communication training essentially teaches individuals to strategize toward joint outcomes by mutually analyzing conflicts and to suppress individualistic strategies.

Confrontation

Confrontive remarks refer to the types of verbally competitive acts that we most associate with hostile, abusive, and destructive conflicts; that is, criticism, demands, hostile jokes and questions, denial of responsibility, "mind-reading," and so forth. There is a heavy attributional element associated with confrontive remarks, as they fix blame, either directly or by implication, on the other party. Not surprisingly, confrontive remarks are used more and are reciprocated more readily when individuals blame one another for a conflict than when they blame themselves. Conciliatory remarks occur more often when people blame themselves (Sillars, 1985). Indeed, hostile conflicts are largely consumed by the question of who is at fault or rather, who is the "victim."

Although clear examples of either style are easy to recognize, there is often a fine line between analytic and confrontive styles. Consequently, the appropriate characterization of a person's remarks is itself a matter of contention. If you asked most people whether their conflict style is mostly confrontive or analytic, they would probably describe themselves as analytic. Further, people sometimes see themselves as collaborating but construe their adversaries as competing during conflicts (Thomas & Pondy, 1977). Individuals do not typically perceive themselves as *choosing* to compete. Even when people openly acknowledge having a competitive orientation in conflict simulations, they may justify their competitive strategy on the basis that the other person can be expected to compete (Kelley & Stahelski, 1970).

The dynamics of incompatible relationships help perpetuate negative attributions about conflict style. Bradbury and Fincham (1987) noted that dissatisfied spouses selectively attend to and remember negative behaviors by the partner, as these behaviors are highly salient and are easily integrated within existing memory structures. Satisfied spouses, on the other hand, are likely to discount negative behavior. Because of their sensitivity to negative behavior, dissatisfied spouses are actually more accurate than satisfied spouses in recalling confrontive and paralinguistically negative statements made by their partner (Sillars, Weisberg, Burggraf, & Zietlow, 1990). Dissatisfied spouses also tend to assign more negative intentions and causes to the partner's messages than reported by the speaker or actor (see Fincham, 1985; Noller, 1984; Sillars, 1985) and they blame one another more for marital conflicts by comparison with satisfied spouses (Fincham, 1985; Sillars, 1985). As suggested, these negative attributional tendencies may cause even further entrenchment of conflict by encouraging additional confrontive messages.

Confrontation by both parties leads to an "escalatory spiral," where each iteration brings forth more hostile, abusive, destructive communication (Hocker & Wilmot, 1991). Such spirals, if unchecked, can result in threats of divorce, walking out, or physical violence. More typically, confrontation is eventually counterbalanced by conciliation, avoidance, or another less intense form of conflict. As with the other styles, it is the joint action by both parties that determines the outcome of the communication, not one remark taken in isolation from the partner's response. These organizational dynamics of conflict are taken up in the next section.

ORGANIZATIONAL PROPERTIES OF CONFLICT

People do not often make a simple choice between one type of message or another in conflict. More typically they use a combination of styles. This is the case partly because people adapt and revise their style as they interact with one another. Further, the goals of individuals in conflict tend to be complex and this contributes to the complexity of conflict patterns. People form more elaborate message strategies primarily to reconcile conflicting goals (O'Keefe & Delia, 1982). Situations that do not involve conflicting goals are unproblematic, so messages tend to be direct and uncomplicated. However, in conflicts people often balance several goals simultaneously. They may, for example, seek to achieve tangible outcomes, insure fair treatment, maintain personal dignity, preserve the health of a relationship, obey situational norms, and respond to time and task pressures. These concerns are frequently at odds, therefore communication patterns may reflect successive changes from one style of conflict to another. For example, because people experience simultaneous desires to engage and avoid, conflict patterns often reflect alternation in and out of engagement and avoidance cycles. Even the most intense confrontation sequences are typically punctuated by instances of denial, equivocation, tangentialism, and humor.

Thus, the moves that a person might initiate at a given point in time only partly define the style of conflict employed. As systems theorists have noted (e.g., Watzlawick et al., 1967), the timing of a move is often as significant as the move per se, as an action is defined largely by the context in which it occurs. At least five important qualities describe the organization of conflict patterns: variety, continuity, symmetry, stationarity, and spontaneity.

Variety

Variety refers to the number of alternate messages that people employ in a given situation. Rigidly patterned sequences of conflict reflect minimal variety, thus leading to one extreme style or another—constant avoidance, never-ending analysis and reanalysis, or rigid escalation. Systems principles suggest that there is some point of optimal variety, where the system is not chaotically patterned (i.e., random shifting from one style to another) but there is adequate flexibility to shift styles as the situation demands. Couples who possess a varied repertoire are more apt to manage the level of engagement at a comfortable level, for example, by counterbalancing small provocations with jokes or questions or by returning to an issue after an interlude of avoidance. Behavioral flexibility thus characterizes the communication of more interpersonally competent individuals and couples (Argyle, 1969; Kieren & Tallman, 1972; Millar & Rogers, 1987; Wiemann, 1977).

Limited variety is demonstrated in at least two ways. First, a particular style of conflict may be missing from a couple's repertoire; for example, a complete absence of humor or an inability to engage without releasing a flood of complaints. Second, the sequence of conflict may be highly patterned. For example, distressed and dissatisfied spouses may have especially high reciprocity of negative nonverbal affect, as conveyed by tone of voice and possibly other channels (Gottman, 1979; Gottman, Markman, & Notarius, 1977; Margolin & Wampold, 1981; Mettatal & Gottman, 1980; Pike & Sillars, 1985; Rubin, 1983). Although these couples do not consistently speak to one another in whines and growls, their likelihood of doing so increases dramatically when the precipitating comment by the partner is also negative.

The restricted repertoire of some individuals and couples may stem from the assumption that conflict is an "all-or-nothing" affair. For example, Zietlow and Sillars (1988) compared the discussions of married couples from different life stage groups. Although elderly, retired couples were more harmonious as a group than young couples, they enacted one extreme pattern of behavior or another, that is, no acknowledgement of conflict whatsoever or constant bickering. Most of the elderly couples were remarkably passive and congenial in their conversations. For example, on the subject of irritability, which nearly always elicits at least mild conflict among young couples, elderly couples often commented that the issue rarely, if ever, came up in their marriage. Remarkably, one woman stated to her husband that she did not recall him ever being irritable in the 50-plus years that the two had been married. Such sentiments could only exist through a combination of thick skin, selective memory, and inexpressive norms for communication. A particular divorce mediation session we encountered also reflected the passive and congenial style of conflict found among some elderly couples. The retired couples in question wanted to get a divorce but not change the overall pattern of their lives, except that they would live in separate houses (co-owned by the couples). She would continue to cook for him, he would do all the yardwork and repairs, and they would spend holidays and vacations with their grown children as always. When the mediator asked what led them to seek a divorce, they replied, "Oh, we've never really gotten along. We're just different people—no reason for her to change or for me to change." The mediation session as a whole continued in this vein, sounding more like a relaxed "chat" than a "conflict episode."

In stark contrast to the congeniality shown by the majority of elderly couples in the Zietlow and Sillars research, a small number of elderly couples argued aggressively throughout the discussions. Thus, the elderly had predictable conversations consisting either of passive (mostly noncommittal) remarks or highly reciprocal confrontive statements. There was little indication, as was the case among young and middle-aged couples, of elderly couples shifting in and out of a problem-focused, analytic style of discussion. As is the case with other traditional family types, some elderly seem predisposed to diffuse potential conflicts by making implicit adjustments to the other spouse (Sillars & Kalbfleisch, 1989; Sillars & Wilmot, 1989). Overall, this pattern was associated with remarkable harmony; however, elderly couples who experienced serious and persistent marital conflicts seemed to lack an adequate communication repertoire for expressing conflict directly.

Continuity

Conflicts may be "about" many different things—food, vacation time, irritating habits, bad breath, respect, love, or arrogance. As conflicts expand, the locus of conflict tends to shift from specific substantive issues to broad relational concerns (e.g., power, self-esteem, trust) and to the ground rules under which conflict is conducted (i.e., violations of expectations concerning interruptions, taboo topics, aggressive tactics, etc.). Although each of these areas may be involved, to some extent, in any conflict, low-intensity conflicts occur within a context of broad consensus about core issues and basic rules in a relationship. Bitter and destructive conflicts are fundamentally conflicts over core relationship issues, such as power, respect, and self-esteem (Altman & Taylor, 1973; Morton, Alexander, & Altman, 1976). Further, due to the abstract and elusive nature of relationship issues (Hocker & Wilmot, 1991; Watzlawick et al., 1967), relationship struggles are generally played out through the proliferation of specific conflicts, many of which may appear to involve minor and insignificant matters. One may generally assume that if a specific content conflict recurs frequently and with increasing intensity, the issue left unresolved is a relationship issue.

Because intense relationship conflicts lead to the proliferation of many specific issues, these conflicts are naturally less orderly, concrete, and focused than mild conflicts. In intense conflicts, conversations by conflicting parties often lack topic continuity, as the focus of conversation will tend to drift from one loosely related issue to another. A divorcing couple may initially face the issue of child visitation during Christmas, but this easily leads to old grudges against in-laws, which brings up the equity of the general custody arrangement, parenting abilities, infidelity prior to the break-up, and so forth. The continual shifting from one issue to another represents one of the most problematic aspects of communication during conflict, as many issues may be raised but none considered adequately for the parties to approach consensus. The inevitable result is escalation of conflict and the propagation of an increasing store of unresolved business.

Extensive strategizing by the conflicting parties probably disrupts topic continuity further, as the speakers may ignore preceding messages in order to carry out their own internal plans of argument (Sillars & Weisberg, 1987). Such plans may consist of internalized monologues that speakers wish to express or interactive ''scripts,'' such as a sequence of leading questions that indirectly leads to the speaker's claim (see the discussion of ''presequences'' by Jackson & Jacobs, 1980). To the extent that the plans of two speakers are incompatible, discussion is apt to appear chaotic as the parties will struggle to define the focus of conversation on their own terms (i.e., their own favorite gripes, arguments, and stories). The individuals are therefore likely to initiate, expand, terminate, and recycle issues without great regularity, further contributing to the difficulty of keeping conflict within manageable limits.

Symmetry

Symmetry is the extent to which parties match styles of conflict. Although there are cases where individuals behave in a compensatory manner, for example, counterbalancing confrontation with avoidance, the dominant tendency is to match styles. A person is much more likely to avoid conflict if the immediate stimulus is an avoidance act by the partner, to confront if the immediate stimulus is a confrontive act, and so forth. To some extent, matching of styles can be expected to moderate inter-speaker differences in communication associated with personality traits and other individual-level characteristics. For example, cooperatively oriented individuals become competitive in conflict simulations when matched with a competitive partner (Kelley & Stahelski, 1970; Rubin & Brown, 1975).

Conflict styles tend to be reciprocal for fairly obvious reasons. Generally, inconsistent styles do not fit together comfortably. It is more difficult and less plausible to deny the presence of conflict, for example, after the partner has disclosed deep-seated feelings of anxiety and resentment. There are also straightforward affective linkages between some styles. Compliments provoke positive feelings and lead to return compliments. Criticism provokes negative feelings that lead to counter-criticism. Compliments do not lead to criticism, unless there are bitter feelings below the surface.

Matching is easiest to observe in statement-by-statement reciprocity in conversations (See Roloff & Campion, 1985). Presumably, matching also occurs on a long-term basis, although the gradual, long-term effects of matching are difficult to demonstrate. By long-term matching we mean gradual adjustment of styles in ongoing relationships, such that the parties become increasingly like one another. The relatively high reciprocity of conflict styles among elderly couples observed by Zietlow and Sillars (1988) might partly reflect accommodation of styles over many years of marriage. Elderly spouses reciprocated the partner's conflict style 60% of the time versus approximately 50% reciprocity among middle-aged and young couples. Many of the middle-aged and elderly couples from this research also mimicked each other through overlapping speaking turns (e.g., repetition, paraphrasing, and completion of one another's statements) and mutual reference to abstract themes (Sillars, Burggraf, Yost, & Zietlow, 1992).

One of two problematic tendencies related to symmetry may occur in troubled relationships. First, the reciprocity rate may be so high as to reflect a rigid, "stimulus-response" structure that precludes constructive strategizing to manage conflict. For example, confrontive acts may lead unmercifully to countercomplaints, threats, and other forms of escalation. Similarly, avoidance may lead rigidly to subsequent avoidance. This type of situation was previously covered during the discussion of variety in conflict patterns. The opposite sort of problem occurs when there is a lack of convergence in conflict styles. Humor, for example, is a constructive resource if it is shared. If, however, two people do not participate in one another's humor, then jokes seem shallow, inappropriate, or cruel. Similarly, Raush et al. (1974) described couples who collaborate in avoiding conflicts. Although these individuals may have difficulty adapting to change, they are sometimes among the most satisfied couples. Underlying such instances of collusive avoidance or collaborative parody is a basic consensus about the nature of the relationship and the way conflict should be carried out. In instances where one person confronts while the other avoids, or one analyzes while the other makes jokes, the rules of conflict themselves are at issue.

A particular type of asymmetrical pattern characteristic of dissatisfied couples might be termed "hit-and-run." In this pattern a person will tend to be confrontive at inappropriate moments, for example, when the partner is being conciliatory or analytic. Confrontive acts, on the other hand, are met with acts of avoidance. Studies by Raush et al. (1974), Peterson (1979), and Pike and Sillars (1985) have observed hit-and-run tendencies among dissatisfied couples. In the Pike and Sillars research, for example, less-satisfied couples used confrontive acts more often than satisfied couples in all circumstances *except* when the partner was confrontive immediately prior. When the partner was confrontive, the spouse was likely to shift to a conciliatory or avoidance style of conflict. Clinicians have long observed similar aggression–withdrawal patterns among discordant couples (Watzlawick et al., 1967). Aggression–withdrawal patterns may result partly from an inner "approach–avoidance" conflict, where an individual experiences the desire to express dissatisfactions but at the same time fears escalation. Consequently, conflict comes out as a tossed salad of confrontation and avoidance.

Stationarity

Conflicting parties do not necessarily begin a discussion with one style of conflict and end exhibiting the same style. Normally, discussions progress through phases (Holmes & Poole, 1991). Couples also vary considerably in this regard. Some conflicts are highly stationary, and others progress through several phases, periodically cycling back through an earlier phase. Further, the sequence of progression is variable (Poole & Doelger, 1986). In some conflicts the partners first avoid and then confront, and in others they confront and then avoid.

Some conflict styles, such as the noncommittal style, seem to be more stationary than others. Although noncommittal remarks are frequently embedded within larger episodes of avoidance or engagement, there are some instances where the noncommittal style is the dominant form of communication. When this happens, the conversation can have an especially stationary quality, because there is little tension compelling a shift from the low disclosure, low-risk noncommittal style to another style. Couples who rely heavily on the noncommittal style are essentially static, as their discussion does not promote any movement either within an episode of conflict or across many episodes. As we noted earlier, the static quality of such relationships is neither absolutely good or bad, as they may be stable and harmonious although inflexible in adapting to problems.

High-intensity conflicts seem to go through phasic changes more rapidly than low-intensity conflicts. Once again, the crucial factor is the extent to which there is fundamental agreement on the nature of the relationship, particularly the rules for carrying out conflict. For example, when one person raises an issue that the partner believes should stay hidden, there is often a struggle to determine the status of the issue and the propriety of discussion. The struggle carries the discussion through phases of avoidance, analysis, confrontation, and further avoidance.

A typical phasic progression observed in research situations is that a couple first enacts a very socially desirable style of conflict (i.e., the analytic style) but this quickly dissolves if the style is not part of the couple's normal conflict repertoire. Some couples are surprisingly argumentative when their conversations are being monitored, because even their best attempts at constructive communication open wounds and evoke criticism. Naturally, dissatisfied couples have a more difficult time maintaining a socially desirable conflict style than satisfied couples. When satisfied couples raise issues they tend to validate one another's view (Gottman, 1979; Krueger & Smith, 1982; Ting-Toomey, 1983) and produce converging lines of argument (Canary, Brossman, Sillars, & LoVette, 1987). When dissatisfied couples raise issues it often leads to refutation sequences and efforts to bolster personal arguments against attack (Canary et al., 1987). Generally it appears that couples cannot jointly sustain an analytic style of conflict unless the style is well practiced and the spouses hold basic assumptions about conflict in common.

Although we have discussed stationarity in terms of phasic stability within an episode of conflict, stationarity or nonstationarity also exists with respect to conflict episodes. If the same sequence of conflict is replayed on different occasions then stationarity exists on an episodic level. Phasic and episodic stationarity are independent of one another. For example, two individuals may begin conflict with a mild inquiry by one party, then escalate, hurl insults back-and-forth, become sullen, make up, and finally promise to always support and love one another in the future. At the phasic level, this process is obviously nonstationary. However, if the same sequence is played over and over at other times then the process is stationary at the episodic level. Watzlawick, Weakland, and Fisch (1974) noted that alterations of the sequence of events (i.e., episodic level change) involve "second-order" change in the system's way of behaving, which is more complex and difficult to accomplish than the simple change from state-to-state (i.e., first-order change, which roughly corresponds to repetitive phasic movement). Third parties may be an effective instrument of second-order change but must be able to recognize abstract, recurring patterns across episodes.

Spontaneity

There is a sense one receives observing audio or videotaped discussions of conflict to the effect that some individuals heavily contemplate and censor their remarks whereas others find the process of discussion incredibly easy. The latter individuals appear more spontaneous, by which we mean that they strategize less and instead speak "off the cuff." Spontaneous interactions are reactive. In the absence of complex, multiturn strategies, individuals are more responsive to the other speaker and to moment-to-moment shifts in conversations. Spontaneity is frequently very obvious to the casual observer but it is a difficult quality to objectify. The impression of spontaneity is evidently given by nonverbal cues, particularly speech hesitation. Slower and more hesitant speech is associated with more reflective and complex thought, according to several studies (Siegman, 1979). Conflict avoidance, which we intuitively associate with less spontaneity, is also related to lower speech productivity, more nervous gestures, more frequent eye glances, and less total other-directed gaze (Sillars et al., 1982). These cues suggest a person who is somewhat reticent, anxious, and concerned about the partner's reactions.

Greater spontaneity may characterize conflict for two opposite reasons. First, individuals who have few or no threatening conflict issues before them seem to show greater spontaneity. Harmonious couples strategize less because the rules of interaction are shared and conflicts are confined to more "peripheral" areas of the relationship. These individuals are apt to find communication about conflict an easy process governed by simple rules of thumb (e.g., "Just say what's on your mind"). From the perspective of such individuals, it may be difficult to see why others find communication so complex and troubling.

Second, conflicts that are very stressful may inhibit moment-to-moment strategizing, as stress above a certain level disrupts one's ability to engage in complex thought. High levels of stress interfere with hypothetical and abstract reasoning, including the ability to differentiate and simultaneously consider multiple points of view (Schroder, Driver, & Streufert, 1967). This ability is utilized extensively in listener-adapted, goal-directed communication (O'Keefe & Delia, 1982; O'Keefe & Sypher, 1981). Communication during stressful conflicts tends to mirror the cognitive deficits associated with high stress, with messages portraying a simplistic, black–white perception of the situation (Holsti, 1965; Sillars & Parry, 1982; Suedfeld & Tetlock, 1977). On an experiential level, high stress may be associated with the feeling that conflict is proceeding under its own momentum, as people revert to a stimulus–response style of escalation (Schroder et al., 1967). Thus, high stress may foster a rigid, negative form of spontaneity.

It is difficult to derive a simple rule concerning the effects of spontaneity, but it appears that either extensive strategizing or complete spontaneity can represent relational problems. Extensive strategizing promotes an excessively individualistic, noncollaborative approach to conflict, whereas complete spontaneity fosters rigidity. Ideally, one would be spontaneous enough to be responsive and collaborative but strategic enough to modify destructive patterns when they arise.

When called to mediate conflicts, third parties are faced with both overly strategic and overly spontaneous patterns of discussion. In the ensuing section we take up the communication strategies used by mediators in their efforts to transform destructive patterns of conflict.

MEDIATION AND CONFLICT ORGANIZATION

Mediation is when a third person joins a conflict to assist the participants in managing the conflict process. It assumes (a) that the conflict parties both are responsible for their conflict, and (b) that the best agreements for ending a conflict should be derived with the conflict parties' full participation. Typically, mediation results in greater satisfaction with the outcome than when other mechanisms of dispute resolution are involved, such as arbitration or judicial action (Kressel, 1987; Pearson & Thoennes, 1984).

Mediators use a variety of strategies designed to move the parties toward productive conflict while discouraging destructive conflict behavior (Haynes & Haynes, 1989; Moore, 1986). There is considerable research and speculation about specific strategies mediators can use such as caucuses, finding interests, establishing the agenda, fractionation, and others (see Blades, 1984; Carnevale, 1986; Donohue, 1991; Haynes & Haynes, 1989; Kressel, 1987; Moore, 1986; Rubin, 1985). Rather than reviewing literature on individual mediator strategies, we build on our notion of system-wide, organizational properties of conflicts and how mediators can use them as a guide for strategy selection. Though system-wide properties are sometimes discussed (Donohue, 1991; Haynes & Haynes, 1989), most writers on conflict and mediation still limit themselves to individualistic perspectives.

Many married couples heading toward a divorce manifest a lack of variety in their conflict behaviors with one another. When this is the case, the mediator can identify their predominant patterns and supply alternatives. For example, many couples coming into divorce mediation have been locked into unproductive patterns of high reciprocity of negative affect. One person says, "He always breaks our agreements," which promptly brings a deep sigh from the partner. Left unchecked this pattern will be repeated. In such a case, the mediator can (a) alter the verbalization from one spouse, and (b) help the other spouse stop emitting nonproductive "deep sighs" that promote the first spouse to continue the attack.

Basically, the lack of variety in divorcing spouses is always present—the mediator just needs to find the patterns that are keeping them from reforming their relationship. Often, as a result of the stress of the divorcing process, couples are not able to see any humor in their predicament. Mediators can purposefully inject carefully timed humor in the later mediation sessions, which helps the couples see some of their unproductive moves in a different light. With one couple, the mediator had used humor sparingly a few times with a positive effect on the parties. Later, the participants began incorporating humor into their repertoire as well. The wife had a habit of always crying during stressful decisions in mediation. During the first session, she was obviously embarrassed by her crying, and it was her embarrassment that kept her from successfully negotiating with her husband. During later sessions, however, she would often say, "Well, if things get tough today I can always cry!", making it apparent that her self-humor helped her both accept herself and provide a defense against debilitating embarrassment. Of course, the humor can be directed at the overall situation too, with a couple finding humor in the midst of their struggle.

At other times, the lack of variety is exemplified by a lack of overt conflict.

Another couple exemplified "civility" with one another, to the point they could not sharpen issues enough to pave the way for negotiation and solutions. In this case, the mediator promoted more variety by helping them escalate. He asked such questions as "Well, that sounds nice and peaceful—but do you think that 5 years from now when he is remarried you will still be doing his laundry?" Whether a couple is in a pattern of too much or too little escalation the mediator plays the same role—increasing the variety and types of responses. In most cases, the mediator has to shape productive responses, showing the couple how to negotiate with one another, illustrating for them how to self-regulate confrontive responses, and moving them into an analytic, problem-solving communication style. One hopes that the couple will get to the point where they can begin an unproductive sequence of interaction, check it themselves, and move into more productive integrative actions. The mediator has thereby limited the variety of unproductive communication moves, and increased the variety of productive forms of communication.

Stationarity, or the movement through phases and episodes over time, is at a more macrolevel of system dynamics than is variety. Basically, the overall sequencing of communication over time identifies the amount of stationarity a couple manifests. In mediation, conflict may be nonstationary because of posturing that takes place early in the discussion when parties seek a competitive advantage in the outcome of a settlement. The role of the mediator is to move the discussion away from this individualistic orientation, for example, by reframing comments and enforcing ground rules of discussion. Conversely, some couples begin well but store up grievances for later when a settlement is approached.

In dealing with stationarity forces, the mediator needs to let sequences "play out" in order to see which ones can be encouraged and which ones extinguished. One couple in divorce mediation manifested an overall pattern of the woman setting the tone for the sessions, with the man remaining relatively silent initially and then engaging in extreme escalation toward the end of the hour. In terms of the earlier discussion, this pattern involved movement through phases but stationarity across episodes. After seeing the pattern repeated twice, the mediator intervened by having the man speak first in the next session. This upset a pattern the couple had come to rely on, and as a result, he did not escalate as much and she did not have to defend her early positions. Of course, some patterns are not easy to see at first glance. One couple came to mediation after a court wait of two years, saying they wanted a divorce. After ten hours of mediation, all property was distributed, child custody and visitation issues were resolved except for one issue they agreed the judge would decide, and the couple left with an agreement. Two months later, they had not yet filed for divorce. Only in retrospect could the overall pattern of avoidance of the divorce be seen. Such macropatterns emerge over time.

More experienced mediators often note that the "couple determines their own time frame,'' meaning that stationarity patterns are variable. Some couples move through phases sequentially, others work on the divorce, let issues sit for months, then come back and work on other issues. One couple took two years to move through the phases, always being cooperative, but the overall stationarity flowing from the system was (a) working cooperatively on one issue, (b) taking no action for a few months, and (c) coming back and working on another issue. Finally, stationarity is often manifested by a consistent tone throughout the mediation until the final few sessions. Often, couples who are cooperative (and sometimes avoidant) will successfully negotiate and move forward until the specter of the final session looms. Then, the anger, frustration, and pain not yet acknowledged may for the first time be surfaced. With such stationarity patterns, the mediator needs to be alert to sudden switching at the end of the process.

Lack of continuity occurs when conflict participants struggle over many different items—ranging from treatment of the children to property settlements. Conflict participants will often begin on one topic area, launch an attack, then move to the next battleground. The mediator can neutralize the unproductive effects of continual topic shifting by fractionation—insisting on taking one topic at a time before bringing in another (Fisher, 1964). When a mediator says ''Well, Carl, you have about three things of concern here. Let's take them one at a time...,'' it provides for exploration of each area and its ramifications. Paradoxically, when a mediator constrains the spouses so they must deal with one topic at a time, it provided an indirect amelioration of the relationship issue. For example, if the woman says, ''He can't be trusted with our child arrangements, he sometimes never shows up, and is usually late, and...'' the mediator may intervene to get her to specify the ''trust'' and work out specific arrangements for exchanging the children. If they can then have a successful agreement so that between sessions the man does live up to the agreements, it helps build relational trust in a step-by-step fashion. To increase continuity of negotiations the mediator must be assertive, often interrupt tangential talk, and otherwise take process control of the discussions.

Symmetrical responses are probably the easiest for a trained mediator to identify. One spouse complains and the other cross-complains, leading the first to issue yet another complaint. The mediator wants to encourage positive symmetry and extinguish examples of negative symmetry. If one spouse offers something that helps move the discussion toward resolution, the mediator may say, ''Well, Sam, Sarah just made quite an offer regarding the disposition of the furniture. Are there some items you could voluntarily give to her to help us continue with this positive step?'' If the couple is cooperating in avoiding an area, the symmetry is altered by the mediator by bringing the topic to their attention.

Finally, mediators can provide needed changes in unproductive conflict systems by altering the degree of spontaneity present in the interactions. Often,

a couple is too strategic. They refuse to make any commitments, offer suggestions for breaking impasse, or move away from a preset position without "consulting my attorney" or "taking time to think about it." When this is the case,
the mediator can persuade the couple to work collaboratively, increase their
flexibility, and become more responsive to the needs of the relationship. If only
one party is overly strategic, the mediator can call a caucus to forcefully point
out the difficulties entailed. On the other hand, if the spouses are interrupting
one another and promoting quick, unthinking responses from the other, the
mediator can slow the process to allow them time to think before talking. In
order to decrease spontaneity the conflict parties can be asked to write down
responses, paraphrase what the partner said before extending the idea, or simply pause before answering. Reaching an optimal level of spontaneity can enhance the chances for a positive settlement. Although these "systemic
suggestions" are beginning excursions, we are convinced that one fruitful direction for research and training of mediators centers on system-wide properties
of conflict. Presently, the emphasis on individual communicative acts limits
our ability to specify emergent patterns in conflict.

CONCLUSION

Interpersonal and intimate conflicts are best described in terms of the communication patterns that unfold between the conflict participants. In the simplest
possible terms the basic communicative moves in conflict reveal an underlying
engagement–avoidance tendency as well as an hostility–friendliness dimension.
However, some styles of conflict (e.g., equivocation and joking) are partially
direct and partially obscure. Similarly, hostility and friendliness are sometimes
revealed in ways that are vague or inconsistent. In this respect, message strategies reflect the ambivalence often associated with conflict; for example, a person may have an urge to vent and at the same time fear the consequences.
 In addition to the individual communicative moves, there are system properties present in any conflict, including variety, continuity, symmetry, stationarity, and spontaneity. System properties describe many additional per-
mutations of conflict not evident from a simple typology of conflict styles
or strategies. System properties result from the fact that individual moves are
used in complex combinations. Further, couples differ in how and how much
they alternate styles. For example, the most static possible pattern would be
characterized by low variety, high symmetry, high continuity, high stationarity, and high spontaneity; in effect, a relationship dominated by a single style
of interaction. We noted that some couples who rely on a noncommittal style
of discussion may approach this extreme. In some cases "static" couples are
extremely harmonious, but a limited repertoire is also associated with inflexi-

bility and an inability to self-regulate destructive patterns. Other communication problems, including asymmetrical conflict, frequent topic shifts, rapid phasic change, or overly strategic interactions, may arise from a lack of agreement about abstract relational issues and interaction rules.

Third parties intervene primarily when there is a lack of basic agreement on the relational level. Mediators help overcome the lack of common assumptions or shared interaction rules by managing the process of discussion. Thus mediators act as "process experts" who facilitate voluntary settlements among disputing parties. The mediator's communicative choices are influenced by the systemic properties we outlined—variety, symmetry, continuity, stationarity, and spontaneity. Mediators can tailor their strategic moves to these systemic variables and thereby enhance their effectiveness.

REFERENCES

Altman, I., & Taylor, D. (1973). *Social penetration.* New York: Holt, Rinehart, & Winston.

Argyle, M. (1969). *Social interaction.* Chicago: Aldine.

Bartos, O. J. (1970). Determinants and consequences of toughness. In P. Swingle (Ed.), *The structure of conflict.* New York: Academic Press.

Bavelas, J. B., Black, A., Chovill, N., & Mullett, J. (1992). *Equivocal communication.* Newbury Park, CA: Sage.

Baxter, L. A., & Philpott, J. (1983). *Planned and emergent strategizing in everyday interaction.* Unpublished manuscript, University of California, Davis.

Blades, J. (1984). Mediation: An old art revitalized. *Mediation Quarterly, 3,* 59–98.

Bradbury, T. N., & Fincham, F. D. (1987). Affect and cognition in close relationships: Towards an integrative model. *Cognition and Emotion, 1,* 59–87.

Burggraf, C. S., & Sillars, A. L. (1987). A critical examination of sex differences in marital communication. *Communication Monographs, 54,* 276–294.

Canary, D. J., Brossmann, B. G., Sillars, A. L., & LoVette, S. (1987, July). *Married couples' argument structures and sequences: A comparison of satisfied and dissatisfied dyads.* Paper presented at the Fifth Summer Conference on Argumentation, Alta, UT.

Canary, D. J., & Cupach, W. R. (1988). Relational and episodic characteristics associated with conflict tactics. *Journal of Social and Personal Relationships, 5,* 426–446.

Carnevale, P. J. D. (1986). Strategic choice in mediation. *Negotiation Journal, 2,* 41–56.

Cupach, W. (1982, February). *Perceived communication competence and choice of interpersonal conflict message strategies.* Paper presented at the Western Speech Communication Association Convention, Denver.

Donohue, W. A. (1991). *Communication, marital dispute, and divorce mediation.* Hillsdale, NJ: Lawrence Erlbaum Associates.

Etzioni, A. (1967) The Kennedy experiment. *The Western Political Quarterly, 20,* 361–380.

Fincham, F. D. (1985). Attributions in close relationships. In J. Harvey & G. Weary (Eds.), *Contemporary attribution theory and research* (pp. 203–234). Hillsdale, NJ: Lawrence Erlbaum Associates.

Fisher, R. (1964). Fractionating conflict. In R. Fisher (Ed.), *International conflict and behavioral science: The Craigville papers* (pp. 91–109). New York: Basic Books.

Fisher, R., & Ury, W. (1981). *Getting to yes: Negotiating agreement without giving in.* Boston: Houghton-Mifflin.

Fitzpatrick, M. A. (1988). *Between husbands and wives: Communication in marriage.* Newbury Park, CA: Sage.

Fitzpatrick, M. A., Fallis, S., & Vance, L. (1982). Multifunctional coding of conflict resolution strategies in marital dyads. *Family Relations, 31,* 611–670.

Folger, J. P., & Poole, M. S. (1984). *Working through conflict: A communication perspective.* Glenview, IL: Scott, Foresman.

Gottman, J. M. (1979). *Marital interaction: Investigations.* New York: Academic Press.

Gottman, J. M., (1982). Emotional responsiveness in marital conversations. *Journal of Communication, 32,* 108–120.

Gottman, J., Markman, H., & Notarius, C. (1977). The topography of marital conflict: A study of verbal and nonverbal behavior. *Journal of Marriage and the Family, 39,* 461–477.

Haynes, J. M., & Haynes, G. (1989). *Mediating divorce.* San Francisco, CA: Jossey-Bass.

Hocker, J. L., & Wilmot, W. W. (1991). *Interpersonal conflict* (3rd ed.). Dubuque, IA: Brown.

Holmes, M. E., & Poole, M. S. (1991). Longitudinal analysis. In B. M. Montgomery & S. Duck (Eds.), *Studying interpersonal interaction* (pp. 286–302). New York: Guilford.

Holsti, O. R. (1965). The 1914 case. *American Political Science Review, 59,* 365–378.

Jackson, S., & Jacobs, S. (1980). Structure of conversational argument: Pragmatic bases for the enthymeme. *Quarterly Journal of Speech, 66,* 251–265.

Katriel, T., & Phillipsen, G. (1981). "What we need is communication": "Communication" as a cultural category in some American speech. *Communication Monographs, 48,* 301–317.

Kelley, H. H., & Stahelski, A. J. (1970). Errors in perceptions of intentions in a mixed-motive game. *Journal of Experimental Social Psychology, 6,* 379–400.

Kieren, D., & Tallman, I. (1972). Spousal adaptability: An assessment of marital competence. *Journal of Marriage and the Family, 34,* 247–255.

Kilmann, R., & Thomas, K. (1975). Interpersonal conflict-handling behavior as reflections of Jungian personality dimensions. *Psychological Reports, 37,* 971–980.

Kressel, K. (1987). *The process of divorce: How professionals and couples negotiate settlements.* New York: Basic Books.

Krueger, D. L., & Smith, P. (1982). Decision-making patterns of couples: A sequential analysis. *Journal of Communication, 32,* 121–134.

Margolin, G., & Wampold, B. E. (1981). Sequential analysis of conflict and accord in distressed and nondistressed marital partners. *Journal of Consulting and Clinical Psychology, 49,* 554–567.

Mettatal, G., & Gottman, J. M. (1980, November). *Affective responsiveness in spouses: Investigating the relationship between communication behavior and marital satisfaction.* Paper presented at the Speech Communication Association Convention, New York.

Millar, F. E., & Rogers, L. E. (1987). Relational dimensions of interpersonal dynamics. In M. E. Rologg & G. R. Miller (Eds.), *Interpersonal processes: New directions in communication research* (pp. 117–139). Newbury Park, CA: Sage.

Moore, C. (1986). *The mediation process: Practical strategies for resolving conflict.* San Francisco: Jossey-Bass.

Morton, T. L., Alexander, J. F., & Altman, I. (1976). Communication and relationship definition. In G. R. Miller (Ed.), *Explorations in interpersonal communication* (pp. 105–125). Newbury Park, CA: Sage.

Noller, P. (1984). *Nonverbal communication and marital interaction.* New York: Praeger.

O'Keefe, B. J., & Delia, J. G. (1982). Impression formation and message production. In M. E. Roloff & C. R. Berger (Eds.), *Social cognition and communication* (pp. 33–72). Beverly Hills, CA: Sage.

O'Keefe, D. J., & Sypher, H. E. (1981). Cognitive complexity measures and the relationship of cognitive complexity to communication: A critical review. *Human Communication Research, 8,* 72–92.

Pearson, J., & Thoennes, N. (1984). Mediating and litigating custody disputes: A longitudinal evaluation. *Family Law Quarterly, 17,* 497–524.

Peterson, D. R. (1979). Assessing interpersonal relationships by means of interaction records. *Behavioral Assessment, 1,* 221–236.

Pike, G. R., & Sillars, A. L. (1985). Reciprocity of marital communication. *Journal of Social and Personal Relationships, 2,* 303–324.

Poole, M. S., & Doelger, J. A. (1986). Developmental processes in group decision-making. In R. Y. Hirokawa & M. S. Poole (Eds.), *Communication and group decision-making* (pp. 35–61). Beverly Hills, CA: Sage.

Putnam, L. L. (1985). Bargaining as task and process: Multiple functions of interaction sequences. In R. L. Street & J. N. Cappella (Eds.), *Sequence and pattern in communicative behaviour* (pp. 225–242). London: Edward Arnold.

Rausch, H. L., Barry, W. A., Hertel, R. K., & Swain, M. A. (1974). *Communication and conflict in marriage.* San Francisco, CA: Jossey-Bass.

Roloff, M. E., & Campion, D. E. (1985). Conversational profit-seeking: Interaction as social exchange. In R. L. Street & J. N. Cappella (Eds.), *Sequence and pattern in communicative behaviour* (pp. 161–189). London: Edward Arnold.

Rubin, J. Z. (1985). Third-party intervention in family conflict. *Negotiation Journal, 1,* 269–281.

Rubin, J. Z., & Brown, B. R. (1975). *The social psychology of bargaining and negotiation.* New York: Academic Press.

Rubin, M. E. (1983). *Differences between distressed and nondistressed couples in verbal and nonverbal communication codes.* Unpublished doctoral dissertation, Indiana University.

Schroder, H. M., Driver, M. J., & Streufert, S. (1967). *Human information processing: Individuals and groups functioning in complex social situation.* New York: Holt, Rinehart, & Winston.

Shelling, T. C. (1960). *The strategy of conflict.* London: Oxford University Press.

Siegman, A. W. (1979). Cognition and hesitation in speech. In A. W. Siegman (Ed.), *Of speech and time: Temporal patterns in interpersonal contexts* (pp. 151–178). Hillsdale, NJ: Lawrence Erlbaum Associates.

Sillars, A. L. (1980). *Communication and attributions in interpersonal conflict.* Unpublished doctoral dissertation, University of Wisconsin.

Sillars, A. L. (1981). Attributions and interpersonal conflict resolution. In J. H. Harvey, W. Ickes, & R. F. Kidd (Eds.), *New directions in attribution research* (Vol. 3, pp. 279–305). Hillsdale, NJ: Lawrence Erlbaum Associates.

Sillars, A. L. (1985). Interpersonal perception in relationships. In W. J. Ickes (Ed.), *Compatible and incompatible relationships* (pp. 227–305). New York: Springer-Verlag.

Sillars, A. L., Burggraf, C. S., Yost, S., & Zietlow, P. H. (1992). Conversational themes and marital relationships: Quantitative and qualitative investigations. *Human Communication Research, 19,* 124–154.

Sillars, A. L., Coletti, S. F., Parry, D., & Rogers M. A. (1982). Coding verbal conflict tactics: Nonverbal and perceptual correlates of the "avoidance-distributive-integrative" distinction. *Human Communication Research, 9,* 83–95.

Sillars, A. L., & Kalbfleisch, P. J. (1989). Implicit and explicit decision-making styles in couples. In D. Brinberg & J. Jaccard (Eds.), *Dyadic decision-making* (pp. 179–215). New York: Springer-Verlag.

Sillars, A. L., & Parry, D. (1982). Stress, cognition, and communication in interpersonal conflicts. *Communication Research, 9,* 201–226.

Sillars, A. L., Pike, G. R., Jones, T. J., & Redmon, K. (1983). Communication and conflict in marriage. In R. N. Bostrom (Ed.), *Communication yearbook 7* (pp. 414–441). Beverly Hills, CA: Sage.

Sillars, A. L., & Weisberg, J. (1987). Conflict as a social skill. In M. E. Roloff & G. R. Miller (Eds.), *Interpersonal processes: New directions in communication research* (pp. 140–171). Newbury Park, CA: Sage.

Sillars, A. L., Weisberg, J., Burggraf, C. S., & Zeitlow, P. H. (1990). Communication and understanding revisited: Married couples' understanding and recall of conversations. *Communication Research, 17,* 500–522.

Sillars, A. L., & Wilmot, W. W. (1989). Marital communication across the life-span. In J. F. Nussbaum (Ed.), *Life-span communication: Normative processes* (pp. 225–253). Hillsdale, NJ: Lawrence Erlbaum Associates.

Suedfeld, P., & Tetlock, P. (1977). Integrative complexity of communication in international crises. *Journal of Conflict Resolution, 21,* 169–184.

Thomas, E. J. (1977). *Marital communication and decision making: Analysis, assessment, and change.* New York: Free Press.

Thomas, K. W., & Pondy, L. R. (1977). Toward an "intent" model of conflict management among principal parties. *Human Relations, 30,* 1089–1102.

Ting-Toomey, S. (1983). An analysis of verbal communication patterns in high and low marital adjustment groups. *Human Communication Research, 9,* 306–319.

Walton, R. E., & McKersie, R. B. (1965). *A behavioral theory of labor negotiations: An analysis of a social system.* New York: McGraw-Hill.

Watzlawick, P., Beavin, J., & Jackson, D. D. (1967). *Pragmatics of human communication: A study of interactional patterns, pathologies, and paradoxes.* New York: Norton.

Watzlawick, P., Weakland, J. H., & Fisch, R. (1974). *Change: Principles of problem formation and problem resolution.* New York: Norton.

Weick, K. E. (1971). Group processes, family processes, and problem solving. In J. Aldous, T. Landon, R. Hall, M. Straus, & I. Tallman (Eds.), *Family problem solving: A symposium of theoretical, methodological, and substantive concerns* (pp. 3–39). Hinsdale, IL: Dryden Press.

Weiss, R. L., Hops, H., & Patterson, G. R. (1973). A framework for conceptualizing marital conflict: A technology for altering it, some data for evaluating it. In L. A. Hamerlynck, L. C. Hundy, & E. J. Mash (Eds.), *Behavior change: Methodology, concepts, and practice* (pp. 309–342). Champaign, IL: Research Press.

Wiemann, J. J. (1977). Explication and test of a model of communicative competence. *Human Communication Research, 3,* 195–213.

Zietlow, P. H., & Sillars, A. L. (1988). Life stage differences in communication during marital conflicts. *Journal of Social and Personal Relationships, 5,* 223–245.

Chapter 7

Deception: Strategic and Nonstrategic Communication

David B. Buller
Judee K. Burgoon
University of Arizona

DEFINITIONS AND PERSPECTIVE

At the heart of the strategic communication perspective is the assumption that people control the information they present in their messages (Turner, Edgley, & Olmstead, 1975). When managing impressions, negotiating conversations, comforting others, gaining compliance, expressing affinity, adapting to another culture, responding to others, resolving conflict, and seeking additional information from others, people must consider what types, how much, and in what order information is communicated.

An important consideration in this information-transmittal process is whether to send information that is entirely honest or to modify it in some way that departs from the truth as the source knows it. Society and most conversations rest on an assumption of veracity in information exchange. That is, the information presented in a message and its intended meaning are assumed to be truthful (Goffman, 1959; Knapp & Comadena, 1979). In actual practice, though, communicators frequently decide that honesty is not the best strategy. Instead, they conclude that some measure of dishonesty will best achieve their desired communication outcomes. Many people, therefore, find the ability to successfully deceive others an indispensible strategy for acquiring goods and services, developing and managing satisfying social relationships, and creating and managing a desired image (Ekman, 1985; Turner et al., 1975; Wolk & Henley, 1970; Zuckerman, DePaulo, & Rosenthal, 1981). Knapp, Hart, and Dennis (1974) explained:

Lying is an adaptive behavior first practiced in situations where it is a harbinger of success . . . its efficiency is in solving interpersonal or other problems. The fact that deception, as a communicative strategy, is often rewarded causes us to resort frequently to varying degrees of fabrication to suit our personal, pragmatic purposes. (p. 16)

Kraut (1980) suggested that the ability to deceive has evolutionary origins. Due to its adaptive benefits, deception has been essential for human survival and naturally selected as a communication skill of the human species. On the other side of the interaction, Kraut also suggested that the ability to detect deception is adaptive and has been selected along with the ability to deceive. Although Kraut's genetic explanation may go too far, it does appear that, at the very least, the ability to deceive can be socially adaptive and an important component of a communicator's repertoire.

Definitions

Typically, deception is defined by scholars and researchers as a communicative act intended to create in the target person a belief that the source considers false, either by causing a false belief to be formed or by altering a preexisting belief to a false state (Knapp & Comadena, 1979; Zuckerman, DePaulo, & Rosenthal, 1981; Zuckerman & Driver, 1985). Some authors have advocated that along with the intent to deceive, a source must verbalize a belief that he or she considers false; that is, actually fabricate a verbal message containing false information (Chisholm & Feehan, 1977). This requirement, though, is too restrictive. Knapp and Comadena (1979), Hopper and Bell (1984), and Buller (1986, 1987c) pointed out, and we concur, that the transmission of false verbal information is not necessary for deception to occur. Communicators can create a false belief in the target's mind by transmitting ambiguous or vague messages, omitting information from truthful messages, varying the intensity of truthful information through exaggeration and minimization, and manipulating environmental cues to create deceptive frames. Moreover, we believe that requiring a verbalized false belief oversimplifies the deception process, which includes many important nonverbal messages. For our discussion, therefore, we define deception as the intent to deceive a target by controlling information (e.g., transmitting verbal and nonverbal messages, and/or manipulating situational cues) to alter the target's beliefs or understanding in a way that the deceiver knows is false. In addition, we rule out of our present discussion self-deceptions, intentionally transparent lies (such as jokes), and mistaken lies (such as unknowingly providing faulty instructions). Self-deceptions are noncommunicative. Intentionally transparent lies are not expected to result in target misunderstanding. And, mistaken lies do not arise from an intent to deceive.

Implicit in our definition is the idea that in actual practice, deception involves more than simple deceptive intent and a single deceptive verbal message. Deceptive intent actually is comprised of one or more motives. As we point out, these motives are not unlike the multiple motives underlying influence messages in general. Similarly, a deceptive message is frequently a composite of several messages. When deceiving, a communicator encodes a deceptive message designed to create the false belief, accompanied by several nonverbal and verbal messages designed to establish the veracity of the central deceptive message or to protect the source in the event that deception is detected. Also, during deception several nonstrategic messages are inadvertently transmitted that communicate that deception is occurring (deception cues in Ekman & Friesen's, 1969, formulation) or that leak the true information being concealed (leakage cues according to Ekman & Friesen, 1969).

Alternative Perspectives

Our approach to deception is slightly unorthodox, because we take an instrumental or functional perspective on deception. In contrast, the vast majority of scholars have adopted, at least implicitly, the perspective that deception is socially reprehensible, generally harmful to the receiver, and an undesirable communication strategy. This perspective parallels a dominant moral value in our culture that ''honesty is the best policy'' and deception is among the most unacceptable communication acts (Turner et al., 1975). Arising from this perspective, most research on deception has been designed to uncover behaviors, mostly nonstrategic, which are reliable indicators of deception or the success with which receivers detect deception.

As communication scholars, we believe that this perspective is too narrow. First, it departs considerably from social reality (Ekman, 1985). Deception is more prevalent than our cultural morality implies. Moreover, like other strategic communication, deception is encoded to achieve a variety of communication goals, some beneficial to the communicator, others to the target, others to the relationship, and still others to a third party (Camden, Motley, & Wilson, 1984; Metts & Chronis, 1986). It is the motivations behind deception, not the deceptive act itself, whose morality should be judged. Second, the prevailing perspective promotes a restricted analysis of the deception process. We believe an amoral perspective on deception is more likely to encourage research and thinking about the broader process of deception, particularly the strategic use of deception, which is only recently gaining the attention of researchers. However, currently we possess extensive information on indicants of deception but relatively less data on what causes people to deceive, how people go about deceiving, and what leads to deception success.

The dominant emphasis on detection and the reprehensibility of deception has also limited our theories about deception. The major theory in deception is concerned with largely nonrational, uncontrollable, and low-awareness cognitive processes that trigger nonstrategic cues indicative of deception. In contrast, we possess almost no theoretical understanding of strategic communication behavior during deception, although we show later that communication researchers have begun to describe typologies of deception messages. In developing a theoretical framework to explain the strategic use of deception, the parallel that comes most quickly to mind is the theory explaining how people strategically use interpersonal influence messages. That deception is a form of social influence is not an idea unique to us. Several scholars writing on the general social influence function have included deception within this function; however, most have not elaborated deception's role in influencing others (Patterson, 1983; Schenck-Hamlin, Wiseman, & Georgacarakos, 1982; Seibold, Cantrill, & Meyers, 1985). Recently, Buller (1987b) noted the similarity between deception and interpersonal influence processes as typically conceptualized:

> interpersonal influence researchers define interpersonal influence as "the process and paths by which individuals reinforce or *alter each others' cognitions, emotions, and behaviors*" [italics added] (Seibold et al., 1985, p. 558) . . . Thus, one might predict that selecting among alternate deception messages follows a process similar to selecting among compliance-gaining messages. Both processes are likely to be goal-directed, premeditated, require cognitive processing, create affective feelings, and determine the verbal and nonverbal cues displayed by the source, and in turn cause cognitive, affective, and behavioral reactions by the target. (pp. 6–7)

A Strategic Perspective

Currently, much research on interpersonal influence is guided by a rational Strategic Choice Model (Seibold et al., 1985). This model appears to be well suited for explaining the use of deception to influence the beliefs of others. Specifically, communicators choose influence messages by (a) assessing their motives, the nature of the influence situation, and their relationship with the target, (b) appraising the alternative influence messages in their communication repertoire, (c) selecting a particular message and foregoing others, and (d) monitoring the reactions of the target in order to formulate subsequent message choices.

There are several reasons to believe that deception follows a rational choice model. First, the fact that deception is considered by some to be socially inappropriate may make the choice to deceive a very conscious, deliberate one in which the communicator takes into account situational, relational, and personal factors before choosing to deceive. Second, deception may require more cognitive effort and planning than truthtelling (Knapp & Comadena, 1979;

Zuckerman, DePaulo, & Rosenthal, 1981; Zuckerman & Driver, 1985). Third, not only are there multiple motives for deception, but communicators have several alternatives when it comes to formulating their deception message. As we review later, researchers are beginning to catalogue deception message types. When the central content of deceptive messages is coupled with the nonverbal and verbal messages designed to substantiate their veracity, the number of alternative deception strategies at a communicator's disposal increases. These multiple decision points necessitate some thought. Finally, feedback from the receiver may be particularly critical to communicators when they deceive. Communicators must guard against and take actions to reduce suspiciousness and incredulity; in other words, they must formulate strategies to minimize the risks of detection when they exist.

Three caveats to our perspective should be mentioned. First, we do not advocate the increased use of deception. Rather, we acknowledge the already prevalent use of deception and call for a more realistic and expanded view of deception to understand its role in human communication. Second, we do not believe that deception is always positive. Instead, we argue that the motive behind the deceptive act, not the act itself, determines its acceptability. Some deception is reprehensible; however, one can deceive for altruistic reasons, as well. Third, our perspective does not trivialize the body of knowledge we already possess about deception, which offers an important database for scholars interested in deception. We believe, though, that it speaks to only one part of the deception process and that the remaining, largely strategic, aspects of deception deserve equal scholarly attention. It is our hope that in adopting this functional, strategic perspective on deception, our discussion will place the current knowledge in proper perspective, provide guideposts for future research within our expanded perspective, and make tentative suggestions aimed at a more elaborated theory of deception that explains why and how people deceive, as well as how people can detect deception.

MOTIVES FOR DECEPTION

Research on the motives for deception reveals that they are very similar to motives behind any message designed to influence another person's beliefs. R. A. Clark (1984), R. A. Clark and Delia (1979), and O'Keefe and Delia (1982) identify three classes of motives for strategically selecting influence messages. *Instrumental objectives* are the specific attitudinal and behavioral changes desired by the communicator. *Interpersonal objectives* concern the establishment and maintenance of a particular interpersonal relationship. *Identity objectives* relate to the image projected by the influencer such as credibility, dominance, expertise, and composure.

Instrumental Motives

Four recent studies have identified several instrumental motives for deception. Turner et al. (1975) reported a set of exploitation motives, including establishing, maximizing, and maintaining power or influence over the target. Similarly, Camden et al. (1984) found that many deceptions were motivated by basic needs, including the acquisition and protection of resources, avoidance of dissonance, and entertainment (practical jokes and exaggeration for effect). Lindskold and Walters (1983) also identified the instrumental objectives of avoiding punishment or disapproval, acquiring or protecting self-gain, and attempting to harm the target for self-gain. In Metts and Chronis' (1986) study, communicators often deceived to protect their resources and to continue receiving some reward or service from the target.

Interpersonal Motives

A much larger set of deception motives is related to the relationship between the deceiver and target. Some of these interpersonal objectives are self-serving, but a significant portion of deceptions are motivated by concerns for the partner and the relationship (Hample, 1980). For instance, respondents in Turner et al.'s (1975) study said they deceived others to maintain, maximize, or terminate relationships, to avoid tension or conflict in relationships, and to maintain, redirect, or terminate social interaction. Camden et al. (1984) identified a group of affiliation motives that included initiating, continuing, and avoiding social interaction, avoiding relational conflict, expressing obligatory acceptance, leave-taking, redirecting the conversation, and avoiding self-disclosure. Lindskold and Walters (1983) found that deception was motivated to protect the target from minor hurt and from punishment or disapproval. Metts and Chronis (1986) reported that deception often was encoded to avoid relational conflict, relational trauma, unpleasant repetitive episodes in relationships, partner worry, and violations of relational role expectations. Also, deception was encoded to protect the target's relationship with a third party.

Identity Motives

Identity objectives are equally important to deception. As with interpersonal objectives, identity objectives can be related to identity needs of a target or third party, as well as the identity needs of the deceiver. Turner et al. (1975) reported a cluster of motives labelled ''saving face,'' either for self, the target, or a third party to the interaction. In Lindskold and Walters' (1983) study, deception was motivated to save the target from shame or embarrassment and to make the deceiver appear better. Similarly, Camden et al. (1984) found that deception was encoded to enhance or protect the self-esteem of the deceiver, target, or third party. This included perceptions of competence, good taste, and social desirability. Finally, Metts and Chronis' (1986) respondents deceived to regulate, constrain, or maintain the target's self-image or self-esteem, and to protect or enhance the deceiver's image in the target's eyes.

Several conclusions arise from these data. First, many deceptions are encoded for selfish reasons; however, not all selfish reasons are vicious or socially undesirable. Second, communicator's often select deception to assist the target, to benefit the relationship with the target, and to maintain the interests of politeness and good taste. Ekman (1985), however, speculated that fewer deceptions are actually motivated by altruistic reasons than are reported. These motives are more socially acceptable, so communicators may prefer to think that their deceptions are altruistic when in fact they are self-serving. Third, the ability to deceive successfully arguably could be considered a socially competent communication strategy (Camden et al., 1984; Lindskold & Walters, 1983). At times, the truth can be very painful to the target, and sparing the target this painful experience may be the socially appropriate course of action. This does not imply that targets desire to be deceived. Simply, not all deceptions are designed to be cruel and self-serving, and not all deceptions should be considered morally reprehensible without considering the motives behind their use. (See Ekman, 1985, and Knapp & Comadena, 1979, for similar arguments).

The Need to Examine Multiple Motives

Unfortunately, few researchers, including the ones cited in this section, have incorporated these multifaceted motives into experiments examining deceptive messages. A few studies have manipulated a deceiver's "motivation to succeed" (Bauchner, Brandt, & Miller, 1977; DePaulo, Lanier, & Davis, 1983; Exline, Thibaut, Hickey, & Gumpert, 1970; Mehrabian, 1972; Zuckerman, DePaulo, & Rosenthal, 1981; Zuckerman & Driver, 1985). These manipulations, however, have concerned the degree of motivation rather than its nature, with most of these experiments limited to manipulating the degree of instrumental motivation. Moreover, the instrumental resource motivating deception in these experiments is generally controlled by the experimenter rather than the target (e.g., offering a prize to the most successful deceiver). The generalizability of these experiments to the instrumental motives identified in this section is open to question, as many of the instrumental objectives noted here are designed to acquire or maintain resources or services provided by the target. The present data also provide very little information about the impact of interpersonal and identity motives in deception, beyond simply highlighting their existence.

One reason interpersonal and identity motives ought to be examined more fully is that they may alter the selection of deception messages. For example,

Metts and Chronis (1986) found that, when deceivers were motivated to avoid hurting the partner, to avoid relational trauma, or to protect the deceiver's image, falsification strategies were common. Interpersonal motivations, especially ones benefiting the target and relationships, also may reduce the negative feelings experienced by many people during deception, reducing the display of negative affect frequently observed in deceivers. Conversely, there may be instances when certain instrumental, interpersonal, and identity motives exacerbate negative feelings, making deception more difficult because more extreme emotional reactions are harder to conceal (Ekman, 1985; Hocking, Bauchner, Kaminski, & Miller, 1979).

Finally, one's personal values and previous experiences may affect the selection and success of deception strategies. Camden et al. (1984) reported that males felt deception was more permissible than females, suggesting that they may deceive more than women. There is some evidence that practice at deception improves the likelihood of success (DePaulo, Stone, & Lassiter, 1985; Zuckerman, DePaulo, & Rosenthal, 1981; Zuckerman & Driver, 1985). If this is true, then males may be more skillful deceivers, in general. By contrast, females in Camden et al.'s study were more likely to deceive for interpersonal reasons than males. Further, females were more likely to deceive to protect the partner's self-esteem (an identity motive), but males were more likely to deceive to protect their own self-esteem, particularly when interacting with a female. Thus, females may be more successful when deceiving for interpersonal reasons and to protect the target's identity, because they have more experience at deceiving for these reasons. Males, meanwhile, may be more skillful at deceiving to protect their own image.

DECEPTIVE ACTS

Surprisingly, the central communication act in the deception process, namely the verbal or nonverbal message designed to create a false belief or alter an existing belief to a false state, has received relatively less research attention than the nonverbal leakage cues that accompany this deceptive message. Until recently, the study of actual deception messages has been relegated to largely intuitive speculation (cf. DePaulo, Zuckerman, & Rosenthal, 1980b; Ekman, 1985; Kraut, 1980). However, researchers have begun the task of documenting a typology of deception strategies.

Types of Deceptive Acts

Turner et al. (1975) reported that 62% of the statements in general conversation exhibited some information control that could be classified as deception. That is, only 38% of the statements were completely honest. Moreover, Turner et al. identified five types of deceptive acts. *Lies* are statements that contain information contradicting information that would be contained in an honest statement. This type of information control was employed in 30% of the statements. *Exaggerations* are statements in which the deceiver creates an overstatement by giving more information than would be given in an honest statement. Exaggerations were encoded in 5% of the deceptive statements. *Half-truths* are statements that omit or conceal part of the truthful information. Frequently these statements contain both truthful and deceptive information. They were used in 29% of deceptive statements. *Secrets* are instances where the deceiver remains silent when possessing information relevant to the conversation. Turner et al. found these to be very rare, occurring in only 3% of the conversations. Finally, *diversionary responses* are statements that are irrelevant to the information the deceiver would have provided in honest discourse. These responses, used in 32% of the statements, conceal actual feelings by diverting the conversation away from the topic that the deceiver finds difficult, embarrassing, or distasteful to address.

More recently, Metts and Chronis (1986) identified three forms of deceptive acts. Like Turner et al.'s (1975) study, *falsifications, half-truths,* and *concealments* comprised the vast majority of deceptive statements reported by Metts and Chronis' undergraduates. However, in a slight departure from Turner et al., falsifications were the most prevalent form of deception (48% of statements). Concealment and half-truths were used less frequently but still occurred in approximately one quarter of the deceptive statements (27% and 23%, respectively). Within these latter two categories, Metts and Chronis distinguished concealment and half-truths dealing with feelings from those dealing with information. This distinction, though, does not seem essential for developing an exhaustive set of deception messages, as it constitutes difference in semantic content rather than structural form. This difference, however, may be relevant to the relational messages discussed in the next section and to the target's efforts to detect deception because of the relative difficulty of concealing emotional information (Ekman, 1985; Hocking et al., 1979).

By far the most exhaustive list of deceptive acts has been provided by Hopper and Bell (1984). Using a "linguistic turn" methodology, they collected a list of English language terms related to deception. From this list, they selected 46 unique forms of deception and submitted them to a group of subjects with the instructions to sort the terms into groups based on their perceived similarity. Six clusters of deceptive acts emerged: fictions (make-believing, exaggerations, myth, irony, tall tale, white lie), playings (joking, teasing, kidding, tricking, bluffing, hoax), lies (dishonesty, fibbing, lie, untruth, cheating), crimes (con, conspiracy, entrapment, spying, disguise, counterfeit, cover-up, forgery), masks (hypocrisy, two-faced, back-stabbing, evasion, masking, concealment), and unlies (distortion, misleading, false implication, misrepresentation). Finally, Hopper and Bell asked another group of subjects to rate each of the 46 terms on an evaluation dimension (right vs. wrong), the degree of detectability, and the amount of premeditation required in each act. Hopper and Bell concluded that fictions and playings constitute a category of benign deceptive acts, whereas lies, crimes, masks, and unlies are exploitative deceptive acts, a conclusion supported by their evaluation ratings.

Most recently, we (Burgoon, Buller, Feldman, Guerrero, & Afifi, 1993) and McCornack (1992) argued that deceptive messages can be created by manipulating several message characteristics with the aim of decreasing detectability or disassociating the sender from the message to provide deniability. The most obvious way of managing information in deception is to reduce its veracity. Beyond this, deception can occur when (a) senders are less informative, syntactically incomplete (i.e., the message is not well-formed and does not meet the minimal requirements for a response); or (b) semantically incomplete (pertinent information is not shared). Senders can also be deceptive by (a) enacting messages that are syntactically ambiguous (obfuscating by being indecipherable because of the language or sentence structure used); (b) semantically ambiguous (obfuscating by presenting content that could be interpreted in multiple ways or that equivocates); (c) syntactically indirect (not being grammatically coherent with the previous utterance); or (d) semantically irrelevant (not giving content that is related to the previous utterance).

The research by these scholars points out that communicators are not limited simply to lying when selecting a deception strategy. At the very least, they can select from among five types of deceptive acts that (a) fabricate false information, (b) conceal truthful information, (c) exaggerate truthful information, (d) mix truthful and deceptive information, or (e) imply false conclusions or misdirect attention. Communicators can also combine several of these deceptive acts in the same deception. Hopper and Bell's (1984) crimes and playings are examples of such multifaceted deceptions. These general categories and specific acts are summarized in Table 7.1.

The choice among deceptive acts doubtless is a function of whether the deception is premeditated, time available to plan, consequences of being detected, and anticipated success in escaping detection (Hopper & Bell, 1984). On the issue of success, Turner et al. (1975) concluded that diversionary responses are the most advantageous deceptive acts. Besides steering the conversation away from the concealed information without actually falsifying information, they reduce the risk of being detected. Ekman (1985) likewise pointed out that concealment may be easier to cover up, once detected, by citing an error in memory, ignorance, failure to see the relevance of the concealed information, or the like. Moreover, although diversionary responses and concealment may be regarded as uncooperative behavior (in the sense of Grice's maxim of quantity in conversational), they are less blatant and reprehensible than outright lying. Similarly, Bavelas, Black, Chovil, and Mullett (1990) argued that *equivocation* is a popular deception strategy because it creates a false belief without

TABLE 7.1
Types of Deceptive Acts

General	Specific
Fabrications	falsifications, dishonesty, fibbing, lie, untruth, cheating
Concealment/Omissions	secrets, hypocrisy, two-faced, back-stabbing, evasion, masking
Exaggerations/Fictions	distortion, make-believing, myth, tall tale, white lie, irony
Half-truths	mix of truthful and dishonest information
Implicit Falsification/Misdirection	diversionary responses, misleading, false implication, misrepresentation
Crimes	con, conspiracy, entrapment, spying, disguise, counterfeiting, cover-up, forgery
Playings	joking, teasing, kidding, tricking, bluffing, hoax

being dishonest. As Chisholm and Feehan (1977) argued, lies are considered wrong, "because unlike the other types of intended deception, [lying] is essentially a breach of faith" (p. 153). That is, the target is assumed to have the right to think that the source believes the statement he or she asserts; in lying, the source has violated the target's right. Such a violation of rights, however, does not occur when truthful information is concealed through omission rather than fabrication.

One of the most serious outcomes of these studies has been to raise questions concerning the generalizability of deception research that focuses exclusively on lying. Though not the first to speculate about this issue (cf. Knapp & Comadena, 1979; Kraut, 1980), Hopper and Bell (1984) voiced one of the most strident calls for expanding deception research:

> We suggest that future investigations of deception should be guided by four premises. First, deception can be carried out via words and/or actions; deceivers are not limited to verbal messages. Second, deceivers can communicate false information but they can also deceive by communicating true information leading to false conclusions; they may also deceive through noncommunication (omission). Third, acts of deception vary tremendously in their consistency with ethical standards . . . their detectability, and their level of premeditation. Fourth, and perhaps most important, not all deceptions are lies. (p. 300)

Deception researchers, however, have defended methodologies that employ lying. DePaulo et al. (1980b) claimed that although several forms of deceptive acts are available to a communicator, deception in actual practice is characterized primarily by lies. Therefore, the data from experiments on lying are generalizable to the broader deception process.

In addition, Buller (1987b) asked research participants faced with hypothetical situations to select responses from among the 46 types of deceptive acts in Hopper and Bell's (1984) typology. He found that communicators did not distinguish between different forms of deceptive acts when making their selections. Rather, they seemed to consider the acceptability of deception within each situation. As the acceptability of deception increased, more deceptive acts were selected. The acceptability dimension underlying the deceptive acts was nonlinear as a result of the communicator's selection threshold. The selection threshold was the point along the continuum of deceptive acts that separated acceptable acts, which were highly likely to be employed, from unacceptable acts, which were less likely to be used by the communicator. The selection threshold was a function of situational factors, not structural differences in the deceptive acts, except that playful deception messages (joking, kidding, and teasing) were selected in a different manner than the other deceptive acts.

These data do not deny the existence of multiple types of deceptive acts, however, they do suggest that when selecting deceptive acts, the overriding concern for communicators is whether or not it is socially acceptable to deceive the target. It may be that the choice between specific types of acts is dictated more by habit, situational, or relational factors, *after* the communicator makes the conscious choice to deceive the target.

Hankiss (1980) suggested that for most people, deception is a spur-of-the-moment decision, and because deception is rarely premeditated, deceivers have little time to select from among a large repertoire of deceptive acts. Consistent with this suggestion, Metts and Chronis (1986) reported that quick selections, caused by a question posed by the target, commonly resulted in fabrication. However, Metts and Chronis also showed that deception is at times premeditated, and that when the deceiver has ample time to plan the deception, concealment strategies increase in frequency. This implies that deceivers select from a broader set of deceptive acts when engaging in premeditated deceptions. Ekman (1985) made the same claim, though he did not provide data relevant to it. Beyond preparation time, Metts and Chronis also showed that the nature of the relationship with the target determined selection. Falsification was most frequent with dating partners and least frequent with spouses, whereas half-truths were employed more with spouses than with dating partners and friends.

To summarize, the findings provided by experiments employing lying should not be devalued or discarded, inasmuch as they provide information about behavior in situations where the decision to deceive has been made. Efforts should be made to manipulate the acceptability of deception through situational and relational factors, as acceptability appears central to the decision to deceive. The situational and relational differences highlighted by Metts and Chronis (1986) and the detectability differences perceived by Hopper and Bell's (1984) subjects suggest that it would be fruitful to explore the selection of deceptive acts under different situational and relational conditions and to assess the success with which different forms of deceptive acts are used. Finally, research on other aspects of the social influence function has shown that often the most effective means of influencing another person is through the careful sequencing of influence messages (M. Burgoon & Miller, 1985; Seibold et al., 1985). The same should be true of deceptive acts. Deceivers may find that they must respond and adapt to statements from the target in order to allay suspiciousness; that a deceptive act at one point in a conversation must be supported by a deceptive act at a later time in the conversation; and that deception during the current conversation may need to be continued in future conversations. The transactional nature of interpersonal encounters warrants much more intensive investigation of how deceptive acts unfold over time and are modified in response to target feedback (J. K. Burgoon, 1989).

STRATEGIC COMMUNICATION
VERSUS NONSTRATEGIC LEAKAGE

When communicators encode these deceptive messages, they are usually accompanied by other communicative behaviors. In addition to the deceptive act itself, deceptions often include verbal and nonverbal behaviors strategically designed to authenticate the deceptive act and/or to protect the source and the interpersonal relationship. Within this group are messages that seek to create intimacy, trust, and good rapport (Buller, 1987a). Other strategic messages function to distance or disassociate the deceiver from the deception. They serve to reduce the deceiver's responsibility for the deceptive act and to reduce the negative consequences if the deception is detected, by creating ambiguity and vagueness and by communicating lower conversational involvement.

Many behaviors emitted by a deceiver, though, are not strategically designed to substantiate the truth of the deception. Instead, they inadvertently leak the deceiver's deceptive intent by signaling cognitive changes that occur when a communicator deceives. Such leakage cues may have relational implications.

The two general categories of strategic communication and nonstrategic leakage can be further subdivided according to the communicative meanings or functions they accomplish. Knapp et al. (1974) originally proposed that deception behaviors (a) signal uncertainty, (b) express vagueness, (c) show reticence or withdrawal, (d) imply greater dependence on others through disassociation from one's own words or actions, (e) leak nervousness, and (f) leak unpleasantness or negative affect. Of these, the first four can be considered strategic relational messages. DePaulo et al. (1985) introduced another possible strategic category—image-protecting behavior. They also include disaffiliation and nonimmediacy among their style classifications. Both of these can be seen as extensions of the reticence idea. The latter two categories proposed by Knapp et al., leaking nervousness and unpleasantness, are related to nonstrategic leakage during deception. Miller and J. K. Burgoon (1982) expanded this set of behavioral style categories to include (g) exhibiting behavior that deviates from a communicator's normal response patterns, and (h) incongruous responses, or behavior in contradiction with actual feelings. When liars are too smooth or too forced, speak far more rapidly than normal, or suddenly suppress their normal body activity, they are displaying deviant behavior. When their facial emotions are contradicted by their verbal behavior, they are displaying incongruous responses. Others have referred to this as discrepant behavior.

If we try to distill these various perspectives into a more parsimonious, single set of relational message categories, cast according to their communicative impact rather than their underlying causes, it is possible to identify four types of general, purposeful communication that liars may employ and three forms of nonstrategic "leakage." The more strategic or intentional communications, which reflect attempted control, are:

1. *Uncertainty and vagueness:* predominantly linguistic behaviors used to create ambiguous, opaque, or intentionally mixed messages.
2. *Nonimmediacy, reticence, and withdrawal:* verbal and nonverbal means used to distance oneself from others, to disaffiliate, and to close off scrutiny or probing communication.
3. *Disassociation:* predominantly linguistic behaviors used to distance oneself from responsibility for one's own statements and actions and to imply dependence on the actions of others. This corresponds in some respects to an external locus of control.
4. *Image- and relationship-protecting behavior:* verbal and nonverbal behaviors used to make oneself appear sincere and trustworthy and to sustain the self-presentation one has created.

Nonstrategic leakage includes:

1. *Revealing arousal and nervousness:* exhibition of nonverbal cues that betray one's heightened state of physiological arousal. The arousal associated with "duping delight"—glee at successfully misleading others—also fits here.
2. *Revealing negative affect:* exhibition of verbal and nonverbal behaviors that leak unpleasant feelings possibly associated with guilt and embarrassment at engaging in deception.
3. *Incompetent communication performance:* verbal and nonverbal behavior patterns such as extreme and nonnormative behavior, awkward conversation, and discrepancies between channels that yield an awkward, substandard communicative performance. These decrements in com-

municative capability may be the result of the cognitive complexity of the deception task or of excessive motivation to succeed, leading to a forced, stilted, halting, or incongruous presentation.

STRATEGIC COMMUNICATION

Let us now review what specific behaviors have been hypothesized and confirmed as associated with each of these strategic and nonstrategic forms. In summarizing this literature, we have relied in part on several meta-analyses and summaries reported by Kraut (1980), DePaulo, Zuckerman, and Rosenthal (1980a), Zuckerman, DePaulo, and Rosenthal (1981), Zuckerman and Driver (1985), and DePaulo et al. (1985). The Zuckerman and Driver analysis, based on 45 studies, includes those previously analyzed by Kraut (1980) and Zuckerman, DePaulo, and Rosenthal (1981) and is one of the more comprehensive syntheses of what nonverbal and verbal cues accompany duplicity. Importantly, Zuckerman and Driver reported that 58% of the behaviors examined in two or more of the studies they analyzed reliably distinguish truthtellers from liars.

However, the meta-analyses don't tell the whole story. They exclude a large number of experiments and analyses, including all those published by communication scholars. We therefore add where necessary those citations that Zuckerman and Driver (1985) and others omitted. Although there are some inconsistencies and contradictions in the findings, there are recurrent patterns in deceivers' verbal and nonverbal relational messages. Table 7.2 summarizes the results of our review.

Uncertainty and Vagueness

Knapp et al. (1974) proposed that liars would express uncertainty through the use of fewer absolute verbs, fewer total different words, and lower confidence ratios, whereas they would express vagueness through such things as avoidance of factual assertions, fewer references to self-experiences, fewer references to the past, and more leveling terms that create broad generalizations (e.g., *all*, *never*). In their experiment, they found support for all of these verbal patterns except the use of absolute verbs. In a study designed to validate the Knapp et al. behavioral indices, Todd-Mancillas and Kibler (1979) showed that the number of different words and confidence ratios were indeed valid indicators of uncertainty.

The Zuckerman meta-analyses (Zuckerman, DePaulo, & Rosenthal, 1981; Zuckerman & Driver, 1985) confirm that liars introduce more irrelevant information into their discourse, reduce their response length (which is equiva-

TABLE 7.2
Strategic Communication and Nonstrategic Leakage

	Specific Nonverbal and Verbal Behavior
Strategic Communication	
Uncertainty and vagueness	fewer different words, lower confidence ratios, fewer factual assertions, fewer references to self-experiences, fewer references to the past, more leveling terms ("all", "never"), more irrelevant information, shorter responses, fewer past tense verbs, less conditional language (males only), greater lexical diversity[1], more frequent hand shrugs, fewer absolute verbs[2]
Nonimmediacy, reticence, and withdrawal	fewer total words, shorter responses[1], more probing questions from receivers, verbal nonimmediacy, more pausing, longer response latencies[1], less gaze[1], more one-sided gazing, less forward lean, greater distance
Disassociation	fewer self-references[1], fewer self-interest statements[1], more other-references[1], verbal nonimmediacy
Image- and relationship-protecting behavior	nodding[1], smiling[1], refraining from interruptions, suppression of leakage cues
Nonstrategic Leakage	
Arousal and nervousness	more blinking, greater pupil dilation or instability, more self- and object-manipulations, higher pitch, vocal nervousness, more speech errors and hesitations, more word repetitions, shorter responses, longer response latencies, less gesturing[1], stiff, restrained trunk and limb positions[1], more leg, foot, head, and posture shifts[1], more body blocks, abortive flight movement, fewer facial changes, more bodily activity[1]
Negative affect	micromomentary facial expressions of displeasure and discomfort, less positive feedback (nodding, smiling), reduced gaze, less pleasant vocal tone, fewer group references, more disparaging remarks, more negative statements
Incompetent communication performance	a pattern of more speech errors, hesitations, word repetitions, postural rigidity, random nervousness movements, and halting, brief messages; faster or slower speaking tempo; channel discrepancies and dissynchrony; exaggerated performances; lack of spontaneity; departure from normal behavior

[1]Some research on this behavior has failed to support this pattern or has found the opposite pattern.
[2]Hypothesized behavior not yet confirmed by research.

lent to using fewer total words), and use more leveling. Other research by Dulaney (1982) likewise demonstrates that liars use fewer words, fewer different words, fewer past tense verbs, and, among men, less conditional language, which might approximate leveling. Surprisingly, that study also showed that liars had a higher type-token ratio (TTR), which is a measure of diversity of lexical choices. This runs contrary to the typical hypothesis that liars, due to their greater anxiety and arousal, will be less capable of generating a diverse vocabulary (see Osgood, 1960). However, Dulaney (1982) demonstrated through a partial correlation analysis that the higher TTR was the result of the smaller number of total words used by liars and thus was an artifact of how the TTR is calculated. Nevertheless, Carpenter (1981) proposed that when people are attempting to be cautious, they may use greater lexical diversity in their effort to dissemble. His conclusions are based on a detailed content analysis of the interrogation of a murder suspect. Whether his calculations of the TTR were artificially affected by the total number of words used is unclear. The conjecture itself is an interesting one that merits further attention.

One final nonverbal cue uncovered through meta-analysis is the greater use of hand shrugs (Zuckerman, DePaulo, & Rosenthal, 1981).

Thus, one of the key ways liars attempt to avoid detection and to successfully perpetrate their deceptions is to make their communication brief, vague, noncommittal, and unverifiable. That this strategy is often successful is indicated by results from DePaulo et al. (1985) showing that highly motivated liars are especially good at hiding their lies through their words; it is their nonverbal behaviors that give them away. (Liars who are less motivated, however, are often betrayed by their verbal behavior.)

Nonimmediacy, Reticence, and Withdrawal

Included in this category are a host of nonverbal behaviors such as physical proximity, eye gaze, body orientation, body lean, and touch that may be used to signal detachment and disaffiliation; vocalic behaviors such as pausing and long response latencies that signal reticence; and verbal behaviors such as shorter responses, use of past rather than present tense verbs, and nonconcrete referents that express nonimmediacy and psychological distance.

Verbally, the use of fewer total words by liars, cited previously as creating vagueness, may also convey reticence. Knapp et al. (1974) also found liars were subjected to more probing questions by their interrogators. Todd-Mancillas and Kibler (1979) confirmed that the number of words spoken, message duration, and probing questions were legitimate measures of nonimmediacy. Other research by Kuiken (1981) showed that people use more nonimmediate language when they fabricate a reply about liked or disliked traits of self or another. The Zuckerman and Driver (1985) meta-analysis supports the use of verbal nonimmediacy as a correlate of lying.

Nonverbally, results have been more conclusive in the vocal domain than in the kinesic and proxemic domains. The use of shorter replies, more pauses, and longer response latencies are consistent with being more reticent and hesitant. Several studies (e.g., Baskett & Freedle, 1974; Buller, Comstock, Aune, & Strzyzewski, 1989; deTurck & Miller, 1985; Feldman, Devin-Sheehan, & Allen, 1978; Goldstein, 1923; Knapp et al., 1974; Krauss, Geller, & Olson,

1976; Kraut, 1978; Mehrabian, 1971; Motley, 1974) showed that these vocalic patterns accompany dissembling. Exceptions include studies showing that some liars increased, some decreased, and some alternated between increasing and decreasing their reaction time (English, 1926; Marston, 1920), and a study (Matarazzo, Wiens, Jackson, & Manaugh, 1970) showing the topic influenced whether liars had shorter or longer answers and response latencies. As for the other codes, Mehrabian (1972) and Knapp et al. (1974) reported that liars decrease the frequency and duration of glances, decrease forward body lean, and increase distance. Buller and Aune (1987) also found that deceivers gaze less overall, gaze more when targets are not looking at them, and engage in less forward lean. However, DePaulo et al. (1985) claimed that liars do not avert their eyes any more than truthtellers do. That conclusion is based on the fact that some experiments have failed to find gaze differences between liars and truthtellers (e.g., Matarazzo et al., 1970; McClintock & Hunt, 1975), although others find increased eye contact from liars (e.g., Riggio & Friedman, 1983). These inconsistencies may stem from the dynamic nature of eye contact. Buller and his colleagues (Buller & Aune, 1987; Buller et al., 1989) recently found that their deceivers initially engaged in less eye contact than their truthtellers, but deceivers increase their eye contact as the conversations progressed. However, deceivers were not always able to mimic truthtellers' level of eye contact (Buller et al., 1989). A more definitive conclusion on gaze behavior awaits a more complete meta-analysis.

The prevailing conclusion is that communicators engaged in deception may attempt to conceal their deceit by becoming more withdrawn and inaccessible to their conversational partners. Zuckerman, DeFrank, Hall, Larrance, and Rosenthal (1979) found that deceptive answers do in fact create impressions of less personal involvement. The greater distance and detachment that results may effectively hinder surveillance and probing by a suspicious partner.

Disassociation

Closely related to vagueness and disaffiliation is the use of verbal behaviors to disassociate oneself from one's actions and to shift the focus of attention on others, which may have the effect of making one seem more dependent on others or that others are responsible for one's behaviors. Knapp et al. (1974) proposed that this would occur, among other things, through the use of fewer self-references and self-interest statements and more references to others. They found support for those predictions. The meta-analyses, however, have failed to yield a statistically significant pattern. It may be instead that verbal nonimmediacy satisfies the dual purposes of reducing scrutiny and distancing oneself from the content of the deceitful message.

Image- and Relationship-Protecting Behavior

DePaulo et al. (1985) suggested that a major objective of deceivers is to protect their image and that they will do so by engaging in innocuous conversational behaviors such as nodding, smiling, and refraining from interruptions. Presumably, such behaviors are designed to deflect attention away from the deceiver and to maintain a positive demeanor. These behaviors also are likely to protect the relationship that exists between the deceiver and target. Although some experiments have found that liars do indeed display fewer interruptions and more smiling, nodding, and more pleasant faces, especially if they are not anxious (e.g., Buller et al., 1989; Ekman, Friesen, & Scherer, 1976; Mehrabian, 1971, 1972), more studies find the opposite or find no differences (e.g., Bennett, 1978; Buller & Aune, 1987; Ekman & Friesen, 1974; Feldman et al., 1978; Hocking & Leathers, 1980; Kraut, 1978; Mehrabian, 1972; Zuckerman, DePaulo, & Rosenthal, 1981). The meta-analyses conclude that smiling generally decreases.

Thus, it is not clear whether or what deceivers do to protect their image. But the proposition is so intuitively appealing, it deserves and surely will receive further investigation.

NONSTRATEGIC LEAKAGE

In predicting what type of leakage cues will be displayed by deceivers, Ekman and Friesen (1969) proposed that when a person deceives, he or she experiences emotional reactions to the act of deception. Generally, these emotional reactions are negative, stemming from guilt about deceiving, eagerness to succeed, and apprehension about detection. The resultant communicative behaviors may signal this underlying negative affect, thus accidentally sending negative feedback to the target. An exception is when the communicator experiences pleasure in the ability to deceive successfully, which may cause the display of inappropriate or unmotivated elation.

Ekman and Friesen (1969) believed that during deception, the deceiver's emotional reactions are ''leaked'' by cues in channels with low sending capacity. A channel with low sending capacity is one that carries fewer discriminable messages, is slower at sending messages, is less visible and salient to both the deceiver and target, and for which the deceiver receives less internal and external feedback about the messages transmitted. As a result, the deceiver exercises less control over the cues in channels with low sending capacities, and these channels are more likely to carry cues indicative of the emotional reactions experienced by the deceiver. Based on this formulation, Ekman and Friesen hypothesized that the body has a lower sending capacity than the face, so body cues are more likely to leak deception than facial cues.

Zuckerman and his colleagues (Zuckerman, DePaulo, & Rosenthal, 1981, 1986; Zuckerman & Driver, 1985) have elaborated on Ekman and Friesen's (1969) "leakage hypothesis." They, too, believed that affective reactions during deception are communicated by nonverbal cues, but they asserted that emotional reactions alone do not account for all the leakage cues observed during deception. They suggested that three additional cognitive processes produce leakage cues: arousal, control, and complex cognitive processing. The idea that deceivers experience arousal comes partly from Ekman and Friesen's assumption that deception creates apprehension, but Zuckerman, DePaulo, and Rosenthal (1981) extended this by identifying three possible ways by which arousal occurs. According to conditioned response theory, deception creates arousal, because the cue evoking the present deception is conditioned to a dishonest traumatic experience in the past or to past deceptions that were unpleasant. Alternately, conflict theory suggests that the arousal is due to conflicting tendencies within the deceiver to tell the truth and to deceive. Finally, punishment theory asserts that arousal is due to the anticipation of punishment if the deception is discovered. Regardless of which explanation is accurate, Zuckerman et al. believed that arousal is present during most deceptive acts and that deceivers display arousal cues in channels with low sending capacities.

Deception also causes the source to emit cues indicative of control. The act of deceiving requires the deceiver to control messages presented to the target. However, based on Ekman and Friesen's (1969) notion of sending capacity, Zuckerman believed that deceivers cannot control all the communication channels equally; therefore, discrepancies between channels often occur, yielding mixed messages. Finally, Zuckerman asserted that encoding deception is a more difficult communicative task requiring more complex cognitive processing than telling the truth. The increased cognitive requirements cause uncontrolled changes in nonverbal cues that signal the performance of abnormally complex cognitive processing.

An implication of the leakage hypothesis is that a leakage hierarchy exists among the various nonverbal and verbal channels. That is, some channels are more likely to display leakage cues than others due to their lower sending capacities. Zuckerman, DePaulo, and associates (DePaulo et al., 1980a; DePaulo et al., 1985; Zuckerman, DePaulo, & Rosenthal, 1981; Zuckerman & Driver, 1985) proposed that verbal and facial cues are most controllable, because they carry the greatest number of discriminable messages, can send messages quickly, and are highly visible and salient to both the deceiver and the target. Thus, verbal and facial cues should leak the fewest deception cues. Early on, they considered the voice a highly controllable, low-leakage channel, because of the high attention speakers and listeners were assumed to devote to the voice and because of the larynx' responsiveness to internal feedback (DePaulo et al., 1980a). Contrary to these suppositions, research has found that the voice is a rich source of leakage cues during deception. The other "leaky" channel in the hierarchy is the body. This channel has a very low sending capacity due to the less specific messages it transmits and the lack of internal and external feedback communicators receive about body cues.

Arousal and Nervousness

One of the most widely held assumptions about deception is that lying increases arousal and anxiety, which results in automatic changes in overt nonverbal displays (Waid & Orne, 1981). In actuality, arousal is bound to differ dramatically, depending on such factors as (a) how serious the lie is, (b) how motivated the deceiver is to avoid detection, (c) how serious the consequences are of being found out, and (d) whether the actor has had time to rehearse the lie (Knapp & Comadena, 1979; O'Hair, Cody, & McLaughlin, 1981; Zuckerman & Driver, 1985). Consequently, when lying occurs under conditions of low arousal, leakage may be far less apparent and the deception may be far less likely to draw suspicion. Moreover, internally experienced arousal need not always yield overt indicators of it. One study showed that subjects could be trained through biofeedback or hypnosis to suppress their arousal and hence to avoid detection (Corcoran, Lewis, & Garver, 1978). To the extent that actors can monitor and exercise control over a communication channel, they may be able to suppress external manifestations of internal arousal states. The degree of control should follow the leakage hierarchy identified earlier, with the least leakage occurring in the face and the most leakage occurring in the body and voice (DePaulo et al., 1985; DePaulo et al., 1980a; Ekman & Friesen, 1969, 1974; Zuckerman & Driver, 1985).

The research on arousal-linked deception cues generally supports the leakage hypothesis in that the leaked indicators are primarily physiologically based behaviors that are less controllable or less monitored by the sender. The meta-analyses, as well as experiments not included in them (Berrien & Huntington, 1943; W. R. Clark, 1975; Ekman et al., 1976; Ekman, Friesen, O'Sullivan, & Scherer, 1980; Hocking & Leathers, 1980; Knapp et al., 1974; McClintock & Hunt, 1975; Mehrabian, 1971; O'Hair et al., 1981; Riggio & Friedman, 1983; Streeter, Krauss, Geller, Olson, & Apple, 1977), found that liars engage in more blinking, pupil dilation or instability, self- and object-manipulations, higher pitch, vocal nervousness, more speech errors and hesitations, more word repetitions, and less gesturing. Research has been mixed on whether liars engage in more or less postural shifting; random leg, foot, and head movement; gestural activity; and other bodily indicators of nervousness (cf. Buller & Aune, 1987; Buller et al., 1989; Ekman & Friesen, 1974; Ekman et al., 1976; Knapp et al., 1974; Hocking & Leathers, 1980; Mehrabian, 1972). It may be that liars attempt to suppress bodily activity so as not to appear nervous. Alternatively, the lesser gestural animation and bodily movement together may be indicative of less involvement and commitment to what one is saying. Either way, the net result is often stiff, restrained trunk and limb positions, indicative of tension. Moreover, consistent with the control hypothesis, Zuckerman and Driver (1985) reported that liars exhibit reduced amount of facial changes (labeled facial segmentation) in the "nonleaky" facial channel and more noticeable changes in body activity (body segmentation). Similarly, Buller and Aune (1987) reported fewer arousal cues by deceivers and a decrease in arousal cues as deceptive conversations progressed; however, deceivers continued to swivel more in their chairs than truthtellers. These results imply that liars attempt to restrict the expressiveness of the face but are less successful at controlling the rest of the body.

Although deception is often accompanied by high arousal, it is important to recognize that high arousal is not always a sign of deception. One of the major difficulties of assessing lies in such anxiety-producing contexts as the courtroom is that a defendant's nervousness at being accused and being placed in unfamiliar circumstances may prompt the same behaviors that are taken to be signs of lying. For instance, Buller et al. (1989) and Buller, Strzyzewski, and Comstock (1991) reported that both truthtellers and liars displayed more speech errors and pauses, long object and body adaptors, and less facial affect when faced with probing questions from targets. Hence, it becomes important to distinguish which behaviors are merely signs of arousal, and not necessarily deception, and those that are truly indicators of deception.

In an effort to parse out these differences, deTurck and Miller (1985) designed an experiment that had three conditions: unaroused truthful, aroused truthful, and deceptive. They found that both deceivers and aroused truthtellers increased their rate of adaptor behaviors and gave shorter answers, but deceivers exhibited these changes to a much greater extent: They decreased their message duration twice as much as aroused truthtellers and showed a 300% increase in adaptor behavior, compared to a 30% increase among nondeceivers. Moreover, deceivers gestured more, made more speech errors, paused more, gave shorter answers, and had longer response latencies compared to aroused truthtellers. DeTurck and Miller concluded that these particular behaviors—adaptors, message duration, gesturing, speech errors, pauses, and response latencies—are specifically linked to deception-induced arousal rather than general arousal, and may be the result of their attempts to mask or control leakage, their affective reactions to their deceit, and/or their increased cognitive effort during deception. Noteworthy is that this study found increased hand gesturing among aroused/deceptive communicators, in contrast to previous studies showing a decrease in gesturing.

Negative Affect

Deception is purportedly an unpleasant experience for most people. Consequently, one of the clues that deception is taking place may be leaked negative affect in the midst of an otherwise pleasant, image-enhancing demeanor.

Ekman and Friesen (1969) proposed that this may be leaked in part through micromomentary expressions: fleeting, barely perceptible facial expressions of displeasure or comfort that precede the more posed, pleasant expressions people affix on their faces.

We have also noted that deception more often than not produces a reduction in smiling and positive head nods. Thus, deceivers may be revealing a state of negative affect by failing to give the normal amount of positive feedback to their conversational partners. The reduction in gaze reported in some studies (e.g., Knapp et al., 1974) and Buller and Aune's (1987) finding that deceivers encoded more negative affect in their tone of voice than in their facial cues, may be a further indication of liars experiencing unpleasant emotional states, which they attempt to mask by closing off the visual channel.

Others have looked to the verbal stream for indicators of negative feelings. Knapp et al. (1974) found that liars use fewer group references and make more disparaging remarks. The meta-analyses (Zuckerman, DePaulo, & Rosenthal, 1981; Zuckerman & Driver, 1985) also conclude that liars increase the number of negative statements they make relative to truthtellers.

In summary, although few studies have directly addressed this issue of negative affect, the data do tend to support this as one by-product of deception.

Incompetent Communication Performance

In many ways, the earlier substantiated behavioral profiles implicitly point to a decrement in communication performance as part of the act of duplicity. The increase in speech errors, hesitations, word repetitions, postural rigidity, and random movement accompanying nervousness and the halting, brief messages that accompany reticence are key indicators that "something has gone astray" with the actor. Other proposed indicators are verbal statements that are inconsistent with other verbal statements or nonverbal behaviors, discrepancies among verbal and nonverbal channels, kinesic behaviors that are "out of sync" with the verbal–vocal stream, exaggerated performances, and general changes in behavior that deviate from one's normal communication pattern (DePaulo et al., 1985; Miller & J. K. Burgoon, 1982; Zuckerman & Driver, 1985; Zuckerman, Larrance, Spiegel, & Klorman, 1981).

Direct, concrete evidence of these behavioral indicators is limited. Zuckerman and Driver (1985) reported evidence that interchannel discrepancy increases with deception. DePaulo et al. (1983) also reported that deceptive answers are viewed as less spontaneous. However, all the mixed findings on such behaviors as gaze, response latency, gesturing, and body activity may be indicative of deviations from one's normal level of activity. Hocking et al. (1979) argued that because deceptive behavior may be idiosyncratic, it is essential that research establish baseline truthful behavior for an actor before determining the direction of the behavior during deception. It is plausible that heightened awareness of one's behavior during deception leads to a disruption of normal behavior and efforts to restore a semblance of normalcy, but with varying degrees of success. Some people may attempt to compensate by becoming more animated and loquacious; others may attempt to mask their deceit by becoming taciturn and less involved. The best measure of whether deception is occurring may therefore be the absolute degree to which the suspected deceptive behavior deviates from the person's normal pattern, rather than the direction of the deviation. The more skillful the communicator, the better he or she should be able to minimize the deviant behaviors. The amount of arousal and anxiety may also mediate the direction of response. For example, under conditions of minimal discomfort (presumably when telling the truth) or maximal discomfort, speaking rate usually is faster; under moderate discomfort, which may typify many deceptive circumstances, speaking rate is usually slower than normal (Mehrabian, 1971). Similarly, when people are highly motivated to lie, they may speak slower than usual (Zuckerman, DePaulo, & Rosenthal, 1981; Zuckerman & Driver, 1985).

In summary, a common occurrence during deception is inconsistency among channels or between prior and current behavior.

FACTORS MEDIATING DECEPTION DISPLAYS

Much of the more recent work on deception has begun exploring how different factors alter these typical display patterns. The following are among the more important factors that determine how pronounced a deceptive display will be and what specific behaviors comprise it.

Channel

We have noted repeatedly that channels differ in their controllability or leakage potential. Other considerations are the extent to which a channel is highly expressive (i.e., the degree to which it expresses spontaneous nonverbal cues) and characterizes a communicator's more stable demeanor (i.e., tends to convey the same impression despite the actual experienced emotion). Research indicates that senders are better able to control, suppress, or exaggerate their facial expressions than their voice (Zuckerman, Amidon, Bishop, & Pomerantz, 1982; Zuckerman, Larrance, Spiegel, & Klorman, 1981). As DePaulo et al. (1985) affirmed, "Facial cues . . . are indeed faking cues" (p. 331). The verbal channel is also highly controllable and more indicative of one's demeanor than expressive or spontaneous changes in emotional states. Consequently, liars should be more successful when using verbal means to deceive than when using nonverbal ones. But in fact, the verbal channel is often very revealing, especially when combined with vocal tone (DePaulo et al., 1985). Finally, the body and voice are the leakiest channels typically (DePaulo et al., 1985; Ekman & Friesen, 1969; Harrison, Hwalek, Raney, & Fitz, 1978; Krauss et al., 1976; Littlepage & Pineault, 1979; Zuckerman, DePaulo, & Rosenthal, 1981).

These channel differences, however, interact with the type of deceptive information being judged and the communicator's motivation to deceive. The body is more likely to betray deception when the actor is lying about emotional states; the face is a better source of leakage about factual lies, such as might occur in the courtroom, or the liking of another; and the voice is better at leaking information about dominance–submission (Hocking et al., 1979; Zuckerman et al., 1982). Ironically, the motivation to deceive may backfire on the sender. When liars are not highly motivated to succeed, they are most readily betrayed by their words; when they are highly motivated, tone of voice or combined audiovisual cues are more likely to give them away (DePaulo et al., 1985). Thus, when highly motivated, communicators are less successful at masking their lies through their nonverbal behavior but may be able to concoct a successful verbal lie.

Motivation and Consequences

In addition to its effect on which channels are more or less readily controlled, motivation affects the complexion of the deceptive display. More cues are actually present under high motivation than low motivation. In a meta-analysis specifically on motivation, Zuckerman, DePaulo, and Rosenthal (1981) found that 9 out of 19 behaviors studied distinguished liars from truthtellers under high motivation, whereas only 5 made a difference under low motivation. Moreover, some of the behaviors changed direction depending on the motivation level. In their later meta-analysis, Zuckerman and Driver (1985) found that 50% of the behaviors they analyzed were significantly associated with deception in the high motivation condition, whereas only 38% were so in the low motivation condition. In general, high motivation leads to a decrease in the frequency and/or intensity of visual behaviors (less blinking, more neutral expressions, fewer head movements, fewer adaptors, fewer postural shifts), shorter responses, a slower speaking pace, and more negative verbal statements. Thus, in their efforts to "cover up" their lies, deceivers unwittingly give themselves away through an unnatural suppression of behavior. Highly motivated liars also exhibit higher pitch and more hand shrugs, two behaviors that are less controllable or less in conscious awareness.

Recently, research suggests three other factors that may motivate deceivers to monitor and control nonverbal cues. One is an established relationship with the target. Buller and Aune (1987) found that strangers display more nonverbal cues to deception (more nonimmediacy, arousal, and negative affect cues) than intimates and friends, although intimates and friends are unable to mask all nonverbal deception cues. They continue to display increased chair twisting, an arousal cue. J. K. Burgoon (1989) similarly found that interviewees take more control of conversations with suspicious strangers than suspicious friends. Perhaps interviewees were unwilling to take command with friends for fear that their dominance would be construed as a deception cue, whereas they had less detection apprehension with strangers and a greater willingness to control the conversation.

Suspicion in general and probing questions in particular may also lead to numerous changes in behavior. Buller et al. (1989) reported that deceivers facing probing questions (a) inhibit some very common deception cues (e.g., shrug emblems, longer response latencies, and speech errors), (b) do not display some nonverbal changes that truthtellers encode (e.g., they do not increase head movement, head nodding, or interruptions), and (c) subsequently control the nonverbal changes that occurred when probing first began (e.g., they increase eye contact, respond to fewer questions). Likewise, Buller et al. (1991) reported that senders who perceived more suspicion and received probing questions enacted fewer pauses, less laughter, and fewer illustrators than senders who perceived less suspicion. Buller et al. speculated that probing signals suspicion by targets that causes deceivers to monitor and control their behavior more carefully. Stiff and Miller (1986) made a similar suggestion in an earlier study in which deceivers receiving suspicious probes encoded fewer arousal cues— fewer blinks and smiles and shorter response latencies—than those receiving accepting probes. Buller et al. (1991) reported that probing in general did not increase senders' perceptions of suspicion, but skeptical probes (questions that indicated disbelief) produced perceived suspicion. J. K. Burgoon (1989) similarly presented evidence that contradicts the motivating effect of suspicion. She found that interviewees become more ambiguous, less pleasant, less immediate, and less serious (but also more anxious) when confronted with suspicion, regardless of whether they are lying or telling the truth. If they are lying, they are even less immediate and spontaneous.

The kinds of verbal tactics that are selected also depends on the nature of one's motivation to lie and the probability of being detected. Metts and Chronis (1986) found that people, when confronted with a request for information or a situation that requires explanation, are more likely to use falsification strategies when they want to avoid hurting the partner, avoid relational trauma, or protect their image with the partner. J. K. Burgoon (1989) showed that liars are less truthful and report a higher percentage of lies when responding to probing questions from a spouse or friend than from a stranger, and their duplicity increases when friends are suspicious. When people instead generate spontaneous lies (i.e., are free to manipulate the truth without the partner's intervention) and presumably expect the falsehood to go unchallenged or undetected (e.g., with strangers), they are more likely to use concealment.

Planning and Rehearsal

The more time actors have to plan a lie, the more they are likely to leak anxiety-related cues. Those who have time to rehearse their lies or have some lag time before having to respond have more dilated pupils, engage in more postural shifts, increase long body adaptors, respond more quickly, give shorter answers, speak faster, exhibit briefer laughter or smiling, and use somewhat fewer gestures than those who give spontaneous, on-the-spot lies (O'Hair et al., 1981; Zuckerman & Driver, 1985). However, they may also attempt to conceal their lie through the use of more affirmative head nods (O'Hair et al., 1981). Thus, just as high motivation may backfire, so may the opportunity to prepare a lie in advance.

Personality and Communication Skill

Finally, a host of studies have explored how one's personality type or social-communicative skills impact deceptive encoding. It is clear that some people are far more successful at lying than others (Miller & J. K. Burgoon, 1982). This individual variability may be partly due to personality. Extroverted, dominant, exhibitionistic, and nonanxious people tend to be more successful at controlling leakage than introverts and the highly anxious (Mehrabian, 1972; Riggio & Friedman, 1983; Riggio, Tucker, & Throckmorton, 1987). These effects in turn are probably due to greater social skill among the more extroverted and nonanxious. Those with greater communication skills and greater self-monitoring are better able to minimize leakage, increase facial animation and head movements, increase verbal fluency, increase eye contact, use more "we" pronouns, and present a believable lie (J. K. Burgoon, Buller, Guerrero, & Feldman, 1993; DePaulo et al., 1985; Riggio & Friedman, 1983; Riggio, Tucker, & Widaman, 1987). In short, they are good actors. However, concern over one's presentation (i.e., self-monitoring) may be important only insofar as one is a skilled communicator and not overly concerned about being scrutinized. Riggio, Tucker, and Widaman (1987) found that people high in public self-consciousness (who are overly concerned with being scrutinized) are less successful liars, encoding less verbal fluency, less eye contact, fewer head movements, and more emotional reactions than subjects low in public self-consciousness. It seems that these people may over-control some nonverbal behaviors, presenting an incompetent performance, and at the same time exhibit inappropriate images (i.e., less serious) or negative emotions (i.e., embarrassment) (Riggio, Tucker, & Widaman, 1987).

One other personality trait that has been frequently hypothesized to affect skill in deceiving is Machiavellianism. The empirical findings are very mixed, but tend to support high Machs being more skilled at perpetrating lies (Christie & Geis, 1970; Exline et al., 1970; Geis & Moon, 1981; Knapp & Comadena, 1979; Knapp et al., 1974; O'Hair et al., 1981). It has been demonstrated, for example, that high Machs increase eye contact and fabricate plausible verbal lies, and low Machs decrease eye contact during deception and produce less convincing lies (Exline et al., 1970).

There is reason to believe that people become more skillful at lying as they get older (Allen & Atkinson, 1978; DePaulo & Rosenthal, 1979; Morency & Krauss, 1982; Zuckerman, DePaulo, & Rosenthal, 1981), although there is some contrary evidence (e.g., Feldman et al., 1978; Feldman, Jenkins, & Popoola, 1979) and the improvement may be confined to women (Feldman & White, 1980).

Interaction

It may be somewhat surprising to see "interaction" listed as one of the factors mediating deception display; however, most of the past research on deception has been characterized by designs that minimized and constrained actual interaction between liars and their targets and looked at aggregate measures of cues to deception. Recently, a few researchers (Buller & Aune, 1987; Buller et al., 1989, 1991; Buller, Burgoon, Roiger, & Buslig, 1993; J. K. Burgoon, 1989; J. K. Burgoon, Buller, Dillman, & Walther, 1992; Toris & DePaulo, 1985) have developed experiments in which deceivers and truthtellers interact in face-to-face conversations with targets and their behavior is measured and analyzed longitudinally. The major outcome of these studies is that cues to deception are dynamic, a less than surprising finding as "a cardinal element in any definition of interpersonal communication is that it is a dynamic process" (J. K. Burgoon, 1989, p. 1). As we have noted in several places in the preceding manuscript, deceivers in these processual studies altered their nonverbal displays as the conversations progressed. In fact, very few changes that occurred early in the conversations were maintained throughout it. Further, some changes arose only after several minutes of communication and still other changes emerged in the middle of the conversations but dissipated before the conversations ended (Buller & Aune, 1987; Buller et al., 1989, 1991; J. K. Burgoon et al., 1992). The data are insufficient to draw strong conclusions about the dynamics of individual cues or sets of cues, but deception researchers are well advised to view deception as a "chain of offensive and defensive maneuvers

on the part of both participants'' (J. K. Burgoon, 1989, p. 2). The promise
of this view is that deception researchers will gain a better understanding of
how cues to deception are withheld, masked, blended, exaggerated, and
minimized in the course of conversation.

SUMMARY

In this chapter, we proposed that deception is part of a communicator's strategic repertoire of message forms. Strategic deception involves a rational, conscious message selection process where verbal and nonverbal messages are
combined to create a false belief. Deception frequently entails multiple motives. Besides serving instrumental and identity objectives, deception may be
designed to achieve such altruistic purposes as maintaining the interpersonal
relationship, preserving the target's self-esteem, and minimizing interpersonal
conflict.

Research on general deception strategies has begun to reveal a wide range
of messages that can be used to deceive. These can be reduced to roughly five
types of strategies: lies or falsifications, exaggerations, half-truths, concealments
or omissions, and misdirections or diversions. Although the primary purpose
in these strategies is to promulgate a belief in the target the communicator knows
to be false, the strategies are also accompanied by a host of meta-communicative
verbal and nonverbal behaviors that have relational implications. Some of this
ancillary "text" may be strategic, intentionally designed to (a) introduce uncertainty and vagueness, (b) signal nonimmediacy, reticence, and withdrawal, (c) disassociate the communicator from the deception or deceptive event,
and (d) protect one's image. In these cases the relational messages are used
to assist with successful deception and to protect the deceiver from possible
risks associated with detection by the target. Other meta-communicative behaviors may be nonstrategic (uncontrolled), communicating (e) arousal and
nervousness and (f) negative affect, and (g) creating an incompetent communication performance. Such behaviors may leak deceptive intent to the target,
as well as carrying relational messages of insincerity, lack of composure, and
negative emotional arousal.

Numerous factors may mediate what specific deception tactics are employed.
These are in need of further research. Another issue deserving exploration is
the sequencing of strategies and tactics in ongoing deceptive interactions. Of
particular interest should be sequencing of messages when the deceiver senses
suspicion from the target and attempts to bolster the believability of the deception. Similarly, detection efforts by the target might be explored from a strategic perspective. Besides identifying what verbal and nonverbal leakage
behaviors can alert targets to deception, detection strategies that involve probing, laying traps, and checking deceptive information against prior messages

or conversations should be examined. The issues of sequencing deception tactics and strategic detection activities are deserving of an entire other chapter.

REFERENCES

Allen, V. L., & Atkinson, M. L. (1978). Encoding of nonverbal behavior by high-achieving and low-achieving children. *Journal of Educational Psychology, 70,* 298–305.

Baskett, G., & Freedle, R. O. (1974). Aspects of language pragmatics and the social perception of lying. *Journal of Psycholinguistic Research, 3,* 112–131.

Bauchner, J. E., Brandt, D. R., & Miller, G. R. (1977). The truth–deception attribution: Effects of varying levels of information availability. In B. R. Ruben (Ed.), *Communication yearbook 1* (pp. 229–243). New Brunswick, NJ: Transaction Books.

Bavelas, J. B., Black, A., Chovil, N., & Mullett, J. (1990). *Equivocal communication.* Newbury Park, CA: Sage.

Bennett, R. (1978, April). Micromoments. *Human Behavior,* 34–35.

Berrien, F. K., & Huntington, G. H. (1943). An exploratory study of pupillary responses during deception. *Journal of Experimental Psychology, 32,* 443–449.

Buller, D. B. (1986). *Selecting deception strategies.* Paper presented to the annual meeting of the International Communication Association, Chicago.

Buller, D. B. (1987a, Nov.). *Detecting deception by strangers, friends, and intimates: Attributional biases due to relationship development.* Paper presented at the annual meeting of the Speech Communication Association, Boston.

Buller, D. B. (1987b). *Selecting deception messages.* Unpublished manuscript, University of Arizona.

Buller, D. B. (1987c, Feb.). *Selecting deception strategies: Implications for research on deception.* Paper presented at the annual meeting of the Western Speech Communication Association, Salt Lake City, UT.

Buller, D. B., & Aune, R. K. (1987). Nonverbal cues to deception among intimates, friends, and strangers. *Journal of Nonverbal Behavior, 11,* 269–290.

Buller, D. B., Burgoon, J. K., Roiger, J., & Buslig, A. (1993, May). *The language of interpersonal deception.* Paper presented at the annual meeting of the International Communication Association, Washington, DC.

Buller, D. B., Comstock, J., Aune, R. K., & Strzyzewski, K. D. (1989). The effect of probing on deceivers and truthtellers. *Journal of Nonverbal Behavior, 13,* 155–170.

Buller, D. B., Strzyzewski, K. D., & Comstock, J. (1991). Interpersonal deception: I. Deceivers' reactions to receivers' suspicions and probing. *Communication Monographs, 58,* 1–24.

Burgoon, J. K. (1989, May). *Toward a processual view of interpersonal deception.* Paper presented at the annual meeting of the International Communication Association, San Francisco.

Burgoon, J. K., Buller, D. B., Dillman, L., & Walther, J. (1992). *Interpersonal deception: Effects of suspicion on perceived communication and nonverbal behavior dynamics.* Manuscript submitted for publication.

Burgoon, J. K., Buller, D. B., Feldman, C., Guerrero, L., & Afifi, W. (1993). *Deceptive message strategies: Verbal dimensions of information manipulation and control.* Manuscript submitted for publication.

Burgoon, J. K., Buller, D. B., Guerrero, L., & Feldman, C. (1993, May). *Viewing deception success from deceiver and observer perspectives: Effects of preinteractional and interactional factors.* Paper presented at the annual meeting of the International Communication Association, Washington, DC.

Burgoon, M., & Miller, G. R. (1985). An expectancy interpretation of language and persuasion. In H. Giles & R. N. St. Clair (Eds.), *The social and psychological contexts of language* (pp. 199–229). London: Lawrence Erlbaum Associates.

Camden, C., Motley, M. T., & Wilson, A. (1984). White lies in interpersonal communication: A taxonomy and preliminary investigation of social motivations. *Western Journal of Speech Communication, 48,* 309–325.

Carpenter, R. H. (1981). Stylistic analysis for law enforcement purposes: A case study of a language variable as an index of a suspect's caution in phrasing answers. *Communication Quarterly, 29,* 32–39.

Chisholm, R. M., & Feehan, T. D. (1977). The intent to deceive. *Journal of Philosophy, 74,* 143–159.

Christie, R., & Geis, F. L. (1970). *Studies in Machiavellianism.* New York: Academic Press.

Clark, R. A. (1984). *Persuasive messages.* New York: Harper & Row.

Clark, R. A., & Delia, J. G. (1979). Topoi and rhetorical competence. *Quarterly Journal of Speech, 65,* 187–206.

Clark, W. R. (1975). *A comparison of pupillary response, heart rate, and GSR during deception.* Paper presented at the annual meeting of the Midwestern Psychological Association, Chicago.

Corcoran, J. F. T., Lewis, M. D., & Garver, R. B. (1978). Biofeedback-conditioned galvanic skin response and hypnotic suppression of arousal: A pilot study of their relation to deception. *Journal of Forensic Sciences, 23,* 155–162.

DePaulo, B. M., Lanier, K., & Davis, T. (1983). Detecting the deceit of the motivated liar. *Journal of Personality and Social Psychology, 45,* 1096–1103.

DePaulo, B. M., & Rosenthal, R. (1979). Telling lies. *Journal of Personality and Social Psychology, 37,* 1713–1722.

DePaulo, B. M., Stone, J. I., & Lassiter, G. D. (1985). Deceiving and detecting deceit. In B. R. Schlenker (Ed.), *The self and social life* (pp. 323–370). New York: McGraw-Hill.

DePaulo, B. M., Zuckerman, M., & Rosenthal, R. (1980a). Detecting deception: Modality effects. In L. Wheeler (Ed.), *Review of personality and social psychology* (pp. 125–162). Beverly Hills, CA: Sage.

DePaulo, B. M., Zuckerman, M., & Rosenthal, R. (1980b). The deceptions of everyday life. *Journal of Communication, 30,* 216–218.

deTurck, M. A., & Miller, G. R. (1985). Deception and arousal: Isolating the behavioral correlates of deception. *Human Communication Research, 12,* 181–202.

Dulaney, E. F., Jr. (1982). Changes in language behavior as a function of veracity. *Human Communication Research, 9,* 75–82.

Ekman, P. (1985). *Telling lies.* New York: Norton.

Ekman, P., & Friesen, W. V. (1969). Nonverbal leakage and clues to deception. *Psychiatry, 32,* 88–105.

Ekman, P., & Friesen, W. V. (1974). Detecting deception from the body or face. *Journal of Personality and Social Psychology, 29,* 288–298.

Ekman, P., Friesen, W. V., O'Sullivan, M., & Scherer, K. (1980). Relative importance of face, body, and speech in judgments of personality and affect. *Journal of Personality and Social Psychology, 38,* 270–277.

Ekman, P., Friesen, W. V., & Scherer, K. (1976). Body movement and voice pitch in deceptive interaction. *Semiotica, 16,* 23–27.

English, H. B. (1926). Reaction-time symptoms of deception. *American Journal of Psychology, 37,* 428–429.

Exline, R., Thibaut, J., Hickey, C., & Gumpert, P. (1970). Visual interaction in relation to Machiavellianism and an unethical act. In R. Christie & F. Geis (Eds.), *Studies in Machiavellianism* (pp. 53–75). New York: Academic Press.

Feldman, R. S., Devin-Sheehan, L., & Allen, V. L. (1978). Nonverbal cues as indicators of verbal dissembling. *American Educational Research Journal, 15,* 217–231.

Feldman, R. S., Jenkins, L., & Popoola, O. (1979). Detection of deception in adults and children via facial expressions. *Child Development, 50,* 350–355.

Feldman, R. S., & White, J. B. (1980). Detecting deception in children. *Journal of Communication, 30,* 121–139.

Geis, F. L., & Moon, T. H. (1981). Machiavellianism and deception. *Journal of Personality and Social Psychology, 41,* 766-775.

Goffman, E. (1959). *The presentation of self in everyday life.* Garden City, NY: Doubleday.

Goldstein, E. R. (1923). Reaction times and the consciousness of deception. *American Journal of Psychology, 34,* 562-581.

Hample, D. (1980). Purposes and effects of lying. *Southern Speech Communication Journal, 46,* 33-47.

Hankiss, A. (1980). Games con men play: The semiosis of deceptive interaction. *Journal of Communication, 30,* 104-112.

Harrison, A. A., Hwalek, M., Raney, D. F., & Fritz, J. G. (1978). Cues to deception in an interview situation. *Social Psychology, 41,* 156-161.

Hocking, J. E., Bauchner, J., Kaminski, E. P., & Miller, G. R. (1979). Detecting deceptive communication from verbal, visual, and paralinguistic cues. *Human Communication Research, 6,* 33-46.

Hocking, J. E., & Leathers, D. G. (1980). Nonverbal indicators of deception: A new theoretical perspective. *Communication Monographs, 47,* 119-131.

Hopper, R., & Bell, R. A. (1984). Broadening the deception construct. *Quarterly Journal of Speech, 70,* 288-302.

Knapp, M. L., & Comadena, M. E. (1979). Telling it like it isn't: A review of theory and research on deceptive communications. *Human Communication Research, 5,* 270-285.

Knapp, M. L., Hart, R. P., & Dennis, H. S. (1974). An exploration of deception as a communication construct. *Human Communication Research, 1,* 15-29.

Krauss, R. M., Geller, V., & Olson, C. (1976). *Modalities and cues in the detection of deception.* Paper presented at the annual meeting of the American Psychological Association, Washington, DC.

Kraut, R. (1978). Verbal and nonverbal cues in the perception of lying. *Journal of Personality and Social Psychology, 36,* 380-391.

Kraut, R. (1980). Humans as lie detectors: Some second thoughts. *Journal of Communication, 30,* 209-216.

Kuiken, D. (1981). Nonimmediate language style and inconsistency between private and expressed evaluations. *Journal of Experimental Social Psychology, 17,* 183-196.

Lindskold, S., & Walters, P. S. (1983). Categories for acceptability of lies. *Journal of Social Psychology, 120,* 129-136.

Littlepage, G. E., & Pineault, M. A. (1979). Detection of deceptive factual statements from the body and the face. *Personality and Social Psychology Bulletin, 5,* 325-328.

Marston, W. M. (1920). Reaction-time symptoms of deception. *Journal of Experimental Psychology, 3,* 72-87.

Matarazzo, J. D., Wiens, A. N., Jackson, R. H., & Manaugh, T. S. (1970). Interviewee speech behavior under conditions of endogenously-present and exogenously-induced motivational states. *Journal of Clinical Psychology, 26,* 141-148.

McClintock, C. C., & Hunt, R. G. (1975). Nonverbal indicators of affect and deception in an interview setting. *Journal of Applied Social Psychology, 5,* 54-67.

McCornack, S. A. (1992). Information manipulation theory. *Communication Monographs, 59,* 1-16.

Mehrabian, A. (1971). Nonverbal betrayal of feeling. *Journal of Experimental Research in Personality, 5,* 64-73.

Mehrabian, A. (1972). *Nonverbal communication.* Chicago: Aldine.

Metts, S., & Chronis, H. (1986). *An exploratory investigation of relational deception.* Paper presented at the annual meeting of the International Communication Association, Chicago.

Miller, G. R., & Burgoon, J. K. (1982). Factors affecting witness credibility. In N. L. Kerr & R. M. Bray (Eds.), *The psychology of the courtroom* (pp. 169-194). New York: Academic Press.

Morency, N. L., & Krauss, R. M. (1982). The nonverbal encoding and decoding of affect in first and fifth graders. In R. S. Feldman (Ed.), *Development of nonverbal behavioral skill* (pp. 181-199). New York: Springer-Verlag.

Motley, M. T. (1974). Acoustic correlates of lies. *Western Speech, 38,* 81-87.

O'Hair, H. D., Cody, M. J., & McLaughlin, M. L. (1981). Prepared lies, spontaneous lies, Machiavellianism, and nonverbal communication. *Human Communication Research, 7,* 325–339.

O'Keefe, B. J., & Delia, J. G. (1982). Impression formation and message production. In M. E. Roloff & C. R. Berger (Eds.), *Social cognition and communication* (pp. 33–72). Beverly Hills, CA: Sage.

Osgood, C. E. (1960). Some effects of motivation on style of encoding. In T. A. Sebeok (Ed.), *Style in language* (pp. 293–306). Cambridge, MA: MIT Press.

Patterson, M. L. (1983). *Nonverbal behavior: A functional perspective.* New York: Springer-Verlag.

Riggio, R. E., & Friedman, H. S. (1983). Individual differences and cues to deception. *Journal of Personality and Social Psychology, 45,* 899–915.

Riggio, R. E., Tucker, J., & Throckmorton, D. (1987). Social skills and deception ability. *Personality and Social Psychology Bulletin, 13,* 568–577.

Riggio, R. E., Tucker, J., & Widaman, K. F. (1987). Verbal and nonverbal cues as mediators of deception ability. *Journal of Nonverbal Behavior, 11,* 126–145.

Schenck-Hamlin, W. J., Wiseman, R. L., & Georgacarakos, G. N. (1982). A model of properties of compliance-gaining strategies. *Communication Quarterly, 30,* 92–100.

Seibold, D. R., Cantrill, J. G., & Meyers, R. A. (1985). Communication and interpersonal influence. In M. L. Knapp & G. R. Miller (Eds.), *Handbook of interpersonal communication* (pp. 551–614). Beverly Hills, CA: Sage.

Stiff, J. B., & Miller, G. R. (1986). "Come to think of it. . . .": Interrogative probes, deceptive communication, and deception detection. *Human Communication Research, 12,* 339–358.

Streeter, L. A., Krauss, R. M., Geller, V., Olson, C., & Apple, W. (1977). Pitch changes during attempted deception. *Journal of Personality and Social Psychology, 35,* 345–350.

Todd-Mancillas, W. R., & Kibler, R. J. (1979). A test of concurrent validity for linguistic indices of deception. *Western Journal of Speech Communication, 43,* 108–122.

Toris, D., & DePaulo, B. M. (1985). Effects of actual deception and suspiciousness of deception on interpersonal perceptions. *Journal of Personality and Social Psychology, 47,* 1063–1073.

Turner, R. E., Edgley, C., & Olmsted, G. (1975). Information control in conversations: Honesty is not always the best policy. *Kansas Journal of Speech, 11,* 69–89.

Waid, W. M., & Orne, M. T. (1981). Cognitive, social, and personality processes in the physiological detection of deception. In L. Berkowitz (Ed.), *Advances in experimental social psychology* (Vol. 14, pp. 61–106). New York: Academic Press.

Wolk, R., & Henley, A. (1970). *The right to lie.* New York: Wyden.

Zuckerman, M., Amidon, M. D., Bishop, S. E., & Pomerantz, S. D. (1982). Face and tone of voice in the communication of deception. *Journal of Personality and Social Psychology, 43,* 347–357.

Zuckerman, M., DeFrank, R. S., Hall, J. A., Larrance, D. T., & Rosenthal, R. (1979). Facial and vocal cues of deception and honesty. *Journal of Experimental Social Psychology, 15,* 378–396.

Zuckerman, M., DePaulo, B. M., & Rosenthal, R. (1981). Verbal and nonverbal communication of deception. In L. Berkowitz (Ed.), *Advances in experimental social psychology* (Vol. 14, pp. 1–59). New York: Academic Press.

Zuckerman, M., DePaulo, B. M., & Rosenthal, R. (1986). Humans as deceivers and lie detectors. In P. D. Blanck, R. Buck, & R. Rosenthal (Eds.), *Nonverbal communication in the clinical context* (pp. 13–35). University Park, PA: Pennsylvania State University Press.

Zuckerman, M., & Driver, R. E. (1985). Telling lies: Verbal and nonverbal correlates of deception. In A. W. Siegman & S. Feldstein (Eds.), *Multichannel integrations of nonverbal behavior* (pp. 129–148). Hillsdale, NJ: Lawrence Erlbaum Associates.

Zuckerman, M., Larrance, D. T., Spiegel, N. H., & Klorman, R. (1981). Controlling nonverbal displays: Facial expressions and tone of voice. *Journal of Experimental Social Psychology, 17,* 506–524.

Chapter 8

Strategies for Effective Communication and Adaptation in Intergroup Contexts

William B. Gudykunst
California State University, Fullerton

Bradford 'J' Hall
University of Wisconsin, Milwaukee

> *See at a distance an undesirable person;*
> *See close at hand a desirable person;*
> *Come closer to the undesirable person;*
> *Move away from the desirable person;*
> *Coming close and moving apart,*
> *how interesting life is.*
> —Gensho Ogura

Even though the cultural diversity of the population in the United States has increased in the last few decades, communication between people from different cultures and/or ethnic groups is still relatively rare. Most people have little contact with members of other cultures/ethnicities in their daily lives that is not role-related. Some people avoid interacting with members of other cultures/ethnicities and/or view them as "undesirable" people. Either response can lead to members of other cultures/ethnicities being treated in a morally exclusive manner (i.e., outside the boundary for which moral values apply; Optow, 1990). When others perceive that they are seen as undesirable and/or believe they are being treated in a morally exclusive fashion, they may respond with frustration or aggression (e.g., the unrest in Los Angeles in 1992). Individually, however, we can make a difference in the relations between groups in society. To improve relations between groups in society, we must individually communicate as effectively as we can with members of other cultures/ethnicities and be able to adapt our communication when necessary.[1] Our purpose in this chapter is to isolate strategies individuals can use to accomplish these goals. We begin with a brief overview of the theoretical perspective used throughout the majority of the chapter.

THEORETICAL FOUNDATIONS

There are several perspectives that could be used to examine the strategies individuals can use to be effective and/or adapt their communication with members of other cultures/ethnicities. Our focus in this chapter is on the theoretical research program being developed by one of the authors and several colleagues (e.g., Gudykunst, 1988, 1991, 1993; Gudykunst & Hammer, 1988b; Gudykunst & Kim, 1984, 1992). We do, however, discuss how these issues are addressed in other theoretical perspectives in the final section of the chapter. In this section we outline the theoretical assumptions and overview the theoretical perspective on effectiveness and adaptation used in the majority of the chapter.

Theoretical Assumptions

There are several theoretical assumptions implicit in the perspective used in the majority of the chapter. Gudykunst and Nishida (1989) argue that there are at least three metatheoretical issues about which any theorist must make assumptions: ontology (e.g., what is the nature of reality), epistemology (e.g., how do we gain knowledge), and human nature (e.g., what is the basis of human behavior). In making metatheoretical assumptions, the perspective used in the majority of the chapter (based on Gudykunst, 1988, 1991, 1993) attempts to avoid extreme "objectivist" and "subjectivist" assumptions (see Gudykunst & Nishida, 1989, for an overview of the positions; the position taken is close to Hooker's, 1987, realistic approach to science).

With respect to ontology, it is assumed that names, concepts, and labels are artificial constructs we use to create our "subjective" realities. Because of our socialization into a culture and ethnic group, we share a large portion of our intersubjective realities with other people in our culture or ethnic group. Our shared intersubjective realities are sufficiently stable that we consider the shared portion as an "objective" reality. The perspective used in the majority of the chapter further assumes that the basic process of communication is the same across cultures. This assumption is consistent with Hamill's (1990) argument that humans are endowed with innate logical structures, but cultures create unique meanings out of this innate knowledge.

---

[1]For the theory of effective interpersonal and intergroup communication on which the majority of this chapter is based, see Gudykunst (1993).

With respect to epistemology, it is assumed that our interpretations of our communication *and* external observations of our communication provide useful data for generating and testing theories, and more generally, understanding the world in which we live. We need to search for underlying regularities in communication and, at the same time, recognize that our explanations will never be perfect because our subjective realities are different. With respect to human nature, the perspective presented in the majority of the chapter assumes that our communication is influenced by our culture and group memberships, as well as structural, situational, and environmental factors. We, nevertheless, have the ability to choose how we communicate. It is the ability to make choices that allows us to be "socially eloquent," to use Pearce's (1989) term.

Theoretical Perspective

Within the theoretical framework used in the majority of the chapter, effective communication refers to minimizing misunderstandings (Gudykunst & Kim, 1992). Minimizing misunderstandings involves accurately predicting and explaining our own and others' behavior. This view is consistent with Triandis' (1977) position that effectiveness involves making "isomorphic attributions." It also is compatible with Powers and Lowrey's (1984) conceptualization of "basic communication fidelity": "the degree of congruence between the cognitions [or thoughts] of two or more individuals following a communication event" (p. 58).

Adaptation is a "consequence of an ongoing process in which a system strives to adjust and readjust itself to challenges, changes, and irritants in [the] environment" (Ruben, 1983, p. 137). Adaptation implies an adjustment to incoming stimuli. The core of adaptation is change (Dyal & Dyal, 1981). Adaptive behavior, therefore, occurs when we change our behavior or perceptions in light of the perceived strangeness in another person or group (Ellingsworth, 1983). To understand effective communication and/or adaptation that occur in intergroup contexts (defined later), it is necessary to recognize that one of the participants is a "stranger." Simmel (1908/1950) introduced the concept, arguing that strangers are physically present and participating in situations (e.g., encountering someone in a foreign culture), but at the same time, are outside the situation because they are from a different place. Schuetz (1944) views a stranger as an "individual who tries to be permanently accepted or at least partially tolerated by the group which he [or she] approaches" (p. 499).

Gudykunst and Kim (1984, 1992) argue that the process of communication between people from different groups (including cultures/ethnicities) is the same as the process of communication between members of the same group. They refer to the process of communicating with people who are different and unknown and in an environment unfamiliar to them as "communicating with strangers" (based on Simmel's, 1950/1908, concept of "stranger").[2] Levine (1979) summarizes the importance of Simmel's concept of stranger in understanding communication between members of different cultures and/or groups. He points out that

> it is the dialectic between closeness and remoteness that makes the position of strangers socially problematic in all times and places. When those who would be close, in any sense of the term, are actually close, and those who would be distant are distant, everyone is "in his [or her] place." When those who would be distant are close, however, the inevitable result is a degree of tension and anxiety which necessitates some special kind of response . . . group members derive security from relating in familiar ways to fellow group members and from maintaining distance from nonmembers through established insulating mechanisms. In situations where an outsider comes into the social space normally occupied by group members only, one can presume an initial response of anxiety and at least latent antagonism. (pp. 29–30)

To manage the antagonistic response when confronting strangers, individuals must understand the strategies they can use to effectively communicate and adapt their behavior when communicating with strangers whom are often viewed as "undesirable" people.

Interacting with strangers is a novel situation for most people. Novel situations are characterized by high levels of uncertainty and anxiety. "The immediate psychological result of being in a new situation is lack of security. Ignorance of the potentialities inherent in the situation, of the means to reach a goal, and of the probable outcomes of an intended action causes insecurity" (Herman & Schield, 1961, p. 165). Attempts to deal with the ambiguity of new situations involves a pattern of information seeking (uncertainty reduction) and tension (anxiety) reduction (Ball-Rokeach, 1973).

When we reduce uncertainty about others and ourselves, understanding is possible. Understanding involves obtaining information, knowing, comprehending, and interpreting. Three levels of understanding can be differentiated: description, prediction, and explanation (Berger, Gardner, Parks, Schulman, & Miller, 1976). Description involves specifying what is observed in terms of its physical attributes (i.e., drawing a picture in words). Prediction involves projecting what will happen in a particular situation, and explanation involves stating why something occurred.

---

[2]Stranger is a figure–ground phenomenon. Who is the stranger depends on the context. To simplify application of the material presented here we use the perspective of a person being approached by a stranger. In presenting the material, we arbitrarily use either the perspective of the "sender" or "receiver." We believe that these processes occur simultaneously, but separating the processes simplifies the presentation.

We make predictions and create explanations all of the time when we communicate. We rarely describe others' behavior, however. When we communicate with others we typically decode messages by attaching meaning to or interpreting them. We do not stop to describe what we saw or heard before we interpret it. Rather, we interpret messages as we decode them. The problem is that we base our interpretations on our life experiences, culture, or ethnic group memberships. Since our life experiences differ from other people's, our interpretations of their behavior may be incorrect. This often leads to misunderstandings.

Anxiety refers to the feeling of being uneasy, tense, worried, or apprehensive about what might happen. It is an affective (e.g., emotional) response, not a cognitive response like uncertainty. While uncertainty results from our inability to predict others' behavior, "anxiety stems from the anticipation of negative consequences. People fear at least four types of negative consequences: psychological or behavioral consequences for the self, and negative evaluations by members of the outgroup and the ingroup" (Stephan & Stephan, 1985, p. 159).

As indicated earlier, the process of communicating with strangers is the same as the process of communicating with people who are familiar. Some factors, however, have more of an influence in one situation than the other. We, therefore, isolate the factors that differentiate interpersonal and intergroup communication in the next section.

INTERPERSONAL AND INTERGROUP COMMUNICATION

In order to discuss strategies for improving effectiveness in intercultural and intergroup encounters, it is necessary to begin by looking at how interpersonal and intergroup encounters differ. We believe that the differences are a function of the portion of the self-concept that serves as the major generative mechanism for behavior. We, therefore, begin by examining self-conceptions.

Self-Conceptions

J. C. Turner (1987) defines the *self-concept* as "the set of cognitive representations of self available to a person" (p. 44). The unique assumptions in this theory are based on the notion of self-categorization. J. C. Turner argues that cognitive representations of the self take the form of self-categorizations in which individuals group themselves into categories with others that they see as similar to themselves on some dimension and different from others on that dimension. He goes on to point out that there are at least three levels of abstraction of self-categorization important in the self-concept: (a) the superordinate level of the self as a human being, the common features shared with other members of the human species in contrast to other forms of life, (b) the intermediate level of ingroup–outgroup categorizations based on similarities and differences between human beings that define one as a member of certain social groups and not others (e.g., 'American', 'female', 'black', 'student', 'working class'), and (c) the subordinate level of personal categorizations based on differences between oneself as a unique individual and other ingroup [or outgroup] members that define one as a specific individual person (e.g., in terms of one's personality or other kinds of individual differences). (p. 45)

The three levels define our human, social, and personal identities.

Following Tajfel (1978), J. C. Turner (1987) argues that the process of evaluating our self-conceptions is one of social comparison. To illustrate, we compare the groups of which we are members with other on value-laden attributes and characteristics. Positive comparisons of the ingroup with an outgroup lead to high prestige, and negative comparisons lead to low prestige (Tajfel & Turner, 1979). The social comparison process also affects how self-conceptions are formed. In the self-categorization theory, Turner also assumes that if the self and others are evaluated positive when they are seen as prototypical members of positively valued groups.

Schlenker (1986) argues that "self-identification constructs and expresses an identity" (p. 23). Identity, as Schlenker uses the concept, is a person's theory of him or herself:

Identity, like any theory, is both a *structure*, containing the organized contents of experience, and an active *process* that guides and regulates one's thoughts, feelings, and actions . . . It influences how information is perceived, processed, and recalled . . . it acts as a script to guide behavior . . . and it contains the standards against which one's behavior can be compared and evaluated. (p. 24)

Our self-conceptions, therefore, influence how we communicate with others and our choices (conscious and unconscious) of those with whom we form relationships. It also should be noted that individuals choose the identity they wish to put forth in an interaction (at least implicitly), and that others also may impose an identity on them. Part of effective communication depends on the parties negotiating the identities they will use in communicating with the other person.

Extensive research suggests that perceived similarity is one of the major factors we use in deciding who to approach (see Berscheid, 1985, for a review of this research). Swann (1983), for example, suggests that similarity is important because we assume that people who are similar to us are more likely to verify our self-conceptions than people who are different. Similarly, Huston

(1973) believes we are not likely to initiate interaction with people we think will reject us.

Differentiating Interpersonal and Intergroup Behavior

Intergroup behavior differs from nonintergroup behavior in that its locus of control is social, not personal, identity. The differences in social behavior due to its locus of control are outlined by Tajfel and Turner (1979) when they describe behavior as varying along a continuum from purely interpersonal to purely intergroup:

> At one extreme . . . is the interaction between two or more individuals which is *fully* determined by their interpersonal relationships and individual characteristics and not at all affected by various groups or categories to which they respectively belong. The other extreme consists of interactions between two or more individuals (or groups of individuals) which are *fully* determined by their respective memberships of various social groups or categories, and not at all affected by the interindividual personal relationships between the people involved. (p. 34)

Tajfel and Turner point out that the purely interpersonal extreme is "absurd" because no instance of it can be found, but some cases (i.e., communication between two lovers) come close. Pure intergroup behavior, in contrast, does exist; for example, an air force bomber crew dropping bombs on an enemy population would be "pure" intergroup, while labor-management negotiations over a new contract are very close to pure intergroup.

Other conceptualizations suggest that the interpersonal–intergroup continuum oversimplifies the nature of the communication involved (Giles & Hewstone, 1982; Stephenson, 1981). Stephenson, for example, treats interpersonal and intergroup salience as orthogonal dimensions and argues that communication occurs in one of four quadrants: (a) low interpersonal and low intergroup salience, (b) low interpersonal and high intergroup salience, (c) high interpersonal and low intergroup salience, and (d) high interpersonal and high intergroup salience. We believe, however, that the four quadrants also oversimplifies the relationship between interpersonal and intergroup salience. This view implies that a specific encounter is either high or low in interpersonal and intergroup salience. This, however, is not necessarily the case. Interpersonal and intergroup salience can and do change within specific encounters (Coupland, 1980). Stated differently, personal and social identity both serve as generative mechanisms for behavior in the same encounter. One, however, often predominates.

Given this overview of the factors that differentiate interpersonal and intergroup communication, we turn to a discussion of the cognitive processes that influence our ability to communicate effectively. Following this, we examine motivations to communicate effectively and adapt our behavior when communicating with strangers. With this background, we isolate the major areas where mindfulness is necessary in order to communicate effectively, including interpreting strangers' behavior, understanding our expectations, making sense of strangers' behavior, adapting our language usage, and managing our uncertainty and anxiety when communicating with strangers.

COGNITIVE PROCESSES INFLUENCING OUR ABILITY TO COMMUNICATE EFFECTIVELY AND ADAPT OUR BEHAVIOR IN INTERGROUP CONTEXTS

When communicating with others, we usually interpret others' messages based on our own frame of reference. In the vast majority of encounters with other members of our culture and/or ethnic group, this is not highly problematic. In encounters with others with whom we have intimate relationships and/or in intergroup encounters, however, using our frame of reference to interpret others' behavior can lead to misunderstanding and miscommunication. Communicating effectively and adapting our behavior in these situations requires that we be aware of our interpretations of our own and others' messages. At least two cognitive processes are important in being able to accomplish this: being mindful and managing our need for closure.

Being Mindful

Much of our communication behavior is habitual. When we are communicating habitually, we are following *scripts*: "a coherent sequence of events expected by the individual involving him [or her] either as a participant or an observer" (Abelson, 1976, p. 33). According to Langer (1978), when we first encounter a new situation, we consciously seek cues to guide our behavior. As we have repeated experiences with the same event, we have less need to consciously think about our behavior. "The more often we engage in the activity, the more likely it is that we rely on scripts for the completion of the activity and the less likely there will be any correspondence between our actions and those thoughts of ours that occur simultaneously" (Langer, 1978, p. 39).

When we are engaging in habitual or scripted behavior, we are not highly aware of what we are doing or saying. To borrow an analogy from flying a plane, we are on "automatic pilot." In Langer's (1978) terminology, we are "mindless" (Bellah, Madsen, Sullivan, Swidler, & Tipton, 1991, and Csikszentmihalyi, 1990, use *paying attention* when discussing what Langer calls *mindfulness*). Recent research, however, suggests that we do not communicate totally on automatic pilot. Rather, we pay sufficient attention so that we can recall key words in the conversations we have (Kitayama & Burnstein, 1988).

In order to communicate effectively in nonscripted situations, we must become mindful of our thought processes. Langer (1989) isolates three qualities of mindfulness: "(1) creation of new categories; (2) openness to new information; and (3) awareness of more than one perspective" (p. 62). She points out that "categorizing is a fundamental and natural human activity. It is the way we come to know the world. Any attempt to eliminate bias by attempting to eliminate the perception of differences is doomed to failure" (p. 154).

Langer (1989) argues that mindfulness involves making more, not fewer, distinctions. To illustrate, Langer uses an example of people who are in the category "cripple." If we see all people in this category as the same, we start treating the category in which we place a person as his or her identity. If we draw additional distinctions within this category (e.g., create new categories) on the other hand, it stops us from treating the person as a category. If we see a person with a "lame leg," we do not necessarily treat her or him as a "cripple."

Openness to new information and awareness of more than one perspective are related to focusing on the process, rather than the outcome. Langer (1989) argues that

> an outcome orientation in social situations can induce mindlessness. If we think we know how to handle a situation, we don't feel a need to pay attention. If we respond to the situation as very familiar (as a result, for example, of overlearning), we notice only minimal cues necessary to carry out the proper scenarios. If, on the other hand, the situation is strange, we might be so preoccupied with the thought of failure ("what if I make a fool of myself?") that we miss nuances of our own and others' behavior. In this sense, we are mindless with respect to the immediate situation, although we may be thinking quite actively about outcome related issues. (p. 34)

Langer believes that focusing on the process (e.g., how we do something) forces us to be mindful of our behavior and pay attention to the situations in which we find ourselves.

Sometimes we become mindful of our communication without any effort on our part because of the circumstances in which we find ourselves. We tend to engage in habitual behavior and follow scripts only when they are available and nothing unusual to the scripts is encountered. There are, however, several factors that will cause us to become mindful of our communication:

> (1) in novel situations where, by definition, no appropriate script exists, (2) where external factors prevent completion of a script, (3) when scripted behavior becomes effortful because substantially more of the behavior is required than is usual, (4) when a discrepant outcome is experienced, or (5) where multiple scripts come into conflict. (Berger & Douglas, 1982, pp. 46–47)

We argue throughout this chapter that choosing to be mindful, or pay attention, is necessary to develop relationships with strangers, to accurately interpret their messages, to create messages they will understand, and to adapt our behavior. If we communicate with strangers on automatic pilot, we create our messages and interpret their messages using our own frame of reference. This inevitably will lead to some degree of misunderstanding. One of the things we need to do when we are mindful is manage our need for closure.

Managing Our Need for Closure

Kruglanski (1989) presents a "lay" theory of human knowledge. He defines knowledge as "propositions (or bodies of interrelated propositions) in which a person has a given degree of confidence" (pp. 9–10). This definition suggests that the acquisition of knowledge involves "hypothesis generation" and "hypothesis validation." Hypothesis generation is the process whereby the content of the propositions is generated; hypothesis validation is the process through which confidence is developed regarding the propositions.

To isolate motivations that influence our desire to generate hypotheses and validate them, Kruglanski (1989) uses two orthogonal dimensions: seek versus avoid closure, and specificity versus nonspecificity. "The first distinction asks whether the individual desires cognitive closure on a topic or wishes to avoid closure and keep an open mind. The second distinction asks whether the desired or avoided closure is of a special kind, or whether any closure or absence of closure will do" (pp. 13–14). When combined, the two orthogonal dimensions yield four motivational orientations.

The need for nonspecific closure involves a motivation to seek a definite answer on some topic. Any form of closure is seen as preferable to the ambiguity that exists. "Such need thus represents a quest for assured knowledge that affords predictability and a base for action" (Kruglanski, 1989, p. 14). Kruglanski points out that the need for nonspecific closure is limited to specific topics in which we have an interest.

Although the need for nonspecific closure will vary as a function of the topic involved and the situations in which individuals find themselves, Kruglanski (1989) also believes that people vary in their need for nonspecific closure. Individual differences in authoritarianism or dogmatism (e.g., Rokeach, 1960), or open-mindedness more generally, should account for differences in the need for nonspecific closure. There also appear to be differences across cultures (e.g., Hofstede's, 1980, uncertainty avoidance dimension of cultural variability).

At times, Kruglanski (1989) argues, people do not want just any answer, they want a particular answer to their questions. The need for specific closure, therefore, is biased in its effect. As with the need for nonspecific closure, the need for specific closure can stem from numerous motives and the degree to which it is aroused will vary from situation to situation.

Kruglanski (1989) does not make the specific point, but it appears reasonable to argue that there also are individual differences in the need for nonspecific closure. Sorrentino and Short (1986) isolate a characteristic, certainty orientation, that appears consistent with this conceptualization. They point out

> that there are many people who simply are not interested in finding out information about themselves or the world, who do not conduct causal searches, who could not care less about comparing themselves with others, and who "don't give a hoot" for resolving discrepancies or inconsistencies about the self. Indeed, such people (we call them certainty oriented) will go out of their way not to perform activities such as these (we call people who *do* go out of their way to do such things uncertainty oriented). (pp. 379–380)

Sorrentino and Short go on to point out that uncertainty oriented people integrate new and old ideas and change their belief systems accordingly. Uncertainty oriented people evaluate ideas and thoughts on their own merit and do not necessarily compare them with others. Uncertainty oriented people want to understand themselves and their environment. Certainty oriented people, in contrast, like to hold on to traditional beliefs and have a tendency to reject ideas that are different. Certainty oriented people maintain a sense of self by not examining themselves or their behavior.

"The need to avoid closure pertains to situations where *judgmental noncommitment* is valued or desired" (Kruglanski, 1989, p. 17). Kruglanski points out that when commitment to a particular position may be "costly," individuals may choose nonclosure as a way to deal with the situation. He also suggests that nonclosure may be used as an intermediate step in the hypothesis validation process in order to reduce the chance that "mistakes" are made.

The need to avoid nonspecific closure may also be a way to avoid the restrictions that closure may impose. Kruglanski (1989) points to Snyder and Wicklund's (1981) research as an illustration. They found that in some situations that definite knowledge connotes dullness and "unattractive" predictability. The need to avoid nonspecific closure, therefore, allows "mystery" and ambiguity to be part of our cognitive system.

We often avoid specific closures because of the undesirable consequences that may follow from the closure. Kruglanski (1989) also points out that "the need to avoid specific closure may occasionally represent the need *for* the opposite closure" (p. 18), but this is not always the case. The difference, according to Kruglanski, lies in the focus of our interest. Do we focus on the thing to be avoided and not care much about its opposite, or do we focus on closure and not be concerned with its opposite?

To develop relationships, be effective, and/or adapt our behavior when communicating with strangers we must mindfully increase our need to avoid closure and decrease our need for closure. If our need for closure takes precedence over our need to avoid closure, we will not be motivated to communicate with strangers (i.e., we will avoid rather than approach strangers).

MOTIVATION TO COMMUNICATE EFFECTIVELY AND ADAPT BEHAVIOR

One important factor in our ability to be effective and adapt our behavior when communicating with strangers is our motivation. If we want to avoid interacting with members of other groups and do not approach them, we will not be able to communicate with those with whom we do come in contact. In this section, we overview the factors that motivate us to want to communicate effectively with strangers.

Understanding Our Needs

J. H. Turner (1987) concludes that certain basic "needs" motivate us to interact with others. Needs are "fundamental states of being in humans which, if unsatisfied, generate feelings of deprivation" (p. 23). The needs that serve as motivating factors are: (a) our need for a sense of group inclusion; (b) our need for a sense of trust (this need involves issue of predictability; I trust you will behave as I think you will); (c) our need for a sense of security as human beings; (d) our need to avoid diffuse anxiety; (e) our need for a sense of a common shared world; (f) our need for symbolic/material gratification; and (g) our need to sustain our self-conception. J. H. Turner argues that we "seek to avoid the deprivations that come from a failure to realize these seven fundamental states of being, and at the same time, to achieve the gratification that comes from meeting them" (p. 23).

The seven needs vary in the degree to which we are conscious of them. We are the least conscious of the needs for security as humans, sense of trust, and group inclusion; moderately conscious of the need to avoid diffuse anxiety; and the most conscious of the needs for a shared sense of the world, symbolic/material gratification, and to sustain our self-conceptions.

Each of the needs, separately and in combination, influences how we want to present ourselves to others, the intentions we form, and the habits or scripts we follow.[3] The needs also can influence each other. Anxiety, for example, can result from not meeting our needs for group inclusion, trust, security, and/or sustaining our self-concept. J. H. Turner (1987) argues that our "overall level

---

[3]J. H. Turner (1987) uses different labels for some of the terms (including the needs). He uses the ethnomethods, for example, to refer to what we call habits or scripts. We believe these terms capture the essence of his idea, but are not as full of academic jargon.

of motivational energy'' is a function of our level of anxiety produced by these four needs.

While avoiding anxiety is an important motivating factor in our communication with people who are similar, it is critical in our communication with strangers. Intergroup anxiety is largely a function of our fear of negative consequences when we interact with people who are different (Stephan & Stephan, 1985; this issue is discussed in more detail later). As our anxiety becomes high, our need for a sense of a common shared world and our need to sustain our self-conception become central (J. H. Turner, 1987). Having a sense of a common shared world and sustaining our self-concept are much more difficult when we communicate with strangers than when we communicate with people who are similar. High anxiety, therefore, leads us to avoid communicating with strangers.

The combination of our need to avoid anxiety and our need to sustain our self-conception leads to an approach–avoidance orientation toward intergroup encounters.[4] Most of us want to see ourselves as nonprejudiced and caring people. We may, therefore, want to interact with strangers to sustain our self-concept. At the same time, however, our need to avoid anxiety leads us to want to avoid interactions that are not predictable. Holding both attitudes at the same time is not unusual.

Most of us spend the vast majority of our time interacting with people who are relatively similar to us. Our actual contact with people who are different is limited; it is a novel form of interaction (Rose, 1981). If our attempts to communicate with strangers are not successful and we can not get out of the situations in which we find ourselves easily, then our unconscious need for group inclusion becomes unsatisfied. This leads to anxiety about ourselves and our standing in a group context (J. H. Turner, 1987). The net result is that we retreat into known territory and limit our interactions to people who are similar.

When we find ourselves limiting our communication to members of our in-groups, we can mindfully choose to change our behavior. This is important because failure to maintain our social bonds with others, including members of other groups, influences our psychological well-being.

Maintaining Intact Social Bonds

Scheff (1990) argues that our need for secure social bonds with others is one of the major factors motivating our behavior. He argues that we need to balance our closeness and distance to others (Bowen's, 1978, concept of differentiation). He claims that ''optimal differentiation defines an intact social bond,

---

[4]Spitzberg and Cupach (1984) also talk about approach avoidance as a factor in motivation. They, however, assume that it is a basic orientation to any encounter rather than deriving it from more basic needs.

a bond which balances the needs of the individual and the needs of the group''
(p. 4).[5] Scheff goes on to suggest that attunement, "mutual understanding
that is not only mental but also emotional" (p. 7), is necessary for a social
bond to exist.[6]

Scheff (1990) believes that pride and shame are the primary emotions that
influence our social bonds with others. Pride is the sign of an intact social bond;
shame is a sign of a threatened social bond.[7] He argues that "shame is the
primary social emotion in that it is generated by the virtually constant monitoring of the self in relation to others. Such monitoring . . . is not rare but almost
continuous in social interaction and, more covertly, in solitary thought" (p.
79). Scheff goes on to define self-esteem as "freedom from chronic shame"
(p. 168).

When our social bonds are not intact and/or we feel unconnected to others,
we will feel shame (Scheff, 1990) and are morally exclusive (Optow, 1990).
Optow points out that "moral exclusion occurs when individuals or groups
are perceived as *outside the boundary in which moral values, rules, and considerations
of fairness apply*. Those who are morally excluded are perceived as nonentities,
expendable, or undeserving; consequently, harming them appears acceptable,
appropriate, or just" (p. 1). When we are morally exclusive, we may think
that it is justified, but it will form what Lewis (1971) calls "unacknowledged
shame."

To be effective and adapt our behavior when communicating with strangers,
we must consciously work toward attunement in our social bonds with them.
Attunement does not imply that our social bonds are highly intimate, but rather
that they involve mutual understanding. If we can achieve attunement, then
the bonds will be intact and we will feel pride, not shame.[8]

INTERPRETING STRANGERS' BEHAVIOR

To be effective and adapt our behavior in communicating with strangers we
must have knowledge the strangers and their groups. Knowledge refers to our
awareness and understanding of what needs to be done to communicate effectively and adapt our behavior (Spitzberg & Cupach, 1984). Two aspects of

---

[5]Brewer (1991) uses a similar idea in her discussion of optimal distinctiveness, which involves
balancing personal and social identities to maximize distinctiveness.

[6]Scheff also argues that there can be attunement between groups and to the extent that this
exists, society can be said to exist.

[7]Following Lewis (1971), Scheff includes embarrassment, guilt, and other related emotions
as part of the shame construct.

[8]On the surface, this claim appears inconsistent with Tajfel's (1978) social comparison process.
Tajfel's conceptualization, however, does not take into consideration the existence of unacknowledged
shame.

knowledge are critical to adapting our behavior to communicate effectively with strangers: understanding that strangers' interpretations are different from ours, and knowledge of similarities and differences between our group and the strangers' groups.

Understanding Strangers' Interpretations

There are at least three interrelated cognitive processes involved when we communicate with others: description, interpretation, and evaluation. Description refers to an actual report of what we have taken in with our senses with the minimum of distortion and without attributing social significance to the behavior. Interpretation involves attaching meaning or social significance to social stimuli. Evaluations involve our judgments of social stimuli.

If we do not distinguish among these three cognitive processes, it is likely that we will skip the descriptive process and jump immediately to either interpretation or evaluation when communicating with strangers. This leads to misattributions of meaning and, therefore, to ineffective communication. If we mindfully distinguish among the three processes, on the other hand, we are able to search for alternative interpretations that are used by strangers, thereby increasing our effectiveness. Differentiating among the three processes also increases the likelihood of our making more accurate predictions and explanations of strangers' behavior.

To decrease the chance of misinterpretations of others' messages based on our unconscious interpretations, we must be aware of our "normal" tendencies. Beck (1988) outlines five principles of cognitive therapy that are useful in understanding how misinterpretations occur:

1. We can never know the state of mind—the attitudes, thoughts, and feelings—of other people.
2. We depend on signals, which are frequently ambiguous, to inform us about the attitudes and wishes of other people.
3. We use our own coding system, which may be defective, to decipher these signals.
4. Depending on our own state of mind at a particular time, we may be biased in our method of interpreting other people's behavior, that is, how we decode.
5. The degree to which we believe that we are correct in divining another person's motives and attitudes is not related to the actual accuracy of our belief. (p. 18)

When we are not mindful of the process of our communication, we assume others interpret stimuli the same as we do. Being mindful of the process of communication is necessary if we are to understand how strangers interpret the messages being exchanged when we communicate. If we understand how strangers interpret messages, we can be effective and adapt our behavior accordingly when communicating with them.

Understanding Similarities and Differences

Making accurate attributions about others' behavior requires that we be able to determine how they are interpreting their own and our messages. To make accurate predictions and explanations, we must understand the "stocks of knowledge" (Scheff, 1990) being used to interpret the messages. We also need to understand the similarities and differences between their groups and ours. The focus here is on how group memberships (e.g., culture, ethnicity, gender) influence the way we interpret stimuli.

In addition to understanding stocks of knowledge, we must seek out commonalities between ourselves and others. Bellah, Madsen, Sullivan, Swidler, and Tipton (1985), for example, point out that we need to seek out commonalities because "with a more explicit understanding of what we have in common and the goals we seek to attain together, the differences between us that remain would be less threatening" (p. 287). Finding commonalities requires that we be mindful of our prejudices.

The position that Bellah and his associates (1985) advocate vis-à-vis cultural and/or ethnic differences is consistent with Langer's (1989) contention that

> because most of us grow up and spend our time with people like ourselves, we tend to assume uniformities and commonalities. When confronted with someone who is clearly different in one specific way, we drop that assumption and look for differences. . . . The mindful curiosity generated by an encounter with someone who is different, which can lead to exaggerated perceptions of strangeness, can also bring us closer to that person if channeled differently. (p. 156)

Langer suggests that once we are able to satisfy our curiosity about differences, understanding can occur. This, however, requires that we are mindful.[9]

UNDERSTANDING OUR EXPECTATIONS

Our expectations of strangers influence how we communicate with them. To be effective and able to adapt our behavior, we must understand what our expectations are and how they influence the way we communicate. In this section,

---

[9]We believe that it is necessary to understand the differences between ourselves and strangers before we can seek out commonalities.

we discuss the nature of expectations, how they are linked to status characteristics (e.g., the other person's ethnicity or gender), and how stereotypes create expectations. We conclude this section by looking at how we can change our expectations.

The Nature of Our Expectations

Expectations involve our anticipations and predictions about how others will communicate with us. Our expectations are derived from social norms, communication rules, and others' personal characteristics of which we are aware. There is a "should" component to most of our expectations. "People who interact develop expectations about each others' behavior, not only in the sense that they are able to predict the regularities, but also in the sense that they develop preferences about how others *should* behave under certain circumstances" (Jackson, 1964, p. 225).

Our culture and ethnicity provide guidelines for appropriate behavior and the expectations we use in judging competent communication. To illustrate, Burgoon and Hale (1988) point out that in the White middle-class subculture[10]

> one expects normal speakers to be reasonably fluent and coherent in their discourse, to refrain from erratic movements or emotional outbursts, and to adhere to politeness norms. Generally, normative behaviors are positively valued. If one keeps a polite distance and shows an appropriate level of interest in one's conversational partner, for instance, such behavior should be favorably received. (p. 61)

It must be recognized, however, that norms for what is a "polite" distance and what constitutes an "emotional" outburst vary across cultures and across subcultures within a culture.

If one person violates another's expectations to a sufficient degree that the violation is recognized, the person recognizing the violation becomes aroused and has to assess the situation (Burgoon & Hale, 1988). In other words, the violation of expectations leads to some degree of mindfulness.

Burgoon and Hale (1988) argue that the degree to which the other person provides us with rewards affects how we evaluate the violation and the person committing the act. As used here, rewards do not refer to money (although it might be consideration if the other person is our boss or a client). Rather, rewards include the benefits we obtain from our interactions with the other person. If the other person provides us with rewards, we choose the most positive of the possible interpretations of violations that have multiple possible

---

[10]Burgoon and Hale do not limit their statement to this group, we do.

interpretations; "for example, increased proximity during conversation may be taken as a sign of affiliation if committed by a high reward person but as a sign of aggressiveness if committed by a low reward person" (Burgoon & Hale, 1988, p. 63).

Positively evaluated violations of our expectations should have positive consequences for our communication with violators (e.g., not lead to misinterpretations, increase intimacy; Burgoon & Hale, 1988). Negatively evaluated violations, in contrast, generally lead to negative outcomes (e.g., misinterpretations, decreases in intimacy). There are, however, exceptions for negative violations. Burgoon and Hale point out that if the other person provides rewards and commits an extreme violation of our expectations, positive outcomes (e.g., higher credibility and/or interpersonal attraction) are possible. Strangers are generally not perceived as providing rewards (Gudykunst & Kim, 1992).

Status Characteristics and Expectation States

Berger, Wagner, and Zelditch (1985) define expectation states as "self–other relational structures that organize behavior among interactants" (p. 32). Expectation states are inferred from known antecedent conditions and consequent observables. Berger et al. point out that "interactants, while engaged in interaction, typically are not aware of how expectation states are formed, what states are formed, and how these states are transformed into behavior" (p. 35). Stated differently, expectation states are outside of participants' awareness—they occur when individuals are behaving mindlessly.

Berger et al. (1985) contend that "expectation states drive behavior . . . differences in underlying states and structures lead to differences in behavior" (p. 35). They also point out that behavioral and information inputs drive expectation states. One important set of informational inputs used in forming expectation states is status characteristics. Driskell and Mullen (1990) succinctly outline the assumptions expectation states theory and status characteristics:

> The basic assumption is that within task groups whose members are differentiated by some valued characteristic (e.g., race, sex, age, ability) individuals form stable conceptions of one another's performance capabilities which are consistent with the distributions of that valued characteristic. These performance expectations, or expectation states, determine the power and prestige structure of the group, including opportunities to perform, deference, and exercise of influence. Status characteristics serve as cues to performance capability because they are culturally evaluated (e.g., it is considered preferable in our culture to be White, male, and professional) and carry performance connotations (e.g., Whites, males, and professionals are thought to do better on most tasks). The external evaluation of a status characteristic is imported into the group and forms the basis for the assignment of performance expectations. (pp. 541–542)

Driskell and Mullen's meta-analysis of previous research supported this conceptualization (i.e., that expectation states is an intervening variable between status characteristics and behavior).

Stereotypes and Expectations

Stereotypes provide the content of our social categories and create expectations for others' behavior. We have social categories in which we place people and it is our stereotype that tells us what people in that category are like. We can draw at least four generalizations about the stereotyping process (Hewstone & Giles, 1986). First, stereotyping is the result of our tendency to overestimate the degree of association between group membership and psychological attributes. Although there may be some association between group membership and psychological characteristics of members, it is much smaller than we assume when we communicate on automatic pilot.

Second, stereotypes influence the way we process information. Research indicates that we remember more favorable information about our ingroups and more unfavorable information about outgroups. This, in turn, affects the way we interpret incoming messages from members of ingroups and outgroups.

Third, stereotypes create expectations regarding how members of other groups will behave. Stereotypes are activated automatically when we have contact with strangers (Devine, 1989). Unconsciously, we assume that our expectations are correct and we behave as though they are. We, therefore, try to confirm our expectations when we communicate with members of other groups. We can, however, control the effects of automatic processing. This occurs especially in conditions where we want to present a "nonprejudiced" identity (Devine, 1989).

Fourth, our stereotypes constrain others' patterns of communication and engender stereotype-confirming communication. Stated differently, stereotypes create self-fulfilling prophecies. We tend to see behavior that confirms our expectations, even when it is absent. We ignore disconfirming evidence when communicating on automatic pilot. If we assume someone else is not competent and communicate with them based on this assumption, they will appear incompetent (even if they are actually competent).

Stereotypes, in and of themselves, do not lead to miscommunication and/or communication breakdown. If, however, stereotypes are held rigidly, they lead to inaccurate predictions of others' behavior and misunderstandings. Simple stereotypes of other groups also can lead to misunderstandings. In order to increase our effectiveness in communicating with strangers, we need to increase the complexity of our stereotypes and question our unconscious assumption that most members of a group fit a single stereotype (Hamilton, Sherman, & Ruvolo, 1990).

Devine (1989) argues that conscious control of our reactions when our stereotypes are activated is necessary to control our prejudice:

> Nonprejudiced responses are . . . a function of intentional controlled processes
> and require a conscious decision to behave in a nonprejudiced fashion. In addi-
> tion, new responses must be learned and well practiced before they can serve
> as competitive responses to the automatically activated stereotype-congruent
> response. (p. 15)

This position is consistent with Langer's (1989) notion that mindfulness is necessary to reduce prejudice.[11]

Changing Our Expectations of Outgroup Members

Brewer and Miller (1988) argue that when we communicate with strangers there
are three ways that our experiences with individual strangers can generalize
to change our attitudes toward stereotypes of their groups:

> 1. *Change in attitudes toward the group as a whole.* This is the most direct form of
> generalization, where positive experiences with individual members of a broad
> social category lead to alterations in the affect and stereotypes associated with
> the group as a whole.
>
> 2. *Increased complexity of intergroup perceptions.* This form of generalization involves
> a change in the perceived heterogeneity of category structure. Instead of per-
> ceiving the out-group category as a relatively homogeneous social group, the in-
> dividual comes to recognize variability among category members. Attitudes toward
> the category as a whole may not be altered, but affect and stereotypes are differen-
> tiated among various "sub-types" of the general category.
>
> 3. *Decategorization.* In this form of generalization, the meaningfulness of the
> category itself is undermined. Based on the frequency or intensity of exposure
> to individual members of a social group, the utility of category membership as
> a basis for identifying or classifying new individuals is reduced. (p. 316)

Each of these forms of generalization deserve brief discussion.

Many people assume that if we have contact with members of other groups,
our attitudes toward those groups will become more positive. This, however,
is not necessarily the case. Research on intergroup contact suggests that contact can promote better relations between groups or increase hostility between
groups. The question that needs to be answered is: When does contact lead
to better relations between groups?

---

[11]Langer's (1989) chapter on prejudice is titled "Reducing Prejudice by Increasing Discrimination." Discrimination refers to creating finer categories.

In his review of research on intergroup contact, Stephan (1985) isolated 13 characteristics of the contact situation that are necessary for positive attitude change toward a social group to occur as a result of our individual contact with specific strangers:

1. Cooperation within groups should be maximized and competition between groups should be minimized.
2. Members of the in-group and the out-group should be of equal status both within and outside the contact situation.
3. Similarity of group members on nonstatus dimensions (beliefs, values, etc.) appears to be desirable.
4. Differences in competence should be avoided.
5. The outcomes should be positive.
6. Strong normative and institutional support for the contact should be provided.
7. The intergroup contact should have the potential to extend beyond the immediate situation.
8. Individuation of group members should be promoted.
9. Nonsuperficial contact (e.g., mutual disclosure of information) should be encouraged.
10. The contact should be voluntary.
11. Positive effects are likely to correlate with the duration of the contact.
12. The contact should occur in a variety of contexts with a variety of in-group and out-group members.
13. Equal numbers of in-group and out-group members should be used. (p. 643)

Although this list is long, Stephan points out that it is incomplete. If we want to design a program to reduce prejudice or ethnocentrism, we, therefore, must make sure that the contact we arrange meets as many of these conditions as possible.

Increasing the complexity of our intergroup perceptions involves seeing the social category as heterogeneous (i.e., different), rather than homogeneous (i.e., alike; Brewer & Miller, 1988). Stated differently, we can increase the complexity of our intergroup perceptions by recognizing how members of a social category are different. Think of the social groups males and females. Are all males and all females the same? Obviously, the answer is no. We see differences among males and females and place them in subcategories. Females, for example, may categorize males into "male chauvinists" and "feminists."

Increasing the complexity of our intergroup perceptions is consistent with Langer's (1989) notion of mindfulness. One aspect of becoming mindful of our communication is the creation of new categories. Creating new categories for Langer involves differentiating among the individuals within the broad social categories we use. This means increasing the number of "discriminations" we make—using specific rather than global labels (e.g., a person with a lame leg, rather than a "cripple"). When we are mindful of differences among the members of the various outgroups with whom we communicate, our expectations are based on the subcategories, not the broader social category.

Decategorization occurs when we communicate with strangers based on their individual characteristics, rather than the categories in which we place them (i.e., communication is interpersonal, not intergroup; Brewer & Miller, 1988). In order to accomplish this, we must differentiate individual strangers from their groups. Differentiation alone, however, is not sufficient for decategorization or personalization to occur. When we personalize or decategorize our interactions with strangers, personal identity takes on more importance than social identity.

All of the strategies discussed in this section to change our expectations of strangers require some degree of mindfulness to be effectively implemented. It is possible for us to change our expectations while communicating on automatic pilot (e.g., if we have repeated contact with strangers under favorable conditions). This, however, is a rare occurrence.

MAKING SENSE OF STRANGERS' BEHAVIOR

To communicate effectively with strangers, we must understand how we make sense of their behavior (i.e., the attribution process). If we understand how we make attributions and use others' group memberships to explain their behavior, we can mindfully manage this process in order to communicate more effectively.

Understanding the Attributions We Make

Heider (1958) originally raised the question of how we make sense of our own and others' behavior and how our interpretations shape our responses to behavior. He believed that we act as "naive" or "intuitive" scientists when we are trying to make sense of the world. Briefly, Heider suggests that we are motivated by practical concerns such as our need to simplify and comprehend our environment, and to predict others' behavior. In order to meet these needs, we try to get beneath external appearances to isolate stable underlying processes, which he called "dispositional properties." Heider believes that others' motives are the dispositions we use most frequently in giving meaning to our experiences. He also pointed out that it is not our experiences per se, but our interpretations of our experiences that constitute our "reality."

Kelley (1967) extended Heider's work by trying to explain when we attribute behavior to internal causes and when we attribute it to external causes.

He argues that when observing others' behavior we attempt to make attributions about the effect of the environment on their behavior by ruling out individual explanations for the behavior. We organize our observations into a cube with three dimensions: Person × Object × Situation. In the person dimension, we compare the person engaging in the behavior with others; in the object dimension, we compare the different objects (things or people) of the person's behavior; in the situation dimension, we vary the context in which the behavior occurs. We then use a "covariation" principle to assess the degree to which the behavior occurs in the presence and absence of the various causes.

Heider (1958) and Kelley (1967) focus on individual attributions. Their perspectives, however, do not take our group memberships into consideration. Social attributions are concerned with how members of one social group explain the behavior of their own members and that of members of other social groups. Hewstone and Jaspars (1984) isolate three propositions regarding the social nature of attributions:

> 1. Attribution is social in origin (e.g., it may be created by, or strengthened through, social interaction, or it may be influenced by social information).
>
> 2. Attribution is social in its reference or object (e.g., an attribution may be demanded for the individual characterized as a member of a social group, rather than in purely individual terms; or for a social outcome, rather than any behavior as such).
>
> 3. Attribution is social in that it is common to the members of a society or group (e.g., the members of different groups may hold different attributions for the same event). (pp. 379–380; italics omitted)

Hewstone and Jaspars argue that we enhance our social identities when we make social attributions. They also point out that our social attributions usually are based on the social stereotypes we share with other members of our ingroups. Our social attributions, however, can also be based on ethnocentrism.

Most writing on individual and social attributions is based on the assumption that observers know what the behavior they are observing means. This assumption, however, is questionable when we communicate with strangers. Hewstone and Brown (1986) argue that when we perceive ourselves and others in individual terms (e.g., our personal identities generate our behavior) or we see an outgroup member as atypical, we tend to make person-based attributions. Person-based attributions, in turn, lead us to look for personal similarities and differences between us and the other person. When we perceive ourselves and others as members of groups (e.g., our social identities generate our behavior), we tend to make category-based attributions. Category-based attributions then lead us to look for differences between our ingroup and the relevant outgroup.

The nature of the attributions we make influences our relations with members of other groups. When members of different groups are working together and fail on their task, members of the ingroup usually blame the outgroup for the failure. Attributions like this do not help to improve intergroup relations and can, in fact, have a negative influence. If ingroup members are somehow "prevented" from blaming the outgroup for the failure, cooperation that results in failure does not result in increased bias against the outgroup (Worchel & Norwell, 1980). This requires that we consciously (i.e., mindfully) avoid automatically placing blame on strangers.

Incorrectly blaming others is only one error in our attribution processes when we communicate on automatic pilot. Pettigrew (1979) combines the "fundamental attribution error" and the "principle of negativity" to propose the "ultimate" attribution error, "a systematic patterning of intergroup mis-attributions shaped in part by prejudice" (p. 464). He points out that our tendency to attribute behavior to dispositional characteristics, rather than situational characteristics, is enhanced when a member of an outgroup is perceived to engage in negative behavior. When members of an outgroup engage in what is perceived to be positive behavior, in contrast, our tendency is to treat the person as an "exception to the rule" and we discount dispositional explanations for the behavior. We, therefore, attribute the behavior to situational factors.

With respect to the ultimate attribution error, Pettigrew (1978) concluded that

> across-group perceptions are more likely than within-group perceptions to include the following:
>
> 1. For acts perceived as antisocial or undesirable, behavior will be attributed to personal, dispositional causes. Often these internal causes will be seen as innate characteristics, and role requirements will be overlooked. ("He shoved the white guy, because blacks are born violent like that.")
>
> 2. For acts perceived as prosocial or desirable, behavior will be attributed either: (a) to the situation—with role requirements receiving more attention ("Under the circumstances, what could the cheap Scot do, but pay the check?"); (b) to the motivational, as opposed to innate, dispositional qualities ("Jewish students make better grades, because they try so much harder"); or (c) to the exceptional, even exaggerated "special case" individual who is contrasted with his/her group—what Allport (1954) called "fence-mending" ("She is certainly bright and hardworking—not at all like other Chicanos"). (p. 39; italics omitted)

We tend to make the ultimate attribution error when communicating mindlessly or on automatic pilot. To reduce the possibility of making the ultimate attribution error when explaining the behavior of strangers, we must be mindful of our interpretations of their behavior.

Using Wide Categories

There is at least one cognitive style that influences the way in which we make attributions. "Category width refers to the range of instances included in a cognitive category" (Pettigrew, 1982, p. 200). Pettigrew suggests that individual differences in category width are related to more general information processing strategies people use. Broad categorizers, for example, tend to perform better than narrow categorizers on tasks that require holistic, integrated, information processing. Narrow categorizers, in comparison, tend to perform better than broad categorizers on tasks that require detailed, analytic, information processing.

Detweiler (1975) studied how category width influences the attributions whites in the United States make about people who are culturally similar (another white from the United States) or culturally dissimilar (a person from Haiti) who engage in either positive or negative behavior. His findings indicate that narrow categorizers

> assume that the effects of behavior of a person from another culture tell all about the person, even though he [or she] in fact knows nothing about the actor's [or actress'] cultural background. He [or she] seems to make strong judgments based on the positivity or negativity of the effects of the behavior as evaluated from his [or her] own cultural viewpoint. Contrarily, when making attributions to a person who is culturally similar, the narrow [categorizer] seems to view the similarity as overshadowing the behavior. Thus, positive effects are seen as intended, and negative effects are confidently seen as unintended. (p. 600)

These findings suggest that narrow categorizers may have trouble making accurate attributions about messages from both people who are culturally similar and people who are culturally dissimilar.

The wide categorizers in Detweiler's (1975) study had a very different orientation. When making attributions about a culturally dissimilar person, a wide categorizer

> seems to assume that he [or she] in fact doesn't know enough to make "usual" attributions. Thus, behaviors with negative effect result in less confident and generally more neutral attributions when judgments are made about a person from a different culture. Conversely, the culturally similar person who causes a negative outcome is rated relatively more negatively with greater confidence by the wide [categorizer], since the behavior from one's own cultural background is meaningful. (p. 600)

Using wide categories, therefore, is necessary to see that there is more than one perspective and to make isomorphic attributions.

ADAPTING OUR LANGUAGE USAGE
IN COMMUNICATING WITH STRANGERS

The language we use is an important component of communicating effectively with strangers. In this section we discuss several important factors including learning a second language, accommodating our speech, switching the code we use, decreasing our communicative distance, and avoiding prejudice in our discourse.

Learning a Second Language

There are numerous explanations of second language learning (see Gardner, 1985, for reviews of major theories), but only the intergroup model takes into consideration the intergroup factors relevant to second language learning. We, therefore, focus on that model here.

The intergroup model of second language learning originally was proposed by Giles and Byrne (1982). They argued that second language learning cannot be explained unless the relations between the groups is taken into consideration. More recently, Garrett, Giles, and Coupland (1989) extended the intergroup model. Garrett et al. isolate five factors that contribute to members of a "minority" group learning the language of the "dominant" group.

The first factor in Garrett et al.'s (1989) model involves how the minority language is viewed. If members of an ethnic group identify weakly within their group or do not view language as an important part of their identity, they are likely to try to learn the dominant language. If members of minority groups view their language as an important part of their identity, they will try to learn the dominant language to the extent that it does not threaten their identity or they have other ways to preserve their ethnic identity.

Second, if members of the ethnic group perceive few alternatives to their "subordinate" status and view the chance of it changing as small, they will try to learn the dominant language (Garrett et al., 1989). They will also try to learn the dominant language if they perceive cognitive alternatives to their status and realize that these can be met by learning the dominant language.

Third, members of minority groups will try to learn the dominant language to the extent that they perceive the boundaries between their group and the dominant group to be soft and open (Garrett et al., 1989). Stated differently, if they believe that learning the dominant language will help them be accepted in the dominant group, they will try to learn the language.

Fourth, members of minority groups will try to learn the dominant language to the extent that they derive satisfactory social identities from other group memberships (Garrett et al., 1989). That is, they are members of other social categories that provide them with satisfactory identities.

Finally, if members of minority groups perceive the vitality of their group to be low, they will attempt to learn the dominant group language (Garrett et al., 1989). They also will try to learn the dominant language if they believe learning it will contribute to the vitality of their ingroup.

In addition to these five intergroup factors, Garrett et al. (1989) isolated three sociolinguistic factors that contribute to second language learning. First, the more similar the dominant language and the majority language, the more likely members of minorities are to learn the dominant language. Second, there must be exposure to the dominant language for it to be learned (e.g., members of the minority group must have contact with speakers of the dominant language). Third, there must be use of the dominant language for it to be learned (e.g., members of the minority group need to have the opportunity to use the dominant language in a variety of contexts).

Before proceeding, it should be noted that the theory outlined here is not limited to members of minority groups learning the dominant language; it applies equally to a person from one culture learning the language of another culture. Once the dominant or second language is learned, there is the remaining issue of what effects its use has on the communication that takes place. If we are competent in strangers' languages, it reduces our uncertainty and anxiety when we communicate with them (Gudykunst, 1988). Linguistic competence also influences our ability to accommodate our communication and code-switch when we communicate with strangers.

Accommodating to Strangers

In attempting to provide a systematic explanation for the persistence of linguistic diversity, Tajfel (1978) suggests that when members of one group interact with strangers of another, they compare themselves on a number of value dimensions with the strangers. He claims that these intergroup social comparisons lead group members to search for characteristics of their own group that will enable them to differentiate themselves favorably from the outgroup. Such positive ingroup distinctiveness not only allows individuals personal satisfaction in their own group membership but also affords them a positive social identity. Applying this psychological process to speech behavior, Giles (1973) describes the tendency to accentuate (e.g., emphasize) linguistic difference as speech divergence. Some individuals in interaction with others shift their speech in their desire for their listeners' social approval. One tactic, consciously or unconsciously conceived, is for them to modify their speech in the direction of the listeners' speech patterns, a process Giles terms *speech convergence*.

Giles, Bourhis, and Taylor (1977) suggest that when members of a subordinate group accept their inferior status, they attempt to converge into the dominant group socially and psychologically by means of speech convergence.

If, on the other hand, they consider their inferior status to be illegitimate and the intergroup situation to be unstable, they seek "psychological distinctiveness" by redefining their group attributes in a socially and psychologically more favorable direction. They also might do this linguistically and hence, in interaction with a member of the outgroup, accentuate their own ingroup characteristics by means of speech divergence using their own dialect, accent, jargon, or other form of speech variation.

There is a tendency for members of ingroups to react favorably to outgroup members who linguistically converge toward them (Giles & Smith, 1979). This, however, is not always the case. Giles and Byrne (1982) point out that as an outgroup's members begin to learn the speech style of the ingroup, ingroup members may diverge in some way to maintain linguistic distinctiveness. Reaction to outgroup members' speech convergence depends on the intent ingroup members attribute to the outgroup members (Simard, Taylor, & Giles, 1976).

Genesse and Bourhis (1982) found that ingroup members' evaluation of outgroup members' language usage in conversations is based on situational norms in the initial stages of conversations and on interpersonal accommodation later in the conversation. Bourhis (1985) discovered that following situational norms is the strategy used most frequently in early stages of hostile intergroup encounters. In later stages of conversations, however, individuals adopt strategies based on their goals, desire to assert their group identity, and their affective response to the other person.

Giles, Mulac, Bradac, and Johnson (1987) argue that communication convergence is a function of a speaker's desire for (a) social approval, (b) high communication efficiency, (c) shared self- or group-presentation, and (d) an appropriate identity definition. In addition, for communication convergence to occur, there needs to be a match between the speaker's view of the recipient's speech style and the actual style used; also, the specific speech style used must be appropriate for both speaker and recipient. Divergence, in contrast, is a function of the speaker's desire (a) for a "contrastive" self-image, (b) to dissociate from the recipient, (c) to change the recipient's speech behavior, and (d) to define an encounter in intergroup terms. Divergence also occurs when recipients use a speech style that deviates from a norm that is valued and consistent with the speaker's expectations regarding the recipient's performance. If strangers accommodate to our communication style and we perceive their intent to be positive, it will reduce our uncertainty and anxiety in communicating with them (Gudykunst, 1993).

Switching Our Codes

The code we use is, in part, a function of the vitality of the languages or dialects we speak and our desire to accommodate to the person with whom we are communicating. There are also "normative" factors that contribute to code choice (see Gudykunst, Ting-Toomey, Hall, & Schmidt, 1989; Sachdev & Bourhis, 1990, for sources). Studies of immigrants in the United States, for example, found that English is used in public formal settings, whereas native language is used in informal, nonpublic settings. This conclusion is supported by research in other countries (e.g., Philippines, Paraguay, Israel, Nigeria) as well. Similarly, the topic of conversation affects the code used. People tend to use their native languages when discussing stressful or exciting topics.

In addition to the topic of conversation and the setting, we may switch languages to show warmth and group identification (Gumperz & Hernandez-Chavez, 1972). Similarly, immigrants tend to use their first language when discussing life in the native country. Using the first language to discuss life in the native country reinforces cultural heritage and fills a need to "identify with compatriots" (Chaika, 1982, p. 239).

Chaika (1982) points out that people sometimes switch codes for emphasis or to see if a stranger belongs to the ingroup. She argues that

> the switch from one language to another, in itself, has meaning. No matter what else a switch means, it reinforces bonds between speakers. Such switching can obviously only occur between those who speak the same language. It may be done in the presence of nonspeakers as a way of excluding them, just as jargon may. (p. 238)

The language or dialect people select, therefore, reinforces their social identity.

Researchers have linked code-switching to ethnic identity in organizations. Banks (1987), for example, examined the influence of language use on ethnic identity. Based on his study of language use in organizations, Banks argued that the "boundary" (e.g., the line separating) between marked (e.g., use of ethnic dialect) and unmarked (e.g., "standard" dialect) ethnic discourse is soft and permeable, whereas the boundary between low- and high-power positions in the organization are more hard and less permeable. Banks draws four conclusions regarding ethnic discourse in organizations. First, members of minority groups must cross the soft boundary from ethnically marked to unmarked discourse before crossing the boundary from low- to high-power positions. Second, crossing the boundary from ethnically marked to unmarked discourse is a function of the strategies individuals use to maximize their rewards, as well as the norms, values for discourse in the organization. Third, there is an implicit promise from the organization he studied that if members of minorities cross the boundary from ethnically marked to unmarked discourse, they will have the opportunity to cross the boundary from low- to high-power position. Finally, individuals who cross the boundary from ethnically marked to unmarked discourse "subtract from" their ethnic identities (i.e., using unmarked discourse takes away from the strength of their ethnic identity).

Decreasing Our Communicative Distances

The attitudes we hold create expectations for how we should speak to other people. The speed with which we talk or the accent we use may be varied in order to generate different feelings of distance for the strangers with whom we communicate (i.e., to make the distance seem smaller or greater). Lukens (1978) argues that "ethnocentric speech" is reflected in three communicative distances: (a) the distance of indifference, (b) the distance of avoidance, and (c) the distance of disparagement. Lukens associates each of the three distances with a different level of ethnocentrism (low, moderate, and high, respectively).

The distance of indifference, according to Lukens (1978), is the speech form used to "reflect the view that one's own culture is the center of everything" (p. 42). This distance, therefore, reflects an insensitivity to strangers' perspectives. One example of the speech used at this distance is "foreigner talk," the form of speech used when talking to people who are not native speakers of a language. It usually takes the form of loud and slow speech patterns, exaggerated pronunciation, and simplification (e.g., deletion of articles). Downs (1971) points out, "We tend to believe that, if we speak slowly enough or loudly enough, anyone can understand us. I have done this myself quite without realizing it, and others have tried to reach me in the same way in Japanese, Chinese, Thai, Punjabi, Navajo, Spanish, Tibetan, and Singhalese" (p. 19).

According to Lukens (1978), the distance of avoidance is established in order to avoid or minimize contact with members of an outgroup. One technique commonly used to accomplish this is the use of an ingroup dialect. "The emphasizing of an ethnic dialect and other linguistic differences between the ingroup and outsiders may be purposefully used by in-group members to make themselves appear esoteric to the out-group thus lessening the likelihood for interaction" (p. 45). At this distance members of the ingroup also may use terms of solidarity. Feelings of cultural pride and solidarity are increased through the use of such terms as "Black power," "Black is beautiful," and "Red power." In establishing this distance, jargon common to the ingroup is used extensively.

The distance of disparagement, according to Lukens (1978), reflects animosity of the ingroup toward the outgroup. It arises when the two groups are in competition for the same resources. This level is characterized by the use of pejorative expressions and ethnophaulisms. Lukens indicates that at this distance imitation and mockery of speech styles are characteristic.

Gudykunst and Kim (1984) argue that cultural relativism, the view that all cultures are of equal value and the values and behavior of a culture can only be understood using that culture's frame of reference, must also be taken into consideration in understanding communicative distances. They contend that there are two additional communicative distances based on moderate and high levels of cultural relativism. The level of moderate cultural relativism reflects a sensitivity to cultural differences. The speech at this level reflects our desire to decrease the communicative distance between ourselves and strangers. This distance is labeled the distance of sensitivity. The level of high cultural relativism reflects our desire to minimize the distance between ourselves and strangers. This distance involves an attitude of equality, one where we demonstrate that we are interpreting the language and behavior of strangers in terms of their culture. This distance is labeled the *distance of equality*. Using a distance of sensitivity and/or equality is necessary to be effective in communicating with strangers.

Avoiding Prejudice in Our Discourse

Crosby, Bromley, and Saxe (1980) argue that Whites in the United States generally try to express nonbigoted ideologies and behave in a nondiscriminatory fashion but, at the same time, they have not internalized the feelings that correspond to the attitudes expressed. Sears (1988) argues that this is due to "symbolic racism" existing in the United States today. According to Sears, symbolic racism is "not racism composed of derogations of and antagonism toward blacks per se, or of support for formal inequality." Rather, it blends "some anti-black feeling with the first and proudest of traditional [North] American values, particularly individualism" (p. 54).

Billig et al. (1988) contend that there is an ambivalence inherent in racial discourse. They point out that even individuals who are highly authoritarian (and, therefore, expected to hold negative views of other groups) tend to verbally qualify the views of other groups they express so that they appear reasonable. They also note that people who appear very liberal "introduce innuendos and . . . cast aspersions in the most polite and outwardly 'reasonable' ways" (p. 107). If people are going to make a negative comment about strangers, for example, they preface their comment with a claim of not being prejudiced. To illustrate, one interviewee in van Dijk's (1984) study responded in this way:

[Interviewer]: Did you ever have any unpleasant experiences [with foreigners]?
[Interviewee]: I have nothing against foreigners. But their attitude, their aggression is scaring. We are no longer free here. You have to be careful. (p. 65)

Billig and his associates (1988) claim that the ambivalence inherent in qualified prejudiced discourse does not simply reflect an inconsistency between attitudes and impression management. Rather, they suggest it indicates that people have "dilemmatic" or dialectical thoughts—they may be prejudiced and tolerant at the same time. We believe that for most people the prejudiced pole of the dialectic is manifested when we communicate "mindlessly," and the tolerance pole of the dialectic is manifested when we communicate "mindfully."

Van Dijk found (1984) that prejudiced talk clusters in four categories: (1) "they are different (culture, mentality)"; (2) "they do not adapt themselves"; (3) "they are involved in negative acts (nuisance, crime)"; and (4) "they threaten our (social, economic) interests" (p. 70). Although van Dijk's study was conducted in the Netherlands, these same types of prejudiced talk consistently are overheard in the United States.

The way we talk about people who are different is, in large part, a function of how we want to be seen by our ingroup. Van Dijk (1984) points out that

> people "adapt" their discourse to the rules and constraints of interaction and communication social settings. Especially when delicate topics, such as "foreigners," are concerned, social members will strategically try to realize both the aims of positive self-presentation and those of effective persuasion. Both aims, however, derive from the position of social members within their group. Positive self-presentation is not just a defense mechanism of individuals as persons, but also as respected, accepted, and integrated social members of ingroups. And the same holds for the persuasive nature of prejudiced talk; people do not merely lodge personal complaints or uneasiness about people of other groups, but intend to have their experiences, their evaluations, their opinions, their attitudes, and their actions shared by other members of the ingroup. (p. 154)

Everyone engages in prejudiced talk to some degree. It is inevitable. We can, however, reduce the degree to which we engage in prejudiced talk if we are mindful of our communication. Further, if we do not engage in prejudiced discourse, those around us are less likely to engage in prejudiced discourse (Blanchard, 1992).

MANAGING UNCERTAINTY AND ANXIETY

Uncertainty refers to our cognitive ability to predict and/or explain strangers' feelings, attitudes, values, and behavior. Anxiety, in contrast, involves our affective or emotional reaction to communicating with strangers. To communicate effectively we must be able to manage the uncertainty and anxiety we experience when communicating with strangers (see Gudykunst, 1988; Gudykunst & Kim, 1992). We discuss uncertainty and anxiety separately, then we link them to effective communication and adaptation.

Managing Our Uncertainty

There are two types of uncertainty that are relevant when we communicate with strangers: predictive and explanatory uncertainty. Predictive uncertainty involves the degree to which we can predict strangers' attitudes, beliefs, feelings, values, and behavior. Explanatory uncertainty, in contrast, involves the degree to which we can accurately explain why they behave the way they do (Berger & Calabrese, 1975). Gudykunst (1988) isolated several factors that influence the amount of uncertainty we experience when we communicate with strangers. These factors include our expectations, our social identities, the perception of similarity between our group and the strangers' groups, the degree to which we share communication networks with strangers, the interpersonal salience of our contact with strangers, and our personality orientations.

Well-defined expectations (e.g., complex stereotypes) help us reduce uncertainty. The more well defined our expectations are, the more confident we will be regarding predicting strangers' behavior (Gudykunst, 1988). We can have either well-defined positive or negative expectations. Well-defined expectations alone, however, do not necessarily increase our explanatory certainty. To reduce our explanatory uncertainty we need to have accurate information regarding the stranger's culture, group memberships, and the individual stranger with whom we are communicating.

Gudykunst (1988) argues that the stronger our social identities are (e.g., the more important our group memberships are to how we define ourselves), the greater our predictive certainty regarding strangers' behavior. This claim, however, has to be qualified. Gudykunst and Hammer (1988a) discovered that strength of social identity reduces uncertainty only when we recognize that the strangers are from another group and when the strangers with whom we are communicating are perceived to be typical members of their group. When the strangers are perceived to be atypical members of their group, we do not treat them based on their group membership; that is, we see them as "an exception to the rule." In this case, our communication is influenced by our personal identities, not our social identities. When communication is based on our personal identities, we need information about the individual stranger with whom we are communicating to reduce uncertainty.

The degree to which our group is similar to strangers' groups also affects uncertainty reduction (Gudykunst, 1988) and through uncertainty reduction to adaptation. Furnham and Bochner (1982), for example, report that cultural similarity is related inversely to the difficulties sojourners experience in another culture. The difficulties experienced are, at least in part, a function of predictive uncertainty. If we perceive that the strangers' groups are similar to our own ingroup, we are able to reduce our predictive uncertainty. Perceived similarity, however, influences only predictive uncertainty because we may perceive similarities when we are actually different or perceive differences when we are actually similar. Knowledge of the actual similarities or dissimilarities between our group and the strangers' groups is necessary to reduce our explanatory uncertainty.

The amount of uncertainty we experience when we communicate with strangers is influenced by the degree to which we share communication net-

works with the strangers (Gudykunst, 1988). The more we know the same people that the strangers with whom we are communicating know, the more we
can reduce uncertainty. Parks and Adelman's (1983) research, for example,
revealed that sharing communication networks with strangers reduces uncertainty. One reason for this is that shared networks provide an opportunity to
gather information about strangers. Adelman's (1988) work also suggests that
developing "fringe" relationships with shopkeepers, bartenders, hairdressers,
or barbers also can provide information on similarities and differences between
our culture and other cultures when we are trying to adapt to new cultures.

The degree to which we want to establish an interpersonal relationship with
the specific strangers also contributes to the reduction of uncertainty
(Gudykunst, 1988). If we are physically or socially attracted to the strangers
with whom we are communicating, our predictive uncertainty will be reduced.
Attraction, however, does not necessarily reduce our explanatory uncertainty
regarding strangers' behavior.

Our cultural and linguistic knowledge of the strangers' cultures also influences our ability to reduce uncertainty (Gudykunst, 1988). The more we
understand and can speak the strangers' language and the more knowledge
we have of their culture, the more our uncertainty will be reduced. Research
indicates that second language competence increases our ability to cope with
uncertainty (Naiman, Frohlich, Stern, & Todesco, 1978). Gudykunst (1985)
found that second language competence influences individuals' ability to reduce
uncertainty in a new culture.

Another factor Gudykunst (1988) isolated is personality factors. We focus
here on one personality factor, self-monitoring. Snyder (1974) characterized
self-monitoring as "self-observation and self-control guided by cues to situational appropriateness" (p. 526). Research indicates that in comparison to low
self-monitors, high self-monitors are better able to discover appropriate behavior in new situations, have more control over their emotional reactions,
and create the impressions they wish (Snyder, 1974). High self-monitors also
make more confident and extreme attributions than low self-monitors (Berscheid, Granziano, Monson, & Dermer, 1976). Given this research, it can be
argued that the more we self-monitor, the more we reduce predictive uncertainty. Because high self-monitors make more extreme attributions than low
self-monitors, we would not expect self-monitoring to be related to reducing
explanatory uncertainty. High self-monitors, however, may not be more accurate than low self-monitors in explaining strangers' behavior.

In addition to the factors isolated in Gudykunst's (1988) theory, Berger
(1979) argues that there are three general types of strategies we can use to gather
information about people in other groups and reduce our uncertainty about
them and the way they will interact with us: passive, active, and interactive
strategies (see Berger & Kellerman's chapter in this volume for a detailed discussion of these strategies). Passive strategies involve us taking the role of

"unobtrusive observers" (i.e., we do not intervene in the situation we are observing). The active strategies for reducing uncertainty require us to do something to acquire information about strangers. When we use active strategies to gather information, we do not actually interact with the people about whom we are trying to gather information. The interactive strategies of verbal interrogation (question asking) and self-disclosure, in contrast, are used when we interact with strangers.

Wilder and Allen's (1978) research further indicates that we tend to seek information regarding dissimilarities for members of outgroups. Wilder and Shapiro (1989) found that when anxiety is too high, we are not able to gather accurate information about strangers. McPherson (1983) also discovered that when we have a low tolerance for ambiguity we tend to seek information that is supportive of our own beliefs, rather than information that is "objective." This finding is compatible with Sorrentino and Short's (1986) description of certainty oriented people.

Managing Our Anxiety

Intergroup anxiety is based on the expectation of negative consequences (Stephan & Stephan, 1985). Stephan and Stephan (1985) isolated three broad categories of antecedents to intergroup anxiety: prior intergroup relations, intergroup cognitions (e.g., stereotypes and intergroup attitudes), and situational factors. The important aspects of prior intergroup relations that influence the amount of intergroup anxiety we experience when communicating with strangers are the amount of contact we have had with the strangers' groups and the conditions under which that contact occurred. Stephan and Stephan argue that the more contact we have had and the clearer the norms are for intergroup relations, the less intergroup anxiety we will experience. If, however, there has been prior conflict between our group and the strangers' groups, or our economic and political interests do not coincide, we are likely to experience intergroup anxiety.

Our intergroup cognitions influence our preconscious or automatic thoughts regarding our affective reactions to strangers. The important intergroup cognitions, according to Stephan and Stephan (1985), are our knowledge of the stranger's culture, our stereotypes, our prejudice, our ethnocentrism, and our perceptions of ingroup–outgroup differences. The less knowledge we have of strangers' groups, the more anxiety we will experience. Negative cognitive expectations (i.e., negative stereotypes and prejudice) lead to intergroup anxiety. The greater our ethnocentrism and the greater the differences (real or imagined) we perceive between our group and the strangers' groups, the more intergroup anxiety we will experience.

The situational factors that contribute to intergroup anxiety include the amount of structure in the situation in which contact occurs, the type of interdependence, the group composition, and the relative status of the participants. Stephan and Stephan (1985) point out that in structured situations, the norms provide guides for our behavior and reduce our anxiety. The more unstructured the situation is, therefore, the greater our intergroup anxiety. Situations in which we cooperate with strangers involve less anxiety than situations in which we compete with them. Further, we will experience less anxiety when we find ourselves in situations where our ingroup is in the majority, than in situations where our ingroup is in the majority. Finally, we will experience less anxiety in situations where our ingroup has higher status than the strangers' groups, than in situations where our ingroup has lower status than their groups.

Stephan and Stephan (1985) isolate cognitive, behavioral, and affective consequences of intergroup anxiety. One of the behavioral consequences of anxiety is avoidance. We avoid strangers because it reduces our anxiety. When we are experiencing anxiety and cannot avoid strangers, we will terminate the interaction as soon as we can. Other behavioral responses depend on whether there are norms guiding intergroup interaction. If there are norms for how to interact with strangers, anxiety will amplify our responses; that is, we will follow the norms more rigidly. To illustrate, "if the norm prescribes or condones politeness, then individuals will be more polite as they become more anxious" (Stephan & Stephan, 1985, p. 166). In the absence of norms guiding intergroup interactions, we will look to ingroup norms for how to deal with people who are unfamiliar and amplify our response. If the ingroup norms, for example, call for us to be suspicious, our suspicion will increase as our anxiety increases. Another behavioral consequence of high anxiety is ineffective communication (Gudykunst, 1988).

Cognitively, intergroup anxiety leads to biases in information processing. The more anxious we are, the more likely we will attune to the behaviors we expected to see (e.g., those based on our stereotypes) and the more likely we are to confirm these expectations (i.e., we will not attune to behavior that is inconsistent with our expectations). The greater our anxiety, the more we will be self-aware and concerned with our self-esteem. When we are highly anxious we, therefore, try to make our own group look good in comparison to other groups.

The intergroup anxiety we experience when communicating with strangers transfers to other emotions we experience in the situation. "Positive interactions will produce strong positive emotions, while negative interactions will have the opposite effect. Among the positive emotions are relief, joy, or even love; negative emotions frequently include fear, hate, resentment, guilt, disgust, or righteous indignation" (Stephan & Stephan, 1985, p. 169). Finally, intergroup anxiety amplifies our evaluative reactions to strangers; for example, the more anxious we are, the more likely we are to evaluate strangers negatively.

Uncertainty, Anxiety, Effective Communication, and Adaptation

In general, as our uncertainty and anxiety decrease, the better we get to know others. Uncertainty and anxiety, however, do not increase or decrease consistently over time. Uncertainty, for example, is not reduced every time we communicate with strangers. We may reduce our uncertainty the first time we communicate, but something may occur the second time we communicate (e.g., the other person does something we did not expect) and our uncertainty might increase. Once we have established a relationship with another person, we can expect our uncertainty and anxiety regarding the other person will fluctuate over time. As the relationship becomes more intimate, nevertheless, there should be a general pattern for uncertainty and anxiety to decrease. To illustrate, there tends to be less uncertainty and anxiety in acquaintance relationships than in relationships with strangers, and there is less uncertainty and anxiety in friendships than in acquaintance relationships. At the same time, within any stage (e.g., acquaintance, friend) of a particular relationship, uncertainty and anxiety will fluctuate over time.

We do not want to try to totally reduce our anxiety and uncertainty. At the same time, we cannot communicate effectively if our uncertainty and anxiety are too high. If uncertainty and anxiety are too high, we cannot accurately interpret strangers' messages or make accurate predictions about strangers' behavior. This line of thinking suggests that there are minimum and maximum thresholds for uncertainty and anxiety, if we are to communicate effectively with strangers.

If uncertainty and anxiety are above our maximum thresholds, as they often are when we first meet strangers, we are too anxious and uncertain to communicate effectively. In most situations, however, there are sufficiently clear norms and rules for communication that our uncertainty and anxiety are reduced below our maximum thresholds. Even if our uncertainty and anxiety are below the maximum threshold, either or both may still be too high for us to communicate effectively. To communicate effectively our anxiety needs to be sufficiently low so that we can accurately interpret and predict strangers' behavior. When anxiety is too high we communicate on automatic pilot and interpret strangers' behavior using our own cultural frame of reference.

If uncertainty and anxiety are low we may not be motivated to communicate. If both uncertainty and anxiety are consistently below our minimum threshold in a particular relationship, for example, the relationship will become boring. Kruglanski (1989) points out that we all have a need to avoid closure on topics or people to allow for ''mystery'' to be maintained. To communicate effectively, our uncertainty and anxiety both must be above our minimum threshold.

Uncertainty and anxiety do not necessarily increase and decrease at the same time. We may reduce our uncertainty and be highly anxious. Consider, for example, a situation in which we predict very confidently that something negative is going to happen. We also may reduce our anxiety and have high uncertainty. To communicate effectively, our anxiety must be sufficiently low (well below maximum threshold, but above minimum) that we can reduce our explanatory uncertainty. If our anxiety is high, we must cognitively "manage" our anxiety (i.e., become mindful) if we are to communicate effectively and adapt to other cultural environments.

Gao and Gudykunst (1990) demonstrate that uncertainty and anxiety moderate the influence of other variables (e.g., knowledge, social contact) on intercultural adaptation. Gudykunst (1993) also argues that mindfulness moderates the influence of managing uncertainty and anxiety on communication. More specifically, if we are not mindful when we communicate with strangers, uncertainty reduction may not lead to effective communication because the predictions and explanations we make will be based on our cultural frame of reference. When we are mindful, we can search for alternative interpretations of strangers' behavior and select the interpretation we believe to have the greatest accuracy.

OTHER THEORETICAL PERSPECTIVES[12]

The preceding discussion focused on one perspective that may be used to isolate strategies for effective communication and intercultural adaptation. Two other theoretical approaches to this concern are considered in this section. These perspectives, commonly referred to as the Ethnography of Communication and the Coordinated Management of Meaning (CMM), diverge dramatically from the perspective adopted thus far in the chapter (see Hall, 1992, for a comprehensive review of these two perspectives).

One common thread between the ethnographic and CMM perspectives in juxtaposition to the traditional scientific perspective is that communication is posited as the primary social process (Carbaugh, 1990; Cronen, Chen, & Pearce, 1988). In other words, "any human creation, from the concepts and actions of 'physicians,' 'friends,' or 'France,' can be explored as resources in, and of, particular communication systems" (Carbaugh, 1990, p. 18). Communication, therefore, ceases to be simply a tool (even a powerful one) for discovering and manipulating the world out there, but rather is how our social world takes on form and sense.

This difference in understanding regarding communication has distinctive implications for the notion of "strategies for adaptation." With the "commu-

---

[12]The earlier version of this chapter focused exclusively on adaptation. This focus is maintained in this section.

nication as tool" perspective, readers are subtly posited into the position of contestants in a game who are presented general techniques for winning and/or specific scouting reports on the other side in hopes of improving their chances for success. When communication is posited as *primary*, strategies are no longer activities that a person may use to deal with *others'* strangeness and enable the accomplishment of some objective (see for example, Copeland & Griggs, 1985; Moran & Harris, 1982).[13] Rather, strategies are the substance of what it means to live a life, inescapably involving not only means but meanings as well.

From the ethnographic perspective, it is life as a member of a particular speech community that a researcher tries to understand. In other words, ethnographers strive to understand the communication system (or parts thereof) that constitutes that particular community. Carbaugh (1990) proposes that any such system is composed of at least three structural elements: personhood, communication (natively named practices), and emotion. Although these three elements are inescapably interwoven together in the fabric of communal life, each one may be brought to the fore in a given study.[14]

The ethnographic perspective, however, does not allow for particular models of personhood, communication, and emotion to be assumed across communities; rather, they must be discovered in each case. Thus, one of the basic goals of ethnographic research is the development and refinement of descriptive frameworks that allow for the expression of community specific contexts and meanings (Carbaugh & Hastings, 1992; Hymes, 1972; Philipsen, 1989). Perhaps the most prominent of these frameworks is the "SPEAKING" framework originated by Hymes (1972). Articulated more as an artist's brush set to be creatively used in the painting of a community portrait than a group of cookie cutters to be rigidly stamped on to each community, it consists of eight potentially interactive components. These include: the Situation (the physical setting and psychological scene), Participants (roles, relations, etc.), Ends (goals and outcomes), Acts (both in terms of form and content), Key (the mood or tone), Instrumentality or channels of communication, Norms of interaction and interpretation, and Genre.

Katriel's (1986) work on speaking *dugri* in Israel's Sabra community provides an excellent example of how Hymes' (1972) framework may assist in painting a community portrait. Of necessity only broad strokes in representing her finely detailed work are presented here. *Dugri* refers to a blunt, straightforward type of talk that grew out of the Sabra's desire to separate themselves

---

[13]Readers should not infer that the perspective presented in the main body of this paper is conceptually similar to Copeland and Griggs or Harris and Moran. Gudykunst (e.g., 1991, 1993) consistently argues against the use of "dos and don'ts" for either effective communication and/or adaptation.

[14]See Weider and Pratt (1990) on being a recognizable Indian, Fitch (1991) on the use of *Madre* terms in Columbian personal address, and Hall and Noguchi (1992) on the enactment of *kenson* in Japan, for respective examples.

from stylistic forms of speech required of them and earlier generations living in Europe. It is generated spontaneously by the demands of a rhetorical exigency marked by the perception of a wrong. *Dugri* is most poignant when performed face to face in public, and when directed toward a person who holds a relatively socially superior position. The speaking of *dugri* signals a suspension of these normally restricting social ties and a foregrounding of the interactants' shared membership within the Sabra community. Although the speaking of *dugri* may allow for the superior to gain useful information, it primarily serves a bonding and cathartic function for the community and individual speaker respectively. For the listener to take offense or to try to turn the moment into a problem-solving time would be to fail in their role; rather it is appropriate to simply acknowledge the comment at that time. To outsiders, *dugri* may sound unusually abrasive and disrespectful to both the listener's personal face and to the position that he or she holds.

A review of Hymes' (1972) framework along with the foregoing description provides just a small sense of how the framework can be used in describing and understanding specific cultural systems. The Hymes framework has proven to be so valuable over the years because it allows for very different types of talk to be articulated. Griefat and Katriel (1989), for example, use it to elaborate an understanding of a type of talk, *musayara*, which is dramatically different than that of *dugri*. *Musayara* is an effusive, yet socially restrained type of talk that is valued within the Arab community in Israel. Indeed, understanding the two ways of being as expressed within these two types of talk provides additional insight into the problems currently facing that region of the world.

It is important at this point to return briefly to the notion of strategies for adaptation. The position argued here suggests that separated from the proper appreciation of a *dugri*'s ends and meanings, the specific means that may be formulated will be static and lack the creative flexibility that marks the speech of a member. Specific suggestions for "dos and don'ts," therefore, are not possible.

Cultures, from the CMM perspective, may be properly viewed as incommensurate systems (Cronen et al., 1988). Intercultural communication is challenging not because members of another culture are playing the same game as we are with different symbols and rules, but because they and we are actually playing different games.

Given the position that people within different cultures are playing different games, the search for universal strategies for dealing with intercultural adaptation becomes a misguided venture. Instead, a sophisticated understanding of the local situation is desirable. Chen and Pearce (1991) capture the flavor of this point in the following:

> In your seaworthy but fragile sailboat, you are entering a harbor on the rocky New England coast for the first time and have no charts. Whom would you rather

have in your crew: a person who knows all the mathematical relationships between the spin of the earth, the movement of the moon, and the rise and fall
of the tides; or a person who has "local knowledge" of many harbors? (p. 21)

What is called for is the ability to be sensitive to the different contexts and
unique aspects of each situation. This point is aptly demonstrated by Chen
(1990/1991) in her study of *Mien tze* (face) in Chinese dinner conversation. She
shows that face is not some objective psychological reality on which stable strategies for action may be based. Rather, it is a negotiated resource expressed and
constructed in the flow of interaction. Indeed, not only the giving of face, but
all forms of human activity may be understood in terms of a fully reflexive
relationship between resources (culture, symbols, institutions, etc.) and practices (communicative conduct such as playing cards, selling cars, etc.) (Pearce,
1989).

Pearce (1989) expresses concern that the "we're all playing the same game"
mentality leads to unnecessary and potentially harmful difficulties over what
is the best way to play it. He refers to efforts to determine and persuade in
regard to which stories of interpretation are best, as rhetorical eloquence. In
contrast he calls for the need to practice social eloquence. Social eloquence refers
to the use of symbolic means to achieve practices that enact getting on with
life in a liberating manner for all concerned. The individual's focus is thus
turned toward the *many* ways in which people live honorable lives and how
they may cooperatively continue to do so.

In order to be cooperative, a person must expand his or her understanding
regarding how it is that others get on in life. Pearce (1989) provides some suggestions for how this may be done. Integral to this process is learning to speak
so that the natives hear you talking as they do. This does not mean a parroting
of the other groups' behaviors, but involves using their resources in a flexible
way. In addition, Pearce and Kang (1988) explain that one must be perceived
as using the native reasoning in one's activities. This requires a view that emphasizes the conjointly produced nature of acculturation, and by implication
adaptation. Strategies for adaptation are cooperative in that they are conjointly produced and ideally should help make the incommensurate resources of
different cultures comparable.

The task of dealing with incommensurate resources is not easy and one may
wonder how it can be accomplished. One illustrative case may be found in
the *Milan* method of family therapy. Pearce (1989) describes how the Milan
team avoids the vocabulary of causes tapped into by such questions as "Why
are you depressed?" Instead they involve the entire family in therapy and use
probes focused on how, when, and to whom a particular problem is shown.
The assumption is that a problem occurs through the coordinated actions of
an entire family. The key is to understand and, change the patterns of coordination that have produced the problem. In a similar manner, a person faced

with a problem in regard to intergroup interaction must understand and deal with the particular practices conjointly produced in that interaction if positive change is to occur.

CONCLUSION

We have overviewed strategies that individuals can use to communicate effectively in intergroup contexts. Effective intergroup communication requires cognitive, affective, and behavioral (including linguistic) adaptations by one or both interactants in an intergroup encounter. The perspective presented in the majority of the chapter suggests that it is our responsibility as participants in a social system to behave in a moral inclusive manner and to try to communicate effectively with members of other groups, adapting our behavior when necessary. To accomplish these goals we must be mindful of the process of our communication with strangers. Even though individuals may be mindful and motivated to communicate effectively with strangers, institutional support is necessary to improve intergroup relations in society. We need to develop social climates in our institutions where the Vulcan salutation—"Greetings. I am pleased to see that you are different. May we together become greater than the sum of both of us."—is "the rule, not the exception," in intergroup encounters.

ACKNOWLEDGMENTS

The original version of this chapter was written in 1986. When given an opportunity to "update" the chapter in May 1992, our thinking had changed sufficiently that we chose to rewrite it completely. To meet the short turnaround allowed, we have used some material published elsewhere (e.g., Gudykunst & Kim, 1992).

REFERENCES

Abelson, R. (1976). Script processing in attitude formation and decision making. In J. Carroll & J. Payne (Eds.), *Cognition and social behavior* (pp. 33–46). Hillsdale, NJ: Lawrence Erlbaum Associates.
Adelman, M. (1988). Cross-cultural adjustment: A theoretical perspective on social support. *International Journal of Intercultural Relations, 12*, 183–204.
Allport, G. W. (1954). *The nature of prejudice.* New York: Macmillan.
Ball-Rokeach, S. (1973). From pervasive ambiguity to definition of the situation. *Sociometry, 36*, 378–389.
Banks, S. (1987). Achieving "unmarkedness" in organizational discourse. *Journal of Language and Social Psychology, 6*, 171–190.

Beck, A. (1988). *Love is never enough*. New York: Harper & Row.

Bellah, R., Madsen, R., Sullivan, W., Swidler, A., & Tipton, S. (1985). *Habits of the heart*. Berkeley: University of California Press.

Bellah, R., Madsen, R., Sullivan, W., Swidler, A., & Tipton, S. (1991). *The good society*. New York: Knopf.

Berger, C. R. (1979). Beyond initial interaction. In H. Giles & R. St. Clair (Eds.), *Language and social psychology* (pp. 122–144). Oxford, England: Blackwell.

Berger, C. R., & Calabrese, R. (1975). Some explorations in initial interaction and beyond. *Human Communication Research, 1*, 99–112.

Berger, C. R., & Douglas, W. (1982). Thought and talk: "Excuse me, but have I been talking to myself?" In F. Dance (Ed.), *Human communication theory* (pp. 42–60). New York: Harper & Row.

Berger, C. R., Gardner, R., Parks, M., Schulman, L., & Miller, G. R. (1976). Interpersonal epistemology and interpersonal understanding. In G. R. Miller (Ed.), *Explorations in interpersonal communication* (pp. 149–172). Beverly Hills, CA: Sage.

Berger, J., Wagner, D., & Zelditch, M. (1985). Introduction: Expectation states theory. In J. Berger & M. Zelditch (Eds.), *Status, rewards, and influence* (pp. 1–72). San Francisco: Jossey-Bass.

Berscheid, E. (1985). Interpersonal attraction. In G. Lindzey & E. Aronson (Eds.), *Handbook of social psychology* (3rd ed., Vol. 2, pp. 413–483). New York: Random House.

Berscheid, E., Granziano, W., Monson, T., & Dermer, M. (1976). Outcome dependency. *Journal of Personality and Social Psychology, 34*, 978–989.

Billig, M., Condor, S., Edwards, D., Gane, M., Middleton, D., & Radley, A. (1988). *Ideological dilemmas*. Newbury Park, CA: Sage.

Blanchard, F. A. (1992, May 13). Combatting intentional bigotry and inadvertently racist acts. *The Chronicle of Higher Education*, pp. B1–B2.

Bourhis, R. (1985). The sequential nature of language choices in cross-cultural communication. In R. Street & J. Cappella (Eds.), *Sequence and pattern in communicative behavior* (pp. 120–141). London: Edward Arnold.

Bowen, M. (1978). *Family therapy in clinical practice*. New York: Arenson.

Brewer, M. B. (1991). The social self: On being the same and different at the same time. *Personality and Social Psychology Bulletin, 17*, 475–482.

Brewer, M., & Miller, N. (1988). Contact and cooperation. In P. Katz & D. Taylor (Eds.), *Eliminating racism* (pp. 315–326). New York: Plenum.

Burgoon, J., & Hale, J. (1988). Nonverbal expectancy violations. *Communication Monographs, 55*, 58–79.

Carbaugh, D. (1990). Toward a perspective on cultural communication and intercultural contact. *Semiotica, 80*, 15–35.

Carbaugh, D., & Hastings, S. O. (1992). A role for communication theory in ethnography and cultural analysis. *Communication Theory, 2*, 156–164.

Chaika, E. (1982). *Language: The social mirror*. Rowley, MA: Newbury House.

Chen, V. (1990/1991). *Mien Tze* at the Chinese dinner table: A study of the interactional accomplishment of face. *Research on Language and Social Interaction, 24*, 109–140.

Chen, V., & Pearce, W. B. (1991). *Even if a thing of beauty, can a case study be a joy forever?* Paper presented to the Speech Communication Association, Atlanta, Georgia.

Copeland, L., & Griggs, L. (1985). *Going International: How to make friends and deal effectively in the global marketplace*. New York: Random House.

Coupland, N. (1980). Style-shifting in a Cardiff work setting. *Language in Society, 9*, 1–12.

Cronen, V. E., Chen, V., & Pearce, W. B. (1988). Coordinated management of meaning: A critical theory. In Y. Y. Kim & W. B. Gudykunst (Eds.), *Theories in intercultural communication* (pp. 66–97). Newbury Park, CA: Sage.

Crosby, F., Bromley, S., & Saxe, L. (1980). Recent unobtrusive studies of black and white discrimination and prejudice. *Psychological Bulletin, 87*, 546–563.

Csikszentmihalyi, M. (1990). *Flow: The psychology of optimal experience*. New York: Harper & Row.

Detweiler, R. (1975). On inferring the intentions of a person from another culture. *Journal of Personality, 43*, 591–611.

Devine, P. (1989). Stereotypes and prejudice. *Journal of Personality and Social Psychology, 56*, 5–18.

Downs, J. (1971). *Cultures in crisis*. Chicago: Glencoe Press.

Driskell, J. E., & Mullen, B. (1990). Status, expectations, and behavior. *Personality and Social Psychology Bulletin, 16*, 541–553.

Dyal, J. A., & Dyal, R. Y. (1981). Acculturation, stress, and coping. *International Journal of Intercultural Relations, 5*, 301–328.

Ellingsworth, H. (1983). Adaptive intercultural communication. In W. B. Gudykunst (Ed.), *Intercultural communication theory* (pp. 195–204). Beverly Hills, CA: Sage.

Fitch, K. L. (1991). The interplay of linguistic universals and cultural knowledge in personal address: Columbian *Madre* terms. *Communication Monographs, 58*, 254–272.

Furnham, A., & Bochner, S. (1982). Social difficulty in a foreign culture. In S. Bochner (Ed.), *Cultures in contact* (pp. 161–198). Elmsford, NY: Pergamon.

Gao, G., & Gudykunst, W. B. (1990). Uncertainty, anxiety, and adaptation. *International Journal of Intercultural Relations, 14*, 301–317.

Gardner, R. (1985). *Social psychology and second language learning*. London: Edward Arnold.

Garrett, P., Giles, H., & Coupland, N. (1989). The contexts of language learning. In S. Ting-Toomey & F. Korzenny (Eds.), *Language, communication, and culture* (pp. 201–221). Newbury Park, CA: Sage.

Genesse, F., & Bourhis, R. (1982). The social psychological significance of code switching in cross-cultural communication. *Journal of Language and Social Psychology, 1*, 1–28.

Giles, H. (1973). Accent mobility. *Anthropological Linguistics, 15*, 87–105.

Giles, H., Bourhis, R., & Taylor, D. (1977). Toward a theory of language in ethnic group relations. In H. Giles (Ed.), *Language, ethnicity and intergroup relations* (pp. 307–348). London: Academic Press.

Giles, H., & Byrne, J. (1982). The intergroup theory of second language acquisition. *Journal of Multilingual and Multicultural Development, 3*, 17–40.

Giles, H., & Hewstone, M. (1982). Cognitive structures, speech, and social situations. *Language Sciences, 4*, 187–219.

Giles, H., Mulac, A., Bradac, J., & Johnson, P. (1987). Speech accommodation theory. In M. McLaughlin (Ed.), *Communication yearbook 10* (pp. 13–48). Newbury Park, CA: Sage.

Giles, H., & Smith, P. (1979). Accommodation theory. In H. Giles & R. St. Clair (Eds.), *Language and social psychology* (pp. 45–65). Oxford: Blackwell.

Griefat, Y., & Katriel, T. (1989). Life demands *Musayara*: Communication and culture among Arabs in Israel. In S. Ting-Toomey & F. Korzenny (Eds.), *Language, communication, and culture* (pp. 121–138). Newbury Park, CA: Sage.

Gudykunst, W. B. (1985). A model of uncertainty reduction in intercultural encounters. *Journal of Language and Social Psychology, 4*, 79–98.

Gudykunst, W. B. (1988). Uncertainty and anxiety. In Y. Y. Kim & W. B. Gudykunst (Eds.), *Theories in intercultural communication* (pp. 123–156). Newbury Park, CA: Sage.

Gudykunst, W. B. (1991). *Bridging differences*. Newbury Park, CA: Sage.

Gudykunst, W. B. (1993). Toward a theory of effective interpersonal and intergroup communication. In R. Wiseman & J. Koester (Eds.), *Intercultural communication competence* (pp. 33–71). Newbury Park, CA: Sage.

Gudykunst, W. B., & Hammer, M. R. (1988a). The influence of social identity and intimacy of interethnic relationships on uncertainty reduction processes. *Human Communication Research, 14*, 569–601.

Gudykunst, W. B., & Hammer, M. R. (1988b). Strangers and hosts. In Y. Y. Kim & W. B. Gudykunst (Eds.), *Cross-cultural adaptation* (pp. 106–139). Newbury Park, CA: Sage.

Gudykunst, W. B., & Kim, Y. Y. (1984). *Communicating with strangers*. New York: McGraw-Hill.

Gudykunst, W. B., & Kim, Y. Y. (1992). *Communicating with strangers* (2nd ed.). New York: McGraw-Hill.

Gudykunst, W. B., & Nishida, T. (1989). Perspectives for studying intercultural communication. In M. K. Asante & W. B. Gudykunst (Eds.), *Handbook of international and intercultural communication* (pp. 7-46). Newbury Park, CA: Sage.

Gudykunst, W. B., Ting-Toomey, S., Hall, B. J., & Schmidt, K. L. (1989). Language and intergroup communication. In M. K. Asante & W. B. Gudykunst (Eds.), *Handbook of international and intercultural communication* (pp. 145-162). Newbury Park, CA: Sage.

Gumperz, J., & Hernandez-Chavez, E. (1972). Bilingualism, bidialectism, and classroom interaction. In C. Cazden, V. John, & D. Hymes (Eds.), *Functions of language in the classroom* (pp. 83-108). New York: Teacher's College Press.

Hall, B. J. (1992). Theories of culture and communication. *Communication Theory, 2*, 50-70.

Hall, B. J., & Noguchi, M. (1992). *Understanding the Japanese concept of kenson*. Paper presented to the International Communication Association, Miami, Florida.

Hamill, J. F. (1990). *Ethno-logic: The anthropology of human reasoning*. Urbana: University of Illinois Press.

Hamilton, D. L., Sherman, S. J., & Ruvolo, C. M. (1990). Stereotyped-based expectancies. *Journal of Social Issues, 46*(2), 35-60.

Heider, F. (1958). *The psychology of interpersonal relations*. New York: Wiley.

Herman, S., & Schield, E. (1961). The stranger group in a cross-cultural situation. *Sociometry, 24*, 165-176.

Hewstone, M., & Brown, R. (1986). Contact is not enough. In M. Hewstone & R. Brown (Eds.), *Contact and conflict in intergroup encounters* (pp. 1-44). Oxford: Blackwell.

Hewstone, M., & Giles, H. (1986). Stereotypes and intergroup communication. In W. Gudykunst (Ed.), *Intergroup communication* (pp. 10-26). London: Edward Arnold.

Hewstone, M., & Jaspars, J. (1984). Social dimensions of attributions. In H. Tajfel (Ed.), *The social dimension* (Vol. 2, pp. 379-404). Cambridge, England: Cambridge University Press.

Hofstede, G. (1980). *Culture's consequences*. Beverly Hills, CA: Sage.

Hooker, C. A. (1987). *A realistic theory of science*. Albany: State University of New York Press.

Huston, T. (1973). Ambiguity of acceptance, social desirability, and dating choice. *Journal of Experimental Social Psychology, 9*, 32-42.

Hymes, D. (1972). Models of the interaction of language and social life. In J. Gumperz & D. Hymes (Eds.), *Directions in sociolinguistics: The ethnography of communication* (pp. 35-71). New York: Holt, Rinehart, & Winston.

Jackson, J. (1964). The normative regulation of authoritative behavior. In W. Grove & J. Dyson (Eds.), *The making of decisions* (pp. 213-241). New York: Free Press.

Katriel, T. (1986). *Talking straight*. Cambridge: Cambridge University Press.

Kelley, H. (1967). Attribution theory in social psychology. *Nebraska Symposium on Motivation, 15*, 192-238.

Kitayama, S., & Burnstein, E. (1988). Automaticity in conversations. *Journal of Personality and Social Psychology, 54*, 219-224.

Kruglanski, A. (1989). *Lay epistemics and human knowledge*. New York: Plenum.

Langer, E. (1978). Rethinking the role of thought in social interaction. In J. Harvey et al. (Eds.), *New directions in attribution research* (Vol. 2, pp. 35-58). Hillsdale, NJ: Lawrence Erlbaum Associates.

Langer, E. (1989). *Mindfulness*. Reading, MA: Addison-Wesley.

Levine, D. (1979). Simmel at a distance. In W. Shack & E. Skinner (Eds.), *Strangers in African societies* (pp. 21-36). Berkeley: University of California Press.

Lewis, H. B. (1971). *Shame and guilt in neurosis*. New York: International Universities Press.

Lukens, J. (1978). Ethnocentric speech. *Ethnic Groups, 2*, 35-53.

McPherson, K. (1983). Opinion-related information seeking. *Personality and Social Psychology Bulletin, 9,* 116–124.

Moran, R., & Harris, P. (1982). *Managing cultural synergy.* Houston, TX: Gulf.

Naiman, N., Frohlich, M., Stern, H., & Todesco, A. (1978). *The good language learner.* Toronto: Ontario Institute for Studies in Education.

Optow, S. (1990). Moral exclusion and injustice. *Journal of Social Issues, 46*(1), 1–20.

Parks, M., & Adelman, M. (1983). Communication networks and the development of romantic relationships. *Human Communication Research, 10,* 55–80.

Pearce, W. B. (1989). *Communication and the human condition.* Carbondale, IL: Southern Illinois University Press.

Pearce, W. B., & Kang, K. (1988). Conceptual migrations: Understanding "Travelers' Tales" for cross-cultural adaptation. In Y. Y. Kim & W. B. Gudykunst (Eds.), *Cross-cultural adaptation* (pp. 20–41). Newbury Park: Sage.

Pettigrew, T. (1978). Three issues in ethnicity. In J. Yinger & S. Cutler (Eds.), *Major social issues* (pp. 25–49). New York: Free Press.

Pettigrew, T. (1979). The ultimate attribution error. *Personality and Social Psychology Bulletin, 5,* 461–476.

Pettigrew, T. (1982). Cognitive styles and social behavior. In L. Wheeler (Ed.), *Review of personality and social psychology* (Vol. 3, pp. 199–233). Beverly Hills, CA: Sage.

Philipsen, G. (1989). An ethnographic approach to communication studies. In B. Dervin, L. Grossberg, B. J. O'Keefe, & E. Wartella (Eds.), *Rethinking communication* (Vol. 2, pp. 258–268). Newbury Park, CA: Sage.

Powers, W., & Lowry, D. (1984). Basic communication fidelity. In R. Bostrom (Ed.), *Competence in communication* (pp. 57–71). Beverly Hills, CA: Sage.

Rokeach, M. (1960). *The open and closed mind.* New York: Basic Books.

Rose, T. (1981). Cognitive and dyadic processes in intergroup contact. In D. Hamilton (Ed.), *Cognitive processes in stereotyping and intergroup behavior* (pp. 259–303). Hillsdale, NJ: Lawrence Erlbaum Associates.

Ruben, B. (1983). A system-theoretic view. In W. B. Gudykunst (Ed.), *Intercultural communication theory* (pp. 131–147). Beverly Hills, CA: Sage.

Sachdev, I., & Bourhis, R. (1990). Bilinguality and multilingualism. In H. Giles & W. P. Robinson (Eds.), *Handbook of language and social psychology* (pp. 293–308). London: Wiley.

Scheff, T. J. (1990). *Microsociology: Discourse, emotion, and social structure.* Chicago: University of Chicago Press.

Schlenker, B. R. (1986). Self-identification. In R. F. Baumeister (Ed.), *Public self and private self* (pp. 21–62). New York: Springer-Verlag.

Schuetz, A. (1944). The stranger. *American Journal of Sociology, 49,* 599–607.

Sears, D. (1988). Symbolic racism. In P. Katz & D. Taylor (Eds.), *Eliminating racism* (pp. 53–84). New York: Plenum.

Simard, L. M., Taylor, D. M., & Giles, H. (1976). Attributional processes and interpersonal accommodation. *Language and Speech, 19,* 374–387.

Simmel, G. (1950). The stranger. In K. Wolff (Ed. and Trans.), *The sociology of Georg Simmel* (pp. 402–408). New York: Free Press. (Original work published 1908)

Snyder, M. (1974). Self-monitoring of expressive behavior. *Journal of Personality and Social Psychology, 30,* 526–537.

Snyder, M., & Wicklund, R. (1981). Attribute ambiguity. In J. H. Harvey, W. Ickes, & R. F. Kidd (Eds.), *New directions in attribution research* (Vol. 3, pp. 197–221). Hillsdale, NJ: Lawrence Erlbaum Associates.

Sorrentino, R., & Short, J. (1986). Uncertainty orientation, motivation, and cognition. In R. Sorrentino & E. T. Higgins (Eds.), *Handbook of motivation and cognition* (pp. 379–403). New York: Guilford.

Spitzberg, B., & Cupach, W. (1984). *Interpersonal communication competence.* Beverly Hills, CA: Sage.

Stephan, W. (1985). Intergroup relations. In G. Lindzey & E. Aronson (Eds.), *Handbook of social psychology* (3rd ed., Vol. 2, pp. 599–658). New York: Random House.

Stephan, W., & Stephan, C. (1985). Intergroup anxiety. *Journal of Social Issues, 41,* 157–166.

Stephenson, G. (1981). Intergroup bargaining and negotiation. In J. Turner & H. Giles (Eds.), *Intergroup behavior* (pp. 168–198). Chicago: University of Chicago Press.

Swann, W. (1983). Self-verification. In J. Suls & A. Greenwald (Eds.), *Psychological perspectives on the self* (Vol. 2, pp. 33–66). Hillsdale, NJ: Lawrence Erlbaum Associates.

Tajfel, H. (1978). Social categorization, social identity, and social comparisons. In H. Tajfel (Ed.), *Differentiation between social groups* (pp. 61–76). London: Academic Press.

Tajfel, H., & Turner, J. (1979). An integrative theory of intergroup conflict. In W. Austin & S. Worchel (Eds.), *The social psychology of intergroup relations* (pp. 33–47). Monterey, CA: Brooks/Cole.

Triandis, H. C. (1977). *Interpersonal behavior.* Monterey, CA: Brook/Cole.

Turner, J. C. (1987). *Rediscovering the social group.* Oxford: Blackwell.

Turner, J. H. (1987). Toward a sociological theory of motivation. *American Sociological Review, 52,* 15–27.

van Dijk, T. (1984). *Prejudice in discourse.* Amsterdam: Benjamins.

Weider, D. L., & Pratt, S. (1990). On being a recognizable Indian among Indians. In D. Carbaugh (Ed.), *Cultural communication and intercultural contact* (pp. 45–64). Hillsdale, NJ: Lawrence Erlbaum Associates.

Wilder, D. A., & Allen, V. L. (1978). Group membership and preference for information about others. *Personality and Social Psychology Bulletin, 4,* 106–110.

Wilder, D. A., & Shapiro, P. (1989). Effects of anxiety on impression formation in a group context. *Journal of Experimental Social Psychology, 25,* 481–499.

Worchel, S., & Norwell, N. (1980). Effect of perceived environmental conditions during co-operation on intergroup attraction. *Journal of Personality and Social Psychology, 38,* 764–772.

Chapter 9

Strategic Functions
of Nonverbal Exchange

Miles L. Patterson
University of Missouri-St. Louis

The study of strategic communication encompasses a very extensive area of research. Topics such as attitude change, conformity, deception, conflict, decision making, and impression management are some of the many issues that relate to strategic communication. For the most part, the research on strategic communication has focused on verbal behavior, or the content side of communication, with less attention paid to the role of nonverbal behavior. That condition has been changing in recent years with the growth of research on nonverbal behavior in interaction.

One of the circumstances that has been conducive to the study of strategic nonverbal behavior is the recognition that nonverbal behavior may serve a variety of functions in interaction. Several different researchers have proposed classifications of functions that apply to nonverbal behavior. For example, Argyle and his colleagues (Argyle, 1972; Argyle & Dean, 1965; Argyle, Lalljee, & Cook, 1968; Kendon, 1967) have emphasized the role of nonverbal behavior in the following areas: (a) synchronizing speech; (b) providing feedback; (c) expressing intimacy; and (d) supporting or replacing verbal communication. Ekman and Friesen (1969) have emphasized the role of nonverbal behavior relative to verbal communication. They suggested that, in addition to regulating interaction, nonverbal behavior may repeat, contradict, complement, or accent verbal communication. In a similar fashion, Harrison (1973) and Burgoon (Burgoon, 1985; Burgoon & Saine, 1978) have employed a communication systems perspective in proposing their classification of functions.

In recent years, I have been working on elaborating a classification of functions of nonverbal behavior in constructing a theoretical model of nonverbal exchange in interaction (Patterson, 1982, 1983, 1991). This functional model has considerable relevance for understanding the nonverbal component of strategic interaction. The purpose of this chapter is to discuss the strategic functions of nonverbal behavior from the perspective of the functional model of nonverbal exchange. The functional model developed as an alternative explanation for nonverbal exchange, one that stresses the complex and varied bases for interactive behavior. In order to set the context for the discussion of the strategic functions, it is useful first to appreciate how the functional approach is different from other theoretical approaches. Consequently, this discussion begins with a brief overview of earlier models of nonverbal exchange.

THEORIES OF NONVERBAL EXCHANGE

Early Approaches

The first attempt at explaining patterns of nonverbal behavior in social interaction was Argyle and Dean's (1965) equilibrium theory. Argyle and Dean proposed that, in any given interaction, there was an appropriate or comfortable level of intimacy between the interactants that was expressed behaviorally. In particular, gaze, interpersonal distance, smiling, and verbal intimacy or self-disclosure were assumed to contribute to the overall behavioral intimacy between the interactants. Equilibrium theory proposed that, over the course of an interaction, there is pressure to maintain a kind of homeostasis or equilibrium in intimacy through adjustments in the behavior of one or both persons. For example, if one member of a pair approached closer than the partner felt appropriate, the partner might decrease gaze, smile less, or decrease verbal intimacy in order to compensate for the uncomfortable level of intimacy and, in the process, restore equilibrium. Although there is a substantial body of empirical research that supports the compensation predictions of equilibrium theory (Cappella, 1981; Patterson, 1973), it was also clear that equilibrium theory could not account for those important exceptions to compensation in which increased behavioral intimacy by one person was reciprocated or enhanced by the partner. That is, sometimes increased intimacy by one person is reciprocated with increased gaze, smiling, or a touch by the partner. Such a reciprocal pattern might be characteristic of good friends, lovers, or parent–child exchanges.

The arousal model of interpersonal intimacy (Patterson, 1976) was an attempt to explain both compensatory and reciprocal changes in interaction. This theory expanded on equilibrium theory by suggesting that patterns of nonverbal exchange were mediated by an arousal-labeling (attribution) process. Specifically, it was proposed that increased or decreased intimacy by one person precipitated arousal change in the partner. This arousal, in turn, was interpreted in a labeling phase, leading to specific feeling states (Schachter & Singer, 1962). In turn, these feeling states determined the behavioral adjustments of the interactants. For example, negative affective states, such as fear or anxiety, would lead to compensatory adjustments, whereas positive affective states, such as liking or love, would lead to reciprocal adjustments. Thus, this model proposed a general mechanism (the arousal-attribution process) that could, potentially, explain both the compensatory and reciprocal patterns of adjustment. Research on this model shows mixed support for its predictions but, in any case, it is probably too simplistic to capture the complexity of nonverbal exchange in interactions.

Expectancy Models

The expectancy models differ from the arousal model in proposing that the actual level of nonverbal intimacy or involvement is less important than the discrepancy between the behavior expected and the behavior initiated by the partner. In both the violations of expectations model (Burgoon, 1978, 1983; Burgoon & Hale, 1988; Burgoon & Jones, 1976) and the arousal-discrepancy model (Cappella & Greene, 1982), individuals make "automatic" comparisons between their expectancies for a partner's nonverbal behavior (based on past experience and social norms) and the partner's actual behavior. For each model, behavior approximating the expectancy level results in little or no arousal, but as the size of the discrepancy increases, so does the level of arousal.

In the violations of expectations model, the reward value of the interaction partner moderates the effect of the discrepancy. Specifically, for rewarding partners, greater discrepancy between the actual and expected behavior (up to some moderate level), should produce more favorable impressions and increased behavioral involvement. In contrast, for nonrewarding partners, conformity to the expected levels of nonverbal involvement should produce more favorable impressions and increased behavioral involvement, whereas substantial deviation from expectancies should produce more negative impressions and decreased behavioral involvement.

In Cappella and Greene's (1982) discrepancy-arousal model, arousal is presumed to be a direct consequence of the degree of discrepancy between the expected and observed level of nonverbal involvement. Small to moderate discrepancies, falling within an acceptable range, are assumed to precipitate small to moderate increases in arousal. Larger discrepancies are likely to fall outside of the acceptable range and precipitate high levels of arousal. Arousal, in turn, is related in a curvilinear manner to the quality of affect. In particular, moderate levels of arousal produce the most positive affect, whereas high levels of arousal produce negative affect. Finally, the degree of positive or negative affect determines the nature of the behavioral response. Positive affect leads to the reciprocation of nonverbal involvement and negative affect leads to compensation.

Limitations of the Theories

The theories discussed up to this point share a common focus. The starting point for each theory is the behavioral pattern initiated by one person in an interaction. The behavior to be explained is the partner's response to the first person's behavior. In other words, these theories are all reactive in nature because they only address how one person might react to the partner's immediately preceding behavior. Of course, we could reverse the perspective and assume that the original behavior was the result of the partner's earlier behavior and so on. Obviously, such a regression backwards is unsatisfactory and still leaves us without an explanation for what we might identify as the initial behavior pattern. Furthermore, some behavioral patterns are not simply reactions to a partner's behavior, but, rather, part of a script simultaneously engaged by both interactants (Abelson, 1981). For example, in greeting exchange, both parties are aware of the behavior sequence required and are not simply responding to one another.

A second limitation of all these theories is that they are affect driven. That is, an individual's affective reaction to the partner's behavior determines the subsequent behavioral response. In general, negative affect leads to compensation whereas positive affect leads to reciprocation. Although affect undoubtedly influences spontaneous reactions, affect can also be quite independent of nonverbal involvement. This is especially the case for strategic behavior where the goal of influencing a partner may be quite independent of feelings toward that person. Thus the boss may be the recipient of very friendly, warm behavior from the employee who thoroughly dislikes him. Salespeople will similarly manage their behavior to influence a customer, independent of their affective reactions to the customer. These examples point to the necessity of moving beyond affect as the sole mediator of patterns of nonverbal exchange. The functional model was an attempt to address these limitations of earlier theories.

FUNCTIONAL MODEL

The functional model (Patterson, 1982, 1983, 1991) proposes that patterns of nonverbal exchange are the product of sequentially linked processes that have their origin in genetic and environmental determinants. These factors, in turn, help to shape the antecedent factors—culture, gender, personality, situation, and relationships. The antecedent factors serve to frame the interaction context through their influence on the preinteraction mediators—behavioral predispositions, arousal, and cognitive–affective expectancies. That is, one's habitual style of interacting (behavioral predispositions), arousal level, and expectancies about the partner and the situation affect how the interaction is construed (perceived function) and how one initially behaves (nonverbal involvement). Figure 9.1 illustrates the relationships among these processes.

Interactions will usually be more stable and predictable when the partners' preferred levels of involvement are similar and their perceived functions are complementary. When a discrepancy occurs between either the preferred levels of involvement or the perceived functions, the interaction will tend to be unstable. This instability, in turn, will lead to arousal change and cognitive reassessment in one or both of the interactants. These mediators then trigger adjustments in nonverbal involvement and a reevaluation of the function of the interaction. If the new involvement level is more compatible and the perceived functions more complementary, then the interaction will tend to be more stable. If not, then there should be another cycling through the interaction mediators. Of course, if the instability and resulting discomfort is sufficiently great, the interaction might be terminated before adjustments are sufficient to stabilize the interaction.

In summary, the functional model proposes that initial patterns of nonverbal exchange are the product of factors antecedent to an interaction that determine both the habitual patterns of involvement and functional expectancies. In terms of strategic behavior, expectancies about the interaction are important determinants of an individual's nonverbal patterns.

Perhaps the most basic of all the functions of nonverbal behavior is providing information. That is, patterns of nonverbal involvement can provide information about a partner's dispositions, momentary reactions, or qualify the meaning of verbal comments. Furthermore, one's own nonverbal behavior may help in specifying attitudes (Bem, 1972) and emotions (Tomkins, 1982). Thus, a person's own nonverbal behavior can be self-informative. The function of *regulating interaction* identifies behavioral patterns that facilitate the initiation and development of the give-and-take in an interaction. For example, the standing features of an interaction (Argyle & Kendon, 1967), in the form of closer distances and more directly facing orientations, tend to facilitate interaction. In addition, changes in gaze, gestures, and paralinguistic cues are related to smooth sequencing in conversations (Duncan, 1972). *Expressing intimacy* refers to the spontaneous expression of interpersonal affect (positive or negative) in the form of nonverbal involvement. Increased gaze between lovers is one example of this function (Rubin, 1970). *Social control* is the managed use of nonverbal involvement to influence others. The use of touch to gain compliance from another person is an example of social control (Patterson, Powell, & Lenihan, 1986).

The *presentational* function may be seen in the typically managed or deliberate use of nonverbal involvement designed to present an image or an identity to surrounding observers (Patterson, 1987). Goffman's (1972) ''tie-signs,'' in

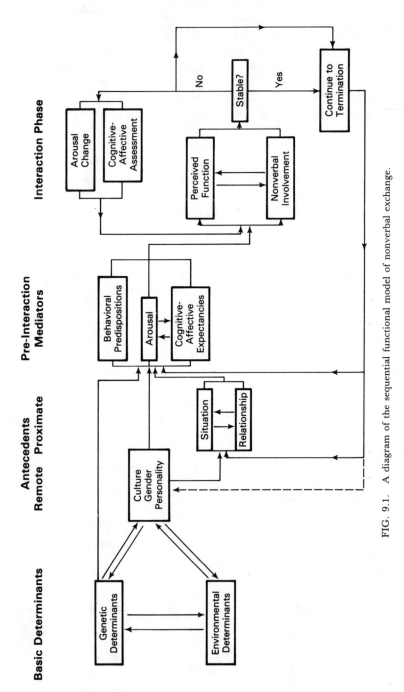

FIG. 9.1. A diagram of the sequential functional model of nonverbal exchange.

the form of a couple's holding hands at a social gathering would be an example of presenting a pair identity. *Affect management* identifies the use of nonverbal involvement in regulating the experience and/or consequences of affect, especially strong affect. Decreased gaze toward others when individuals are embarrassed is an example of affect management (Edelmann & Hampson, 1979, 1981). Finally, the *service-task* function includes the variable use of nonverbal involvement in a variety of service and task relationships. This function identifies the impersonal basis for high or low involvement with others, such as the close approach and touch of a physician administering a physical exam.

Not all of the functions described here are relevant for an analysis of strategic behavior. Relatively spontaneous behavior patterns reflecting either internal states (providing information) or interpersonal affect (expressing intimacy) are not representative of the managed patterns characteristic of strategic behavior. In addition, although service relationships (e.g., physician-patient) and task constraints (e.g., working in close proximity with others) affect the manner in which people relate to one another, such patterns are not strategic in nature. Strategic behavior can occur in such settings, but the service-task function itself simply refers to the regularities imposed by service relationships and task constraints. The remaining functions, regulating interaction, social control, the presentational function, and affect management are relevant for strategic behavior and each is discussed in the next section.

INTERACTION REGULATION

One important aspect of interaction regulation may be seen in the smooth give-and-take in conversations. For example, turn taking in conversations is facilitated by a variety of vocal and nonverbal cues by both the speaker and listener, including changes in gaze direction, vocal amplitude, gestures, and other behaviors (Duncan, 1972; Duncan & Niederehe, 1974; Kendon, 1967; see Cappella, 1985, for a review). Because these patterns typically develop automatically and are outside of the awareness of both the speakers and listeners, they would not be classified as strategic.

There are, however, other ways in which interaction regulation can be considered strategic in nature. Specifically, this would involve the deliberate or managed use of nonverbal behavior to control interaction. There are basically two ways in which interaction regulation may be strategic. In the first, an individual can manipulate the physical or arrangement features (e.g., distance and orientation in seating) so as to facilitate or inhibit interaction. In general, it might be expected that an individual would typically exercise such options only in primary or secondary territories, for example, home, office, private social club (Altman, 1975). Thus, individuals can manipulate the physical environment so as to control the access others have to them. In fact, this might be viewed as a form of privacy regulation (Altman, 1975). On a broader scale, the choice of secluded versus open homes or offices or even the choice of an occupation can determine the habitual level of contact we have with others. Of course, one's ability to implement such preferences may be dependent on money and status. In fact, it is typically the case, for obvious reasons, that high-status, wealthy people are more likely to structure their environments to limit unwanted contacts from others.

The second form of strategic interaction regulation includes specific behavioral adjustments designed to facilitate or inhibit interaction. At times this may involve anticipating a partner's reaction and then acting to control the undesirable consequences of that behavior. For example, Bond (1972) manipulated "warm" versus "cold" expectancies about an individual subjects were going to meet. Subjects who received the cold expectancy acted more warmly with their partners (as rated by independent judges) than did those who received the warm expectancy. Presumably, the cold-expectancy subjects acted more warmly in order to avert an unpleasant interaction with their partners. Thus the subjects compensated for the negative expectancy by behaving more warmly. It is interesting to note that, in this study, the partners (confederates) of the cold-expectancy subjects increased their own behavioral warmth (also rated by judges). Thus, the confederates who were instructed to maintain a constant demeanor reacted more positively in response to the subjects' strategic behavior. In two other experiments that examined the effect of interaction expectancies on specific behavioral patterns, further evidence was found for this kind of compensatory strategy. Specifically, both experiments showed that unfriendly or negative expectancies led to higher nonverbal involvement, especially in terms of increased smiling, than did friendly or positive expectancies (Ickes, Patterson, Rajecki, & Tanford, 1982). Furthermore, this increased involvement occurred even though the negative-expectancy subjects rated their partners much more negatively than did the positive-expectancy subjects.

In a similar study, Honeycutt (1989) manipulated expectancies in pairs of unacquainted subjects. Unfriendly-expectancy subjects not only initiated conversation more frequently than did subjects in other conditions, they also reported that they compensated more for their partner's failure to initiate conversation than did the friendly-expectancy subjects. In addition, a *post hoc* analysis showed that the unfriendly-expectancy subjects who actually initiated conversation also reported higher levels of compensation for their partner's failure to initiate conversation. This suggests that these subjects were apparently aware of what they were doing in trying to manage the conversation. Thus, in both the Ickes et al. (1982) and Honeycutt (1989) studies, subjects invested greater effort into the interactions because they anticipated that the interactions would *not* go well.

It seems likely that a contrasting compensatory strategy may also be enacted when one anticipates too much interaction or unwanted interaction. Deliberately decreasing gaze, orienting away from a partner, or being less responsive facially can serve to control attempts to initiate an intense and/or prolonged exchange. In one study of ignoring an interaction partner, the effects of such behaviors were clear. In three person groups, the two confederates ignored the subject by enlisting the following tactics: (a) decreasing gaze toward the subject; (b) responding only to direct questions and then only briefly; (c) showing little interest in the subject's remarks; and (d) interrupting the subject or changing the topic of discussion (Geller, Goodstein, Silver, & Sternberg, 1974). Compared to the normal conversation condition, ignored subjects initiated about one fourth as many comments and judged their reactions to the session more negatively on an adjective checklist. In addition, ignored subjects rated themselves and two confederates lower on a set of social presentation ratings than did the subjects in the normal conversation. Clearly, deliberately decreasing involvement from some normal or expected level can limit the resulting exchange between interactants and affect the perceptions of the target individual.

Another example of strategic interaction regulation is flirting. Here one manages carefully controlled, but fleeting, signs of interest in a potential partner (e.g., a brief gaze, smile, or postural change). These behaviors are designed to encourage the other person to make the "first move." The obvious advantage of signaling interest nonverbally is that a person does not have to verbalize interest and risk rejection. Furthermore, because nonverbal cues are ambiguous, one can deny any interest if the initial contact is disappointing.

When might interaction regulation strategies be initiated? Ickes et al. (1982) suggested that when individuals are faced with an expectancy for an unfriendly or negative interaction *and* there is some reason to believe that the partner's behavior is modifiable, a compensatory strategy of increased involvement is likely. Furthermore, such a compensatory strategy should be more likely with a high-status than with a low-status partner. In contrast, if there is little or no hope for affecting the partner's behavior and the partner is low, rather than high, status, then one is more likely to reciprocate the anticipated unfriendly or negative reaction. In other words, because there is less incentive to make the interaction more comfortable, this circumstance can develop into a kind of self-fulfilling prophecy (Rosenthal, 1966) or behavioral confirmation process (Snyder & Swann, 1978; Snyder, Tanke, & Berscheid, 1977). That is, subjects act in the same manner that they expect of their partners. In turn, such behavior tends to confirm the initial expectancy.

Thus far, this discussion has concentrated on face-to-face conversational exchanges, or what Goffman (1963) termed *focused interactions*. In contrast, in *unfocused interactions*, people share a common presence but they do not typically expect to converse with one another. Nevertheless, one may strategically manage behavior even in these situations to insure adequate comfort or privacy. This may be common in many public settings such as train stations, airports, doctors' waiting rooms, or libraries. Frequently, when people use such settings by themselves, they select arrangements (or standing positions) and manage their gaze patterns and body orientation to discourage contact with others in the setting (see Patterson, 1983). Specifically, this might involve selecting positions that are more distant from others and not in the line of direct visual regard from them. In some cases, coats, books, or other material may be placed in adjacent locations to discourage others from taking those positions. In contrast, choosing a more central location, or one that is in the line of visual regard from others, or simply sitting adjacent to another person, provides an opportunity for initiating interaction with others in the setting. One factor that may contribute to this type of affiliative strategy is the experience of fear (Schachter, 1959). That is, fear provides an incentive for increased contact with others.

In summary, nonverbal involvement may be used strategically to facilitate or inhibit the initial social contract with others and to manage the intensity and amount of interaction with them. First, the design and arrangement features of a social setting can serve to constrain the range of involvement possible with others. In addition, in the interaction itself, behavioral patterns may be strategically managed to increase or decrease the involvement with others.

SOCIAL CONTROL

A second strategic function of nonverbal involvement is that of social control. In general, social control may be described as the managed expression of nonverbal involvement that is designed to influence an interaction partner (Edinger & Patterson, 1983; Patterson, 1982). There are several distinct processes that may reflect social control motives, including: (a) power and dominance, (b) compliance and persuasion, (c) feedback and reinforcement, (d) impression management, and (e) deception. Burgoon (1985) discussed a similar set of processes that may be described as strategic, but she identified them as distinct functions. Burgoon's categories included (a) social influence, (b) impression formation and management, and (c) mixed messages and deception as separate functions. Whether these processes are described as separate functions or components of a single function, there is considerable evidence that nonverbal behavior may be used strategically to influence an interaction partner. The following discussion considers the ways in which nonverbal behavior may be used in influencing others.

Power and Dominance

In general, an individual's direct power to influence others is usually a product of the person's position or status in a social hierarchy. Of course, through various ingratiation tactics, the lower status member of a pair may practically exert power or control over the higher status person. In addition, if the higher status person is committed to and feels responsible for the lower status person, this provides an opportunity for the latter to influence the former.

In the circumstances in which status provides a power difference within a pair, the resulting dominance pattern can be manifested in a variety of ways. For example, higher rank in formal hierarchies, like the military, would typically permit staring at or touching the lower ranked person. The use of non-reciprocal touch by physicians toward staff members in a hospital setting is another example (Goffman, 1967). Even outside of formal hierarchies, characteristics such as being male, older, and having a higher socioeconomic status, all factors related to overall status, are predictive of a greater frequency of initiating touch (Henley, 1973, 1977). Gender-based differences in nonverbal power displays may, however, be qualified by relative expertise. In a series of studies by Dovidio and his colleagues, verbal and nonverbal power displays were related to the gender typing of the discussion topic (Dovidio, Brown, Heltman, Ellyson, & Keating, 1988; Dovidio, Ellyson, Keating, Heltman, & Brown, 1988). That is, although males showed more verbal and nonverbal power displays on both masculine and neutral topics, females showed more verbal and nonverbal power displays on feminine topics.

Usually individuals who gaze more at a partner are judged more dominant or potent (Thayer, 1969; Zimmerman, 1977), but status differences are not always manifested in such a straightforward manner. Exline and his colleagues (Exline, 1972; Exline, Ellyson, & Long, 1975) found that the higher status person interacting in pairs actually gazed less at the lower status person than vice versa, especially when each was in the listener role. One approach to understanding gaze and dominance is to consider both gazing while speaking and while listening. Dovidio and his colleagues defined visual dominance as the ratio of looking while speaking to looking while listening (Dovidio, Ellyson, Keatirg, Heltman, & Brown, 1988). That is, more dominant individuals gaze at their partners relatively more while speaking than while listening.

Persuasion and Compliance

Attempts to influence the behavior or attitudes of others in face-to-face interactions, or even in televised presentations, can be substantially affected by the behavioral patterns of the communicator. For example, in one study in which subjects were instructed to be more persuasive, increases were found in (a) gaze, (b) nodding, (c) gesturing, (d) facial activity, and (e) speech volume and rate (Mehrabian & Williams, 1969). In a separate study of perceived persuasiveness in counseling interactions, LaCrosse (1975) found that a set of behaviors similar to those identified by Mehrabian and Williams (i.e., higher levels of gaze, smiling, head nods, and gestures) was judged more persuasive than a contrasting set of low involvement behaviors.

Unfortunately, the perception of persuasiveness and actual persuasion on a particular topic are not identical. Albert and Dabbs (1970) found that subjects perceived speakers to be more expert when they were at a moderate distance (4–5 ft) than when they were at either a close (1–2 ft) or far (14–15 ft) distance. Because a separation of only 1 or 2 ft is very close and probably stressful, it should not be surprising that perceived expertise was low in that condition. What may be more surprising about the results of this study is that actual attitude change *increased* with distance. Albert and Dabbs suggested that increased distance may have lowered subjects' defenses about the issue and, consequently, increased attitude change.

In any case, it seems appropriate to offer some caution about a "more is better" principle in using nonverbal behavior to increase attitude change. Extreme violations of normative expectancies regarding nonverbal involvement may be both stressful and distracting and, consequently, lead to less attitude change. Burgoon (1978, 1983) offered a different kind of qualification, one that is grounded in individual differences among communicators. Specifically, when rewarding communicators increase the discrepancy between the actual and expected levels of involvement (up to some moderate level) they should be viewed more positively and, presumably, exercise greater influence over the target person. In contrast, when nonrewarding communicators increase the discrepancy between the actual and expected levels of involvement, they should be viewed more negatively and have decreased influence over the target person. Support for the expectancy violations predictions has been mixed thus far (Burgoon & Hale, 1988; Hale & Burgoon, 1984).

When the focus of an influence attempt is only behavioral compliance rather than attitude change, different dynamics may be involved. In general, it might be expected that increased pressure from a communicator will typically produce increased behavioral compliance. That does not, however, insure that the target of the influence attempt accepts the corresponding attitude. In fact, the increased pressure may result in reactance against the communicator and the message, even though behavioral compliance is achieved (Brehm, 1966).

How might pressure in terms of nonverbal involvement affect compliance? A number of studies show that the initiation of gaze or touch increases the probability of complying to a simple request, such as returning a "lost" dime (Kleinke, 1977, 1980), signing a petition (Willis & Hamm, 1980), and donating money to a charity (Bull & Gibson-Robinson, 1981). In a study conducted in our laboratory, we found that the initiation of touch increased compliance, as measured by the total time spent scoring a set of bogus personality inventories (Patterson et al., 1986). It is interesting that the compliance did not extend to the number of inventories scored, only to the time spent scoring inventories. This may, in fact, indicate a kind of reactance against the influence attempt. That is, subjects nominally complied by spending more time on the task, but they did not work very hard at it. The compliance effect did not seem to be mediated by increased liking of the experimenter because touch did not affect attraction toward the experimenter. Instead, it is possible that the touch indicated status or power differences that, in turn, produced compliance. An alternative explanation is simply that increased involvement was stressful and compliance represented an easy way to terminate the interaction and its associated stress.

Feedback and Reinforcement

A number of nonverbal cues may be used to provide feedback and/or reinforcement regarding performance on various tasks. Contingent nonverbal warmth, in the form of increased smiling and touching, can improve classroom behavior and learning (Kazdin & Klock, 1973; Kleinfeld, 1973) and even increase intelligence test scores (Isenberg & Bass, 1974; Sheckart & Bass, 1976). In addition, contingent nonverbal warmth can increase overall talking duration (Reece & Whitman, 1962) and specific classes of verbal behavior (Banks, 1974; Stewart & Patterson, 1973). Although the contingent initiation of nonverbal warmth can clearly serve to reinforce specific categories of behavior, increased noncontingent warmth can also facilitate performance in other ways. For example, the initiation of touch, gaze, or smiling may reduce anxiety that might otherwise lower performance levels. Alternatively, nonverbal warmth may signal approval, acceptance, or even liking by the teacher (boss, therapist) toward the student (employee, client). The communication of such positive affect can also increase the motivation to perform well or be more productive.

Impression Management

It is obvious from personal experience, in addition to being well documented in research, that an individual's nonverbal behavior is an important factor affecting impressions (Schneider, Hastorf, & Ellsworth, 1979). Consequently, successful impression management is, at least, partially a product of one's nonverbal behavior. Counseling or therapy exchanges represent one type of situation in which the actor's (counselor's, therapist's) nonverbal behavior may be managed to facilitate influence over the partner (client). The results of one set of studies show that increased nonverbal involvement by the counselor, combined with objective evidence (diplomas or certificates) of qualifications, increases the perceived expertise of the counselor. In addition, counselors were judged to be warmer when there was a higher level of gaze, nodding, gestures, and facial expressiveness (Sobelman, 1974; Strong, Taylor, Bratton, & Loper, 1971). Increased involvement is not invariably better. For example, Kleinke and Tully (1979) found that counselors were judged to be more dominant and potent the more they talked but, at the same time, they were liked less.

In general, a similar pattern emerges in impression studies of interview behavior. For example, increased involvement, manifested in behaviors such as a high level of gaze, smiling, and head movement, produced more favorable impressions (Imada & Hakel, 1977; McGovern, 1977) and hiring decisions (Forbes & Jackson, 1980; Young & Beier, 1977). Some caution is needed in evaluating the generalizability of such results. When the quality of the verbal content is manipulated, verbal behavior may be a more important factor in hiring decisions than is the nonverbal behavior (Hollandsworth, Kazelskis, Stevens, & Dressel, 1979). Furthermore, Forbes and Jackson (1980) suggested that nonverbal cues may become important only when other factors such as tests or resumes do not discriminate among the applicants. When the more objective data are available and also differentiate among applicants, hiring decisions may be made relatively easily without sensitivity to nonverbal cues. In a recent review, DePaulo (1992) addressed many of these issues from a self-presentational perspective.

Deception

A final area of social control behavior is that of deception, a topic that has been the focus of extensive research in recent years. In attempted deception an actor may be seen as trying to manage his or her nonverbal behavior to be as consistent as possible with the false verbal content. In fact, one might even view deception as a special case of impression management. That is, the impression that the actor intends to portray is one of sincerity or spontaneity in the delivery of the verbal message. The research on deception is not reviewed here because a comprehensive analysis is provided in the Buller and Burgoon chapter of this volume.

PRESENTATIONAL FUNCTION

The presentational function, like the social control function, entails strategic behavior designed to influence other people. The critical difference between the two functions is in the target of the influence attempt. Social control is focused toward the interaction partner, whereas the presentational function is focused toward the surrounding observers. Furthermore, the presentational function involves an attempt to present or enhance an image or identity, either at the individual or relationship level. In the latter instance, two or more people may collaborate in managing their behavior in order to construct a particular identity or image. For example, a couple in conflict may still wish to maintain a public image of "wedded bliss" by holding hands and being attentive to one another, even though they are both consulting with their respective lawyers. Once again, as in other forms of strategic behavior, the nonverbal display may be quite inconsistent with the underlying affect toward the partner.

Demonstrating a relationship identity serves a useful purpose in social settings. Goffman (1972) described behaviors such as holding hands as "tie signs," in that they tied or linked individuals together into a pair identity. A similar set of behaviors (including talking briefly, sharing gaze, or touching) has been called "with" signals because they identify the individuals who constitute a couple (Scheflen, 1974; Scheflen & Ashcraft, 1976). Furthermore, Scheflen (1974) proposed that such signals facilitate order and communication in larger groups by defining the relationships of individuals within the larger group.

In general, it might be expected that the initiation of increased involvement to signal a relationship might be more common the less well known the couple is in a given setting. An example of this may be seen in a field study of reactions of males in cross-gender pairs approached by an interviewer. The setting for the study was the sidewalk outside a movie theatre where people waited in line. When the interviewer was a female and when the interview questions became more intimate, males initiated more tie-signs with their partners (Fine, Stitt, & Finch, 1984). The specific behaviors included increased gaze, more direct orientation toward the partner, and increased talking with the partner. Apparently these behavioral adjustments served to reinforce the pair identity. A different purpose may be served by increased involvement in social settings where the couple is known. Specifically, in the presence of friends, acquaintances, or even family, a couple may be concerned about *appearing* to be intimate, even if that intimacy no longer characterizes the relationship.

Not all instances of the presentational function may be characterized by increased involvement. At times, the desired image may be one of independence from or indifference toward one's partner. In such circumstances, decreased involvement with a partner is likely to be enacted to portray that independence. Like the contrasting form of the presentational function, the exaggerated pattern of decreased involvement is triggered by the presence of others who are judged to value a specific identity or image.

In summary, the presentational function is characterized by interactive behavior that is enacted to influence observers, not one's partner. Goffman's (1959, 1963, 1967, 1972) perspective and terminology for analyzing social behavior can be usefully applied to the presentational function. Specifically, Goffman's dramaturgical approach views social behavior as a "performance" that "actors" deliver to impress or influence an "audience." In general, it might be predicted that the greater the actors' concern about both the audience acceptance and their own image or identity, the more likely that interactive behaviors will reflect the presentational function.

AFFECT MANAGEMENT

The affect management function is reflected in patterns of nonverbal behavior that manage or regulate the experience or affect, especially intense affect. In addition, affect management may also modulate the interpersonal consequences of emotional expression. An example in which both of these purposes may be served is the experience of negative affect, such as embarrassment, that produces a high level of public self-consciousness (Buss, 1980). Intense and acute embarrassment is likely to produce temporary avoidance of others in the form of decreased gaze (Edelmann & Hampson, 1979, 1981) or possibly even turning or moving away from others. Such a reaction of decreased involvement may lessen the intensity of negative affect by separating the individual from the bystanders. At the same time, however, the embarrassed person may increase movement and gestural activity and increase smiling (Edelmann & Hampson, 1979, 1981). The smiling and gestures that occur in such situations are not, however, the same kinds of behaviors that may occur in an animated, friendly exchange. The embarrassed individual may be blushing and have a "silly" smile, often with downcast or covered eyes (Buss, 1980). This type of reaction may even constitute an appeasement pattern that could, in turn, limit any additional critical evaluation (and laughing) by the observers.

Taken as a whole, the overall reaction might both lessen the negative affect and reduce additional negative social consequences. Although much of this pattern may be spontaneous, some components, especially the smile and the increased gestural activity, may be managed and appropriately described as strategic. In this case, the purpose would be to minimize the negative evaluation of others, or at least, bring it to a conclusion more quickly.

Although many instances of affect management are probably spontaneous and, consequently, not strategic, there are other important exceptions that take on an almost ritual character. For example, "high fives," fanny slapping, or embraces among athletes following scores or in celebrating victory seem too predictable to be completely spontaneous.

At the other end of the emotional spectrum, some patterns of consoling sad or grieving individuals are probably quite deliberate too. For example, sharing an embrace or holding hands shows concern and support for the grieving person, and is not simply an expression of shared grief. Similar patterns may be enacted when one person is afraid or sad. In each of these cases, the pattern of close contact may serve to provide an outlet for the expression of negative affect and, eventually, reduce its intensity.

CONCLUSIONS

The functions discussed in this chapter—interaction regulation, social control, the presentational function, and affect management—describe categories of purposes or motives served by the strategic use of nonverbal involvement. In contrast to nonverbal displays that are more spontaneous in nature and affectively based, strategic displays are more deliberate and managed. Furthermore, such patterns can be independent of interpersonal affect. That is, strategic displays can override the affective reactions that might normally determine our behavior. Thus, disliking a boss does not prevent an employee from initiating a friendly encounter with such a person. It should also be noted that characterizing strategic patterns as deliberate and managed does not mean that the actor necessarily has awareness of what he or she is doing during a strategic display. Well-learned or scripted influence attempts may be initiated automatically when situation calls for it. Nevertheless, these automatic displays would be deliberate and managed in their origin. That is, in learning such patterns, actors have some awareness of their intention and, in most cases, awareness of their behavior. Over time, with learning, this kind of awareness can become unnecessary for the successful implementation of strategic displays.

This distinction between spontaneous and deliberate or managed behavior is also one that has relevance for evaluating the effectiveness of strategic behavior. In general, strategic behavior should be more effective (in terms of the desired influence or creating a specific impression), if the targets of the influence perceive the behavior to be spontaneous and not deliberate. In contrast, if a behavioral routine is perceived as managed and not sincere, its influence should be diminished. An obvious example of this principle is that of successful deception. That is, the managed and deceptive behavioral routine should be seen as spontaneous and consistent with the deceptive verbal message. If the behavior is judged deceptive then it is likely that the verbal message will also be judged deceptive.

There are undoubtedly exceptions to such a generalization. With sufficient status or power, one probably does not have to worry about appearing to be sincere or spontaneous. That is, power alone is sufficient to exact compliance. Of course, the blatant use of power may produce reactance that, in turn, reduces the overall effectiveness of the influence attempt. In addition, the occasional transparent attempt to influence a partner may be so obvious as to be amusing, disarming, and remarkably effective. An example of this might be a 3-year-old child's exaggerated display of affection toward his father just before asking for a special toy.

A final concern that merits attention here might be described as the collateral costs of strategic behavior. Recent results from our own research suggest that when subjects are given more difficult impression management tasks, sensitivity in judging their partners' reactions decreases (Patterson, Churchill, Farag, & Borden, 1991/1992). Presumably, as greater attention is directed toward the management of one's own behavior, less attention is paid to the reactions of the partner. If successful influence requires not only the implementation of the appropriate behaviors, but also sensitivity to their effect on the partner, more difficult strategic patterns may be ineffective because they decrease sensitivity to the partner.

Underlying this relationship between the encoding, or behavioral production processes, and the decoding, or impression formation processes, is the assumption that the cognitive resources required for attention to and processing of both the encoding and decoding of behavior come from a common pool (Patterson, 1992). Thus, as more attention to and monitoring of a strategic display is required, fewer cognitive resources are available for attention to and processing of information about the partner. In general, anything that directs attention toward the self or towards the monitoring of one's own strategic behavior is likely to affect sensitivity to the partner adversely. For example, socially anxious and depressed individuals are more self-focused than their normal counterparts. Furthermore, strategic patterns that are not well learned or scripted require closer monitoring than more automatic patterns. Again, the result is a decrease in cognitive resources available for social inference processes. It is also possible that closely managed and monitored strategic displays will appear less spontaneous and, consequently, lose some of their impact.

Finally, the issues addressed here point to the importance of going beyond a simple classification of strategic behavior to relating parallel, but related, processes in social influence. Such a perspective may be useful, not only in understanding strategic behavior but, more generally, in pursuing the complexities of social interaction.

REFERENCES

Abelson, R. P. (1981). Psychological status of the script concept. *American Psychologist, 36*, 715–729.
Albert, S., & Dabbs, J. M. (1970). Physical distance and persuasion. *Journal of Personality and Social Psychology, 15*, 265–270.
Altman, I. (1975). *The environment and social behavior.* Monterey, CA: Brooks/Cole.
Argyle, M. (1972). Non-verbal communication in human social interaction. In R. A. Hinde (Ed.), *Non-verbal communication* (pp. 243–269). Cambridge: Cambridge University Press.
Argyle, M., & Dean, J. (1965). Eye-contact, distance, and affiliation. *Sociometry, 28*, 289–304.
Argyle, M., & Kendon, A. (1967). The experimental analysis of social performance. In L. Berkowitz (Ed.), *Advances in experimental social psychology* (pp. 55–91). New York: Academic Press.
Argyle, M., Lalljee, M., & Cook, M. (1968). The effects of visibility on interaction in a dyad. *Human Relations, 21*, 3–17.
Banks, D. L. (1974). A comparative study of the reinforcing potential of verbal and nonverbal cues in a verbal conditioning paradigm. *Dissertation Abstracts International, 35*, 2671A. (University Microfilms No. 74-25, 819).
Bem, D. J. (1972). Self-perception theory. In L. Berkowitz (Ed.), *Advances in experimental social psychology* (Vol. 6, pp. 1–62). New York: Academic Press.
Bond, M. H. (1972). Effect of an impression set on subsequent behavior. *Journal of Personality and Social Psychology, 24*, 301–305.
Brehm, J. W. (1966). *A theory of psychological reactance.* New York: Academic Press.
Bull, R., & Gibson-Robinson, E. (1981). The influences of eye-gaze, style of dress, and locality on the amounts of money donated to charity. *Human Relations, 34*, 895–905.

Burgoon, J. K. (1978). A communication model of personal space violations: Explication and an initial test. *Human Communication Research, 4*, 129–142.

Burgoon, J. K. (1983). Nonverbal violations of expectations. In J. M. Wiemann & R. P. Harrison (Eds.), *Nonverbal interaction* (pp. 77–111). Beverly Hills, CA: Sage.

Burgoon, J. K. (1985). Nonverbal signals. In M. L. Knapp & G. R. Miller (Eds.), *Handbook of interpersonal communication* (pp. 344–390). Beverly Hills, CA: Sage.

Burgoon, J. K., & Hale, J. L. (1988). Nonverbal expectancy violations: Model elaboration and application to immediacy behaviors. *Communication Monographs, 2*, 131–146.

Burgoon, J. K., & Jones, S. B. (1976). Toward a theory of personal space expectations and their violations. *Human Communication Research, 2*, 131–146.

Burgoon, J. K., & Saine, T. (1978). *The unspoken dialogue: An introduction to nonverbal communication.* Boston, MA: Houghton-Mifflin.

Buss, A. H. (1980). *Self-consciousness and social anxiety.* San Francisco, CA: Freeman.

Cappella, J. N. (1981). Mutual influence in expressive behavior: Adult–adult and infant–adult dyadic interaction. *Psychological Bulletin, 89*, 101–132.

Cappella, J. N. (1985). Controlling the floor in conversation. In A. W. Siegman & S. Feldstein (Eds.), *Multichannel integrations of nonverbal behavior* (pp. 69–103). Hillsdale, NJ: Lawrence Erlbaum Associates.

Cappella, J. N., & Greene, J. O. (1982). A discrepancy-arousal explanation of mutual influence in expressive behavior for adult and infant–adult interaction. *Communication Monographs, 49*, 89–114.

DePaulo, B. M. (1992). Nonverbal behavior and self-presentation. *Psychological Bulletin, 111*, 203–243.

Dovidio, J. F., Brown, C. E., Heltman, K., Ellyson, S. L., & Keating, C. F. (1988). Power displays between women and men in discussion of gender-linked tasks: A multichannel study. *Journal of Personality and Social Psychology, 55*, 580–587.

Dovidio, J. F., Ellyson, S. L., Keating, C. F., Heltman, K., & Brown, C. E. (1988). The relationship of social power to visual displays of dominance between men and women. *Journal of Personality and Social Psychology, 54*, 233–242.

Duncan, S., Jr. (1972). Some signals and rules for taking speaking turns in conversations. *Journal of Personality and Social Psychology, 23*, 283–292.

Duncan, S., Jr., & Niederehe, G. (1974). On signaling that it's your turn to speak. *Journal of Experimental Social Psychology, 10*, 234–247.

Edelmann, R. J., & Hampson, S. E. (1979). Changes in nonverbal behavior during embarrassment. *British Journal of Social and Clinical Psychology, 18*, 385–390.

Edelmann, R. J., & Hampson, S. E. (1981). Embarrassment in dyadic interaction. *Social Behavior and Personality, 9*, 171–177.

Edinger, J. A., & Patterson, M. L. (1983). Nonverbal involvement and social control. *Psychological Bulletin, 93*, 30–56.

Ekman, P., & Friesen, W. V. (1969). The repertoire of nonverbal behavior: Categories, origins, usage, and codings. *Semiotica, 1*, 49–97.

Exline, R. V. (1972). Visual interaction: The glances of power and preference. In J. K. Cole (Ed.), *Nebraska Symposium on Motivation* (Vol. 19, pp. 163–206). Lincoln, NE: University of Nebraska Press.

Exline, R. V., Ellyson, S. L., & Long, B. (1975). Visual behavior as an aspect of power role relationships. In P. Pilner, L. Krames, & T. Alloway (Eds.), *Advances in the study of communication and affect* (Vol. 2, pp. 21–51). New York: Plenum Press.

Fine, G. A., Stitt, J. L., & Finch, M. (1984). Couple tie-signs and interpersonal threat: A field experiment. *Social Psychology Quarterly, 47*, 282–286.

Forbes, R. J., & Jackson, P. R. (1980). Nonverbal behaviour and the outcome of selection interviews. *Journal of Occupational Psychology, 53*, 65–72.

Geller, D. M., Goodstein, L., Silver, M., & Sternberg, W. C. (1974). On being ignored: The effects of the violation of implicit rules of social interaction. *Sociometry, 37*, 541–556.

Goffman, E. (1959). *Presentation of self in everyday life*. New York: Anchor Books.

Goffman, E. (1963). *Behavior in public places*. New York: The Free Press.

Goffman, E. (1967). *Interaction ritual*. Garden City, NY: Anchor.

Goffman, E. (1972). *Relations in public*. New York: Harper Colophon.

Hale, J. L., & Burgoon, J. K. (1984). Models of reactions to changes in nonverbal immediacy. *Journal of Nonverbal Behavior, 8*, 287–314.

Harrison, R. P. (1973). Nonverbal communication. In I. S. Pool, W. Schramm, N. Maccoby, F. Fry, E. Parker, & J. L. Fern (Eds.), *Handbook of communication* (pp. 93–115). Chicago: Rand McNally.

Henley, N. M. (1973). Status and sex: Some touching observations. *Bulletin of the Psychonomic Society, 2*, 91–93.

Henley, N. M. (1977). *Body politics: Power, sex, and nonverbal communication*. Englewood Cliffs, NJ: Prentice-Hall.

Hollandsworth, J. G., Jr., Kazelskis, R., Stevens, J., & Dressel, M. E. (1979). Relative contributions of verbal, articulative, and nonverbal communication to employment decisions in the job interview setting. *Personnel Psychology, 32*, 359–367.

Honeycutt, J. M. (1989). Effect of preinteraction expectancies on interaction involvement and behavioral responses in initial interaction. *Journal of Nonverbal Behavior, 13*, 25–36.

Ickes, W., Patterson, M. L., Rajecki, D. W., & Tanford, S. (1982). Behavioral and cognitive consequences of reciprocal versus compensatory responses to pre-interaction expectancies. *Social Cognition, 1*, 160–190.

Imada, A. S., & Hakel, M. D. (1977). Influence of nonverbal communication and rater proximity on impressions and decisions in simulated employment interviews. *Journal of Applied Psychology, 62*, 295–300.

Isenberg, S. J., & Bass, B. A. (1974). Effects of verbal and nonverbal reinforcement on the WAIS performance of normal adults. *Journal of Consulting and Clinical Psychology, 42*, 467.

Kazdin, A. E., & Klock, J. (1973). The effect of nonverbal teacher approach on student attentive behavior. *Journal of Applied Behavior Analysis, 6*, 643–654.

Kendon, A. (1967). Some functions of gaze-direction in social interaction. *Acta Psychologica, 26*, 22–63.

Kleinfeld, J. S. (1973). Effects of nonverbally communicated personal warmth on the intelligence test performance of Indian and Eskimo adolescents. *Journal of Social Psychology, 91*, 149–150.

Kleinke, C. L. (1977). Compliance to requests made by gazing and touching experimenters in field settings. *Journal of Experimental Social Psychology, 13*, 218–223.

Kleinke, C. L. (1980). Interaction between gaze and legitimacy of request on compliance in field settings. *Journal of Nonverbal Behavior, 5*, 3–12.

Kleinke, C. L., & Tully, T. B. (1979). Influence of talking level on perceptions of counselors. *Journal of Counseling Psychology, 26*, 23–29.

LaCrosse, M. B. (1975). Nonverbal behavior and perceived counselor attractiveness and persuasiveness. *Journal of Counseling Psychology, 22*, 563–566.

McGovern, T. V. (1977). The making of the job interviewee: The effect of nonverbal behavior on an interviewer's evaluations during a selection interview. *Dissertation Abstracts International, 37*, 4740B–4741B. (University Microfilms No. 77-6239)

Mehrabian, A., & Williams, M. (1969). Nonverbal concomitants of perceived and intended persuasiveness. *Journal of Personality and Social Psychology, 13*, 37–58.

Patterson, M. L. (1973). Compensation in nonverbal immediacy behaviors: A review. *Sociometry, 36*, 237–252.

Patterson, M. L. (1976). An arousal model of interpersonal intimacy. *Psychological Review, 83*, 235–245.

Patterson, M. L. (1982). A sequential functional model of nonverbal exchange. *Psychological Review, 89*, 231–249.

Patterson, M. L. (1983). *Nonverbal behavior: A functional perspective*. New York: Springer-Verlag.

Patterson, M. L. (1987). Presentational and affect management functions of nonverbal involvement. *Journal of Nonverbal Behavior, 11*, 110–122.

Patterson, M. L. (1991). A functional approach to nonverbal exchange. In R. S. Feldman & B. Rime (Eds.), *Fundamentals of nonverbal behavior* (pp. 458–495). Cambridge: Cambridge University Press.

Patterson, M. L. (1992, June). *An interaction model of person perception.* Paper presented at the annual convention of the American Psychological Society, San Diego.

Patterson, M. L., Churchill, M. E., Farag, R., & Borden, E. (1991/1992). Impression management, cognitive demand, and interpersonal sensitivity. *Current Psychology: Research & Reviews, 10*, 263–271.

Patterson, M. L., Powell, J. L., & Lenihan, M. G. (1986). Touch, compliance, and interpersonal affect. *Journal of Nonverbal Behavior, 10*, 41–50.

Reece, M. M., & Whitman, R. N. (1962). Expressive movements, warmth, and verbal reinforcement. *Journal of Abnormal and Social Psychology, 64*, 234–236.

Rosenthal, R. (1966). *Experimenter effects in behavioral research.* New York: Appleton-Century-Crofts.

Rubin, Z. (1970). Measurement of romantic love. *Journal of Personality and Social Psychology, 16*, 265–272.

Schachter, S. (1959). *The psychology of affiliation.* Stanford, CA: Stanford University Press.

Schachter, S., & Singer, J. E. (1962). Cognitive, social, and physiological determinants of emotional state. *Psychological Review, 69*, 379–399.

Scheckart, G. R., & Bass, B. A. (1976). The effects of verbal and nonverbal contingent reinforcement upon the intelligence test performance of black adults. *Journal of Clinical Psychology, 22*, 826–828.

Scheflen, A. E. (1974). *How behavior means.* Garden City, NY: Anchor.

Scheflen, A. E., & Ashcraft, N. (1976). *Human territories: How we behave in space-time.* Englewood Cliffs, NJ: Prentice-Hall.

Schneider, D. J., Hastorf, A. H., & Ellsworth, P. C. (1979). *Person perception* (2nd ed.). Reading, MA: Addison-Wesley.

Snyder, M., & Swann, W. (1978). Behavioral confirmation in social interaction: From social perception to social reality. *Journal of Experimental Social Psychology, 14*, 148–162.

Snyder, M., Tanke, E. D., & Berscheid, E. (1977). Social perception and interpersonal behavior: On the self-fulfilling nature of social stereotypes. *Journal of Personality and Social Psychology, 35*, 656–666.

Sobelman, S. A. (1974). The effects of verbal and nonverbal components on the judged level of counselor warmth. *Dissertation Abstracts International, 35*, 273A. (University Microfilms No. 74-14, 199)

Stewart, D. J., & Patterson, M. L. (1973). Eliciting effects of verbal and nonverbal cues on projective test responses. *Journal of Counseling and Clinical Psychology, 41*, 74–77.

Strong, S. R., Taylor, R. G., Bratton, J. C., & Loper, R. G. (1971). Nonverbal behavior and perceived counselor characteristics. *Journal of Counseling Psychology, 18*, 554–561.

Thayer, S. (1969). The effect of interpersonal looking duration on dominance judgments. *Journal of Social Psychology, 79*, 285–286.

Tomkins, S. S. (1982). *Affect, imagery, consciousness: Vol. 3. Cognition and affect.* New York: Springer-Verlag.

Willis, F. N., & Hamm, H. K. (1980). The use of interpersonal touch in securing compliance. *Journal of Nonverbal Behavior, 5*, 49–55.

Young, D. M., & Beier, E. G. (1977). The role of applicant nonverbal communication in the employment interview. *Journal of Employment Counseling, 14*, 154–165.

Zimmer, L. E. S. (1977). First impressions as influenced by eye contact, sex, and demographic background. *Dissertation Abstracts International, 37*, 6414B–6415B. (University Microfilms No. 77-12, 978)

Author Index

Subject Index